Cambridge IGCSE™ and O Level

Business

Sixth Edition

Karen Borrington
Peter Stimpson

Endorsement indicates that a resource has passed Cambridge International Education's rigorous quality-assurance process and is suitable to support the delivery of their syllabus. However, endorsed resources are not the only suitable materials available to support teaching and learning, and are not essential to achieve the qualification. For the full list of endorsed resources to support this syllabus, visit www.cambridgeinternational.org/endorsed-resources

Any example answers to questions taken from past question papers, practice questions, accompanying marks and mark schemes included in this resource have been written by the authors and are for guidance only. They do not replicate examination papers. In examinations the way marks are awarded may be different. Any references to assessment and/or assessment preparation are the publisher's interpretation of the syllabus requirements. Examiners will not use endorsed resources as a source of material for any assessment set by Cambridge International Education.

While the publishers have made every attempt to ensure that advice on the qualification and its assessment is accurate, the official syllabus, specimen assessment materials and any associated assessment guidance materials produced by the awarding body are the only authoritative source of information and should always be referred to for definitive guidance.

Our approach is to provide teachers with access to a wide range of high-quality resources that suit different styles and types of teaching and learning.

For more information about the endorsement process, please visit www.cambridgeinternational.org/endorsed-resources

Cambridge International Education material in this publication is reproduced under licence and remains the intellectual property of Cambridge University Press & Assessment.

Third-party websites and resources referred to in this publication are not endorsed.

All questions have been written by the authors.

Although every effort has been made to ensure that website addresses are correct at time of going to press, Hachette Learning cannot be held responsible for the content of any website mentioned in this book. It is sometimes possible to find a relocated web page by typing in the address of the home page for a website in the URL window of your browser.

Hachette UK's policy is to use papers that are natural, renewable and recyclable products and made from wood grown in well-managed forests and other controlled sources. The logging and manufacturing processes are expected to conform to the environmental regulations of the country of origin.

To order, please visit www.hachettelearning.com or contact Customer Service at education@hachette.co.uk / +44 (0)1235 827827.

ISBN: 978 1 0360 1064 5

© Karen Borrington and Peter Stimpson 2025

First published in 1999
Second edition published in 2002
Third edition published 2006
Fourth edition published 2013
Fifth edition published 2018
This edition published in 2025 by
Hachette Learning,
An Hachette UK Company
Carmelite House
50 Victoria Embankment
London EC4Y 0DZ
www.hachettelearning.com

The authorised representative in the EEA is Hachette Ireland, 8 Castlecourt Centre, Dublin 15, D15 XTP3, Ireland (email: info@hbgi.ie)

Impression number   10 9 8 7 6 5 4 3

Year   2028   2027   2026   2025

All rights reserved. Apart from any use permitted under UK copyright law, no part of this publication may be reproduced or transmitted in any form or by any means, electronic or mechanical, including photocopying and recording, or held within any information storage and retrieval system, without permission in writing from the publisher or under licence from the Copyright Licensing Agency Limited. Further details of such licences (for reprographic reproduction) may be obtained from the Copyright Licensing Agency Limited, www.cla.co.uk

Cover photo © Sergey Nivens - stock.adobe.com

Illustrations by Oxford Designers and Illustrators Ltd, Aptara Inc. and Integra Software Services

Typeset in ITC Officina Sans 11.5/13 pts. by Aptara Inc.

Printed in the UK by Bell & Bain Ltd, Glasgow

A catalogue record for this title is available from the British Library.

Contents

	Introduction	iv
	How to use this book	iv
	Assessment	vi

SECTION 1 Understanding business activity
1. Business activity and economic sectors — 1
2. Enterprise, business growth and size — 12
3. Types of business organisations — 31
4. Business objectives and stakeholder objectives — 47

SECTION 2 People in business
5. Human resource management (HRM) — 61
6. Organisation and management — 81
7. Methods of communication — 100
8. Motivating employees — 114

SECTION 3 Marketing
9. Marketing and the market — 132
10. Market research — 144
11. The marketing mix: product — 159
12. The marketing mix: price — 172
13. The marketing mix: place — 181
14. The marketing mix: promotion — 188
15. Ecommerce — 198
16. Marketing strategy, entering new markets in other countries and legal controls — 205

SECTION 4 Operations management
17. Production of goods and services — 217
18. Technology and production of goods and services — 230
19. Sustainable production of goods and services — 237
20. Costs, scale of production and break-even analysis — 243
21. Quality of goods and services — 258
22. Location decisions — 264

SECTION 5 Financial information and decisions
23. Business finance — 278
24. Cash flow forecast — 293
25. Profit and loss — 304
26. Statement of financial position — 313
27. Analysis of accounts — 321

SECTION 6 External influences on business activity
28. Economic issues — 335
29. Business and the international economy — 346
30. Business and the environment — 358
31. Business and ethical issues, and pressure groups — 365

Glossary	373
Index	379
Acknowledgements	383

Introduction

This Cambridge IGCSE™ and O Level Business Sixth Edition Student Book provides coverage of the Cambridge IGCSE/IGCSE (9–1)/O Level Business syllabus (0264/0774/7081) for examination from 2027. It fully covers the Cambridge International Education syllabus content and provides the detail and guidance that are needed to support you throughout the course and help you to prepare for assessment. It will also prove to be of great use to anyone who wants to learn more about the key concepts of business.

This book will prove to be valuable to students of Business whether you are:

- studying the subject for the first time through your school or college and need a comprehensive and clearly written textbook
- revising the subject before an assessment and need a study guide to help you with key definitions, techniques and examination advice
- learning the subject on your own through distance or open learning and need a complete programme of supportive questions, activities and suggested answers to these.

Building on the successful formula of the previous five editions, this sixth edition updates all existing chapters, including removing material that is no longer in the syllabus and adding new subject material with additional chapters and a new feature.

How to use this book

To make your study of Business as rewarding and successful as possible, this textbook, endorsed for the Cambridge Pathway, offers the following important features:

Content
Each chapter starts with an outline of the subject material to be covered and ends with a checklist to confirm what you should have learned and understood.

Organisation
The content is in the same order as the syllabus: chapter titles and chapter section headings match those of the Cambridge IGCSE and O Level Business syllabuses.

Approach
The subject material is written in an informative yet lively way that allows for complete understanding of each topic to be gained.

How to use this book

Extend your skills of analysis
The authors have provided the questions in this feature to show how you can develop an answer to make it more detailed. Each question is applied in some way, such as for a certain product. The authors have then provided a simple answer to the question. This is a statement but does not develop the explanation. There are prompts to suggest how you might extend your explanation and then an example of how you might develop the statement so you answer the question in greater detail. This section aims to encourage you to think about how you can make your answers more detailed, rather than them being just simple statements.

Study tips
Tips to help you make key points when answering questions.

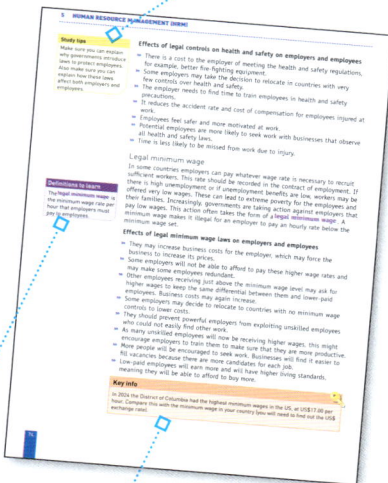

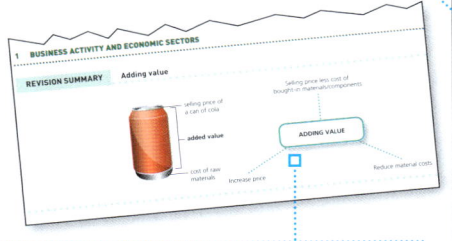

Revision summary
Revision summaries in the form of helpful 'spider diagrams' that highlight key topics and issues.

Activity
Numerous activities support your learning and check your progress at each important stage of every chapter.

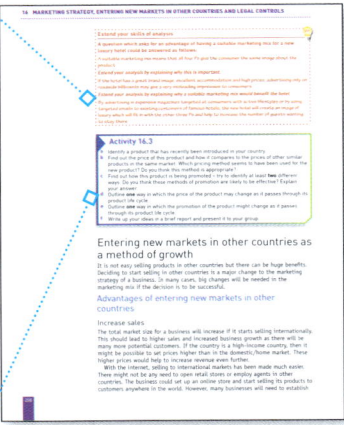

Definitions to learn
Definitions of the key words you need to know are given, with terms highlighted in the text.

Key info
Key info boxes provide further explanation of the key concepts you need to know, with real-world examples.

International business in focus
Case studies of businesses from around the world and discussion points to help confirm understanding.

Case study
Case studies based on a range of international businesses/examples put concepts into a real-world context to help you understand and think about how they work in practice.

Calculations to learn
The formula for each calculation you will need to be able to use will be highlighted. A worked example of each calculation will show how the formula is used.

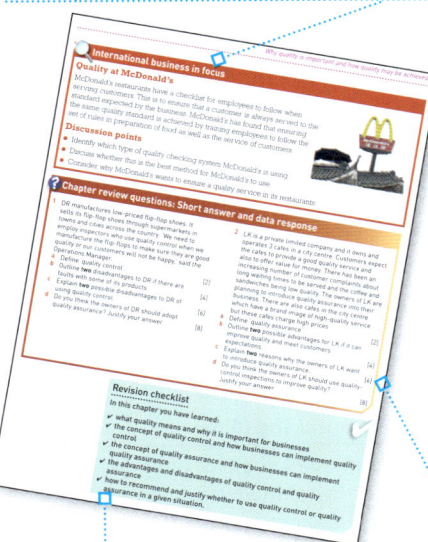

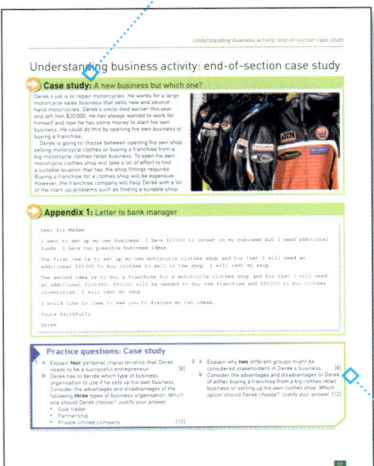

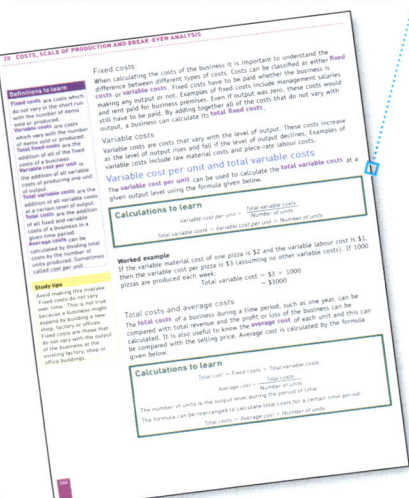

Revision checklist
This checklist lists the key concepts and topics you have covered in the chapter and the key points you will need to know.

Chapter review questions
Practice questions written by the authors at the end of each chapter allow you to gain essential practice at answering questions.

Practice questions
Further case study questions written by the authors at the end of each group of chapters provide practice for a specific section of the curriculum content.

v

Assessment

Revision

You should be able to perform to the best of your ability if you:

» ensure that you have worked through all of the activities and practice questions in this book
» revise thoroughly before assessment – allow plenty of time for this and avoid leaving it until the last minute.

You can also help yourself greatly if you take the following steps:

» Obtain a copy of the syllabus. You should also be able to obtain past papers and mark schemes. It is very important that you check the progress of your learning and revision by 'ticking off' each topic against the syllabus content.
» Make sure that you know the number and length of each of the papers you will have to sit. The style and nature of the questions often differ between papers so you must be quite clear about the type of questions likely to appear on each paper.

For Cambridge IGCSE and O Level Business the papers are:

	Length	Type of paper	Type of questions
Paper 1	1 hour 30 mins	Short answer and data response	Four data response questions based on four different businesses. The questions are structured a) to d)
Paper 2	1 hour 30 mins	Case study	Four structured questions (i.e. a) and b)) all based on a case study provided in an insert

In examinations

Make sure you check the instructions on the question paper, the length of the paper and the number of questions you must answer. Allocate your time sensibly between each question. Students often let themselves down by spending too long on some questions and too little time (or no time at all) on others. You will be expected to spend longer writing an answer to a question worth 8 marks than you would when writing an answer worth 4 marks. There are key command words at the beginning of the questions. Make sure you understand what they are asking you to do. They are listed in the following table.

Key command words you need to know

Command word	Meaning
Calculate	As in 'Using the figures provided, calculate the break-even level of output.' This means 'Using the figures provided, work out the following'
Consider	As in 'Consider the advantages and disadvantages of expanding the car manufacturer by opening another factory or by taking over a competitor.' This is asking you to show advanced skills. The best approach to answer this type of question is to explain the advantages and disadvantages of the two options – using any case material about the business to help you
Define	This is asking you to clearly show that you know what a term means. A single sentence answer is nearly always sufficient

In examinations

Command word	Meaning
Explain	As in 'Explain two ways in which the hotel could promote its services.' The question is asking you to give more detail than just identifying points. Your answer must also be **applied to the business in question – in this case, a hotel**. So, billboards by the side of the road in another town would not be appropriate for this hotel as they might not be seen by potential customers. A better answer would be: 'The hotel could contact all guests who have stayed at the hotel before by email to give them details of a special offer. The hotel could also use a colourful and effective website to promote its services to customers who book hotel accommodation online.'
Identify	As in 'Identify two factors that could affect the price of a product.' Identify means write down, without explanation or discussion, the required number of points. So the answers to the question above might be: 'Costs of production. Prices of competitors' products.'
Justify	As in 'Do you think taking over a smartphone manufacturer or a chain of shops selling smartphones is the best way for TelCom to expand? Justify your answer.' In questions like this you need to consider both options for expansion, giving advantages and disadvantages for both. Finally, you should weigh up the points for and against each option and come to a final decision based on the most important points. For longer questions you should also justify why the alternative(s) was rejected. Answers should also be **applied to the business in the context**
Outline	As in 'Outline two advantages to Jameel of operating his business as a sole trader.' This is asking you to set out two advantages of operating as a sole trader and how they relate to Jameel and his business
State	As in 'State two examples of promotion for XYZ company.' This question only requires two examples to be given and no explanation is required

Finally …

Learning Business should be both rewarding and challenging. We hope that this textbook will help you overcome the challenges of the Cambridge IGCSE and O Level courses so that you can achieve the success you are seeking. In particular, we want the book to encourage you to develop a real interest in – even a passion for – finding out more about how the world of business really works.

Business activity is so crucial to the future wellbeing of us all and it offers great opportunities for all well-motivated students. Success in Cambridge IGCSE and O Level Business can help you take the first important steps towards playing a leading role in managing and directing business activity in your country. We are confident that this book will fully support you during your course.

Wishing you all the best in your studies,

Karen Borrington

Peter Stimpson

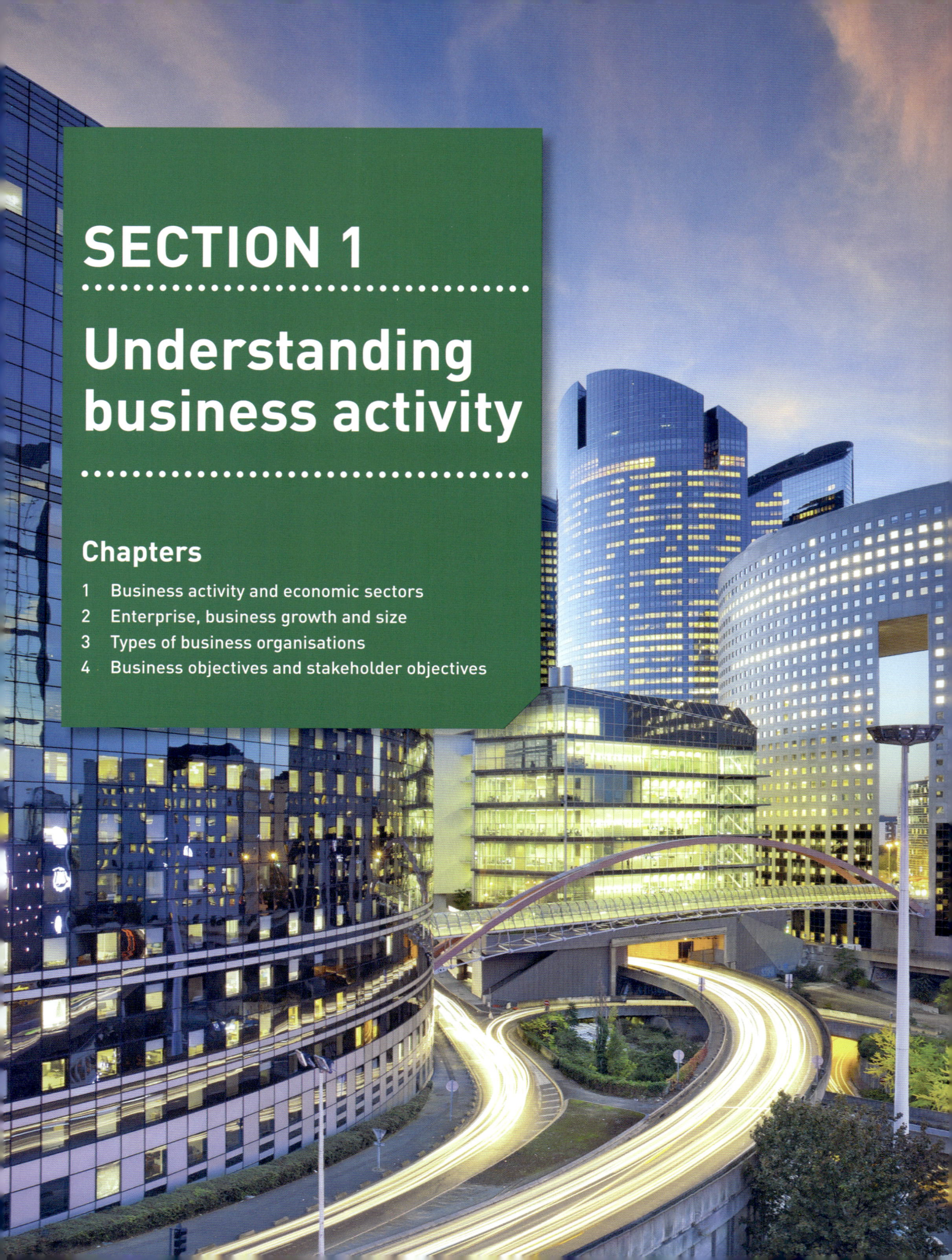

1 Business activity and economic sectors

> This chapter will explain:
>
> The nature of business activity:
>
> ★ factors of production: land, labour, capital and enterprise
> ★ the concept of adding value and how added value can be increased
> ★ the concept of opportunity cost.
>
> Types of economic sector:
>
> ★ primary, secondary and tertiary sectors
> ★ private and public sectors.

The nature of business activity

What would life be like without **business** activity? In a simple economy, businesses do not exist. Everyone attempts to do everything for themselves – they are self-sufficient. With their own plot of land and by their own efforts, such as hunting and farming, they attempt to survive and produce enough for their own needs. This is a very basic existence and living standards are low.

Through the slow process of specialisation, people began to concentrate on what they were best at. They then traded the **goods** they produced for other goods, such as shoes, made by people who had different skills. In this way, businesses began to be formed, and trade and exchange of goods expanded. In today's world, most people specialise by working in one job for a weekly or monthly wage. With this money, they are able to purchase a wide range of goods and **services** produced by many different businesses that specialise in different products. Many businesses specialise in producing one or just a few types of goods or services.

Business activity therefore:

» **combines scarce factors of production** to make or provide goods and services
» **produces goods and services** which satisfy the needs and wants of the population
» **employs people** as workers and pays them wages to allow them to consume products made by other people working for other businesses.

Definitions to learn

A **business** is an organisation that combines factors of production to make products (goods and services) which satisfy people's wants.
Goods are tangible products made by businesses to be sold to customers, such as cars and clothes.
Services are intangible products, such as banking or transport, that are provided by businesses to customers.
Factors of production are those resources needed to produce goods or services. There are four factors of production and they are in limited supply.

Factors of production

To produce these goods and services, businesses need 'factors of production'. There are four **factors of production**:

» **Land** – this term includes all of the natural resources provided by nature that are used in the production of goods and services. This includes fields and forests, oil, gas, metals and other mineral resources.
» **Labour** – this is the number of people available to make products and the skills they have.
» **Capital** – this is the finance, machinery and equipment needed for the manufacture of goods or the provision of services.

1 BUSINESS ACTIVITY AND ECONOMIC SECTORS

» **Enterprise** – this is the skill and risk-taking ability of the person who brings the other resources or factors of production together to produce a good or service, for example, the owner of a business. These people are called entrepreneurs. See Chapter 2 to understand the role of entrepreneurs.

Study tips

Definitions of the key terms in this book can be found in the left-hand margins.

These definitions will be very useful to you as you study the course, so it is important that you learn these by heart.

Whatever their size and whoever owns them, all businesses have one thing in common: in order to produce goods and services that satisfy customer needs, they must combine these four factor of production.

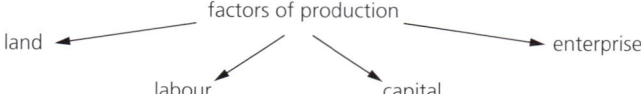

Definitions to learn

Capital is the money invested into a business by the owners.

In any one country, and in the world as a whole, these factors of production are limited in supply. As there is never enough land, labour, **capital** or enterprise to produce all the needs and unlimited wants of a whole population, there is an economic problem of scarcity.

▲ Businesses in all economic sectors produce goods and services by combining factors of production

The concept of adding value

This is a very important idea. All businesses attempt to add value. This is done by selling a product for more than the cost of materials and resources used to produce the good or provide the service. If value is not added to the materials and components that a business buys in, then:

» other costs cannot be paid for
» no profit will be made
» the business is likely to fail.

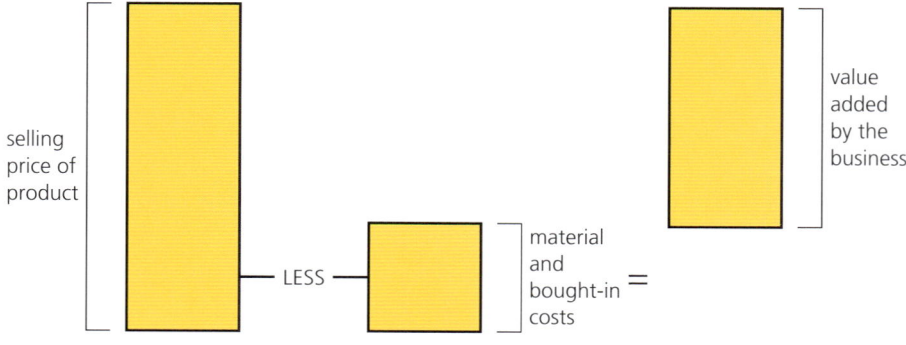

▲ Value added

The nature of business activity

Example:
- The selling price of a newly built house is $200 000.
- The value of the bought-in bricks, cement, wood and other materials was $35 000.
- The added value of the building firm was $165 000. This is not all profit – out of this the builder must pay wages and other costs too.

Why adding value is important

Added value is important because revenue from selling the product is greater than the cost of materials and resources bought in by the business. This means the business:

- can pay other costs such as labour costs, management expenses, advertising and power
- may be able to make a profit if these other costs come to a total that is less than the added value
- may be able to grow, as a profit will provide the finance for expansion.

How added value can be increased

There are two main ways in which a business can try to increase its added value.

1. Finding ways to charge a higher price for the product, such as:
   - creating an effective brand image that customers are prepared to pay higher prices to own. This could be done by advertising the product with celebrities or by having very innovative products
   - adding a new feature to the product that costs less than the increase in price
   - improving customer service, for example, by offering free delivery. Again, the cost of this must be less than the price increase
   - improving packaging, which gives the product a much higher quality image.

2. Reducing the cost of materials, such as by:
   - using a lower-cost supplier of materials and keeping the price the same. Customers must not experience a reduction in quality or they may think the product has fallen in value
   - buying supplies in larger quantities to obtain bulk discounts which reduce cost per unit. However, this could lead to higher storage costs.

Definitions to learn
Added value is the difference between the selling price of a product and the cost of bought-in materials and resources needed to produce it.

Key info
Children around the world are playing with more mini LEGO® people than there are human beings on the planet. The LEGO Group adds value by putting LEGO bricks into themed building sets, such as spaceships or superheroes. Some sets are also linked to successful movie series such as Harry Potter and Marvel's Avengers. When the LEGO Star Wars *Summer Vacation* movie was released, it further strengthened the brand and encouraged consumers to pay a high price for the building sets.

Study tips
Apply your answers to the business in the question. Adding value will be achieved by different businesses in different ways. Improving the reliability of cars will lead to a better brand image for the car manufacturer which could allow it to raise prices. An internet service provider might focus on achieving the highest rating for customer service in the industry. Increased customer loyalty resulting from this will add value. The costs of attracting new customers will fall.

Extend your skills of analysis

A question which asks how a bicycle manufacturer could increase added value to its products could be answered as follows:

Trying to give the products a more sports-focused brand image by promoting the fastest models with well-known sportspeople could help add value.

Extend your analysis by explaining how this helps the business improve its brand image.

Consumers link the bicycle to the well-known sports stars and associate a better, faster performance with the brand image. If they hope they will also improve their performance when using the bicycle, consumers may be prepared to pay a higher price.

Extend your analysis by explaining how this increases added value for the business.

By being able to charge higher prices, the bicycle manufacturer will be increasing the difference between the price charged and the cost of the materials used to make the bicycles.

1 BUSINESS ACTIVITY AND ECONOMIC SECTORS

REVISION SUMMARY — Adding value

Case study: Rakesh's bakery

Rakesh owns a small bakery selling bread, cakes and biscuits. His business is just making enough money to survive. His wife, Neeta, had the idea of serving customers tea and coffee at 2 small tables that could be fitted into the bakery shop. 'Customers will pay more for each cake and biscuit if we sell them with tea or coffee – just like a little cafe.' Rakesh bought some second-hand cafe equipment and furniture and tried what Neeta had suggested. She was right! Some of his customers not only bought teas and coffees, but they paid higher prices for the cakes and biscuits they bought as they were served them on a plate!

Rakesh had increased the value added to the flour, sugar and butter he used to make these cakes and biscuits.

Activity 1.1

Refer to the case study above.

a If the bestselling cake in this bakery uses 50 cents worth of flour, sugar and butter and Rakesh sells each one for $1.50, calculate the value added.
b If customers are prepared to pay $2.00 when this cake is served on a plate at a table within the bakery, what is the new value added per cake?
c Does the opening of the small cafe mean that Rakesh must have increased his weekly profit? Explain your answer.

Case study: Starbucks

Starbucks adds value in several ways, not just by selling coffee.

- It has a brand image for quality, environmental awareness and social responsibility. It sells high-quality coffee that is ethically sourced.
- Customers can personalise their drinks with different milk options, syrups, flavouring and toppings.
- Starbucks cafes are designed to be spaces to relax, socialise, work or study. The cafes have comfortable seating and provide access to free Wi-Fi.

All of these things allow Starbucks to charge a much higher price for its drinks and other products than the prices charged by many other cafes.

The concept of opportunity cost

> **Definitions to learn**
>
> **Opportunity cost** is the value of the next best alternative given up when choosing one option over another.

Have you bought anything this week? A pen or book or perhaps a pizza? If you have, you have experienced **opportunity cost**. By choosing what to buy, you had to give up buying other goods and services. Why? Because, unless you are unbelievably rich, you have limited resources. To be precise, opportunity cost means the next most desired product you would have bought if you had not bought that pen, book or pizza – or whatever you chose. So, by buying a book – assuming this was your choice – you gave up the chance of buying the product you next most desired. This was your opportunity cost – it is the value of what you did not choose.

Opportunity cost always occurs when choices are made about the use of limited resources. All economic decision makers – individuals, businesses and governments – will experience opportunity cost when they decide how to allocate the limited resources at their disposal.

Individual	Business	Government

Holiday or car?	Machine A or Machine B?	New road or new school?
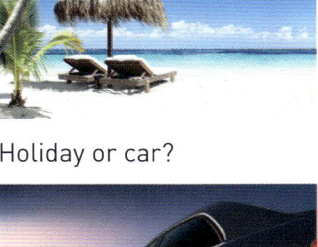		
If the individual chooses to buy the holiday, the value of the car becomes the opportunity cost.	If the company decides to buy Machine A, the value of Machine B becomes the opportunity cost.	If the government chooses to build the road, the value of the school becomes the opportunity cost.

▲ Examples of opportunity cost

Types of economic sectors

Primary, secondary and tertiary sectors

The production of all goods and services can be split into three types of business activity. Many products pass through all three sectors as they are converted from unprocessed materials into goods and services for customers to buy. As you read this book you are probably sitting at a table. Many tables are made of wood. How many different types of business activities have been involved in converting trees into a finished table ready to be sold to the final customer? What 'economic

1 BUSINESS ACTIVITY AND ECONOMIC SECTORS

sectors' – or stages of production – has the wood from trees passed through to arrive at the finished table?

The diagram below shows the most likely stages in the production and sale of a wooden table.

stage	activity	business involved
primary		woodcutter
secondary		furniture maker
tertiary		retailer

▲ The stages involved in making and selling a wooden table

You will notice that there are three main stages from the cutting down of the tree to the sale of the completed table. These stages are typical of the production of nearly all tangible goods and they are called economic sectors.

Stage 1 is called the primary stage of production. This stage involves the Earth's natural resources. Activities in the **primary sector** of industry include farming, fishing, forestry and the extraction of natural materials, such as oil and copper ore. All businesses that operate in these industries are in the primary sector.

Stage 2 is called the secondary stage of production. This stage involves taking the materials and resources provided by the primary sector and converting them into manufactured or processed goods. Activities in the **secondary sector** of industry include building and construction, aircraft and car manufacturing, mobile phone assembly and bread baking. All manufacturing businesses operate in the secondary sector.

Stage 3 is called the tertiary stage of production. This stage involves providing goods and services to both consumers and other businesses. Activities in the **tertiary sector** of industry include transport, banking, retailing, insurance, hotels, entertainment (e.g. film making, music, theatre) and hairdressing. All service providers operate in the tertiary sector.

> **Definitions to learn**
>
> The **primary sector** of industry extracts and uses the natural resources from the Earth to produce raw materials used by other businesses.
> The **secondary sector** of industry manufactures goods using the raw materials provided by the primary sector.
> The **tertiary sector** of industry provides goods and services to consumers and the other economic sectors.

Types of economic sectors

▲ The three types of economic sector: rice farming in Vietnam, clothes production in China and retailing in Kenya

> ### Activity 1.2
> Copy this table. Indicate with a tick which economic sector each business is in.
>
> | Business | Primary | Secondary | Tertiary |
> |---|---|---|---|
> | Insurance | | | |
> | Forestry | | | |
> | Lithium mining | | | |
> | Electronics equipment assembly | | | |
> | Airline | | | |
> | Bakery | | | |
> | Housebuilder | | | |

Study tips

If you are asked which economic sector(s) a business operates in, do not forget that many businesses operate in more than one!

Many businesses do not limit their operations to just one economic sector. For example, a few large UK supermarket groups own their own farms, producing, for example, milk (primary activity). They process farm output in their own factories to make finished goods such as yoghurt (secondary activity). They then sell these goods in their own retail stores (tertiary activity). Such businesses often claim that there are advantages in being able to control all the suppliers of these products.

Private and public sectors

Nearly every country in the world has an economy which combines both a private sector and a public sector.

Private sector

Definitions to learn

The **private sector** is the part of the economy owned and operated by individuals and companies, usually for profit, and is not state/government controlled.

The **private sector** is made up of businesses that are not owned by the government but by private individuals. The individuals who own these businesses will make their own decisions about what to produce, how it should be produced and what price should be charged for it. Most businesses in the private sector will aim to make a profit. Even so, there are likely to be some government controls over these decisions and these are explained in later chapters in this book.

7

1 BUSINESS ACTIVITY AND ECONOMIC SECTORS

Potential advantages of private sector businesses

- Owners of private sector businesses will aim to make a profit – this will encourage owners to operate the business as efficiently as possible to reduce costs and not waste resources.
- Customers are likely to benefit from competition between private sector businesses. Competition should help to keep prices low and customer service levels high, as well as encourage the business to introduce new products to increase demand.
- The profit motive encourages entrepreneurs to set up new businesses which creates new products and a dynamic business environment.

Potential disadvantages of private sector businesses

- Owners may agree with competitors to fix prices and make higher than normal profits.
- Some businesses might become so large that they dominate their industries as monopolies. This again could lead to high prices and high profits.
- Many important goods and services will not be provided to everyone – only those customers who can afford them. If there are only a small number of potential customers for a product, then it may not be profitable for businesses to produce it.

Public sector

> **Definitions to learn**
>
> The **public sector** is made up of organisations in the economy that are owned and controlled by the government.

The **public sector** is made up of government (or state) owned and controlled businesses and organisations. The government, or other public sector authority, makes decisions about what to produce and how much to charge consumers. Some goods and services are provided free of charge to the consumer in many countries, such as state health care and education services. The money for these comes not from the customers but from taxpayers. The objectives of private sector and public sector businesses are often different.

Potential advantages of public sector businesses

- Private monopolies will be prevented from making higher than normal profits, if a profit is made at all.
- Some important goods and services can be provided to all people who need them as consumption will not depend on ability to pay.
- Government ownership and control may mean that the business organisation takes decisions that benefit the whole community. These might include using low polluting production methods.

Potential disadvantages of public sector businesses

- The cost of providing important goods and services to everyone will be high. This may lead to high taxation.
- Public sector businesses may operate with social objectives and not the profit motive as the key aim. This might mean that they are less efficient and more wasteful than private sector businesses.
- The lack of competition in an industry in the public sector may lead to less innovation and few new products being developed.

Types of economic sectors

Which business activities are usually in the public sector?

In many countries the government owns and controls the following important industries or activities:

- health
- education
- defence
- public transport
- water supply
- electricity supply.

Activity 1.3

For each of the examples of key industries or activities listed above, suggest **three** possible reasons why the government of a country might decide to own and control that industry or service.

Activity 1.4

Find out whether, in your own country, the government owns and controls the following businesses:

a railway system
b local bus services
c water supply
d electricity supply
e TV and radio stations
f hospitals
g libraries.

Extend your skills of analysis

A question which asks why a government might want to improve the economy by encouraging expansion of the private sector, such as car manufacturing, could be answered as follows:

Expanding the private sector will result in more car manufacturers owned and controlled by private individuals and not the government.

Extend your analysis by explaining what will happen if the private sector grows.

More private sector businesses will mean more competition and more new cars produced.

Extend your analysis by explaining how this will help the economy.

More competition should encourage businesses to keep car prices as low as possible to encourage sales. Competing businesses will also want to bring out new products and this should increase jobs and output in the economy.

Study tips

The advantages and disadvantages of both the private sector and public sector are important to remember.

Activity 1.5

A government is considering moving the postal service from being in the public sector to being in the private sector (privatisation). You decide to write to the government minister in charge, explaining your views on this matter and stating your opinion. Your letter should contain:

- an explanation of the difference between private sector businesses and public sector businesses
- the possible advantages of the postal service being in the private sector
- the possible disadvantages of the postal service being in the private sector
- your recommendation to the minister on whether to keep the postal service in the public sector or not.

1 BUSINESS ACTIVITY AND ECONOMIC SECTORS

REVISION SUMMARY   Economic sectors

Primary, e.g. fishing, farming, extracting raw materials

Secondary, e.g. processing, manufacturing

Tertiary, e.g. retailing, banking

BY ACTIVITY

BY OWNERSHIP

Private sector, owned by private individuals

Public sector, owned by government or state agencies

International business in focus

Tourism in Mauritius

Mauritius is a small island in the Indian Ocean with a land area of just 2000 km². The Mauritian economy is dominated by the tertiary sector. In 2023 tourism, finance and other services accounted for approximately 66% of total national output (gross domestic product). In contrast, the secondary sector accounted for 18% and primary industries – mainly sugar production – approximately 3%. The government is planning for up to 1.5 million visitors from other countries. These tourists spend a great deal of money on food, drink, travel and holiday gifts.

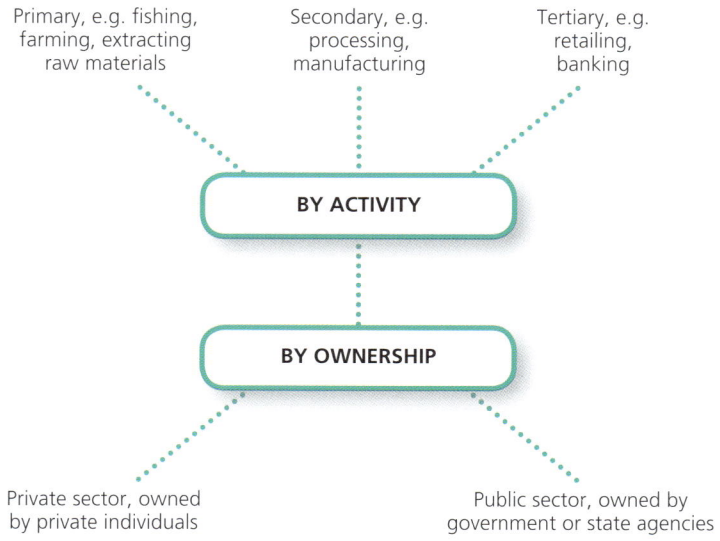

Air Mauritius is one of the businesses that has benefited greatly from the expansion of tourism in the country. The airline is partly owned by private owners and the Mauritian government. It has been nominated in the 'Best Airline in Africa' category in recent years.

Air Mauritius not only has an extensive network of air routes but it also offers services to other airlines operating in the region. There are hundreds of hotels and guesthouses in Mauritius and these employ many local workers. Some of the largest hotel groups in the world operate in Mauritius, including Radisson and Hilton.

Discussion points

- Why do you think the primary sector of the Mauritian economy is relatively small?
- Explain three ways in which tertiary sector industries contribute to the Mauritian economy.
- Do you think that increasing numbers of tourists will bring only benefits to Mauritius?
- Why do you think the Mauritian government still owns a part of Air Mauritius?

Types of economic sectors

Chapter review questions: Short answer and data response

1. Ade's Engineering Company (AEC) operates in the secondary sector. It uses the 4 factors of production to make parts for cars and trucks. These goods are sold to car and truck manufacturers in many countries. The parts include metal brake components and rubber seals to fit around windows. To be successful, AEC requires raw materials supplied by other businesses to make car parts.
   a. Define 'goods'. [2]
   b. Outline **two** examples of tertiary sector businesses AEC is likely to use. [4]
   c. Explain **two** reasons why it might be important for AEC to increase added value. [6]
   d. Explain **two** ways AEC could increase added value. Which way should it choose? Justify your answer. [8]

2. The government of Country Y owns and controls many businesses. 'The public sector always produces goods and services, such as electricity, more efficiently than privately owned businesses,' a government minister recently said. Other ministers disagree and want some businesses that are owned by the state to be sold to the private sector. The private sector businesses in Country Y produce 55% of total output of goods and services – mainly in services such as transport, tourism and finance.
   a. Define 'private sector'. [2]
   b. Outline **two** reasons why the government owns some businesses. [4]
   c. Explain **two** possible reasons why government ministers want some businesses to be sold to the private sector. [6]
   d. Do you agree with the government minister's view that: 'The public sector always produces goods and services more efficiently than privately owned businesses'? Justify your answer. [8]

Revision checklist

In this chapter you have learned:

- ✔ the nature of business activity and the four factors of production
- ✔ the concept of adding value
- ✔ how added value can be increased
- ✔ the concept of opportunity cost
- ✔ the differences between primary, secondary and tertiary sectors
- ✔ the differences between the private and public sectors.

NOW – test your understanding with the revision questions in the Student etextbook and the Workbook.

2 Enterprise, business growth and size

This chapter will explain:

Enterprise and entrepreneurship:

★ characteristics of successful entrepreneurs
★ the purpose and key elements of a business plan
★ the importance of having a business plan
★ why and how governments support business start-ups.

The methods and problems of measuring business size:

★ methods of measuring business size
★ problems when measuring business size.

Why some businesses grow and others remain small:

★ why the owners of a business may want to grow the business
★ how and why businesses can grow internally
★ how and why businesses can grow externally
★ advantages and disadvantages of methods of growth
★ problems linked to business growth
★ why some businesses remain small.

Why some businesses succeed and others fail:

★ reasons why businesses succeed or fail.

Enterprise and entrepreneurship

What will you do when you leave school or college? Maybe you will go to university or get a job. Some of you may decide to take the risk of setting up your own business – this could be full-time or part-time. If you decide to do this then you will become an **entrepreneur**! Table 2.1 outlines the advantages and possible disadvantages of starting your own business.

Definitions to learn

An **entrepreneur** is a person who has an idea for a new business, starts it up and accepts the risks of the new business venture.

Table 2.1 Advantages and disadvantages of being an entrepreneur

Advantages of being an entrepreneur	Disadvantages of being an entrepreneur
• Independence – able to choose how to use time and money	• Risk – many new entrepreneurs' businesses fail, especially if there is poor planning
• Able to put own ideas into practice	• Capital – entrepreneurs have to put their own money into the business and they could lose this if the business fails
• May become successful if the business grows	
• May be profitable and the income may be higher than if working as an employee for another business	• Lack of knowledge and experience in operating a business
• Able to make use of personal interests and skills	• Opportunity cost – lost income from not being an employee of another business

Enterprise and entrepreneurship

Study tips

Think about why successful entrepreneurs are important to the country they are based in. You should be able to explain why governments want to encourage more entrepreneurs to set up in business.

For many successful entrepreneurs, starting up their own business has led to great wealth. Table 2.2. outlines the main business interests of five well-known entrepreneurs. How many of these business leaders have you heard of? They all started out as an entrepreneur with their own business idea.

Table 2.2 Some well-known entrepreneurs

Entrepreneur	Nationality	Main business interests
Victoria Haihambo	Namibian	Founded a start-up in Namibia called Agelvipa Online. Agelvipa Online supports small businesses run by women and offers them business management training. In 2020 she was inducted into the Namibia Business Hall of Fame
Mukesh Ambani	Indian	Continues to start up new ventures within the Reliance Industries business (originally founded by his father, Dhirubhai), which is now one of the largest companies in Asia. Businesses include chemicals, IT and retailing
Howard Yang	Chinese	Named the Chinese mainland winner of the Ernst and Young Entrepreneur Of The Year 2023 award. He is Chairman, CEO and Chief Scientist of Montage Technology Company (chip design and data processing)
Oprah Winfrey	American	Has built a large media empire throughout her career. She co-founded Oxygen Media in 2000 and continued hosting her talk show until 2011. She then created OWN: Oprah Winfrey Network, which she leads as CEO
Mark Zuckerberg	American	Co-founded the social networking site Facebook

Case study: Dr Wedu Tose Somolekae

In an interview with *Forbes Africa*, Tose Somolekae said, 'When I started medical school in 2011, I dreamed of eventually becoming a paediatrician.' However, this changed after Tose Somolekae visited a medical aesthetics clinic in Johannesburg, South Africa, and she began researching aesthetics and medicine instead.

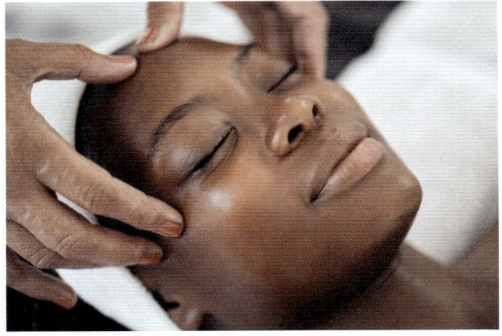

In 2021 Tose Somolekae decided to resign from her job as a medical officer in Masunga, Botswana. She set up Medi-Glow Aesthetics, the first full-time facility of its kind in Gaborone, the capital of Botswana. It provides beauty treatments and aesthetic services that are medically approved.

Tose Somolekae needed to be innovative, hard-working and optimistic to introduce something different to the medical and beauty industry.

Source: Adapted from www.forbesafrica.com/under-30/2023/04/12/forbesafrica30under30-class-of-2023meet-cover-star-dr-wedu-tose-somolekae-aesthetic-medicine-and-entrepreneurship-were-the-furthest-thing-on-my-mind/

Characteristics of successful entrepreneurs

What are the characteristics of successful entrepreneurs? Would everyone make a good entrepreneur? Probably not – some people do not like taking risks or working independently and may prefer to be an employee of a large business instead. Table 2.3 outlines the important characteristics of successful entrepreneurs.

2 ENTERPRISE, BUSINESS GROWTH AND SIZE

Table 2.3 Characteristics of successful entrepreneurs

Characteristics of successful entrepreneurs	Reasons why important
Hard working	Long hours and short holidays are typical for many entrepreneurs. It is essential for entrepreneurs to work hard to meet customers' demands to make their business successful
Risk taker	Entrepreneurs risk losing their own capital if the business fails. However, new ideas and projects which carry the most risk can also bring the greatest profit if the market demand is high
Optimistic	Overcoming setbacks and staying positive is important. Looking forward to a better future is essential – if you think only of failure, you will fail!
Self-confident	Self-confidence is necessary to convince other people of your skills and to convince banks, other lenders and customers that your business is going to be successful
Innovative	Being able to put new ideas into practice in interesting and different ways is also important. A new business is most likely to be successful if it introduces new ideas for goods and services. The entrepreneur needs to make the business and what it offers stand out from the competition
Independent	Entrepreneurs will often have to work on their own before they can afford to employ others. Entrepreneurs must be highly motivated and able to work without any help. Being able to work without orders or instructions from anyone else will mean that effective decisions can be taken by the entrepreneur alone
Effective communicator	Talking clearly and confidently to banks, other investors, customers and government agencies about the new business will raise the profile of the new business. Communicating details about the new business and its products will be key to attracting new customers, lenders and investors

Extend your skills of analysis

A question that asks why a particular entrepreneurial characteristic might help an entrepreneur be successful in starting up a fast-food cafe could be answered as follows:

Being innovative means being able to think of new ideas and put them into effect.

Extend your analysis by explaining how this helps an entrepreneur to be successful.

The entrepreneur's ideas need to be different to those of competitors so the business can possibly attract customers. For example, an entrepreneur operating a fast-food cafe might start to offer free childcare facilities for parents who use the cafe.

Extend your analysis by explaining how offering this helps the business to be successful.

This will encourage more people with children to visit and stay longer, spending more money on food and drink, which will increase sales and revenue.

Activity 2.1

Research the background and business activities of two well-known entrepreneurs in your own country. Identify the personal characteristics that you believe have helped them to succeed. Write a brief report on each entrepreneur and be prepared to present your reports to the rest of your class.

Enterprise and entrepreneurship

REVISION SUMMARY Entrepreneurs

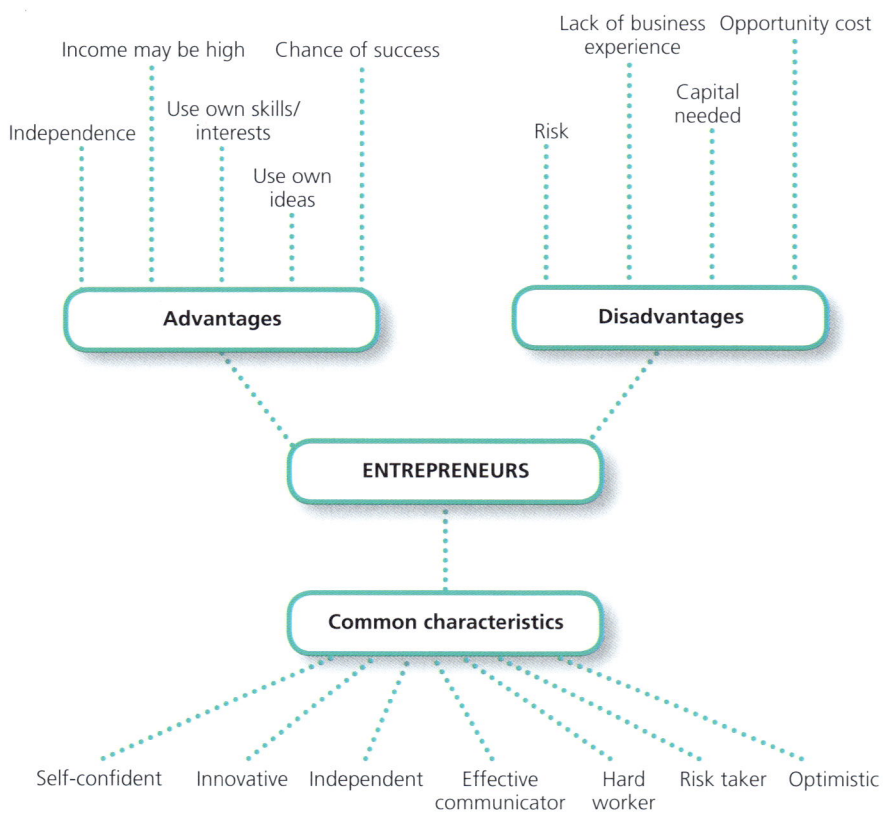

Purpose and key elements of a business plan

Definitions to learn

A **business plan** is a written document that describes a business, its objectives, its strategies, the market it is in and its financial forecasts.

The most important purpose of a **business plan** is to force the entrepreneur to think ahead and prepare carefully for the first few years of the new business. In addition, an effective business plan will be important to persuade banks or investors to provide the necessary finance to get the business started. Business plans are also used by existing businesses if a major new project is being planned.

The entrepreneur will have to consider the following when preparing the business plan:

» What products or services do I intend to provide and which consumers am I 'aiming at'?
» What are my objectives for the business?
» What will be my main costs and will enough products be sold to pay for them?
» Where will the business be located?
» What resources will be required in the business?
» How much finance will be needed and what will the forecast cash flow look like?

Every business plan contains similar headings. The key elements of a business plan will usually include the following:

1. **Summary (or Overview)**
   The summary provides a brief description of the business, including the goods or services it intends to offer to customers. The relevant skills and experience of the entrepreneur are outlined.
2. **Objectives of the business**
   The entrepreneur needs to think carefully about what they hope the business will achieve within a given time period. Examples of objectives include a certain level of profit or a target level of sales.
3. **Resources**
   The business is likely to need premises, equipment, materials and, possibly, employees. These must be planned for and costed.
4. **Market research**
   This research helps the entrepreneur to establish:
   - total market size
   - likely target market
   - main competitors
   - forecast sales of the product (the good or service)
   - predicted market growth.
5. **Marketing**
   This section covers how the good or service is to be sold to customers, the prices to be charged and the main promotion methods to be used.
6. **Human resources plan (people)**
   This section explains whether employees are needed from the start of the business. If so, the number of them and the skills they need is given.
7. **Operations**
   This section covers issues such as:
   - What is the best location for the business? Many very small start-up businesses may operate from the entrepreneur's own home.
   - Will the business make the product or will it be bought in from suppliers?
   - What levels of inventory might be needed?
8. **Finance**
   This is the most important element of the plan and includes:
   - forecast profit or loss and statement of financial position of the business for at least the first year of operation
   - sources of capital, for example, entrepreneur's capital, revenue, bank loans
   - predicted costs
   - forecast cash flow.

Enterprise and entrepreneurship

The importance of having a business plan

A business plan gives the entrepreneur a clear set of guidelines and objectives. These are helpful when key decisions have to be made because they ensure the decision fits with the plan itself. By setting objectives and outlining expected expenditure, the entrepreneur can keep a check on progress. At the end of the first year, they can assess whether the plan has been carried out successfully. If it has not, changes can be made to the plan or different decisions made to put the business back on track.

Without such a detailed plan, banks and other investors will be reluctant to provide loans or other finance to the business. This is because there is no evidence that the owners of the new business have thought seriously about the future and planned for the challenges that the business will certainly face. Even with a detailed business plan, banks might not offer a loan if the bank manager believes that there is not enough research to support the plan or if the financial forecasts are too optimistic.

Key info

In 2022 there were over 6.2 million millionaires in China. Most of these are successful entrepreneurs. There have been many new start-ups by Chinese entrepreneurs who have studied abroad and returned to the country, people who have left their jobs to start their own businesses, migrant workers who have returned to their home towns to start their own businesses, and university students. China is second after the USA for the highest number of millionaires (in $US).

REVISION SUMMARY — **Business plans**

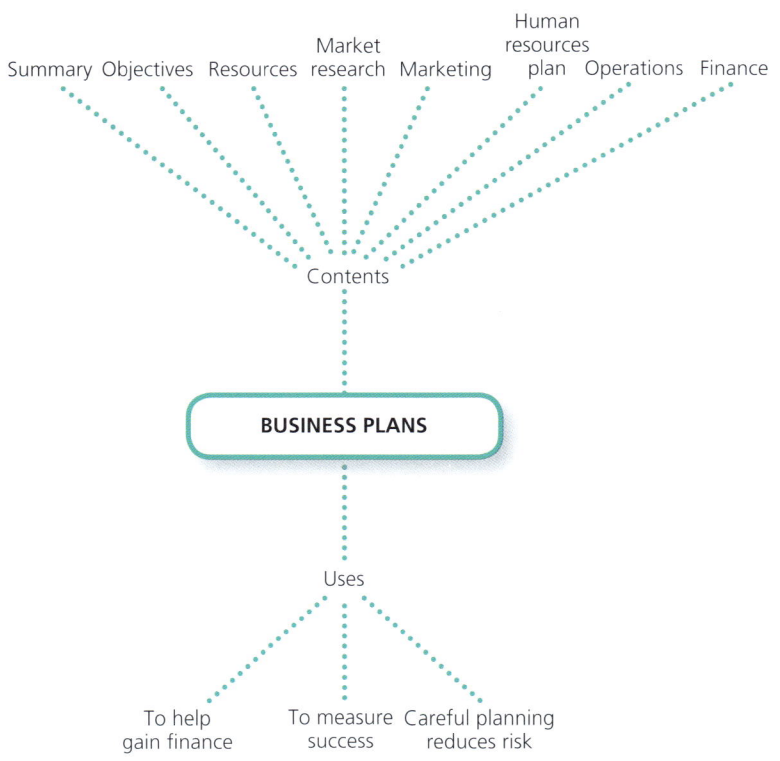

2 ENTERPRISE, BUSINESS GROWTH AND SIZE

An example of a business plan is shown in Table 2.4. It was completed by two entrepreneurs planning to open a takeaway pizza restaurant.

Case study: A business plan for Pizza Palace

Table 2.4 A typical business plan

Summary	Pizza Palace will provide a high-class pizza restaurant and takeaway service including home delivery. Rashid Gupta is a qualified accountant and has 10 years' experience in supermarket management. James Sanchez is a chef who has worked in several different types of restaurant
Business objective	To achieve a profit equal to 10% of capital invested in the business within the first 2 years
Resources required	Small high-street restaurant – rented
	Catering equipment
	3 motorcycles for delivery service
Market research	Total market size in the region: $250 million per year, rising by 10% per year
	Target market: young people and families with above average incomes
	Four competing pizza cafes and restaurants within 10 kilometres of proposed location but all aimed at low-income consumers
	Unemployment in the area is very low
	Sales for Pizza Palace are forecasted to be $220 000 in first year
Marketing	Prices set 10% below main competitors for first 4 months
	From month 5, prices set 10% above competitors
	All promotion on social media with a budget of $5000 per year
Human resources plan	The 2 business owners, plus 3 delivery drivers to be employed on weekly wage of $50 each
Operations	Main suppliers of raw materials: P&P Wholesalers
	Fixed costs of operations: $50 000 per year
	Variable costs: approximately $2 per pizza sold
	Site of restaurant to rent in shopping street (Brunei Avenue) near to the town centre
Finance	Main fixed costs:
	Rent of premises $10 000 per year
	Second-hand kitchen equipment: $6000
	3 second-hand motorcycles: $3000 each
	Forecast profit:
	In the first year of operations the total costs are forecast to be $205 000 with revenue of $220 000
	Forecast profit: $15 000
	Level of output to break even: 30 000 pizzas per year
	Cash flow:
	Due to the high start-up and promotion costs there will be negative cash flow in the first year
	Finance sources:
	$10 000 invested by each owner
	Request to bank for a further $15 000 plus an overdraft arrangement of $6000 per month

Enterprise and entrepreneurship

Study tips
You need to know the main elements of a business plan and be able to explain why a particular business might benefit from developing such a plan.

> ### Activity 2.2
> Read the business plan for Pizza Palace on the previous page. Explain why, if you were a bank manager reading this plan, each of the following would be important to consider before you gave the entrepreneurs a loan:
> - market research results
> - experience of business owners
> - forecast profit.

> ### Activity 2.3
> Draw up another business plan. It should be based on your own idea for a business that is operated within your school or college (for example, a stationery store, confectionery store or cake store).

Why governments support business start-ups

Most governments offer support to entrepreneurs. This encourages them to set up new businesses. The main reasons this support is given include:

» Reducing unemployment – new businesses will often create jobs which helps reduce unemployment.
» Increasing competition – new businesses give consumers more choice and compete with already established businesses.
» Increasing output – the economy will benefit from increased output of goods and services and government tax revenue will increase.
» Benefiting society – entrepreneurs may create social enterprises which offer benefits to society other than jobs and profit, for example, supporting disadvantaged groups in society.
» Encouraging future business growth – all large businesses were small at one time! By supporting today's new entrepreneurs, the government may be helping businesses that will grow to become very large and important in the future.

How governments support business start-ups

The most common ways governments support business start-ups are shown in Table 2.5.

Table 2.5 How governments support business start-ups

What business start-ups need	Support provided
Grants	These are a form of financial support for new businesses which reduces the size of loans they need to start up. This will increase their chance of being successful. Some grants are available to businesses that start up in areas of high unemployment
Advice	Advice and support sessions are offered by experienced business people to help entrepreneurs understand what problems may arise and how they may be overcome
Premises	'Enterprise zones' provide low-cost premises to start-up businesses
Low-cost loans	Loans for small businesses at low interest rates
Employee training	Schemes financed by the government to help start-up businesses to train employees and increase their productivity
Entrepreneur training	Governments often support training in essential business skills for entrepreneurs which is given by senior managers (some of them retired but very experienced). This could include financial and people management training. It reduces the risk of errors being made by entrepreneurs soon after starting up

2 ENTERPRISE, BUSINESS GROWTH AND SIZE

The methods and problems of measuring business size

Businesses vary greatly in terms of size. On the one hand, a small business can be owned and run by a single individual. At the other extreme, some businesses employ hundreds of thousands of workers all over the world. Some produce output worth hundreds of dollars a year, while the biggest businesses sell goods valued at billions of dollars each year.

Who would find it useful to compare the size of businesses?

- Investors – before deciding which business to put their savings into.
- Governments – often there are different tax rates for small and large businesses.
- Competitors – to compare their size and importance with other businesses.
- Employees – to have some idea of how many people they might be working with.
- Banks – to see how important a loan to the business is compared to its overall size.

There are several different methods of measuring business size:

- number of people employed
- value of output/sales
- volume of output/sales
- value of **capital employed**.

They all have uses and problems.

> **Definitions to learn**
>
> **Capital employed** is the total amount of capital invested in a business for the purpose of generating profits.

Number of people employed

This method is easy to calculate and compare with other businesses, especially when they operate in the same industry. For example, in 2023 Tesla, the US-based electric car manufacturer, employed 140 473 workers. In the same year the Japanese-based car manufacturer Toyota had 375 235 employees. This suggests that Toyota is over 2.5 times bigger than Tesla but this is only true if the number of people employed is an accurate measure of business size.

Problems

This measure may not be an accurate measure of business size, especially when comparing businesses in different industries. A retailing business with 1000 employees is likely to have lower sales and much less capital employed than a nuclear power station employing about the same number of workers.

Some businesses use production methods which employ very few people but produce high output levels. This is true for automated factories which use the latest computer-controlled equipment. These businesses are called capital-intensive and they use a great deal of high-cost capital equipment to produce their output. Therefore, a business with high output levels could employ fewer people than a business which produces less output.

Another point to consider is whether two part-time employees, who each work half of a working week, should be counted as one employee or two.

Value of output/sales

Calculating the value of output produced is a common way of comparing business size in the same industry – especially in manufacturing industries. In 2023 Tesla's total output of vehicles was valued at US$82.2 billion. In the same year, Toyota's output was valued at US$274.9 billion. The value of sales is often used when comparing the size of retailing businesses – especially retailers selling similar products, such as supermarkets. It allows market share for each business to be calculated.

Problems

A high level of output does not mean that a business is large when using the other methods of measurement. A business employing few people might produce several very expensive computers each year. This might give higher output figures than a producer selling cheaper products but employing more workers.

The value of output in any time period might not be the same as the value of sales if some goods are not sold.

It could be misleading to use total sales as a measure when comparing the size of businesses that sell very different products, for example, a market stall selling sweets and a retailer of luxury handbags or perfumes.

Volume of output/sales

When making comparisons of business size between businesses in different countries the volume of output or sales is often used. This avoids the problem of using exchange rates (which often fluctuate) to measure the value of output or sales. In addition, comparisons of value are affected by inflation over time. The volume of output uses actual units and so is not distorted by inflation. In 2023 Tesla produced and sold 1.85 million vehicles. In the same year, Toyota produced and sold 11.23 million vehicles.

Problems

This method can only be used to compare business size within the same industry. It would be very misleading to compare the number of bicycles made by Business A with the number of ships built by Business B, for example.

Value of capital employed

Capital employed is the total value of capital invested into the business. By comparing the amount of capital invested in a business it should be clear which businesses use a great deal of capital in production or selling and which use less. In 2023 Toyota's total capital employed was US$316 341 billion. This was over 4.5 times greater than the capital employed of Tesla at US$66 749 billion. This measure can be used, when compared to profit, to assess how effective a business is in using its finance.

Problems

This measure has a similar problem to that of the 'number of people employed' measure. A company employing many workers may use labour-intensive methods of production to manufacture handcrafted and high-priced output. These businesses may have relatively high numbers of employees and value of sales but use little capital equipment.

▲ A capital-intensive and a labour-intensive business

Activity 2.4

You are employed by Company A, which makes motorcycles. You have been asked to write a brief report to the Managing Director comparing the size of your company with three others in the same industry. Use the following information in your report. State the problems of using each method of comparing business size.

	Workers employed	Capital employed ($m)	Value of output ($m)
Company A	20 000	50	100
Company B	5 000	150	300
Company C	3 000	60	160
Company D	15 000	180	150

REVISION SUMMARY Comparing business size

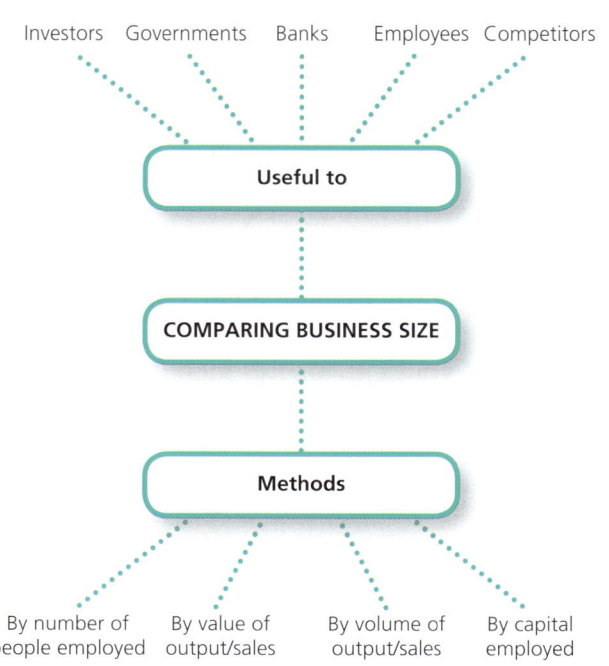

Why some businesses grow and others remain small

Why the owners of a business may want to grow the business

The owners of a business often want their business to grow. What advantages will a business and its owners gain from expansion? Here are some likely benefits:

- the possibility of higher profits for the owners
- more status and prestige for the owners and managers – higher salaries are often paid to managers who control bigger businesses
- lower average costs (see page 248, 'The concept of economies of scale')
- larger share of its market – the proportion of total market sales it makes is greater. This gives a business more influence when dealing with suppliers and distributors, and consumers are often attracted to the 'big names' in an industry.

How and why businesses can grow internally

Internal growth means that a business expands what it is currently doing without joining up with another business. Internal growth can be achieved in different ways:

- **Developing new products.** A common way to expand an existing business is to develop new products. For example, a bicycle manufacturer might start to produce and sell e-bikes with built-in batteries. Many businesses will add to their existing range of products with new products, or developments of existing ones, to increase sales and expand the business. For example, Apple is up to version 16 of its iPhone.
- **Developing new markets.** Instead of expanding existing premises or product ranges to serve more customers in the existing market, businesses often choose to develop new markets to increase sales and grow. For example, a restaurant owner could open additional restaurants in other towns. In this example the business would be taking advantage of new markets and customers in other locations. The market in these new locations could be growing more rapidly than in the original location.

Internal growth is much more gradual and easier to manage than external growth.

How and why businesses can grow externally

External growth means that a business combines operations with another business. This can either involve a **takeover** or a **merger**.

The two most common ways of achieving external growth are:

- **Horizontal integration**. When one business merges with or takes over another one in the same industry at the *same* stage of production.

> **Definitions to learn**
>
> **Internal growth** occurs when a business expands its existing operations.
> **External growth** is when a business takes over or merges with another business. It is often called integration as one business is integrated into another one.
> A **takeover** is when one business buys out the owners of another business, which then becomes part of the 'predator' business (the business which has taken it over/become the new owner).
> A **merger** is when the owners of two businesses agree to join their businesses together to make one business.
> **Horizontal integration** is when one business merges with or takes over another one in the same industry at the same stage of production.

2 ENTERPRISE, BUSINESS GROWTH AND SIZE

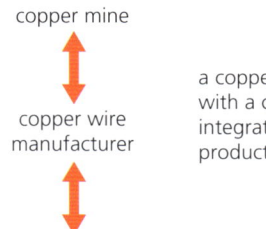

▲ An example of horizontal integration

Definitions to learn

Vertical integration is when one business merges with or takes over another one in the same industry at a different stage of production. Vertical integration can be forward or backward.

» **Vertical integration.** When one business merges with or takes over another one in the same industry at a *different* stage of production. Vertical integration can either be **forward** or **backward**. Forward vertical integration is when a business integrates with another business which is at a later stage of production which is closer to the consumer. An example would be a copper wire manufacturer taking over an electrical product manufacturer. Backward vertical integration is when a business integrates with another business at an earlier stage of production (closer to the sources of supplies the business needs). An example would be a copper wire manufacturer merging with a copper mining business.

You should notice that these two examples of integration are very different, even though they both involve two businesses joining together.

copper mine
↕
copper wire manufacturer
↕
electrical product manufacturer

a copper wire manufacturer merges with a copper mine (backward integration) and with an electrical product manufacturer (forward integration)

▲ Backward and forward integration

Activity 2.5

Identify the form of business growth which is used in each of these situations.

a A vehicle garage agrees to merge with another garage.
b A bicycle retailer expands by buying a bicycle shop in another town.
c A fruit juice business buys a fruit farm.
d A business making electrical goods agrees to join with a business with retail shops specialising in electrical goods.
e A mining company takes over a company supplying mining equipment.

Activity 2.6

In each of the cases in Activity 2.5, explain the likely reason(s) for the expansion.

Why some businesses grow and others remain small

Advantages and disadvantages of methods of growth

The advantages and disadvantages of the methods of business growth are explained in Table 2.6.

Table 2.6 Advantages and disadvantages of methods of growth

Method of growth	Advantages	Disadvantages
Internal	- Relatively gradual and therefore easy to manage - Often financed from profit so may not need to take out loans - Existing owners/managers keep control	- Relatively slow form of growth – competitors might grow more rapidly - No new ideas brought into the business through merger and takeover
External: horizontal	- Reduces competition - Opportunities for cost reductions (see page 247, 'The concept of economies of scale') - Larger market share	- It might be difficult to obtain the finance required to merge or take over a competitor - Different styles of leadership might lead to employee uncertainty about how they are being managed
External: vertical – forward	- Ensures an outlet for the products/services of the business - The business is now 'closer to the customer' and might benefit from better communications with the people who buy its products - The price to the customer can be controlled	- A rapid form of growth which might be difficult to finance and manage - Managers might lack the skills needed to produce effective marketing plans and promotions for a retailing business, for example
External: vertical – backward	- Gives an assured supply of important materials/components - The supplier might be prevented from providing products to competitors - The cost of supplies can be controlled and profit margin absorbed	- Management might lack the skills needed to operate a business manufacturing advanced technology components, for example - The cost of taking over a supplier might be higher, in the long term, than just purchasing the supplies, making the business less competitive

Extend your skills of analysis

A question that asks why a supermarket might benefit from taking over another supermarket could be answered as follows:

Horizontal integration is taking over a business at the same stage of production, in this case retailing.

Extend your analysis by explaining why this is an advantage.

Now the business is larger with a bigger market share, it could insist on bigger discounts from suppliers. This will reduce the cost of supplies.

Extend your analysis by explaining why this will benefit the business.

Lower cost of supplies will help the larger supermarket business increase profit on each item sold (gross profit margin) and total profits of the business are likely to increase.

2 ENTERPRISE, BUSINESS GROWTH AND SIZE

Activity 2.7

Read the case study on the right.

a Is this takeover an example of horizontal or vertical integration? Explain your answer.

b Explain **two** possible reasons why INOX Leisure merged with PVR.

c Do you think consumers in India will benefit from this merger? Explain your answer.

Case study: PVR merger with INOX Leisure

PVR Cinemas, 1 of the largest multiplex cinema chains in India, merged with INOX Leisure, its rival competitor, in February 2023 to create the largest cinema chain in India. These 2 businesses were the leading cinema chains in India. This $1.46 billion deal aimed to strengthen PVR's market position against competition and provide economies of scale for better pricing and better films at the cinemas. The new business aims to open new cinemas in smaller cities but close cinemas in places where previously both had cinemas.

Problems linked to business growth

Not all business expansion leads to success. There are several reasons why business expansion can fail to increase profit or achieve the other objectives set by managers and owners. These reasons are explained in Table 2.7.

Table 2.7 Problems linked to business growth

Problem resulting from expansion	Possible ways to overcome problem
Larger business is difficult to control (see also page 248, 'The concept of diseconomies of scale')	Operate the business in small units, for example, separate product divisions. Each unit will operate on a smaller scale
Co-ordination is more difficult in a larger business	Set clear and specific objectives Senior management team should meet frequently to ensure all departments and units are working towards these objectives
Larger business can lead to poor communication (see Chapter 7)	Operate the business in smaller units Use latest IT equipment and telecommunications to communicate with employees/customers
Expansion costs so much that business is short of finance	Expand more slowly – use profits from slowly expanding business to pay for further growth Arrange long-term finance to spread the cost of the expansion over a longer period of time
Integrating with another business is more difficult than expected, perhaps because different leadership styles lead to different opinions on how to run the business	Identify differences in styles before merger or takeover and set common objectives and ways of achieving them

Why some businesses remain small

Not all businesses grow. Some stay small, employing few people and using relatively little capital. There are several reasons why many businesses remain small, including:

- the type of industry the business operates in
- market size
- owners' objectives
- limited availability of capital.

The type of industry the business operates in

Industries with very many small businesses include hairdressing, car repairs, window cleaning, local shops, plumbers, catering. Businesses in these industries offer personal services or specialised products. If they were to grow too large, they would find it difficult to offer the close and personal service demanded by consumers. There are also few cost advantages from expansion. In these industries it is often very easy for new businesses to be set up and this creates new competition. This helps to keep existing businesses relatively small.

Market size

If the market – that is, the total number of customers – is small, the businesses are likely to remain small. This is true for businesses, such as shops, which operate in rural areas far away from cities. It is also why businesses which produce goods or services of a specialised kind, which appeal only to a limited number of consumers – such as very luxurious cars or expensive fashion clothing – remain small.

Owners' objectives

Owners' objectives sometimes include keeping their business small. They could be more interested in keeping control of a small business and knowing all their employees and customers than managing a much larger business. Owners sometimes want to avoid the stress and worry of running a large business.

Limited availability of capital

If finance is difficult to obtain or if interest rates on new loans are high, owners of a small business may be unable to afford to expand the business. They may not want to take on new partners or investors if this means they lose control and ownership of the business.

> **Key info**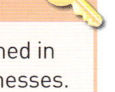
>
> There were 5.6 million private sector businesses in the UK in 2023. Small businesses (defined in the UK as those with 0–49 employees) accounted for 99.2% of all these private sector businesses. Total employment in these businesses was 13.1 million, which is 61% of all private employment in the UK. How many small businesses are there in your country?

> ### Activity 2.8
> In groups, visit or research the central area in your nearest town or city. List the main businesses in this area. Which of these are large businesses and which are small businesses? You may be able to identify this by whether they are part of a chain of shops or businesses or single, individual businesses. What products or services do the small businesses offer? Can you conclude what makes these businesses small?

Why some businesses succeed and others fail

What makes a business successful? By 'success', business analysts are usually referring to the growth and increasing profitability of businesses. There is no magic formula to explain why some businesses become very successful but here are a few examples:

- **New, innovative products:** Dyson electrical products. A high proportion of its income is invested in developing new and ever more innovative products.
- **Management skills:** Toyota cars. Its management skills and processes allow this manufacturer to produce cars at a lower unit/average cost than most other car companies.
- **Lack of competition:** Google search engine. Google dominates the search engine market with more than 85% of global online search volume. Competition is low because of Google's excellent reputation and range of services.
- **Brand image:** Apple iPhones. The high demand for the latest version of Apple's phones always exceeds supply because of the brand image and range of features the products have.

However, not all businesses are successful. The rate of failure of newly formed businesses is high – in some countries, over 50% close within five years of being set up. Even old, established businesses can close down because they make a loss or run out of cash.

The main reasons why some businesses fail include:

- **Lack of management skills.** This is a common cause of new business failures. Lack of experience can lead to bad decisions, such as locating the business in an area with high costs but low demand. Family businesses can fail because the sons and daughters of the founders of a business do not necessarily make good managers – and they might be reluctant to recruit professional managers.
- **Lack of available finance.** Shortage of cash (lack of liquidity) means that employees, suppliers, landlords and governments cannot be paid what they are owed. Failure to plan or forecast cash flows can lead to this problem and is a major cause of businesses of all sizes failing.
- **Unsuitable products.** This will lead to low demand from customers. If the business has failed to research the market and customers' needs accurately, it is likely that the products will fail to meet sales targets. Falling sales and revenue are common reasons for business failure.
- **The demand for the product can be low.** This can happen for reasons other than the poor suitability of the product. If the price is set too high or if lack of promotion means that not enough customers are aware of the product, falling sales and profit will lead to the business eventually closing.

Why some businesses succeed and others fail

- » **Changes in the economy.** Failure to plan for change is a feature in many of the later chapters. It adds to the risk and uncertainty of operating a business. Major economic changes, such as high interest rates or increased unemployment, which reduce demand for many products, can lead to business failures if they are not responded to effectively.
- » **High level of competition.** Some industries and markets are quite easy for new competitors to enter. Examples include fast-food cafes and nail bars. The greater the level of competition, the greater the risk of a business failing as it might not attract enough customers.

Activity 2.9

Using the internet, research one business you know that has stopped operating or gone bankrupt. Try to find out why it failed. Share your findings with the rest of the class.

International business in focus

AstraZeneca takeover of Chinese cancer therapy company Gracell

In 2024 the Anglo-Swedish pharmaceutical business, AstraZeneca, took over a Chinese cancer therapy company, Gracell Biotechnologies, for $1.2 billion. AstraZeneca is Britain's biggest drug manufacturer and about a third of its work is focused on cancer treatments. The company is expanding in China. Gracell Biotechnologies produces a type of cancer therapy known as CAR-T and the takeover provides further investment in cancer research and treatment.

▲ Medical research requires scientists and specialist facilities

China is the second biggest market for AstraZeneca after the USA – more than 10% of the company's revenue in 2023 came from China. By acquiring Gracell, AstraZeneca is not only increasing its number of customers in China but also hoping to work with local Chinese businesses that can sell more of its drugs to other markets in the country.

Source: Adapted from www.theguardian.com/business/2023/dec/26/astrazeneca-buys-chinese-cancer-therapy-firm-gracell-for-12bn

Discussion points

- What are some of the benefits to AstraZeneca of taking over a company in China?
- Why do you think AstraZeneca has used a takeover as a method of growth?
- If AstraZeneca was to take over a chain of retailers selling drugs, what form of integration would this be? Do you think this would be a good idea?

2 ENTERPRISE, BUSINESS GROWTH AND SIZE

❓ Chapter review questions: Short answer and data response

1 Sabrina was bored with her job in a clothing factory. Her main passion was fashion and she had always been good at selling since helping her father on his market stall. She encouraged her parents and some friends to invest in her idea for opening a shop selling good quality women's clothes. Sabrina, as the entrepreneur behind the idea, was prepared to risk her own savings too. She had some exciting ideas for the shop layout and presentation of clothes.
   a Define 'entrepreneur'. [2]
   b Outline **two** characteristics that Sabrina seems to have that might lead to the success of her business. [4]
   c Explain **two** advantages to Sabrina of keeping her business small. [6]
   d 'I think I should draw up a business plan before I start,' said Sabrina to a friend.
   'I think it would be best if you set the business up now – you don't need a plan as the shop will be so small,' said her friend.
   Which view do you agree with? Justify your answer. [8]

2 TelCom owns a phone network and provides phone network services to many consumers. The business does not manufacture phones and it does not own retail stores selling them. It has grown through horizontal integration. Senior managers at TelCom are considering a takeover of either a phone manufacturer or a chain of phone shops. TelCom has 4000 employees and, last year, recorded total sales of $300 million.
   In contrast, the largest manufacturer of mobile phones, PhonTec, has 450 employees and recorded total sales last year of $1200 million.
   a Define 'horizontal integration'. [2]
   b Outline **two** problems of measuring the size of TelCom. [4]
   c Explain **two** possible reasons why senior managers at TelCom want to expand the business. [6]
   d Do you think it would be better for TelCom to expand by taking over one of its suppliers or a chain of phone shops? Justify your answer. [8]

Revision checklist

In this chapter you have learned:

- ✔ the characteristics of successful entrepreneurs
- ✔ the purpose, key elements and importance of a business plan
- ✔ why and how governments support business start-ups
- ✔ methods for measuring the size of businesses and the problems with these methods
- ✔ why owners of a business may want it to grow
- ✔ why and how a business can grow internally and externally
- ✔ the advantages and disadvantages of each method of growth and problems resulting from growth
- ✔ why some businesses remain small
- ✔ why some businesses succeed and others fail.

NOW – test your understanding with the revision questions in the Student etextbook and the Workbook.

3 Types of business organisations

This chapter will explain:

Different types of business organisation:

★ sole traders, partnerships, private limited companies and public limited companies
★ advantages and disadvantages of different types of business organisation
★ how to recommend and justify a suitable type of business organisation to owners/management for a given situation
★ different forms of business organisations: franchises, joint ventures and social enterprises
★ advantages and disadvantages of franchises for the franchisor and franchisee
★ advantages and disadvantages of joint ventures.

Different types of business organisations

There are several main types of business organisations in the private sector. These are:

- sole traders
- partnerships
- private limited companies
- public limited companies.

Sole traders

Sole trader is the most common form of business organisation. It is a business owned and operated by just one person. One of the reasons it is such a common form of organisation is because it is so quick and easy to set up. There are only a few legal regulations which must be followed:

- The owner must register with, and send annual accounts to, the government tax office.
- The name of the business is significant. In some countries the name must be registered with the Registrar of Business Names. In other countries, such as the UK, it is sufficient for the owner to put the business name on all of the business's documents and to put a notice in the main office stating who owns the business.
- In some industries, the sole trader must observe laws which apply to all businesses in that industry. These include health and safety laws and obtaining a licence, for example, to operate a taxi.

What are the advantages and disadvantages to sole traders of running their own business rather than having other people join in with them? If you wanted to set up your own business, why might you choose to create a sole trader organisation? Table 3.1 explains the main advantages and disadvantages of the sole trader type of business organisation.

> **Definitions to learn**
> A **sole trader** is a business owned and controlled by one person.

> **Study tips**
> A sole trader can employ other people but there is only one person who owns the business.

3 TYPES OF BUSINESS ORGANISATIONS

Table 3.1 Advantages and disadvantages of a sole trader

Advantages of a sole trader	Disadvantages of a sole trader
It can be started at very low cost with very few legal requirements	There is unlimited liability so if the business fails and owes money, all of the owner's wealth is at risk (Explained later in this section)
The sole owner has complete control over the decisions made – they are their own boss	The sole owner has no other owner to discuss important business matters with
The owner can choose what hours to work and when to take breaks or holidays – there is complete independence	Start-up capital may be limited. Most start-up capital is often provided by the owner, family and friends and these sources could be insufficient
There is a high incentive to work hard as the owner keeps all the profit (after tax, of course!)	If the owner is ill, there are no other owners to step in to take over
The owner has close contact with customers and can respond quickly to their needs. There can be personal satisfaction from knowing regular customers	If the owner dies or wants to stop working then, legally, the business ceases to exist and it cannot be passed on, for example, to a family member. This is because the business has no separate legal identity
Apart from informing the tax authorities of profit made, business accounts are not made available to the public – there is complete secrecy in business matters	Business growth may be limited as it may be hard to obtain the capital required for expansion

Partnerships

A **partnership** is a group of at least two people who agree to own and run a business together. In some countries, such as India, there is a maximum limit of 100 people. The partners will:

- contribute to the capital of the business
- usually have a say in the running of the business
- share any profits made.

Partnerships can be set up very easily. A sole trader could ask someone they know to become a partner in the business. This would be called a verbal agreement. However, partners are advised to create a written agreement with each other called a **partnership agreement** or deed of partnership. Without this formal document, partners could disagree on who put most capital into the business or who is entitled to more of the profits. A written agreement will provide clear evidence to settle these matters and will include details of:

- the amount of capital invested in the business by each partner
- the management tasks to be undertaken by each partner
- the way in which the profits will be shared out
- how long the partnership will last
- arrangements for absence, retirement and how new partners can be admitted.

> **Definitions to learn**
>
> A **partnership** is formed when two or more people agree to jointly own a business.
> A **partnership agreement** is the written and legal agreement between business partners. It is not essential for partners to have such an agreement, but it is always recommended.

Different types of business organisations

Sole traders and partnerships are **unincorporated businesses**. Table 3.2 explains the main advantages and disadvantages of a business partnership.

Table 3.2 Advantages and disadvantages of a business partnership

Advantages of a partnership	Disadvantages of a partnership
More capital compared to a sole trader as the partners each contribute capital into the business. It should be easier to finance expansion of the business	The partners do not have limited liability – their own wealth is still at risk if the business fails
It is easy to set up as there are few legal formalities	The business has no separate legal identity – it is an unincorporated business, which means the partners are responsible for the business debts and can be sued personally
Profit (after tax) is shared between the partners. This motivates each partner to work hard to make the business a success. The proportion of profit to each partner will be stated in the partnership agreement	There is less independence than if a sole trader operated the business. All major decisions have to be agreed by a majority of the partners
Responsibilities in running the business and making decisions are shared, so it may be more successful. More ideas may be introduced to the business	There is potential for conflict if major disagreements occur between the partners. This could even stop some important business decisions being taken at all
It could improve the decisions taken, as different partners bring different skills and experiences into the business. Between them, they might have many contacts in the business world, for example, in advertising, which could be useful for the partnership	Lack of continuity is a common problem when a partner dies or decides to leave. These changes will disrupt the business and the partnership could then be dissolved. A new partnership agreement will need to be drawn up
Partners do not all have to be closely involved in managing the business – the partnership agreement will outline who does what. A potential partner who wants to invest does not have to help manage the business	If one partner makes a mistake or makes bad decisions, then the other partners are responsible for these mistakes and decisions as well. They are all responsible for the actions of the other partners

> **Definitions to learn**
>
> An **unincorporated business** is one that does not have a separate legal identity to the owners of the business.
> **Unlimited liability** means that the owners of a business can be held responsible for the debts of the business they own. Their liability is not limited to the investment they made in the business.
> **Limited liability** means that the liability of shareholders in a company is limited to only the amount of money they invested.

Limited liability

This is a very important concept. Sole traders and partners in a partnership have **unlimited liability**. If the business fails it may owe money to banks and other lenders. The owners may be forced to use their personal wealth to pay back these loans. They have unlimited liability to pay these debts.

Shareholders, the owners of companies, have **limited liability**. This means that if the company fails and owes money, shareholders can only lose the money they originally invested when they bought the shares. They have limited liability. This is a very important advantage that only the owners of companies have.

3 TYPES OF BUSINESS ORGANISATIONS

> ### Activity 3.1
>
> Your friend, Amin, is an expert computer engineer. He currently works for a large computer manufacturer that operates in an expanding industry. He thinks that he could run his own successful business. He has no experience of running a business. He has very few savings to invest into a business.
>
> Amin has a rich uncle who knows nothing about computers. He is a retired businessman. He is friendly but rather bossy as he always thinks he knows best.
>
> Amin asks for your advice about whether he should set up his own business and what form of organisation he should choose. He asks for your help on 3 issues that are worrying him.
>
> a Explain **two** advantages and **two** disadvantages to Amin of operating his own business rather than working for the computer manufacturer.
> b Do you think he should set up a sole trader business? Explain your answer.
> c His uncle would like to become his partner in the business if Amin decides to go ahead. Explain **two** advantages and **two** disadvantages to Amin of forming a partnership with his uncle.

REVISION SUMMARY Sole traders and partnerships

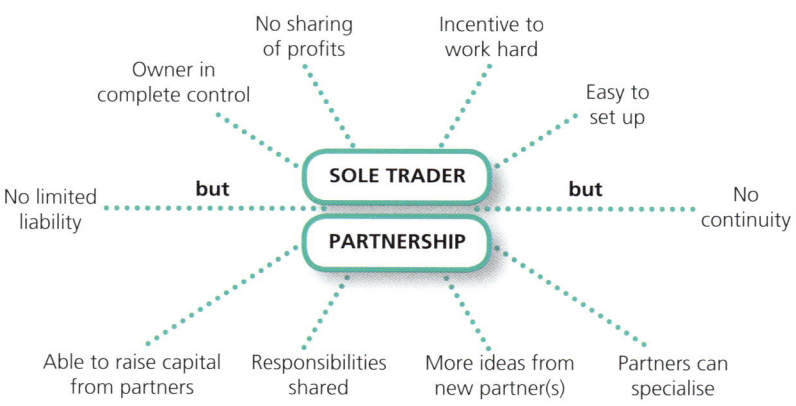

Definitions to learn

Incorporated businesses are companies that have separate legal identity from their owners.

Shareholders are the owners of a limited company. They buy shares which represent part-ownership of the company.

Private limited companies are businesses owned by shareholders but they cannot sell shares to the public – only to family, friends or specialist business investors.

Companies

There is one essential difference between a company and an unincorporated business, such as a sole trader or partnership. A company is a separate legal unit from its owners – it is an **incorporated business**. This means that:

» companies exist separately from owners and will continue to exist if one of the owners dies or wants to leave the business
» a company can make contracts or legal agreements
» company accounts are kept separate from the accounts of the owners.

Companies are jointly owned by the people who have invested in the business. These people buy shares in the company and they are therefore called **shareholders**. These shareholders appoint directors to run the business. In a **private limited company**, the directors are usually the most important or majority shareholders.

Different types of business organisations

There are significant legal matters which have to be dealt with before a company can be formed. In particular, two important documents have to be sent to the Registrar of Companies:

» **Memorandum of Association.** This contains very important information about the company and the directors. The official name and the address of the registered offices of the company must be stated. The objectives of the company must be stated as well as the number of shares to be bought by each of the directors.
» **Articles of Association.** This contains the rules under which the company will be managed – the rights and duties of all of the directors, rules concerning the election of directors and the holding of official meetings, and the procedure to be followed for the issuing of shares.

Both of these documents are intended to make sure that companies are correctly run and to reassure shareholders about the purpose and structure of the company. Once these documents have been received by the Registrar of Companies, a Certificate of Incorporation will be issued to allow the company to start trading.

Private limited companies

These businesses are often owned by one or a small number of shareholders – in many cases they are members of the same family. They can be very large businesses but most private limited companies are much smaller than the majority of public limited companies. The advantages and disadvantages of a private limited company are explained in Table 3.3.

Table 3.3 Advantages and disadvantages of a private limited company

Advantages of a private limited company	Disadvantages of a private limited company
Shares can be sold to family members, friends or specialist business investors (but NOT the general public). The ability to raise finance in this way gives private limited companies more growth opportunities than sole traders or most partnerships	Legal formalities have to be completed before a company can start trading. These will involve some costs
Limited liability is given to all shareholders. This encourages people to buy shares in private limited companies as their personal possessions are not at risk of being taken if the company fails and owes money	Shares cannot be sold to the general public so, unlike with public limited companies, the chance to raise very large amounts of capital is more limited
Private limited companies are often seen as being more secure and having higher status than sole traders and partnerships. When customers buy goods or award contracts, they want to be confident that the business has the resources to provide a reliable good or service	The shares in a private limited company cannot be sold or transferred to anyone else without the agreement of the other shareholders. This means some people do not want to invest in private companies. They may not be able to sell their shares quickly if they need their investment back
Legal identity – the company continues to exist if a shareholder dies. If their shares are then sold, they are often bought by other existing shareholders. There is continuity as the business continues if shareholders leave the business	The accounts of a company are less private than for sole traders or partnerships. Each year the latest accounts must be sent to the Registrar of Companies (as well as the tax office). Members of the public and even competitors can see the accounts

3 TYPES OF BUSINESS ORGANISATIONS

REVISION SUMMARY Private limited companies

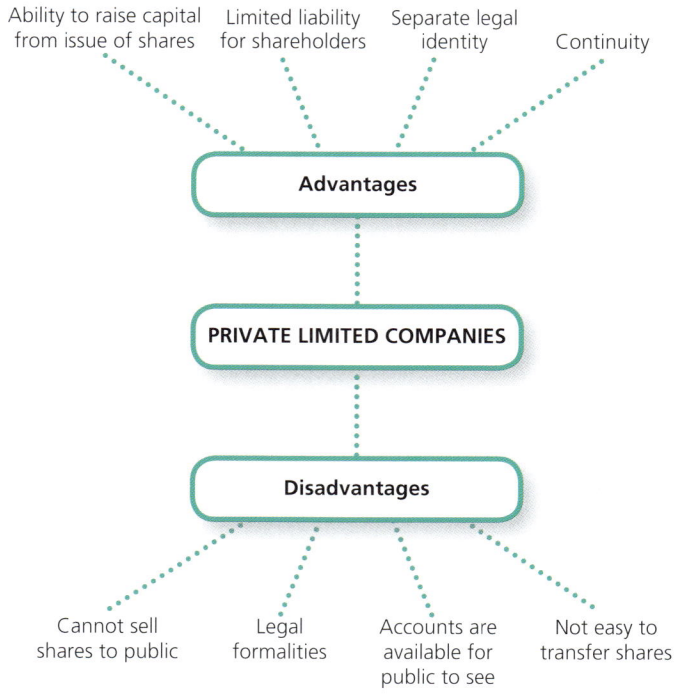

Study tips
When answering questions that refer to 'companies', the business must be either a private limited company or a public limited company. The term 'companies' should not be used when referring to sole traders or partnerships.

Activity 3.2
Read Activity 3.1 (see page 34) again.

Amin decided not to form a partnership with his uncle. Instead, 5 years after setting up his business, he is thinking of forming a private limited company. Amin would sell shares in this new company to friends and relatives, but he wants to keep most shares himself. He is very busy repairing computers and installing new computer systems. His many customers appreciate Amin's IT skills and like the personal service he offers.

Amin wants to raise capital to pay for a bigger workshop and 2 new vans. He plans to employ at least 2 other IT engineers. He is also planning to recruit a manager to help him deal with customers and the accounting side of the business. Amin has been told that when he creates a private limited company his personal risk will be reduced but he will still own most of the business.

a Explain **two** advantages and **two** disadvantages to Amin of converting his business into a private limited company.
b Do you think that a private limited company is the most suitable form of organisation for Amin's business? Justify your answer.

Definitions to learn
Public limited companies are businesses owned by shareholders but, unlike private limited companies, they can sell shares to the public. Their shares are traded on stock exchanges.

Public limited companies
This form of business organisation is most suitable for very large businesses. Most large, well-known businesses are **public limited companies** as they have been able to raise the capital to expand nationally or even internationally.

Public limited companies are not in the public sector of industry and are not owned by the government. They are owned by private individuals and as a result they are in the private sector.

Different types of business organisations

Most public limited companies are formed by converting from existing private limited companies. They then apply for stock exchange listing – which means the shares can be bought and sold on the country's stock exchange. This process can be costly and time-consuming as:

» The private limited company has to be re-registered as a public limited company.
» Advisers and company lawyers have to be paid to ensure correct procedures are carried out.
» The accounts of the company have to be produced in a very detailed form.
» A prospectus must be prepared, giving potential shareholders accurate and honest information about the operations of the business, its potential for growth and future plans.
» The public are invited to buy shares through an Initial Public Offering (IPO).

The advantages and disadvantages of a public limited company form of organisation are explained in Table 3.4.

Table 3.4 Advantages and disadvantages of a public limited company

Advantages of a public limited company	Disadvantages of a public limited company
They have the ability to raise large amounts of capital through the sale of shares to the public. This capital then allows previously small private limited companies to expand to a large scale. Sale of shares could make the original owners wealthy	Accounts have to be published and are made available to the public. The accounts can also be seen by competitors. Detailed accounts have to be produced at regular intervals and these are available for anyone to obtain and analyse
Status, stability and the image of public limited companies are often high. They receive a great deal of media coverage – especially when their shares are rising rapidly in value	The original owners of the business that has been converted may lose control of it. This will happen if the number of shares bought by the public means that the original owners have less than 50% of shares
There is limited liability for all shareholders	It can be costly and time-consuming to establish a public limited company, especially if the company is to be listed on a stock exchange
These companies have the resources to employ professional directors and managers throughout the business. These should be able to make the business more successful and profitable	In large public limited companies there will be a division or split between the control of the company (directors and managers) and ownership (shareholders)
There will be continuity if shareholders want to leave the business, as the business continues because it has its own identity	There are many legal formalities to complete to become a public limited company

Control and ownership in a public limited company

In all sole trader businesses and partnerships the owners have control over how their business operates. They take all the decisions to try to make the business achieve the objectives that they set. This is also the case in most private limited companies which have relatively few shareholders. The directors are often the majority shareholders so they can ensure that their decisions are passed at all meetings.

The situation is very different in public limited companies. There are often thousands of shareholders – even millions in the case of the largest companies.

3 TYPES OF BUSINESS ORGANISATIONS

Definitions to learn

An **Annual General Meeting (AGM)** is a legal requirement for all public limited companies. Shareholders may attend and vote on who they want to be on the Board of Directors for the coming year.

Dividends are payments made to shareholders from the profits (after tax) of a company. They are the return to shareholders for investing in the company.

It is impossible for all these people to be involved in taking decisions – although they are all invited to attend the **Annual General Meeting (AGM)**. The only decision that shareholders can have a real impact on at the AGM is the election of company directors. These directors are given the responsibility of running the business and taking decisions. They will only meet with the other shareholders at the annual AGM. The directors cannot control all of the business by themselves, so they appoint other managers to take day-to-day decisions. The diagram below explains this situation.

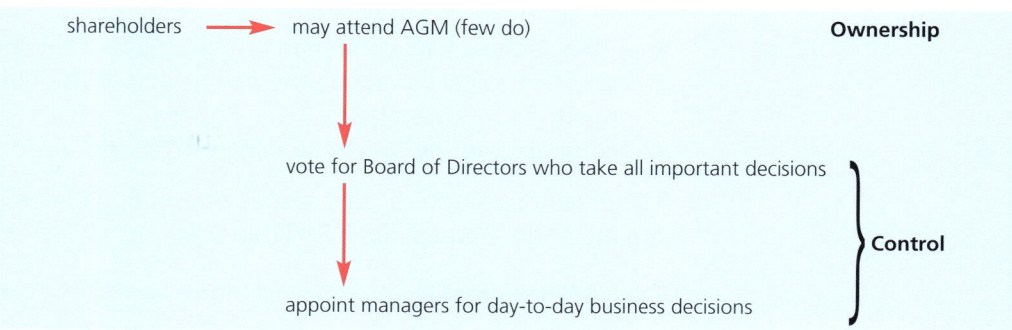

▲ Control and ownership in a public limited company

So, the shareholders own, but the directors and managers control the business. This is sometimes called the divorce between ownership and control.

Does this matter? It might be important for the shareholder. It means that the directors and managers may operate the business to meet their own objectives. These objectives could be increased status, growth of the business which would lead to higher management salaries, or reducing **dividends** paid to shareholders to pay for expansion plans instead. The shareholders are not able to influence these decisions other than by replacing the directors at the next AGM. Doing this would result in very bad publicity and the business may be less successful as the new directors may be inexperienced.

Key info

In 2023 the total number of publicly listed companies in the world was 55 214. The stock exchange with the highest number of companies was in India, with over 5500 companies, and the highest market capitalisation was in the USA, with $26.2 trillion.

Key info

In 2024 the largest company in the world by market value was Apple at $3.287 trillion and the largest company by revenue was US retailer Walmart, with 2.1 million employees and a revenue of $648 billion.

▲ Walmart and Apple are public limited companies

Different types of business organisations

REVISION SUMMARY — Public limited companies

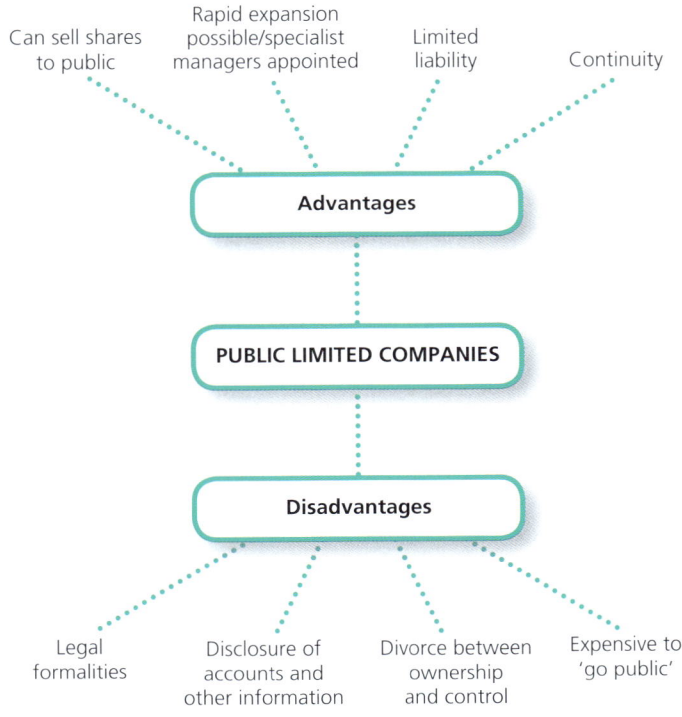

Activity 3.3

a How does the existence of limited liability benefit an individual shareholder?
b Does limited liability make it easier or more difficult for companies to attract new shareholders? Explain your answer.
c Explain why a private limited company might not want to convert the business into a public limited company.
d It is possible to convert a public limited company back into a private limited company. This is done by individuals buying up a majority of the shares. Why is it difficult to do?

How to recommend and justify a suitable type of business organisation for a given situation

How do the owners of a business decide on the most suitable type of business organisation? This is a very important decision because it has an impact on:

» how finance can be raised
» how much finance can be raised
» the ability of the business to expand
» the independence and level of control of the original owner(s)
» the status and image of the business.

When making a decision about the most suitable type of business organisation, the owners (or senior management in large companies) must first consider the following factors:

39

» Should an entrepreneur operate as a sole trader or form a partnership? This depends on the answers to the following questions:
  - Is the sole trader prepared to lose some independence and control to partners?
  - Does the business need more capital than the sole trader can afford to provide?
  - Does the sole trader lack important management skills that potential partners might have?
  - Does the sole trader want other people to help manage the business for them and share risks?

If the answer to most of these questions is YES, then a partnership could be more suitable for the entrepreneur than operating as a sole trader. If the answer to all of these questions is NO, then the entrepreneur should operate as a sole trader.

» Should a sole trader or partners in a partnership set up a private limited company? This depends on the answers to the following questions:
  - Does the business lack capital?
  - Are the existing owners worried about the risk of unlimited liability?
  - Is the business likely to have large debts such as when buying a factory?
  - Are the owners prepared to allow public access to business accounts?
  - Would the business benefit from greater status?
  - Do the owners want to pass on the business when they die or no longer wish to own the business?

If the answer to most of these questions is YES, then a private limited company could be more suitable for the business than remaining as a sole trader or partnership. If the answer to all of these questions is NO, then the owner(s) should consider keeping the business as a sole trader or partnership.

» Should the owners/directors of a private limited company convert it to a public limited company? In large private limited companies, the recommendation to convert to a public limited company is likely to be made by professional directors, who may not be the majority shareholders. The final decision will be taken by all shareholders voting on the decision. The main factors to consider are:
  - Does the business need access to large sums of capital?
  - Would the publicity given to public limited companies benefit the business?
  - Do the existing owners want to make money for themselves from the sale of shares?
  - Are the existing owners prepared to risk losing control over the management of the business?
  - Are the existing owners prepared to risk having the company taken over by another business that buys a majority of its shares?

If the answer to most of these questions is YES, then a public limited company could be more suitable for the business than remaining as a private limited company. If the answer to all of these questions is NO, then the directors and shareholders should consider keeping the business as a private limited company.

Different types of business organisations

Table 3.5 gives a summary of the points that should be considered when recommending a suitable form of business organisation.

Table 3.5 Points to consider when recommending a suitable form of business organisation

Business organisation	Risk of losing personal possessions	Control of business	Availability of finance
Sole trader	Carried by sole owner – unlimited liability	One person	Likely to have access to a small amount of capital
Partnership	Carried by all partners – unlimited liability	Two or more partners	Limited amount of capital available but partners can all contribute capital – likely to be more than for a sole trader
Private limited company	Shareholders – up to their original investment	Directors, who are likely to be shareholders too	Shares can be sold to gain capital but not to the general public – only to family, friends or specialist business investors
Public limited company	Shareholders – up to their original investment	Directors, but most are unlikely to own a majority of shares	Access to large amounts of capital – shares can be sold to the public

- **Extend your skills of analysis**

- A question which asks for an advantage of a clothing manufacturer being a private limited company could be answered as follows:
- Shareholders (the owners) of a private limited company have the advantage of limited liability, which sole traders or partners do not have.
- *Extend your analysis by explaining why this is an advantage to shareholders.*
- If the clothing manufacturer fails or has debts, then the shareholders' total personal wealth is not at risk, only the investment they made in buying the shares.
- *Extend your analysis by explaining why this is an advantage for the business.*
- It should be easier to raise more capital for the clothing company from selling shares to shareholders whose wealth is not now at risk, compared to attracting more partners, for example. The capital raised can be used to expand the business.

Definitions to learn

A **franchise** is a business based upon the use of the brand name, promotional logo and product ideas of an existing successful business.
A **franchisor** is the original business that sells the right to a franchisee to use its name and idea. The franchisor sells the right to open stores and sell products or services using its brand name.
A **franchisee** buys the licence to operate an outlet of an existing business from the franchisor.

Different forms of business organisations

Franchises

Not all entrepreneurs start up businesses with their own products or business names. They often buy a **franchise** licence. Buying a licence to operate a franchise under the name of another business is a very common type of business operation. The **franchisor** is a business owner with a product or service idea that it does not want to sell to consumers directly. Instead, **franchisees** can use the idea, brand name and product to sell to consumers. Two of the best-known international examples of a franchise are McDonald's and Taco Bell.

Why do franchisors want to sell licences for other people to operate a business under their name? Why do some business owners want to operate a franchise

3 TYPES OF BUSINESS ORGANISATIONS

business rather than one based on their own ideas? The advantages and disadvantages to a franchisor are explained in Table 3.6.

Table 3.6 Advantages and disadvantages to a franchisor

Advantages to a franchisor	Disadvantages to a franchisor
The franchisor earns revenue from the sale of franchise licences	Loss of management control over the operations of each franchised outlet
Management costs are reduced for the franchisor as each franchisee manages their own outlet(s). Franchisees might know more about local consumers' tastes and needs than the franchisor	Poor management of one franchised outlet could lead to a bad reputation for the whole business. The franchisor must monitor each outlet carefully and this is costly
The franchisor earns revenue by insisting that the franchisee purchases essential supplies only from them	Profits from operating the outlets are kept by each franchisee (although some franchisors demand a proportion of profit made)
Expansion of the business is quicker and less costly for the franchisor. Capital for each new outlet is provided by the franchisee	There will still be costs, including: • training franchisees in the management of each outlet. They all need to be made aware of the quality and legal standards expected by the franchisor • national/international advertising for the whole business

> **Study tips**
>
> Many well-known international businesses (multinational companies) use franchising as a way of expanding into new markets in other countries. The combination of a large well-known business and the local knowledge of the franchisees can lead to very successful operations.

There are also advantages and disadvantages to a franchisee and these have to be carefully considered by entrepreneurs and others thinking of buying a franchise. Could they make a higher profit by operating their own independent business than by controlling a franchised outlet? The main advantages and disadvantages to a franchisee are explained in Table 3.7.

Table 3.7 Advantages and disadvantages to a franchisee

Advantages to a franchisee	Disadvantages to a franchisee
The risks of business failure are reduced because the franchisor already has an established, and often well-known, business name, product and reputation	There is much less independence for the franchisee than if they were operating their own named business. All sales and finance records must be shared with the franchisor, for example
Banks may be more willing to lend if business risks are lower	Supplies might only be obtainable from the supplier at quite high cost
The main source of supplies will be the franchisor so there will be fewer suppliers to deal with	It might be difficult to source supplies for products demanded by local consumers, perhaps for religious or cultural reasons. It may be more difficult to meet local demand which could lead to lower sales
National or even international marketing and promotion costs are paid for by the franchisor. This means that not only should the business be well known but also that the franchisee does not pay for most of the marketing	The franchisee has less control as many management decisions are taken centrally by the franchisor – such as prices, store layout, products sold
Employee training programmes are offered by the franchisor which help each outlet operate efficiently and to the standards set by the franchisor – but often at a cost to the franchisee	There is often a high cost for buying the franchise licence. In addition, many franchisors demand a share of annual revenue or profit

Different types of business organisations

Key info

Opening a McDonald's franchise requires a total investment of between $0.5 million and $2.3 million.

Extend your skills of analysis

A question which asks for an advantage of a franchise to a new entrepreneur setting up a fast-food restaurant could be answered as follows:

Franchisors are often established businesses with well-known brand names and products. An entrepreneur who becomes a franchisee will benefit from the well-known name and products of a fast-food restaurant.

Extend your analysis by explaining why this is an advantage to the entrepreneur.

Less money will have to be spent on advertising and other promotions as the franchisor's name and products are already well known. A new entrepreneur will have limited finance.

Extend your analysis by explaining why this is an advantage for the business.

By keeping advertising costs low, the franchisee may be more likely to have higher profit from the restaurant. It may also mean more could be spent on employee training, which would improve customer service and, therefore, sales of the restaurant. This would be particularly important for an entrepreneur setting up in business for the first time.

▲ Franchised businesses give advantages to both the franchisor and the franchisee – but they must both contribute too

Activity 3.4

Ashanti has a successful business selling specially designed cakes. She has 10 shops which have a good brand image for selling high-quality cakes for special occasions such as birthdays. Ashanti wants to expand the business further and is considering becoming a franchisor.

a   Why would someone want to become a franchisee of Ashanti's business?
b   Do you think Ashanti should grow her business by becoming a franchisor? Justify your answer.

Definitions to learn

A **joint venture** is where two or more businesses start a new project together, sharing capital, risks and profits.

Joint ventures

Businesses sometimes do not compete with their main rivals but join with them to form a **joint venture**. This is when two or more businesses agree to start a new project together, sharing the capital, the risks and the profits. Many European companies have set up joint ventures with Chinese businesses in China, as the local managers have good knowledge of market needs and consumer tastes.

43

3 TYPES OF BUSINESS ORGANISATIONS

However, it can sometimes be difficult to work with businesses from other countries that manage businesses in different ways. The main advantages and disadvantages of a joint venture are explained in Table 3.8.

Table 3.8 Advantages and disadvantages of a joint venture

Advantages of a joint venture	Disadvantages of a joint venture
Sharing of costs for a new project such as a new aircraft. This can be very important as some projects might be too costly for any one business	If the new project is successful, then the profits have to be shared with the joint venture partner
When planning to expand to another country, local knowledge of the country can be important. A joint venture with a local company could provide this important information	Disagreements over important decisions might occur. This is more likely when the joint venture is with a business from another country and communication problems occur
Risks of the new project are shared. These risks might be reduced if the two businesses have skills in different tasks that can help the project succeed	The two joint venture partners might have different ways of operating a business, perhaps due to different cultures. The management of the joint project might lack common objectives

> **Case study:** BMW Brilliance Automotive Ltd
>
> In 2022 a joint venture in China between BMW and Brilliance China Automotive was extended until 2040. BMW is the world's leading manufacturer of high-quality premium cars and has over 30 production sites around the world. The main activity of Brilliance China Automotive is the design, production and sales of passenger cars in China. The joint venture produces, sells and provides after-sales services of BMW cars in China.
>
> Source: www.press.bmwgroup.com/global/article/detail/T0367992EN/

> **Activity 3.5**
>
> Read the case study above.
>
> a Define 'joint venture'.
> b Explain **two** advantages to BMW of setting up a joint venture to sell its cars in China.
> c Explain **two** disadvantages that BMW might have from this joint venture in China.

Different types of business organisations

Social enterprises

> **Definitions to learn**
>
> A **social enterprise** has social objectives as well as an aim to make a profit to reinvest back into the business.

These are some business organisations that do not just aim to make a profit. They are formed by people who want to do good for their society in ways that do not damage – or could actually improve – the environment. **Social enterprises** are not charities, as they still aim to make some profit. However, this profit will largely be used to expand the business to benefit society and the environment even further. The main advantages and disadvantages of a social enterprise are explained in Table 3.9.

Table 3.9 Advantages and disadvantages of a social enterprise

Advantages of a social enterprise	Disadvantages of a social enterprise
Positive consumer reaction to the social and environmental objectives of the business. This should result in higher sales	There may be a lack of finance as investors and banks might be reluctant to invest in a business that does not put profit as its main objective
Grants from government and environmental agencies might be easier to obtain than for other businesses that put profit first	Social and environmental objectives might take a great deal of management time to achieve. This could reduce the financial returns to the business
Social enterprises attract employees with similar social and environmental objectives. Management and workers will be working towards the same targets	Lower profit might mean that the business cannot afford high wages which could reduce employee motivation

International business in focus

Initial public offering of shares by a private limited company to become a public limited company

Often a private limited company will be changed to a public limited company because it needs more capital to pay back debt or expand the business. Some successful examples are the Saudi Arabian oil giant Saudi Aramco, which raised $25.6 billion in 2019, Alibaba Group, which raised $21.7 billion in 2014 and Facebook, which raised $16.01 billion in 2012.

Not all examples of companies that have converted to public limited companies have been successful. For example, in 2019 Uber failed to attract enough people wanting to buy its shares to achieve the share price it set when launched. The owners of many private limited companies decide against 'going public'.

▲ Share prices in public limited companies can fluctuate daily

Discussion points

- Why do you think people were willing to buy shares in businesses such as Saudi Aramco or Facebook when they converted to a public limited company but were less willing to buy shares in Uber?
- Why are some business owners reluctant to convert their companies into public limited companies?

3 TYPES OF BUSINESS ORGANISATIONS

? Chapter review questions: Short answer and data response

1 When Jameel lost his job in a fruit and vegetable shop that closed down, he opened his own store. He had good contacts with suppliers. They gave him 1 month's credit before he paid for supplies. Jameel had $10 000 in savings to invest in the shop. He thought this would be sufficient to start the business. He is an independent person – he never liked taking the manager's orders in the fruit and vegetable shop! He wanted to operate his new business as a sole trader. Jameel has only been operating for 2 years but he hopes to expand his business. He is unsure whether to open a second shop under his own name or buy a franchise from a large food retailing business.
   a Define 'sole trader'. [2]
   b Outline **two** advantages to Jameel of operating his business as a sole trader. [4]
   c Explain **two** disadvantages to Jameel of operating his business as a sole trader. [6]
   d Do you think Jameel should open a second shop under his own name or buy a franchise from a large food retailer? Justify your answer. [8]

2 Aurelie and Nadine set up the A and N Partnership 10 years ago. It specialises in making handmade shoes and boots. The business now employs around 20 people. Demand for these products is increasing rapidly. The partners need to invest much more capital in the business, but they need to avoid a lot of risk as they both have families that depend on the income from the business. Their main competitor is ShoeWorks, a public limited company which has a much larger market share than A and N and can afford extensive advertising and specialist shoe-making equipment.
   a Define 'partnership'. [2]
   b Outline **one** advantage and **one** disadvantage to ShoeWorks of being a public limited company. [4]
   c Explain **one** advantage and **one** disadvantage to Aurelie and Nadine of being in a business partnership. [6]
   d Do you think Aurelie and Nadine should convert their partnership into a private limited company? Justify your answer. [8]

Revision checklist
In this chapter you have learned:

- ✔ the main features of sole traders, partnerships, private limited companies and public limited companies
- ✔ the advantages and disadvantages of different types of business organisations
- ✔ how to recommend and justify a suitable type of business organisation to owners/management for a given situation
- ✔ the main features of franchises, joint ventures and social enterprises
- ✔ the advantages and disadvantages of franchises for the franchisor and franchisee
- ✔ the advantages and disadvantages of joint ventures.

NOW – test your understanding with the revision questions in the Student etextbook and the Workbook.

4 Business objectives and stakeholder objectives

> This chapter will explain:
>
> **Business objectives:**
>
> ★ businesses can have several objectives
> ★ the importance of business objectives.
>
> **The role of stakeholder groups:**
>
> ★ internal stakeholder groups: owners (sole traders, partners and shareholders), managers, employees
> ★ external stakeholder groups: customers, suppliers, lenders/banks, government, local community
> ★ objectives of different stakeholder groups
> ★ how these objectives might conflict with each other.

Businesses can have several objectives

Business objectives

Definitions to learn

Business objectives are the aims or targets that a business works towards.

An **objective** is an aim or a target that is worked towards. All businesses should have objectives. They help a business achieve success – although just setting an objective does not, of course, guarantee success.

Not all businesses have the same objectives. A business may have been formed by an entrepreneur to provide employment and security for themselves or their family. It could have been started to make as big a profit as possible for the owner. On the other hand, the business might have a more socially focused objective.

The most common objectives for businesses in the private sector are:

» survival
» growth
» profit
» market share
» providing a service to the community.

Survival

When a business starts up, the objectives of the owner(s) will be more concerned with survival than anything else. Many new businesses fail in the first few months of operation. The reasons for this were explained in Chapter 2.

Business failure of well-established businesses can also occur if new competitors quickly attract customers away from existing businesses.

A major economic recession that leads to unemployment and reduced customer spending could lead to managers focusing on business survival more than any other objective.

How could the chances of survival of a business be increased in these situations? Usually, managers will focus on keeping costs as low as possible and looking for new markets with less competition or in countries not experiencing

4 BUSINESS OBJECTIVES AND STAKEHOLDER OBJECTIVES

> **Key info**
>
> You may think of Google as just a search engine. However, its objective of growth has expanded it far beyond its original claim to fame as a search engine. Through its holding company Alphabet Inc., Google has bought more than 250 companies, including those involved in artificial intelligence, robotics, cybersecurity, mapping, video broadcasting, telecommunications and smoke alarms.

> **Definitions to learn**
>
> **Profit** is the surplus after total costs have been subtracted from revenue.

recession. Perhaps short-term survival is the most important of all business objectives at certain times. After all, if a business fails to survive it cannot achieve any other objectives it might have.

Growth

Business growth is measured by a rise in the value of output or sales. Owners and managers may aim for business growth to:

» increase the salaries and status of managers as the business expands
» spread the risks of the business by moving into new products and new markets
» gain a higher market share
» achieve cost advantages, called economies of scale, from business expansion (see Chapter 20). These could make the business more competitive.

Growth will be achieved only if the business's customers are satisfied with the products or services being provided. For this reason, it will be important for the business to put meeting customers' needs as a very high priority.

Profit

Private sector businesses must aim to make a **profit** in the long term. How else will the investors that risked their capital in the business make a return? How will the entrepreneur be rewarded for their hard work and risk taking if the business makes no profit? How will the business expand if no surplus or profit is made from its operations?

Profit is needed to:

» **pay a return** to the owners of and investors in the business for the capital invested and risks taken
» **provide finance** for further investment in the business.

A business might be able to survive in the short term without making a profit. However, without any profit at all in the long term, the owners are likely to close the business.

Will a business try to make as much profit as possible? It is often assumed that this will be the case but there are dangers in trying to do this. Take the example of a business that raises its prices to increase profit. It may find that consumers stop buying its goods. Other entrepreneurs will be encouraged to set up in competition, which will reduce profit in the long term for the original business.

The owners of a business may just aim for a satisfactory level of profit. This provides them with an adequate return for the risk they are taking but avoids them having to work too many hours or pay too much in tax to the government.

As Chapter 3 explained, limited companies are owned by shareholders. The senior managers of companies will often set the objective of increasing returns to shareholders. This can be done in two ways:

» **increasing dividends** paid to shareholders from higher profit made by the business
» **increasing share price**. Managers can try to achieve this not just by making profits but by making decisions that give the business a good chance of growth and higher future profits.

Higher returns to shareholders can discourage them from selling their shares and helps managers keep their jobs!

Businesses can have several objectives

Market share

The **market share** of a business is an important measure. Many businesses have the objective of increasing market share. Increased market share gives a business:

» good publicity, as it could claim that it is becoming 'the most popular'
» increased influence over suppliers, as they will be very keen to sell to a business that is becoming relatively larger than others in the industry
» increased influence over customers (for example, in setting prices).

Definitions to learn

Market share is the percentage of total market sales held by one brand or business.

Calculations to learn

$$\text{Market share (\%)} = \frac{\text{Sales revenue of business}}{\text{Total sales revenue for whole market}} \times 100$$

Worked example:

The annual sales revenue of a business is $20 m. Total sales revenue for the whole market is $100 m.

$$\text{Market share} = \frac{\text{Sales revenue of business}}{\text{Total sales revenue for whole market}} \times 100$$

$$= \frac{\$20\,m}{\$100\,m} \times 100$$

$$= 20\%$$

Providing a service to the community

Social enterprises are operated by private individuals and they are in the private sector. They do not, however, just have profit as an objective. Managers of social enterprises often set three objectives for the business:

» **Social.** To provide jobs and support for disadvantaged groups in society, such as people with disabilities or those experiencing homelessness
» **Environmental.** To protect the environment
» **Financial.** To make a profit to invest back into the social enterprise to expand the social work that it performs.

Study tips

You should not suggest that social enterprise businesses 'do not want to make a profit'. Most of them do have this aim – but they have other objectives that could lead to benefits for the local community.

An example of a social enterprise is Rangsutra Foundation in India. It was established by Rangsutra Crafts India Limited to provide a sustainable source of income for people in very poor village communities by helping them develop skills in craft work and clothing products. It also helps them market their products at a fair price.

▶ A display of Rangsutra products. Rangsutra's core value is 'respect for both the producer and the customer'. It ensures a fair price to the producer as well as quality products for the customer. Profits earned from sales ensure a better life for the communities, as the producers are also the owners of Rangsutra

Source: https://rangsutra.com/en-gb/pages/rangsutra-foundation

4 BUSINESS OBJECTIVES AND STAKEHOLDER OBJECTIVES

Why business objectives could change

It is most unusual for a business to have the same objective forever. Here are some examples of situations in which a business might change its objective:

» A business that started up three years ago has survived the riskiest period for any business. The owner now aims to work towards higher profit.
» A business has achieved higher market share and now has the objective of earning higher returns for shareholders.
» A profit-making business operates in a country facing a serious economic recession so now has the short-term objective of survival.

> ### Activity 4.1
> Here are brief details of four businesses:
> - A builder with a small business has noticed more competitors being set up in the building industry.
> - A recently established business, owned by 2 young and ambitious entrepreneurs, operates in the rapidly expanding computer industry.
> - A large book publisher which dominates the market in textbooks in your country.
> - A social enterprise that is concerned about the lack of clean water provided to poor communities.
>   a Explain the most likely main objective of the owners or managers of each of these businesses.
>   b For each example, explain the decisions that could help the business to achieve this objective.

Study tips

Do not suggest that 'making as much profit as possible' is always the most likely objective of a business. It might depend on economic conditions and the original aims of the owners – for example, they could have been more focused on helping groups in society than making money.

The importance of business objectives

Setting an objective helps guide future actions. This is true for individuals as well as businesses. If you have set yourself the objective of attending university then you will need to:

» allocate time to study rather than taking part in social activities
» study hard to pass examinations
» research universities and the courses they offer.

If you are successful in going to university, then you can congratulate yourself for having achieved your objective – and then think about the next goal to aim for!

A similar process applies to businesses. A clear objective gives them a target to reach within a certain time limit. This means that decisions will have to be taken to move the business towards achieving this aim. At the end of the time period, the business can review whether its objective has been achieved or not. If it has not, further actions will be needed. If it has, then another goal will be set for the future.

Here are the main reasons why business objectives are important:

» They give all employees – workers and managers – a clear target to work towards and this helps motivate people.
» Decision making will focus on whether something will help to achieve the objectives, and these decisions are more likely to result in success.

» Clear and measurable objectives, which are shared with employees, help unite the whole business towards the same goal.
» Managers and owners can compare how the business has performed against its objectives. They can then see if the business has been successful or not.

> **Extend your skills of analysis**
>
> A question which asks why having an objective is important to a sole trader business that cleans cars could be answered as follows:
>
> A sole trader might set business growth as their business objective.
>
> *Extend your analysis by explaining why this is important to the business.*
>
> By setting this target the sole trader can now decide on the best ways they might expand the business and clean other vehicles as well as cars with the limited finance they have available. This would help achieve the objective.
>
> *Extend your analysis by explaining why setting an objective is important to the business.*
>
> The sole trader will now have a clear focus towards their goal. Explaining this to their bank will help the sole trader obtain finance. They might take the decision to take out a loan to buy a new cleaning machine. This could help increase output and therefore sales for the business. The objective will have guided the sole trader's decision.

The role of stakeholder groups and their objectives

Many groups of people have a direct interest in how a business performs and the decisions it takes. These groups are called **stakeholders** and they can either be internal or external to the business.

Internal and external stakeholder groups

Internal stakeholders are individuals or groups who work within or own the business. They have a direct interest in the performance and activities of the business. Internal stakeholders are:

» owners of sole traders and partnerships
» shareholders in limited companies
» managers
» other employees.

External stakeholders are individuals or groups who are separate from the business but have a direct interest in the performance and activities of the business. External stakeholders are:

» customers
» suppliers
» lenders/banks
» government
» local community.

> **Definitions to learn**
>
> A **stakeholder** is any person or group with a direct interest in the performance and activities of a business.
>
> **Internal stakeholders** are individuals or groups who work within or own the business. They have a direct interest in the performance and activities of the business.
>
> **External stakeholders** are individuals or groups who are separate from the business but have a direct interest in the performance and activities of the business.

4 BUSINESS OBJECTIVES AND STAKEHOLDER OBJECTIVES

Why are these groups of people important to business? What objectives do these stakeholders have? Consider Tables 4.1 and 4.2.

Table 4.1 Internal stakeholder groups and their objectives

Internal stakeholder group	Role of stakeholder group and its importance to the business	Objectives of the stakeholder group
Owners: Sole traders and partnerships	• They provide capital to start up and expand the business • They accept the risks of investing in unlimited liability businesses	• Share of the profits so that they gain a rate of return on the money put into the business • Growth of the business so that the value of their investment increases
Owners: Shareholders – limited companies	• They own the business and invest capital when buying shares in the company	• Regular share of profits, called dividends • Growth and rising profitability of the business to raise the value of shares
Managers	• They are also employees of the business and control the work of other employees • They take important decisions which could impact on the success or failure of the business	• High salaries as their work is important • Job security • Business growth so they control a big and successful business. This gives them more status and power
Other employees	• They perform tasks within the business to provide goods and services	• Regular payment for their work • Job security • Work that gives satisfaction and provides motivation

Table 4.2 External stakeholder groups and their objectives

External stakeholder group	Role of stakeholder group and its importance to the business	Objectives of the stakeholder group
Customers	• They are buyers of the goods and services and this provides revenue to the business	• Safe and reliable products • Value for money with well-designed products of good quality • Reliability of service and maintenance
Suppliers	• They provide essential materials and services to the business so that it can make products available for sale	• Have regular orders from the business • Receive prompt payment
Lenders/banks	• They provide essential finance for the business to allow it to, for example, buy premises and equipment	• Receive regular payments of interest for the finance provided • Be repaid in the agreed time period
Government	• It should provide a legal system and management of the economy that allows the business to operate in a stable environment • It may provide grants and other financial support	• Business growth that creates jobs for the working population • Greater business output that increases the income of the country (and which may lead to increased tax revenue) • Safe products and production methods that are socially responsible/protect the environment
Local community	• It provides infrastructure to allow business to operate effectively e.g. good roads • It provides potential workforce	• Jobs for local population • Safe production processes that do not damage the environment • Business growth that does not damage local environment

The role of stakeholder groups and their objectives

REVISION SUMMARY — Business objectives

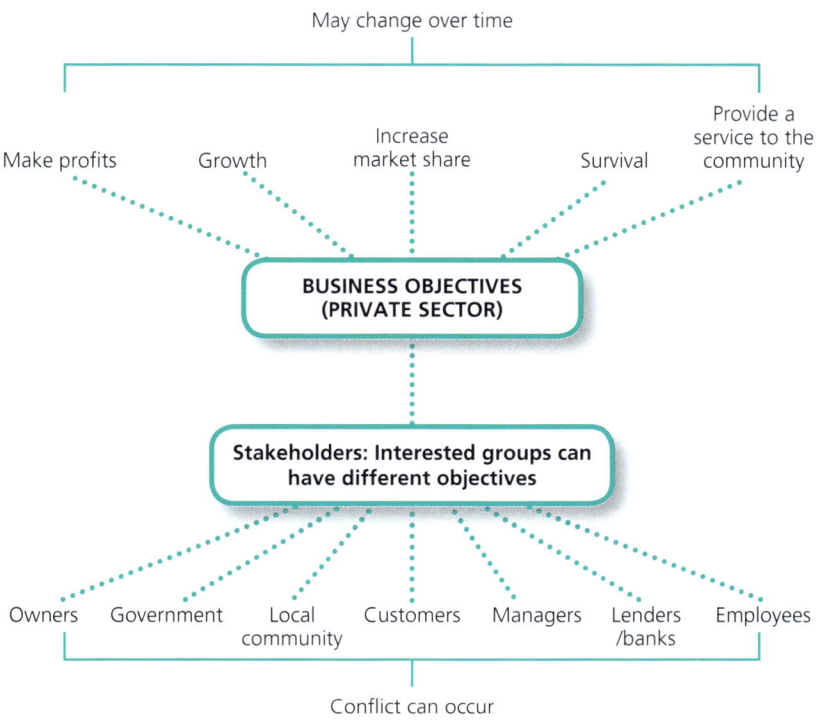

Activity 4.2

Coca-Cola's senior managers have set the objective of increasing returns to owners of the company – that is, its millions of shareholders. However, the managers believe that this can only be achieved if Coca-Cola meets three other objectives:

- Remain the world's largest soft-drinks company by value of sales.
- Continue to satisfy consumers with a top-value and clearly branded product.
- Protect the environment by making its packaging more sustainable.

a Why do you think the senior managers believe that 'increasing returns to owners' is important?
b Explain why Coca-Cola has set three other objectives as well as 'increasing returns to owners'.
c By referring to the market in your own country, explain how you think Coca-Cola could achieve its aim of remaining the world's largest soft-drinks company.

▲ Senior managers set clear objectives for Coca-Cola

4 BUSINESS OBJECTIVES AND STAKEHOLDER OBJECTIVES

How stakeholder objectives might conflict with each other

In the previous section we assumed that a business would set one objective and pursue activities to achieve it. However, life is not that simple and most businesses are trying to satisfy the objectives of more than one group, as the diagram below shows.

Likely conflicts between stakeholder objectives

Some of the most likely conflicts between stakeholder objectives are:

- Owners' objective is high profits BUT customers want good value products which satisfy their needs at reasonable prices.
- Owners' objective is high profits BUT using low-cost production methods (which may be polluting and creating waste) to raise profits could damage the environment for the local community.
- Owners want the business to grow to become more profitable BUT expansion may lead to bigger premises and more traffic which could damage the environment for the local community.
- Employees' objective is to see an increase in wages BUT higher wages, without more output per person, will raise costs and this will reduce profit for owners.
- Managers want the business to make higher profits so they may receive higher salaries BUT this could lead to higher prices which customers will not want.
- The government's social and environmental objectives often result in legal controls such as minimum wage or limits on pollution BUT these will raise business costs and reduce the profit available to pay for business growth.

These conflicts may cause real problems for businesses if they are not overcome. Local communities could restrict business growth if the business damages

Study tips

Make sure you do not confuse stakeholders with shareholders. Shareholders can be stakeholders but there may be other stakeholders.

the environment. Employees may go on strike if wages are not increased. The government might take legal action against a business that puts profit before social or environmental objectives. Managers and owners may have to compromise when they come to decide on the best objectives for the business they operate or own. They would be unwise to ignore the objectives of other stakeholder groups with an interest in the operation of the business.

Perhaps the most successful businesses in the long term are those that aim to make a profit by satisfying the objectives of their most important stakeholders. How could this approach actually lead to higher profits?

- Paying employees a satisfactory wage. This could motivate employees to produce more efficiently, reducing costs per unit.
- Producing safe products at prices that customers recognise as being good value. This could increase profit by resulting in an excellent reputation that leads consumers to buy more products from the business.
- Respecting all laws, especially on employees' rights, product safety and the environment. This could increase profit by creating positive media publicity for the business which improves brand image. Sales should increase as a result.
- Communicating with people in the local community and responding to their worries over pollution, for example. This could increase profit by leading to local community support when the business asks for improved infrastructure or approval for an expansion plan.

Extend your skills of analysis

A question which asks for one reason why conflict between stakeholder objectives might occur in an oil company could be answered as follows:

Stakeholder groups have a direct interest in the activities of a business but their objectives often differ – for example, profit objective for owners and low pollution objective for the local community.

Extend your analysis by explaining how this causes conflict.

By aiming for higher profits, owners and senior managers might expand the business using low-cost production methods that result in much waste. The local community wants more jobs but not at the cost of oil pollution and a damaged environment.

Extend your analysis by explaining why this is important to the business.

If this conflict is not overcome, the local community may try to prevent expansion of the oil company. A compromise by owners could overcome the conflict – for example, agreeing to use less polluting production methods if the local community makes land available for expansion.

Case study: Business stakeholders

Oilco is a large oil company operating in your country. The following stakeholder groups are interested in the work of this company:

- Owners of the company. They are likely to want the business to work towards as much profit as possible.
- Directors (senior managers of the company appointed by the owners). They will be interested in growth of the business as their salaries are likely to depend on this.
- Employees. They will want as high a wage as possible with security of employment.
- Local community. It will be concerned about jobs too, but it will also be worried about pollution from the oil refinery.
- Consumers. They will want reasonably priced products of appropriate quality – or they may buy goods from competitors.

In practice, these stakeholder objectives could conflict with each other. For example:

- It could be that a cheap method of production increases profits but causes more pollution.
- A decision to expand the refinery could lead to a dirtier, noisier local environment.
- A decision to introduce new machines could reduce the number of jobs at the refinery but lead to higher profits.
- Expansion could be expensive, reducing payments to owners, and this could reduce short-term profits.

4 BUSINESS OBJECTIVES AND STAKEHOLDER OBJECTIVES

Study tips

Be prepared to explain how a business objective might satisfy some stakeholders but not others.

Activity 4.3

Read the case study on the previous page.

a Define 'stakeholder group'.
b Explain **one** other possible conflict of objectives between Oilco's stakeholders.

Key info

Billions of plastic bottles are thrown away each year but many are not recyclable or biodegradable, and many end up in the oceans. This garbage is harming fish and spoiling the coastlines of many countries. Manufacturers want a cheap way to package their products but people also want an unpolluted place to live. Can these two objectives be achieved at the same time?

REVISION SUMMARY — Business stakeholders and their aims

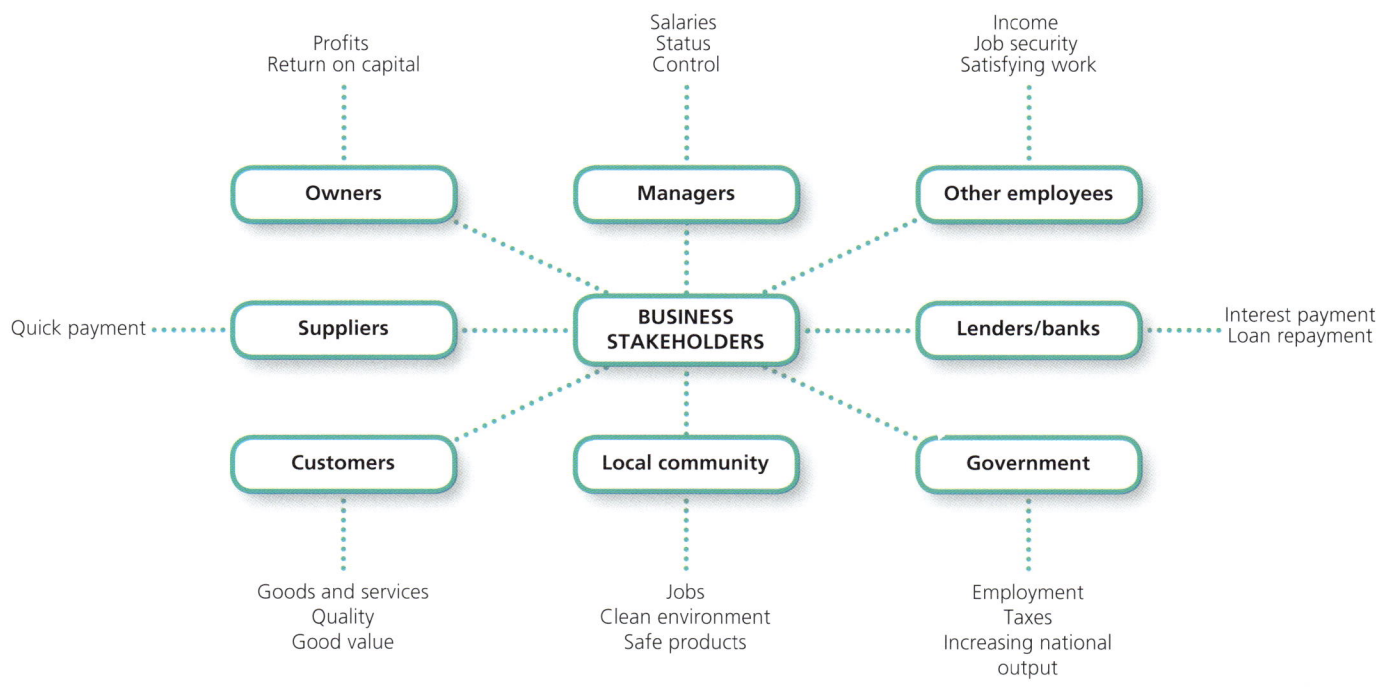

The role of stakeholder groups and their objectives

International business in focus

Toyota makes clear its business objectives

▲ A Toyota concept car showing the style of cars for the future

One of Toyota's objectives is to produce a range of cars that help to reduce global carbon emissions from new cars.

Toyota has a set of objectives, to be achieved by 2050, to reduce the negative impact of manufacturing and the driving of vehicles as much as possible. Its objectives include:

- **Producing ever-better cars.** Toyota is developing electric and hybrid cars. Hydrogen-powered vehicles, such as the Mirai, are important to Toyota's strategy for promoting widespread use of fuel-cell vehicles. Toyota's plan is to reduce global average new-vehicle carbon emissions by 90% by 2050.

- **Using ever-better manufacturing.** Toyota wants to reduce carbon emissions from its factories to zero by 2050. This will be achieved through the use of low-carbon methods of production. The company will also use renewable power, such as wind, biomass and hydroelectric to run its factories.

- **Sales growth in the emerging markets of Asia, Africa and South America.** Although profits are important, Toyota sets quite low earnings targets, preferring to focus on growth in a competitive market. The most popular Toyota car models worldwide were the Rav4 and Corolla. These were the second and third bestselling car models in the world in 2023.

Sources: www.toyota-global.com/pages/contents/investors/ir_library/annual/pdf/2012/p16_20.pdf; https://mag.toyota.co.uk/toyota-environmental-challenge-2050/

Discussion points

- Why did Toyota set objectives for the coming years?
- Why do you think developing new models seems to be more important than making as much profit as possible?
- Which stakeholder groups will be affected – positively or negatively – by Toyota working towards these objectives?
- Do any of these objectives conflict with each other?

4 BUSINESS OBJECTIVES AND STAKEHOLDER OBJECTIVES

Chapter review questions: Short answer and data response

1 Sunita and her partner Sunil decided to start a business selling flowers called S and S Blooms. They agreed on the business objectives they would set. There are several other flower shops in their town and there is much competition. Sunita and Sunil had very little cash to start their shop. However, 5 years after being set up, it is still open. Business objectives have changed. There are plans to open 2 or 3 more shops – perhaps by taking over some of their competitors. The business now employs 5 workers and uses several local flower growers as suppliers.
   a Define 'business objective'. [2]
   b Outline **two** likely business objectives for S and S Blooms when the business was first established. [4]
   c Explain **two** likely reasons why Sunita and Sunil have changed the business objectives of S and S Blooms. [6]
   d Do you think that setting a business objective for S and S Blooms will make sure that the business is successful? Justify your answer. [8]

2 The Big Pit Mining business (BPM) owns and operates coal and gold mines in several different countries. It has thousands of employees. Most of them work in very dangerous conditions for low pay. Waste from the mines is often dumped in local rivers. 'Making higher profits and raising returns to our shareholders are our most important objectives,' said the Managing Director of BPM to his other senior managers recently. 'Shareholders are our most important stakeholder group,' he added.
   a Define 'stakeholders'. [2]
   b Outline **two** possible reasons why BPM has profit as an objective. [4]
   c Explain how **two** stakeholder groups might be affected by the decision to open a new BPM mine. [6]
   d Do you agree with the Managing Director when he says that shareholders are the most important stakeholder group? Justify your answer. [8]

Revision checklist

In this chapter you have learned:

✔ the different business objectives that can be set
✔ the importance of business objectives
✔ what internal and external stakeholder groups are and their objectives
✔ how the objectives of stakeholder groups might conflict with each other.

NOW – test your understanding with the revision questions in the Student etextbook and the Workbook.

Understanding business activity: end-of-section case study

Case study: A new business but which one?

Derek's job is to repair motorcycles. He works for a large motorcycle sales business that sells new and second-hand motorcycles. Derek's uncle died earlier this year and left him $20 000. He has always wanted to work for himself and now he has some money to start his own business. He could do this by opening his own business or buying a franchise.

Derek is going to choose between opening his own shop selling motorcycle clothes or buying a franchise from a big motorcycle clothes retail business. To open his own motorcycle clothes shop will take a lot of effort to find a suitable location that has the shop fittings required. Buying a franchise for a clothes shop will be expensive. However, the franchise company will help Derek with a lot of the start-up problems such as finding a suitable shop.

Appendix 1: Letter to bank manager

```
Dear Sir/Madam

I want to set up my own business. I have $20 000 to invest in my business but I need additional
funds. I have two possible business ideas.

The first one is to set up my own motorcycle clothes shop and for that I will need an
additional $25 000 to buy clothes to sell in the shop. I will rent my shop.

The second idea is to buy a franchise for a motorcycle clothes shop and for that I will need
an additional $100 000. $50 000 will be needed to buy the franchise and $50 000 to buy clothes
inventories. I will rent my shop.

I would like to come to see you to discuss my two ideas.

Yours faithfully

Derek
```

Practice questions: Case study

1   a Explain **four** personal characteristics that Derek needs to be a successful entrepreneur. [8]
    b Derek has to decide which type of business organisation to use if he sets up his own business. Consider the advantages and disadvantages of the following **three** types of business organisation. Which one should Derek choose? Justify your answer.
       • Sole trader
       • Partnership
       • Private limited company [12]

2   a Explain why **two** different groups might be considered stakeholders in Derek's business. [8]
    b Consider the advantages and disadvantages to Derek of either buying a franchise from a big clothes retail business or setting up his own clothes shop. Which option should Derek choose? Justify your answer. [12]

SECTION 2

People in business

Chapters

5 Human resource management (HRM)
6 Organisation and management
7 Methods of communication
8 Motivating employees

5 Human resource management (HRM)

This chapter will explain:

Recruiting and selecting employees:

★ stages in the recruitment process
★ selection methods
★ advantages and disadvantages of internal and external recruitment
★ how to recommend and justify who to employ in a given situation.

Employment contracts and legal controls over employment issues:

★ the main contents of an employment contract
★ the benefits of employment contracts for employers and employees
★ legal controls over employment issues
★ effects of legal controls over employment issues on employers and employees.

Training:

★ the importance of training to a business and to employees
★ types of training
★ advantages and disadvantages of the three types of training.

> **Definitions to learn**
>
> **Recruitment** is the process that starts with identifying that the business needs to employ someone, up to the point at which applications have arrived at the business.
>
> **Employee selection** is the process of evaluating applicants for a specific job and selecting an individual for employment based on the needs of the organisation.

Recruiting and selecting employees

Recruitment and **employee selection** are perhaps the most familiar roles of human resource management (HRM). However, there are other responsibilities, as shown in the figure below, such as training and meeting legal requirements regarding employing workers.

Recruitment and selection
Involves attracting and selecting the best candidates for vacancies that arise

Wages and salaries
These must attract and retain the right people and be sufficiently high to motivate employees

Industrial relations
There must be effective communication between representatives of the management and of the workforce. This may be to resolve grievances and disputes but also to put forward ideas and suggestions for improvements

HUMAN RESOURCES DEPARTMENT

Training programmes
Involves assessing and fulfilling the training needs of employees. This should be linked to the future plans of the business

Health and safety
The business needs to make sure that it complies with all the laws on health and safety

Redundancy and dismissal
This involves releasing employees either because the business changes in some way or because the employee is not satisfactory. The business must observe all legal controls on unfair dismissal and discrimination

▲ The responsibilities of the Human Resources department

5 HUMAN RESOURCE MANAGEMENT (HRM)

Businesses need to start the process of recruitment and selection when:

» an employee leaves their job and they need to be replaced
» a new business starts up and needs employees
» a successful business wants to expand by employing more people.

In a large business the process of recruiting and selecting new employees is usually undertaken by the HRM department. Small businesses do not have enough employees to justify having a separate HRM department and usually the managers who will be supervising the employee will be responsible for recruiting and selecting new workers. For example, in a small hotel the restaurant manager might recruit the employees who serve customers in the restaurant.

The stages in the recruitment process are summarised in the diagram below.

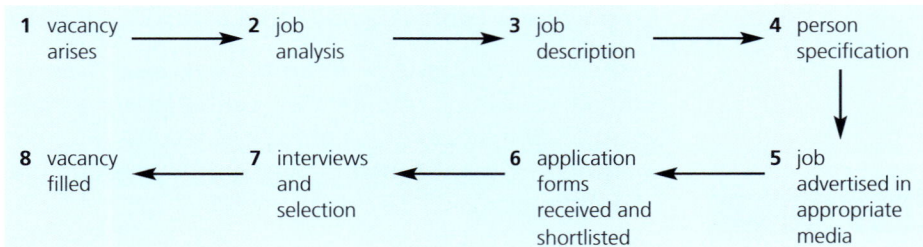

▲ The recruitment process

Stages in the recruitment process

Job descriptions

The first stage of the recruitment process is to carry out a **job analysis** of the vacancy to be filled. This involves studying the job's tasks and activities that will be carried out by the new employee. This will help create both a job description and a person specification.

Once the job has been analysed, a **job description** will be produced. A job description has several functions:

» It is given to the applicants for the job so they know exactly what the job involves.
» It allows a **person specification** to be drawn up, to see if the applicants 'match up' to the skills required to do the job effectively.
» Once someone has been employed, it can help show whether they are carrying out the job effectively. If a dispute occurs about the employee's tasks, the employee and employer can refer to the job description to settle the problem.

The exact structure and content of a job description varies from business to business. Generally it will contain the headings outlined in the following case study.

Definitions to learn

A **job analysis** identifies and records the responsibilities and tasks related to a job.
A **job description** outlines the responsibilities and duties to be carried out by someone employed to do a specific job.
A **person specification** is a document which outlines the requirements, qualifications, expertise and personal characteristics a successful applicant should have.

Recruiting and selecting employees

> **Case study:** Housekeeper job description
>
> Here is a job description for a housekeeper in a hotel.
>
> | Job title: | Housekeeper |
> |---|---|
> | Department: | Housekeeping |
> | Responsible to: | Hotel manager |
> | Responsible for: | Cleaners, room attendants |
>
> **Main purpose of the job:**
> - Responsible for domestic services in the hotel, aiming to keep accommodation clean and well maintained for the hotel guests
> - Responsible for supervising the cleaners and room attendants
>
> **Main duties:**
> - Allocation of duties, such as cleaning
> - Advising employees when queries arise
> - Sending dirty linen to the laundry
> - Organising repairs and replacement of worn items from rooms
> - Checking that belongings have not been left in rooms
> - Checking that the rooms are ready to receive guests
> - Informing reception when rooms are ready for occupancy
>
> **Occasional duties:**
> - Selection of new employees
> - Training new employees in their tasks and handling of equipment
> - Disciplining employees as and when required

Job descriptions often also contain information about:

» the conditions of employment – salary, hours of work, pension scheme and employee welfare
» training that will be offered
» opportunities for promotion.

Person specifications

Once a job description has been drawn up, the qualifications and qualities necessary for a person to undertake the job can be specified. This list of desirable and essential requirements is called a person specification. The typical requirements for applicants included in a person specification are:

» level of educational qualifications
» amount of experience and type of experience
» special skills, knowledge or particular aptitude
» personal characteristics, such as type of personality.

Study tips

Make sure you know the difference between a job description and a person specification and what they are each used for.

5 HUMAN RESOURCE MANAGEMENT (HRM)

> **Case study:** Housekeeper person specification
>
> Here is a person specification for a housekeeper in a hotel.
>
> | Job title: | Housekeeper |
> |---|---|
> | Department: | Housekeeping |
>
> **Qualifications:** Essential: 4 IGCSEs (A–C) including Maths and English
> **Experience:** Desirable: Minimum 1 year's experience of working in hotels
> **Skills:**
> - Communicates effectively with people
> - Ability to manage people
> - Knowledge of cleaning machines and cleaning materials
>
> **Personal characteristics:**
> - Honest and responsible
> - Friendly, helpful, organised

> **Activity 5.1**
>
> a Draw up a job description for one of the following:
>   - accountant
>   - shop assistant
>   - hotel manager
>   - teacher.
>
>   Research information to help you by asking someone who does the job or by looking at careers information.
> b Now draw up a person specification for your chosen job. The same research should help you to complete this task. Show which are essential and which are desirable requirements for the job.
> c How do a job description and a person specification help to ensure the most suitable person for the job is recruited?

Job advertisements

Advertising job vacancies can be done in several ways:

- **Newspapers.** Local newspapers are often used for advertising vacancies for jobs which do not require high skill levels, such as clerical (office) or manual (factory) positions. It is likely that many people locally could fill these vacancies. National newspapers are usually used for senior positions where there may be few, if any, local people who have the right experience, skills and qualifications to do the job. For senior positions, which are highly paid, people will be willing to move to another part of the country.
- **Specialist magazines.** These will usually be used for specialist technical employees, such as scientists. These people will read the specialist magazines and see the advertisements.
- **Online recruitment sites, such as LinkedIn and Totaljobs.** These offer the ability to create online job adverts for vacant positions in a business. These can be searched by job seekers through their networks. For example, the LinkedIn network has millions of members worldwide. Vacancies can be recommended to potential applicants through the 'Jobs You May Be Interested In' feature. Social media is now one of the most commonly used ways of publicising vacancies. More young people access social media than read newspapers!

Recruiting and selecting employees

> **Study tips**
>
> You should be able to give examples of jobs which could be advertised using each of the different methods.

- **Employment agencies.** These are specialist organisations that recruit potential employees for other businesses. These specialists can help businesses draw up job descriptions and person specifications. They will advertise vacancies widely, including using their own website. They will collect details of all applications and then will, if requested, begin the selection process.

  Employment agencies hold details of qualified people looking for another job. When a suitable vacancy arises, they will put forward applicants to be interviewed for the job. Some businesses outsource the recruitment process to agencies to reduce the need to employ their own recruitment team. If a person is successfully appointed to the job, the agency will charge a fee for recruiting them, based on a percentage of the salary for the vacancy.

- **Centres run by the government (Job Centres).** These are places where job vacancies can be advertised. Details of vacancies are given to interested people. The vacancies are usually for unskilled and semi-skilled jobs.

Activity 5.2

On a large sheet of paper, copy out the table below and then fill in the gaps.

Method of advertising	Advantages	Disadvantages	Examples of jobs suitable for this method
Newspapers			
Specialist magazines			
Online recruitment sites			
Employment agencies			
Government-run Job Centres			

Case study: Job advertisements

Night Cashier for busy gas (petrol) station, 38 hours per week, Wed to Sat, 22:00–07:30, $12.50 per hour. Start immediately. Tel.1122 44551

Industrial Engineering Professional

Multi-site role throughout the country: based in New City. Competitive rate of pay with fringe benefits.

Qualityfoam Ltd is a leading manufacturer of polyurethane foam, operating in 16 countries, and is a major supplier to the home country's furniture industry.

Appealing to a results-orientated professional, responsibilities will include performance improvement, business analysis, project management and capital expenditure appraisal.

You will be a university graduate, numerate and IT literate, with at least 3 years' experience in manufacturing.

Please write with full CV to: Mr M. Ahmed, MD, Qualityfoam Ltd, New Road, New City, 3412 8769.

Administration Assistant required, $18.00 per hour

Good all-round administration skills needed to undertake a variety of duties within the organisation. Knowledge of Word or similar package essential. Immediate start.

Please write or telephone for an application form from:

Mr S. Singh, ZYT Ltd, 2341 Old Road, New City, 456723. Tel. 0892 557739

5 HUMAN RESOURCE MANAGEMENT (HRM)

Activity 5.3

Read the case study on page 65.

a Which advert would have appeared in a national newspaper and which would have been in a local newspaper? Explain your choices.
b Design your own advertisement for the job for which you drew up a job description and person specification (page 64). Where would you place this advertisement and why?
c Compare your advert with that of the other students in your group. Which would be most likely to attract the best people to apply for the job and why?

Activity 5.4

Study this job advertisement and the information from three application forms below.

Consider the advantages and disadvantages of the **three** applicants. Which applicant should be chosen for the job and why should the other two applicants be rejected? Justify your answer.

> **Personal Assistant (PA)**
>
> Salary in excess of $30 000 per year.
>
> The General Manager at our New City office requires an experienced and highly skilled Personal Assistant to provide a complete support service. In a typically busy day you will manage the General Manager's office, word-process a variety of documents, maintain an accurate diary and liaise with customers, clients and corporate contacts.
>
> You will need to be able to demonstrate excellent IT skills, knowledge of Microsoft Office and associated programs, a good standard of numeracy and literacy, and have previous experience in a similar role.
>
> *If you enjoy working with a friendly team, please send your CV to Corinne Ogunbanjo, Human Resources, NYDB plc, 3286 New Street, New City, 467813*

	Applicant 1	Applicant 2	Applicant 3
Name	Caroline Sharma	Pablo Gitano	Sara Gherman
Address	2144 Main Road, New City	4245 Long Row, New City	9876 New Road, New City
Educational qualifications	5 IGCSEs, including English, Maths and Information and Communication Technology. Administration qualifications – Level 1	6 IGCSEs, including English, Maths and Information and Communication Technology. Administration qualifications – Levels 1 and 2	5 IGCSEs, including English and Maths. Administration qualifications – Levels 1, 2 and 3
Previous employment	6 months as a junior administration assistant with NYDB	1 year as office junior 3 years on reception 6 years as Personal Assistant to Senior Manager of DFG	Reception – 3 years Head of Administration section – 6 years Personal Assistant within RET Ltd – 6 years
Interests/ hobbies	Playing sports – member of several local teams, going to see friends, voluntary helper with a youth group	Reading, member of local football team, playing piano, rock climbing	Reading, going to the cinema, watching television

Recruiting and selecting employees

Selection methods

Once people have applied for a job vacancy, the business must select the best applicant for the job. This involves the use of one or several methods of selection.

Application forms

These are usually filled in online. The business asks each applicant to answer questions about their qualifications, skills and relevant experience. There are often questions such as: 'Why are you applying for this job?' and 'What personal qualities do you have which will suit this job?'

Curriculum vitaes (CVs)

These are also known as 'résumés'. These are documents that list a job applicant's educational record and qualifications and also include details of relevant skills, work experience, posts of responsibility held and personal qualities.

References

The applicants who are shortlisted and invited for interview will be asked to provide the names and addresses of referees. These are people who will be asked to provide a reference – to give their opinion on the applicant's character, honesty, reliability and suitability for the job. References are usually confidential, which means the applicant does not see what has been written about them.

If the applicant is a school-leaver, it is normal to give the school as a referee. If the applicant is older, usually a former employer will be used.

Testing/assessment centres

Some businesses include tests in their selection process, for example:

>> **Skills tests** aim to show the ability of the applicant to carry out certain tasks.
>> **Aptitude tests** aim to show the applicant's potential to gain additional skills. Either general intelligence tests or more specific tests are used to assess the applicant's ability to train for a particular job.
>> **Personality tests** are used if a particular type of person is required for the job, if the job requires the ability to work under stress or if the person will need to fit in as part of a team of people.
>> **Group situation tests** give tasks to applicants to complete in group situations and the group is observed. Each applicant will be assessed on the way they work as a member of the team, how they approach the task and their potential leadership qualities.

Interviews

Once business managers have read the application forms and CVs, a shortlist of the most suitable applicants is drawn up. This is done by comparing the application form responses and the CVs with the original person specification. Those applicants who closely match the person specification will make up the shortlist and will be invited for interview.

> **Study tips**
>
> Make sure you can explain how the information from these tests might be helpful in choosing between applicants.

5 HUMAN RESOURCE MANAGEMENT (HRM)

Interviews are still the most widely used form of selection. The main purposes of an interview are to assess, in the shortest possible time:

» the applicant's ability to do the job
» the personal qualities the applicant has which could aid their ability to do the job
» the general character and personality of the applicant – will they fit in well with other people in the business?

Interviews can be one-to-one, two-to-one or involve a panel of people to interview the applicant. Panel interviews are usually used for more senior positions.

Interviews are not always the most reliable way of choosing the best person for the job. This would be the case if the interviewee was very nervous and failed to give a good impression of themselves or if the interviewer was prejudiced.

> ### Activity 5.5
>
> Imagine that you are now going to interview applicants for the vacancy that you advertised in Activity 5.3. You have drawn up the following 6 questions to ask the interviewees:
>
> 1 What is it about the job that attracted you to apply for it?
> 2 What do you know about the company?
> 3 Tell me more about your hobbies and interests.
> 4 Why do you feel you are particularly suitable for the job?
> 5 Where do you see yourself in five years' time?
> 6 Do you have any questions?
>
> a What is the purpose of each of these questions? What are you hoping to find out?
> b What other questions ought to be asked?
> c Get other students in your class to apply for the job you have advertised and then carry out a mock interview. Would you offer them the job?

Study tips

Make sure you can explain why particular interview questions might be asked. You need to be able to explain what the interviewer is hoping to learn about the applicant from the questions being asked. Do not just repeat the question if you are asked to explain why an interview question is being asked.

Definitions to learn

Internal recruitment is when a vacancy is filled by someone who is an existing employee of the business.
External recruitment is when a vacancy is filled by someone who is not an existing employee and is new to the business.

Key info

It is estimated that over 50% of employers are prepared to check applicants' social media profiles before offering them a job. Increasingly, perhaps, people who are seeking employment will think carefully about the information and images they upload to sites such as Facebook, Instagram and TikTok and the comments they make on X (Twitter) and similar social media sites.

Advantages and disadvantages of internal and external recruitment

An important factor in the selection process is whether to choose an internal or external applicant. When an applicant who already works for the business is selected it is called **internal recruitment**. When someone who does not currently work for the business is chosen it is called **external recruitment**.

Recruiting and selecting employees

> **Study tips**
> Be prepared to analyse why a business might recruit a senior manager externally rather than from internal applicants.

> **Key info**
> An increasing proportion of leading global companies are recruiting new Chief Executive Officers (CEOs) externally. The trend is greatest among those businesses that face rapid and significant changes. In 2023 research of large US companies found that 75% of new CEOs were recruited externally.

There are advantages and disadvantages to internal recruitment – see Table 5.1.

Table 5.1 Advantages and disadvantages of internal recruitment

Advantages of internal recruitment	Disadvantages of internal recruitment
It is usually quicker and cheaper than external recruitment which can involve costly advertising	The quality of the applicants may be lower than if the recruitment was external
The person is already known to the business. Managers will already know their reliability, work performance and potential	It could lead to jealousy from other existing employees if a work colleague is promoted above them. This rivalry could reduce motivation
There is less need for induction training (see below) as the person already knows how the business works, its structure and senior personnel	New ideas or experience from other organisations, which could help to improve productivity and efficiency, are not brought into the business
By giving a promotion to an existing employee, workers can become more motivated. They can see that their hard work and effort can be rewarded by the business	By recruiting internally, another post now becomes vacant. The recruitment and selection process must start again to fill this post, which might take time and resources to do

Many businesses, especially those that are growing rapidly or which operate in a fast-changing market, will often only use external recruitment. Table 5.2 explains the advantages and disadvantages of external recruitment.

Table 5.2 Advantages and disadvantages of external recruitment

Advantages of external recruitment	Disadvantages of external recruitment
It opens up a much larger pool of potential applicants. Their quality might be higher and their skills greater than those of internal applicants	It takes longer and costs more than internal recruitment
There is less likely to be internal conflict or jealousy than if an internal applicant was selected	All new external recruits must undergo induction training during which they may not actually be working or producing any output
New ideas and working practices can be brought into the business. This could help it keep up to date and develop new products and ways of working	An externally recruited manager might use very different leadership styles and insist on different methods of working to those that employees are used to. This can cause conflict and uncertainty, leading to reduced motivation
It helps avoid complacency among existing employees as they realise that 'just moving up' the organisation to gain promotion is not a certainty	External recruits may leave the business quite soon after being appointed if they have other promotion chances. They may have lower levels of loyalty to the business than internal recruits

> **Study tips**
> If a question asks about internal and external recruitment, be careful not to state an advantage of internal recruitment and the same point but as a disadvantage of external recruitment, i.e. one may cost less and the other may cost more.

On balance, most businesses use a combination of internal and external recruitment. The method used for each job vacancy will depend greatly on the nature of the post to be filled and the quality of existing employees.

5 HUMAN RESOURCE MANAGEMENT (HRM)

How to recommend and justify who to employ in a given situation

You should now understand the process of recruitment and selection. The final decision of who to employ depends on several factors:

» **Work experience.** How important is it that the applicant has direct experience of the job?
» **Educational and other qualifications.** Are these essential for filling the post, for example, for a doctor?
» **Salary.** What salary level will the new recruit expect? This is particularly an issue with external recruits.
» **Personality.** Will they be able to form good working relationships with existing employees?
» **Internal.** How important is it that the applicant has a good understanding of how the business operates?
» **External.** How important is it that the new employee has experience and skills gained from outside the business?

The relative importance of these and other factors will depend on the situation. It is important to understand the type and size of business being considered and the nature of the job vacancy.

> **Study tips**
>
> If a question asks you to recommend and justify who to employ, you should always link your answer back clearly to the business and the nature of the job to be filled.

> **Extend your skills of analysis**
>
> A question which asks why recruiting an external applicant might be recommended for a robot manufacturer could be answered as follows:
>
> External recruitment means employing someone who is not an existing employee of the business. They could have new ideas to benefit the business.
>
> *Extend your analysis by explaining why this is the result of external recruitment.*
>
> People who have experience working for another robot manufacturer might have useful ideas about new products or more efficient ways of producing robots, which internal recruits might not have.
>
> *Extend your analysis by explaining why this is important to the business.*
>
> New ideas for robot manufacturing brought into the business from an external recruit could help the business be more competitive and attract new customers.

Activity 5.6

a An international construction company has just won a contract to build a dam in an African country. How might the HRM department recruit the following employees for the contract?
   - Experienced engineers
   - Labourers

b An international airline is expanding its operations in South America. It needs to recruit employees to be based only in this continent, as the flights will not go all around the world. What recruitment and selection methods would it use to appoint the following?
   - Airline pilots
   - Cabin crew (flight attendants)

REVISION SUMMARY — Stages in the recruitment and selection process

1. Job analysis – the exact nature of the job and the duties to be undertaken
2. Prepare a job description – the tasks and duties to be undertaken by the successful applicant
3. Prepare a person specification – details of the type of person required, qualifications, experience and personal qualities
4. Advertise the vacancy – using employment agencies, online recruitment sites and other media
5. Prepare application forms to be completed by applicants. Select shortlist of applicants
6. Use selection methods – such as curriculum vitae (CV)/résumé, application form, references, testing/assessment centres, interviews
7. Select the most suitable applicant – they will then receive a contract of employment and may require induction training

Employment contracts and legal controls over employment issues

In many countries governments have passed laws that affect the relationship between employers and employees. The most important employment issues affected by legal controls are:

» employment contracts
» unfair dismissal
» discrimination
» health and safety
» legal minimum wage.

5 HUMAN RESOURCE MANAGEMENT (HRM)

> **Definitions to learn**
>
> A **contract of employment** is a legal agreement between an employer and an employee, listing the rights and responsibilities of employees.
>
> **Unfair dismissal** occurs when an employer ends an employee's contract of employment for a reason that is not covered by that contract.

The main contents of an employment contract

A written **contract of employment** between employer and employee is a legal requirement in most countries. The key contents of this contract are:

- job title and the main duties and responsibilities of the employee
- working hours – for example, 8 hours per day, 5 days per week
- rate of pay
- any other benefits, such as sick pay, pension, bonus
- holiday entitlement
- length of notice that the employer or the employee must give to end the employment.

The benefits of employment contracts for employers and employees

- Both employers and employees know what is expected of them. If a dispute arises over, for example, what work the employee must do or how much they will be paid, the conditions of the contract should make these points clear.
- It provides some security of employment to the employee – they cannot just be asked to leave the business immediately unless they break the terms of the contract.
- If the employee does not meet the conditions of the contract, then legal/fair dismissal is allowed.
- If the employer fails to meet the conditions of the contract, for example, does not offer the holidays the employee is entitled to, then the employee can seek legally binding compensation.

Legal controls over employment issues

Unfair dismissal

Unfair dismissal may occur for a number of reasons. These include discrimination (see next page) or it might be that the employer wants to reduce employee numbers but does not want to pay redundancy compensation. Unfair dismissal means the employer is not keeping to the contract of employment and this is illegal in many countries.

Effects of legal controls on unfair dismissal on employers and employees

- Employers will have legal costs and compensation costs to pay if found guilty of unfair dismissal.
- Employers might find it more difficult to recruit employees if they have a reputation for unfair dismissal.
- Employees have the right to ask for a court of law to decide whether dismissal has been unfair. If the court rules that it is unfair dismissal, the employee has the right to either compensation or be offered their previous job back.

Discrimination

Discrimination at work is when an employer makes decisions affecting employees that are based on unfair reasons. The main examples are when workers are treated differently because they:

- are of a different race or colour
- belong to a different religion
- are of a different sex
- are considered too old/young for the job
- are disabled in some way.

In most countries many of these forms of discrimination are illegal. If they were not illegal, many sections of society would find it very difficult to gain jobs or to achieve promotion at work. Businesses can also lose out by practising unfair discrimination. They could fail to select a very good employee just because they used one of the reasons above not to select the person.

Effects of legal controls on discrimination on employers and employees

- Employers have to be careful when wording an advertisement for a job. For example, they cannot advertise for a 'man' or a 'woman' – they must say 'person'.
- When selecting an employee for a job, an employer must treat all applicants equally. If a business does not do this it could be prosecuted and fined.
- By following these laws carefully, businesses should recruit and promote staff on merit alone and this should help to increase motivation at work.
- Employees should be treated equally in the workplace and when being recruited, and they should be paid equal amounts for similar work.
- If a man and a woman are both equally well qualified for a job they should be treated equally. It should not be the case that one rather than the other is given the job simply because of their sex.
- Employees who have a disability, are from different races or of different religions should be treated in the same way as all other employees.

Health and safety at work

Many years ago, most employers were not concerned about the safety of their employees. Machines did not have safety cages. Protective clothing was not issued. Conditions were often very hot or cold, noisy and unpleasant. The arguments often used by employers to explain such conditions were that it would cost too much to make workplaces safe, and if the existing employees did not like the conditions, then they could leave as there were many unemployed people who would do their work!

In the modern world such attitudes are no longer acceptable. Most employers now care for their employees' safety. One reason for this is that many laws have been passed that have forced them to improve health and safety at work. In most countries there are now laws which make sure that all employers:

- protect employees from dangerous machinery
- provide safety equipment and clothing
- maintain reasonable workplace temperatures
- provide hygienic conditions and washing facilities
- do not insist on excessively long shifts and provide breaks in the work timetable.

5 HUMAN RESOURCE MANAGEMENT (HRM)

Study tips

Make sure you can explain why governments introduce laws to protect employees. Also make sure you can explain how these laws affect both employers and employees.

Effects of legal controls on health and safety on employers and employees

- There is a cost to the employer of meeting the health and safety regulations, for example, better fire-fighting equipment.
- Some employers may take the decision to relocate in countries with very few controls over health and safety.
- The employer needs to find time to train employees in health and safety precautions.
- It reduces the accident rate and cost of compensation for employees injured at work.
- Employees feel safer and more motivated at work.
- Potential employees are more likely to seek work with businesses that observe all health and safety laws.
- Time is less likely to be missed from work due to injury.

Legal minimum wage

In some countries employers can pay whatever wage rate is necessary to recruit sufficient workers. This rate should be recorded in the contract of employment. If there is high unemployment or if unemployment benefits are low, workers may be offered very low wages. These can lead to extreme poverty for the employees and their families. Increasingly, governments are taking action against employers that pay low wages. This action often takes the form of a **legal minimum wage**. A minimum wage makes it illegal for an employer to pay an hourly rate below the minimum wage set.

Definitions to learn

The **legal minimum wage** is the minimum wage rate per hour that employers must pay to employees.

Effects of legal minimum wage laws on employers and employees

- They may increase business costs for the employer, which may force the business to increase its prices.
- Some employers will not be able to afford to pay these higher wage rates and may make some employees redundant.
- Other employees receiving just above the minimum wage level may ask for higher wages to keep the same differential between them and lower-paid employees. Business costs may again increase.
- Some employers may decide to relocate to countries with no minimum wage controls to lower costs.
- They should prevent powerful employers from exploiting unskilled employees who could not easily find other work.
- As many unskilled employees will now be receiving higher wages, this might encourage employers to train them to make sure that they are more productive.
- More people will be encouraged to seek work. Businesses will find it easier to fill vacancies because there are more candidates for each job.
- Low-paid employees will earn more and will have higher living standards, meaning they will be able to afford to buy more.

Key info

In 2024 the District of Columbia had the highest minimum wages in the US, at US$17.00 per hour. Compare this with the minimum wage in your country (you will need to find out the US$ exchange rate).

> ### Activity 5.7
>
> Consider the way in which Gowri Kumaran was treated by her employer.
>
> She applied for a job as machine operator in a television assembly factory. The employer offered her the job and said that her contract of employment would be sent to her after 1 month's trial. After 1 month, Gowri received her wages but was surprised to see that her wage rate was much less than expected. She was also earning much less than other employees doing the same work. There had been several deductions from her wages which she did not understand. She did not receive a contract of employment as had been promised.
>
> Gowri had complained to her supervisor that there were some loose electrical wires on her machine but no action had been taken. She worked 10-hour shifts with only one break. Gowri decided to join a trade union (a group that represents workers rights) but when the manager heard about this he called her into his office. He told her that her work was unsatisfactory and she was no longer required. Gowri was very upset about the way she had been treated. She asked for your advice, as her legal adviser, on what she should do.
>
> **a** Do you think that Gowri has been badly treated by her employer? Give reasons for your answer.
> **b** As Gowri's legal adviser, write a letter to the manager of the factory where she used to work. Explain to the manager all of the points of law which you think they have broken.
> **c** What might be the advantages to employers of treating their employees well?

Training

The importance of training

There are advantages to businesses and employees from training. Training is important to a business as it may be used to:

» introduce a new process or new equipment
» improve the efficiency of the workforce
» make unskilled employees more productive for the business
» decrease the supervision of employees needed
» improve the flexibility of employees to do different tasks
» decrease the chances of accidents which can halt production.

Employees should understand the advantages of the training or they will not work hard or take the training seriously. The benefits to employees from being trained include:

» increased skills and knowledge which might lead to internal promotion
» making work more interesting and challenging as more difficult tasks can now be undertaken
» increased motivation as they feel that the business is investing in their future careers
» improved employee attitudes to encourage them to accept change and raise awareness, for example, the need to improve customer service.

5 HUMAN RESOURCE MANAGEMENT (HRM)

> **Definitions to learn**
>
> **Induction training** is an introduction given to a new employee, explaining the business's activities, customs and procedures and introducing them to fellow employees.
>
> **On-the-job training** occurs when a trainee observes and practises with an experienced employee at the workplace.
>
> **Off-the-job training** involves being trained away from the workplace, usually by specialist trainers.

> **Extend your skills of analysis**
>
> A question which asks why having a trained workforce is important to a toy manufacturing business could be answered as follows:
>
> A trained workforce means that the business will be more efficient and could be more profitable.
>
> *Extend your analysis by explaining why this is the result of training.*
>
> Training workers means that they will be able to operate the latest high-technology machinery, which could increase the output of toys per employee.
>
> *Extend your analysis by explaining why this is important to the business.*
>
> Increasing output per employee through training increases efficiency and will reduce the costs of making each toy. This should allow the manufacturer to be more competitive and make a higher profit.

Types of training

There are three types of training:

» **induction training**
» **on-the-job training**
» **off-the-job training**.

Induction training

This is carried out when an employee is new to the business. When a new employee starts work, they will not know the working methods of the business, who people are or what is expected of them.

> **Case study:** Induction programme
>
> The following is an induction programme for a shop assistant.
>
> | Time | Activity |
> |---|---|
> | 08:30 | Introduction |
> | 08:45 | Company history and company structure |
> | 09:30 | Administration details:
• Company regulations
• Health and safety in the workplace |
> | 10:30 | Break |
> | 10:45 | Workplace:
• Map of the premises – places of work
• Staffroom/staff canteen
• First aid point/fire exits |
> | 11:45 | Conditions of employment:
• Rate of pay, bonus, hours to be worked and breaks
• Sickness and holiday pay, and holiday entitlement
• Pensions
• Length of notice period
• Staff purchases/discounts |
> | 12:45 | Training opportunities |
> | 13:00 | Lunch |
> | 13:30 | Job training:
• Customer service and dealing with difficult customers
• Stacking shelves/presentation of shelves
• Pricing goods, using barcode reader and using tills |
> | 17:00 | Close |

The advantages of induction training are that it:

» helps new employees to settle into their job quickly and become part of their team
» may be a legal requirement to give health and safety training at the start of a job
» means employees are less likely to make mistakes.

The disadvantages of induction training are that it:

» is time-consuming
» means wages are paid but no work is being done by the employee
» delays the start of the employee commencing their job.

On-the-job training

This is where a person is trained by observing and practising with a more experienced employee doing the job within the business. They are shown what to do and are often given a chance to practise the main tasks that they will have to perform. This method of training is, generally, only suitable for unskilled and semi-skilled jobs.

The advantages of on-the-job training are that:

» Individual tuition is given and it is in the workplace so the employee does not need time away from the workplace to attend college or a training centre.
» It ensures there is some production from the employee while they are training.
» It usually costs less than off-the-job training courses.
» It is tailored to the specific needs of the business.

The disadvantages of on-the-job training are that:

» The trainer will not be as productive as usual because they are showing the trainee what to do instead of getting on with their job.
» The trainer may have bad habits and they may pass these on to the trainee.
» It may not lead to training qualifications recognised outside the business and this could be demotivating.
» No new ideas on work methods are brought into the business from external training courses.

Off-the-job training

This is where the employee is trained away from the normal place of work. This may be in a different part of the building or it may be at a different location altogether, such as a college or specialist training centre. The techniques used to train employees can be more varied and up to date than on-the-job training. Off-the-job training often involves classroom learning, using lectures, role play, case studies or computer simulations.

The advantages of off-the-job training are that:

» a broad range of skills can be taught using these techniques
» if these courses are taught in the evening after work, they are cheaper for the business because the employee will still carry out their normal duties during the day. The business will only need to pay for the course and it will not also lose the output of the employee

5 HUMAN RESOURCE MANAGEMENT (HRM)

» employees may be taught a variety of skills, becoming multi-skilled, and this makes them more versatile – they can be moved to different sections of the business when the need arises
» it often uses expert trainers who have up-to-date knowledge of business practices.

The disadvantages of off-the-job training are that:

» costs can be high
» wages are paid but no work is being done by the employee if training takes place during the working day
» the additional qualifications gained mean it is easier for the employee to leave and find another job.

Study tips

Make sure you can explain and give examples of when on-the-job and off-the-job training are suitable for particular jobs.

Training is necessary for the success of most businesses. It is a form of investment but in human capital not physical capital. Investment in training usually leads to greater output per worker and better-qualified, more motivated employees.

REVISION SUMMARY Training (management/business)

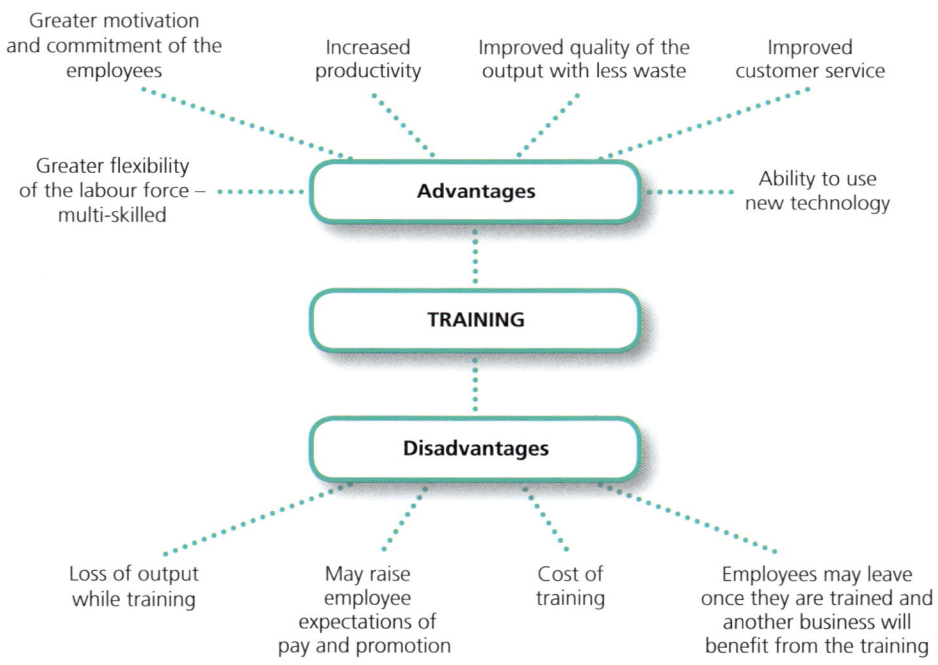

Training

> **REVISION SUMMARY**   Training (employee)

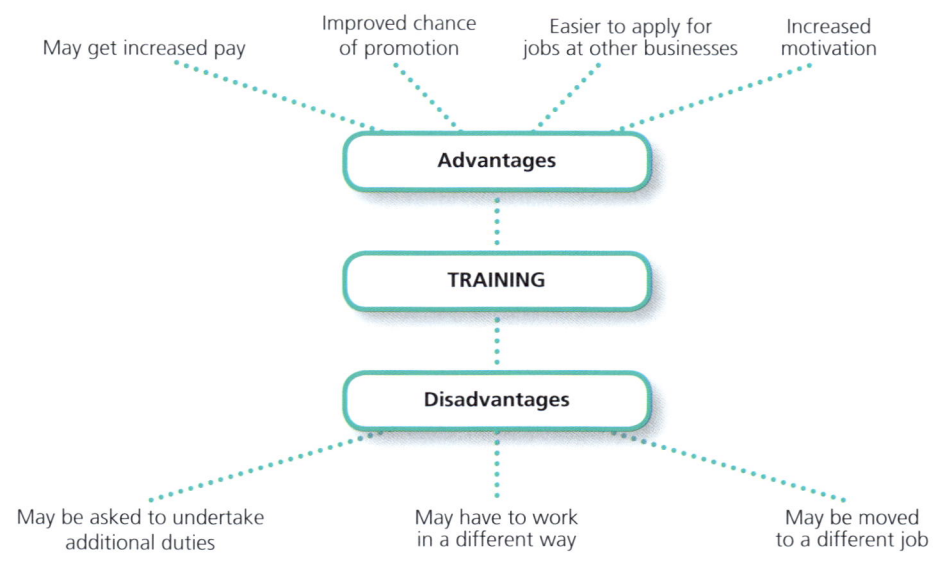

> ### Activity 5.8
> For each of the examples below, decide what type of training would be most appropriate and why.
>
> a S&S is a public limited company and has just introduced a new computer program into the Accounts offices. All the Accounts employees will need to know how to use the new software.
> b Sandeep has been given a job as a trainee manager at a large retail company. The training will last for about 2 years.
> c James has just got a job as a hotel porter. He has never done this type of job before. He is starting work next week.

International business in focus

Malaysia Airlines

Malaysia Airlines Academy provides a wide range of courses, from airline training and aviation services training to digital and innovation learning, all led by experienced trainers. It has its own flight simulator centre for training pilots. It aims to provide excellent education and training to internal and external trainees, which means other airline employees can be trained at the Academy.

Source: www.malaysiaairlines.com/in/en/mh-media-centre/news-releases/2024/unveils-new-mab-academy-campus-corporate-website.html

Discussion points

- Why do you think that Malaysia Airlines uses off-the-job training for its employees?
- Why do you think that effective training is important to both Malaysia Airlines and its employees?
- Suggest ways in which Malaysia Airlines could recruit and select appropriate people, such as Marketing Managers.

5 HUMAN RESOURCE MANAGEMENT (HRM)

Chapter review questions: Short answer and data response

1 Sarah owns a business which manufactures musical instruments. There has been an increase in sales and profits over the last 2 years and there has been a big increase in demand for some products. She employs 50 skilled production workers. She wants to recruit 5 more factory workers to make pianos and 3 skilled violin makers. She has prepared a person specification for both roles. Sarah uses on-the-job training for new factory workers joining the business.
   a Define 'person specification'. [2]
   b Outline **two** questions which Sarah could ask the job applicants at interview. [4]
   c Explain **two** advantages to Sarah of on-the-job training for her new factory employees. [6]
   d Do you think Sarah should use internal recruitment or external recruitment to fill the violin maker vacancies? Justify your answer. [8]

2 Mr Gupta owns an insurance company. He gives advice to clients and arranges insurance policies for customers, who pay a fee for his services. He employs 10 well-qualified employees who offer a high level of customer service. His business needs to recruit an extra 5 well-qualified employees and he will need to draw up a job description. All new employees will have a written contract of employment.
   a Define 'job description'. [2]
   b Outline **two** benefits of Mr Gupta providing a written contract of employment for his employees. [4]
   c Explain why **two** features in an induction training programme would be included by Mr Gupta for his new employees. [6]
   d Do you think that interviews with new applicants will be the best way for Mr Gupta to select new employees? Justify your answer. [8]

Revision checklist

In this chapter you have learned:

- ✔ the role of human resource management
- ✔ the stages in the recruitment process
- ✔ the different methods of selecting employees
- ✔ the advantages and disadvantages of internal and external recruitment
- ✔ how to recommend and justify who to employ in a given situation
- ✔ the main contents of an employment contract
- ✔ the benefits of employment contracts for employers and employees
- ✔ legal controls over employment issues
- ✔ the effects of legal controls over employment issues on employers and employees
- ✔ the importance of training to a business and employees
- ✔ types of training
- ✔ the advantages and disadvantages of the three types of training.

NOW – test your understanding with the revision questions in the Student etextbook and the Workbook.

6 Organisation and management

This chapter will explain:

How to understand simple organisational structures:

★ the main functional areas of a business
★ simple hierarchical structures
★ how to interpret simple organisational charts
★ different ways of flexible working
★ advantages and disadvantages of part-time and full-time employees.

The functions of management:

★ planning, organising, co-ordinating, commanding and controlling
★ advantages and disadvantages of delegation.

Leadership styles:

★ the main leadership styles
★ advantages and disadvantages of the main leadership styles
★ how to recommend and justify an appropriate leadership style for a given situation.

Why reducing the size of the workforce might be necessary:

★ the concept of downsizing
★ why reducing the size of the workforce might be necessary
★ the concept of redundancy
★ how to recommend and justify which employee(s) to make redundant in a given situation.

The role of trade unions:

★ what a trade union is
★ benefits to employees of being a trade union member.

Understanding simple organisational structures

The main functional areas of a business

Most businesses, other than very small ones, will have different departments. In these departments, managers and employees will specialise in different types of work – or functions. The main functional departments are:

» **Operations.** This department is responsible for making the product or providing the service. The managers and employees in Operations have to ensure that the product or service is of the required quality to satisfy the customer. Specific tasks include: ordering materials, holding inventory, manufacturing the product or providing the service, and maintaining quality.

6 ORGANISATION AND MANAGEMENT

- **Marketing.** This department is responsible for researching the market for the product or service and promoting and selling it to customers. Specific tasks include: market research, promoting products and services, setting prices and supporting sales employees.
- **Finance.** This department has responsibility for ensuring the business has adequate finance for both its day-to-day transactions and for longer-term investments. Specific tasks include: checking the inflows and outflows of cash, recording all purchases and sales, providing accounts information for senior managers and arranging loans.
- **Human resource management.** This department has responsibility for the effective management of the workforce of the business. Specific tasks include: recruiting and selecting employees, training, pay negotiations and ensuring the business observes legal requirements for employee management.

Simple hierarchical structures

The best way to explain what the term **hierarchical structure** means is to study a simple **organisational chart**, as shown below.

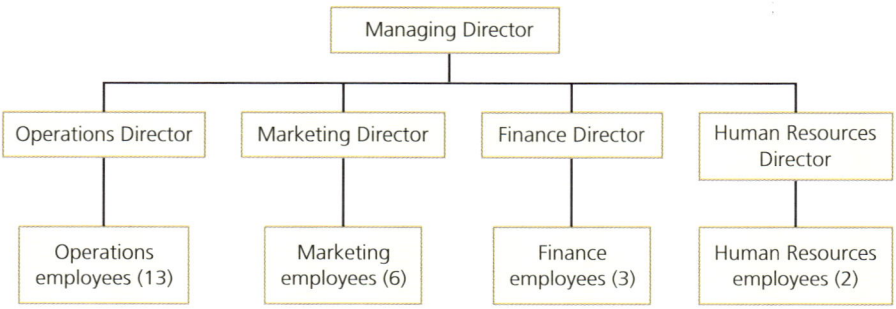

> **Definitions to learn**
>
> **Hierarchical structure** is one with different levels of authority and a chain of command.
>
> **Organisational chart** refers to a diagram that outlines the departmental and management structure.
>
> **Level of hierarchy** refers to managers/supervisors/other employees who are given a similar level of responsibility in an organisation.
>
> **Directors** are senior managers who lead a particular department or division of a business.
>
> **Chain of command** is the way in which authority, control and instructions are passed down from senior management to lower levels.
>
> **Span of control** is the number of subordinates working directly under a manager.

You should be able to identify the following points from this chart:

- There are three levels in the chart. These are called **levels of hierarchy**. The Managing Director has authority and control over the other **directors** and they, in turn, have direct power and control over the other employees.
- There is a **chain of command** from the Managing Director, through the departmental directors, to the other employees. The chain of command is the way that power and control pass through the organisation. This business has a short chain of command as there are only three levels for instructions to pass through.
- The number of employees each director is responsible for is different in the four departments. This means the **span of control** of each director is different.

Advantages of organisational charts

- The charts show how everybody is linked together in the organisation. All employees are aware of how the communication links through the chain of command are used to reach them.
- Every individual can see their own position in the organisation. They can identify who they are accountable to and who they have authority over. Employees can see who they should take orders from.
- They show the links and relationships between different departments within an organisation.
- Everyone is in a department and this gives them a sense of belonging.

Interpreting simple organisational charts

Look at the two organisational charts below. There are two essential differences between them:

» Business A has a tall hierarchy and a long chain of command.
» Business B has a flat hierarchy and a short chain of command.

As a result of these two different structures, the span of control (the number of subordinates working directly under a manager) is wider in Business B than in Business A – in Business A this number is two and in Business B it is five.

There is therefore an important link between the span of control and the chain of command. Tall hierarchies will often have long chains of command but narrow spans of control. Flat hierarchies will often have shorter chains of command but wider spans of control.

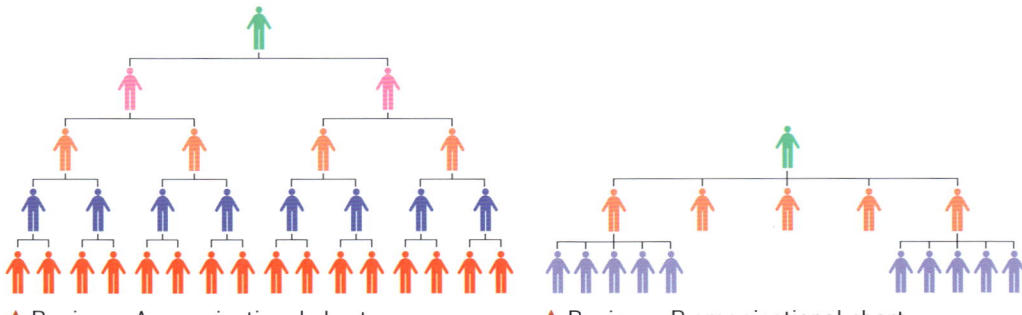

▲ Business A organisational chart   ▲ Business B organisational chart

The two examples above assume that the span of control in each organisation is the same for all managers. This is rarely true in real organisations.

There is no perfect **organisational structure**. In recent years many organisations have made their structure flatter and with a shorter chain of command. In some cases, this has been done by removing a whole level of management – called delayering.

The possible advantages and disadvantages of the different features of hierarchical structures are explained in the following sections.

Definitions to learn

Organisational structure refers to the levels of management and division of responsibilities within an organisation.

Advantages of a short chain of command and flat hierarchy

» Communication is quicker and more accurate. Each message has fewer levels to pass through before reaching the intended person.
» Top managers are less remote from the lower levels of the hierarchy. These top managers should be more in touch with people below them as there are fewer management levels to get to know.
» Spans of control will often be wider. This means that each manager is responsible for more subordinates, but subordinates are likely to have more responsibility and more challenging work which is motivating.
» Decision making is quicker with a short chain of command. There are fewer management levels involved in taking each decision. Each level of hierarchy will have greater decision-making powers than each level in a tall hierarchical structure.

Advantages of a long chain of command and tall hierarchy

» Employees gain more support and guidance from their manager as each manager has fewer people to control.
» There will be more opportunities for promotion to higher levels of the hierarchy. This could have a positive motivational impact.

6 ORGANISATION AND MANAGEMENT

- There is likely to be less workplace stress, as the management function tasks and decision making will be divided between more managers.
- Employees can be more closely supervised as the average span of control will be small.

Advantages of a wide span of control

- If superiors have more people to manage, it will encourage managers to delegate more (see page 91). This is because, as their department is larger, they cannot possibly do all the important work by themselves.
- There will be less direct control of each employee and they will feel more trusted. They will be able to take more decisions by themselves. They may obtain more job satisfaction.

Disadvantages of a wide span of control

- Wide spans of control will mean that each manager is supervising more people. This could result in managers not knowing what each employee is doing and losing control over them.
- To be effective, wide spans of control require employees to be trained to take more responsibility for their own work. This will require further training which will add to business costs.
- Not all employees benefit from being responsible for their own work. Some people prefer close supervision and frequent support from management.

> **Study tips**
> Make sure you can choose a suitable organisational chart for a particular business.

> **Case study:** Organisational structure
>
> Mustafa was bored with his work. He was a customer service adviser for a large online retailer. The business received calls from customers who had queries about their orders.
>
> Mustafa worked in a team, called Team A, with other colleagues, Hammed and Asif. They were supervised by Aziz, who was under the authority of Imran. There were two other groups of customer service advisers, Team B and Team C. These two teams were the same size as Team A. They also had their own supervisors who reported to Imran.
>
> All calls were recorded and supervisors could listen in to make sure that all employees were polite and helpful to customers. Customer service advisers were only allowed to do certain tasks for customers. Other jobs, such as refunds, had to be referred to a supervisor or manager. Customer service advisers had to aim to answer 20 calls each hour. No wonder Mustafa was bored with his work!

> **Activity 6.1**
>
> Read the case study above.
>
> a Draw the organisational chart for this large online retailer.
> b What is the span of control of the supervisors?
> c What would be the advantages and disadvantages of removing the supervisors altogether? Your answer should include references to:
>   - chain of command
>   - span of control.

> **Definitions to learn**
> **Flexible working** allows employees to choose when to start and stop work and where to work, as long as the contracted hours are completed.

Different ways of flexible working

Flexible working gives employees more choice about what time they start work, where they work and what time they stop work. The idea is to help them manage

Understanding simple organisational structures

> **Definitions to learn**
>
> **Home working** means that employees are given the option to work from home rather than at the normal place of employment.

the balance between work and leisure time while they still work the numbers of hours per week stated in the contract of employment.

The two most common examples of flexible working are:

» flexible hours
» **home working**.

Flexible hours

Contracts of employment state the total number of hours that an employee should work each week. Sometimes, this is calculated over a year and this is known as annualised hours. Normally, employees will be expected to work a certain number of these hours each working day, for example, between 08.00 and 16.00. This is an inflexible system.

In recent years, many employers have allowed employees to work at times that best suit them – as long as the total hours stated in the contract are undertaken. For example, an employee might work 10 hours for 4 days a week and not work the 5th day. In other cases, an employee might start work earlier or later some days of the week. This flexible working system has both advantages and disadvantages for employees and employers, as explained in Table 6.1 and Table 6.2.

Table 6.1 Advantages of flexible hours to employees and employers

Advantages to employees	Advantages to employers
Being able to choose when to work gives better work–life balance and this flexibility can be very motivating and improves job satisfaction	A more motivated workforce can lead to higher output and creativity. These benefits could lead to a more efficient business
Many employees have care responsibilities, for example, for young children. Being able to choose work times allows these other responsibilities to be met	Some businesses might be able to open earlier and close later in the day if some employees are on flexible hours. This could increase revenue for a shop or cafe, for example
Greater trust is being shown in employees to choose work times which meet contracted hours. This is empowering and improves self-esteem	The cost of premises could be reduced. If two office employees choose different flexible hours, they could use the same desk and work space at different times

Table 6.2 Disadvantages of flexible hours to employees and employers

Disadvantages to employees	Disadvantages to employers
There could be a reduced feeling of belonging to an organisation if employees do not meet up at the same time. The social benefits to employees of meeting people at work may be reduced	It will be more difficult to communicate with the whole team of employees if they are not all in work at the same time. Important messages might not be received by some employees
By sometimes missing important meetings, because of flexible hours, there could be less involvement in the organisation which can be demotivating	There could be less team working and less collaboration because team members might not all be at work at the same time. New ideas from the team might not be generated effectively

Home working

Two factors have led to a significant increase in the proportion of employees who work some or all of the time from home. Firstly, the widespread use of IT in many employees' jobs means that many of them can undertake their work from a laptop with less need to attend the office. They are able to communicate electronically with their managers and other employees easily and frequently. Secondly, the COVID-19 pandemic of 2020–2022 meant that millions of employees were told to stay at home or had their movements very restricted. Employers often still expected work to be done so encouraged their employees to work from home. Home working has advantages and disadvantages for both employees and employers, as explained in Table 6.3 and Table 6.4.

Table 6.3 Advantages of home working to employees and employers

Advantages to employees	Advantages to employers
No time or money is wasted on travelling to work	The cost of premises may be lower as fewer employees will need to be at the place of work. This could lower office rent costs, for example, and increase profit
They have more control and flexibility over when to work which can help improve the balance between work and leisure	Job satisfaction and motivation will increase. Employees might actually do more work from home than when in the business premises
Employees have no office distractions so may be better able to focus on work	Working from home can be combined with the requirement for employees to work in the office one or two days per week. This flexibility could therefore benefit both employee and employer
Employees may be able to relocate to another part of the country – perhaps with lower house prices or lower rents – and keep working with the same employer	Employees might be less likely to leave an organisation that offers them home working, leading to lower recruitment costs

Table 6.4 Disadvantages of home working to employees and employers

Disadvantages to employees	Disadvantages to employers
They have to pay the cost of home heating or air conditioning	There may be less effective team working and collaboration. This might lead to fewer new ideas and less creativity from employees
Lack of social contact with fellow employees could lead to a feeling of isolation and reduced job satisfaction	It is more difficult to monitor work or the hours being worked. Managers lose some control and autocratic leaders are unlikely to accept employees working from home
They are less likely to meet up with managers and supervisors so there may be less chance of promotion as the employee's personal qualities will be less obvious	It is not suitable for all jobs, such as security or catering workers. There might be conflict within an organisation between those who are allowed to work from home and those who cannot
They have to be very well motivated to work at home and avoid the distractions that exist, such as from other family members	It is more difficult to communicate with employees other than by using IT methods. Sometimes, personal face-to-face communication is better

Case study: Organisational structure

GDX Retail Stores is a public limited company. It owns over 100 food stores in Country A and has just opened its first 3 stores in France. The directors have plans to open more stores in France and other European countries. In addition to its retail business, GDX has a food processing factory. This produces a range of pizzas, pies and desserts for sale in GDX's shops. These products can be produced at a lower cost than buying them from other suppliers.

The current organisational chart of GDX is shown below.

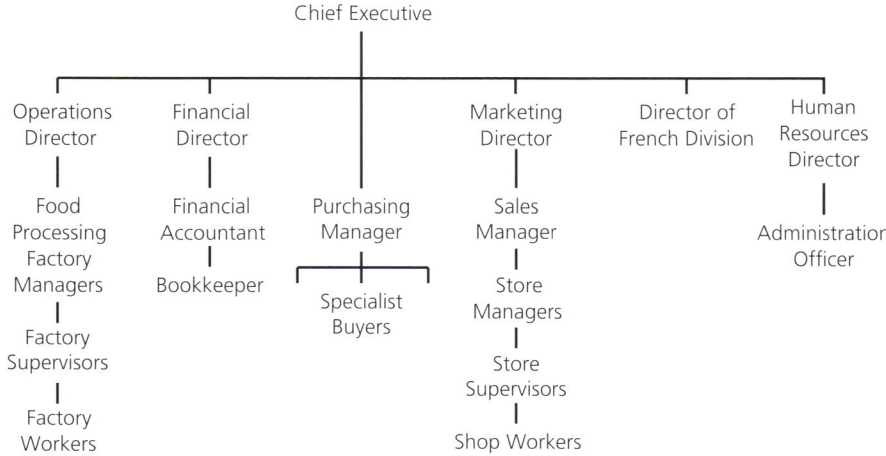

The structure is largely organised into functional departments such as Finance and Marketing, although there is also a French Division led by its own director. The employees in each department often have loyalty towards their own managers and supervisors rather than to the company as a whole.

Food quality and health and safety are very important to GDX. All employees are trained in food handling and hygiene. Standards are very high and the directors believe that close supervision of all retail employees is important. Labour turnover is above the average for retail stores.

Some employees have complained that they often hear about important decisions affecting the stores several days after they have been made. Store supervisors have to report to their managers every day.

GDX directors think that having a senior manager responsible for each country that the company plans to expand into will be an advantage. Using their specialist knowledge of the country will allow managers to take effective local decisions, especially as tastes and cultures differ between countries.

Some directors of GDX want to allow flexible working for food store employees to help reduce labour turnover.

Activity 6.2

a Identify the number of levels of hierarchy in the Marketing department.
b Identify the span of control of the Purchasing Manager.
c Explain **two** advantages to GDX of its tall organisational structure.
d Explain **two** disadvantages to GDX of its tall organisational structure.
e Do you think it is a good idea to have a separate division and director for each country that GDX expands its operations into? Justify your answer.
f Do you think GDX should introduce flexible working for its food store employees? Justify your answer.

6 ORGANISATION AND MANAGEMENT

> **Extend your skills of analysis**
>
> A question which asks for a benefit to a retail business of allowing flexible hours could be answered as follows:
>
> Flexible hours allow employees to choose when they start and end their working day.
>
> *Extend your analysis by explaining why this is an advantage.*
>
> This helps the retail business retain sales employees who, for example, may have care responsibilities and would otherwise leave the business if they could not work flexible hours.
>
> *Extend your analysis by explaining why this is important to the business.*
>
> The business would lose some hard-working and efficient retail sales employees if flexible working was not offered. These employees might be popular with customers. There would also be costs of recruiting new sales employees. Business costs would rise, possibly leading to lower profits.

Advantages and disadvantages of part-time and full-time employees

A **part-time employee** is someone who works fewer hours than a **full-time employee**. There is no specific number of hours that makes someone full-time or part-time, but a full-time employee will usually work 35 hours or more a week. The number of full-time hours which employees usually work in a week will vary from one country to another. The contract of employment will show a different number of hours depending on whether it is a part-time or full-time job. Some employees prefer part-time contracts, for example, students who also have college work to do or parents with childcare responsibilities. Combining two or more part-time jobs can give an employee more variety in their working life.

> **Definitions to learn**
>
> A **part-time employee** is someone who works fewer hours than a full-time employee. This is often less than 35 hours a week.
> **Full-time employees** will usually work 35 hours or more a week.

Advantages to a business of employing part-time employees

- Employees can just be employed to work at busy times.
- Business opening/operating hours can be extended at evenings or weekends.
- Part-time contracts are often suitable for parents with young children. The number of applicants for each vacant post might therefore be greater.
- It reduces business costs compared to employing and paying a full-time employee.
- In some countries it is easier to make part-time workers redundant.

> **Key info**
>
> In many countries, the proportion of employees with a part-time contract is increasing. In the UK and India 24% of workers are employed part-time. In Bangladesh the figure is 21%, in Nigeria 33% of employees are part-time and in Germany the figure is 43%.

Disadvantages to a business of employing part-time employees

- Some part-time employees may see the job as temporary and this may mean they are more likely to leave to get another job.
- Some part-time employees may be less committed to the business if they have more than one part-time job.
- It takes longer to recruit two part-time employees than one full-time employee.
- Part-time workers may be less suitable for promotion because they will not have gained the same skills and experience as full-time employees.
- It may be more difficult to communicate with part-time employees when they are not in work.

Advantages to a business of employing full-time employees

- It may be easier to communicate with full-time employees because they are in work more.
- Full-time employees make it easier to establish effective teamwork.

- Full-time employees will offer continuity of service to regular customers.
- Full-time employees may be more efficient as they spend longer on their work role.

Disadvantages to a business of employing full-time employees
- Having full-time employees reduces flexibility for busy or quiet periods.
- The business must pay full-time wages even if it is not busy.

The functions of management

All organisations, including businesses, have managers. They may not be called managers because different titles can be used – leader, director, headteacher and so on. The main functions of management are outlined below.

Planning

Planning for the future of the organisation involves setting aims or targets, for example: 'The school will aim to increase its sixth form to over 200 students in two years' time' or 'We should plan to increase sales of our new fruit juice range by 50% in three years.'

These aims or targets will give the organisation a sense of direction or purpose. There will be a common feeling in the organisation of having something to work towards. A manager who is not good does not plan for the future at all.

Managers must also plan for the resources that will be needed. For example: 'To achieve our aim of increasing student numbers in the sixth form, we will need to build a new sixth form centre' or 'Increased advertising expenditure will be needed to increase sales of our fruit juices.' These are two examples of plans that are designed to help the organisation achieve the aims set for it.

Organising

A manager cannot do everything. Tasks must be delegated to others in the organisation. These people must have the resources to be able to do these tasks successfully. It is therefore the manager's responsibility to organise people and resources effectively.

An organisational chart can help to show who has the authority to do different jobs. It also helps to make sure that specialisation occurs and that two people do not end up doing the same task. An effective manager will organise people and resources very carefully.

Co-ordinating

Co-ordinating means 'bringing together'. A manager may be very good at planning and organising but may have failed to bring people in the organisation together. This is a real danger with functional departments in an organisation. Different departments can be working away in their own specialist area without making contact with people from other departments. For example, there is no point in the Marketing department planning the launch of a new product unless it has worked with (co-ordinated with) the Operations department. It is the Operations department that will have to produce the product at the right time, in the right quantities.

A good manager will therefore make sure that all departments in the organisation work together to achieve the plans originally set by the manager.

Commanding

Many people think that this is all managers do! In fact, the task of management is more concerned with guiding, leading and supervising people than just telling them what to do – although this may be important too. Managers have to make sure that all supervisors and employees keep to targets and deadlines. Instructions and guidance must be provided by managers and it is also their responsibility to make sure that the tasks are carried out by people below them in the organisation.

Controlling

This is a never-ending task of management. Managers must try to measure and evaluate the work of all individuals and groups to make sure that they are on target. There is little point in planning and organising if managers then fail to check that the original aims are being met. If it seems that certain groups are failing to do what is expected of them, then managers may have to take some action to correct this. This is not necessarily disciplining staff – although that might be important. There might be reasons for poor performance other than inefficient employees – it is the manager's job to find out why targets are not being met and then to correct the problem.

By understanding these five key functions of management it is clear why management is necessary to any organisation. Without clear and effective management, a business will:

» lack a sense of control and direction
» lack co-ordination between departments, leading to wastage of effort
» lack control of employees
» lack organisation of resources, leading to low output and sales.

Activity 6.3

Naomi is a student at a sixth form college. She recently took part in a work shadowing exercise to find out what it is like to be a manager. Work shadowing means that a student follows a manager for a day or more to experience the work that they do. Naomi 'shadowed' Sabrina Choolun, who is the manager of the sportswear section in Suresave, a large retail store. Naomi kept the following diary for one day.

08.30 Attended meeting with other departmental heads and Chief Executive to agree targets for the next 2 years. Departmental heads told to plan their own strategy to meet these goals.

09.15 2 employees failed to turn up for work. Sabrina asked other employees to cover these absences by working longer shifts today.

10.00 Meeting with Sales Manager from big sports manufacturer. Sabrina discussed the range of goods she may purchase next year to meet the store's targets.

11.00 New employee did not cope well with awkward customer. When customer had gone, Sabrina reminded the shop assistant of the correct procedure that should be followed. Asked employee to always follow company policy in these matters.

14.30 Details of individual employee sales figures were studied. 1 employee in particular has failed to meet sales targets and it was agreed with him that further product training was necessary.

16.00 Email received from Sabrina's line manager. There was a problem with another department selling clothing including sports clothes. It was now possible for customers to find the same goods in the store in 2 departments at different prices! Sabrina needed to meet with the other departmental manager to agree on a common policy.

For each of the tasks that Sabrina carried out, identify whether it was concerned with planning, organising, co-ordinating, commanding or controlling.

The functions of management

Advantages and disadvantages of delegation

Managers cannot usually do all of the work within an organisation. They have to decide which tasks they undertake themselves and which they ask subordinates to do. The process of giving subordinates (less senior employees) the authority to perform certain tasks is called **delegation**.

It is important to remember that it is the authority to perform a task which is being delegated – not the final responsibility. If the job is done badly by the subordinate, then it is the manager who has to accept the responsibility for this.

The advantages of delegation to both employees and managers are explained in Table 6.5.

> **Definitions to learn**
>
> **Delegation** means giving a subordinate the authority to perform particular tasks.

Table 6.5 Advantages of delegation to employees and managers

Advantages to employees	Advantages to managers/employers
The tasks delegated should make the employee's work more interesting and rewarding. This will increase their motivation and efficiency	Managers can now focus on other functions such as taking important decisions. This should help to improve the manager's performance/decision making
A good performance by the employee in completing delegated tasks could lead to promotion	Managers do not have all the good ideas. Delegation can encourage employees to show more creativity and initiative, making the business more successful
Delegation can help to train employees in new skills which increases their career opportunities	Managers can measure the performance of the employees more easily. Success in completing delegated tasks shows that they have good potential
Employees feel more important. The trust shown in them to perform a delegated task increases self-esteem	Successful delegation can help managers identify which employees to promote

Delegation can have disadvantages too. It would be unwise of a manager to delegate important business decisions to subordinates, for example, who lack necessary skills and experience. When deciding what to delegate and to whom, managers need to analyse the potential disadvantages of delegation. These are explained in Table 6.6.

Table 6.6 Disadvantages of delegation to employees and managers

Disadvantages to employees	Disadvantages to managers/employers
Some employees prefer to do the jobs they have always been given and become very worried if given new, more challenging tasks	Managers have to show confidence and trust in employees when delegating tasks. Some managers want to keep control over employees so will be reluctant to delegate
Delegation can lead to frustration and a lack of achievement if the employee fails to complete the task well	To do more challenging delegated tasks, employees will need training and this can increase costs
Employees can believe that they are just 'being given more work to do' without any incentive or recognition	Mistakes might be made by employees, especially if the most appropriate employees have not been chosen to do the delegated tasks or they have not been trained effectively to carry out these tasks

6 ORGANISATION AND MANAGEMENT

REVISION SUMMARY — Delegation

Leadership styles

There are many leaders in society – from politicians, religious leaders and captains of sports teams, to leaders of large businesses. An effective business leader is someone who can inspire and get the best out of the workforce, getting them to work towards a common goal.

There are three different **leadership styles** managers can use:

» autocratic leadership
» democratic leadership
» laissez-faire leadership.

Definitions to learn

Leadership styles are the different approaches to dealing with people and making decisions when in a position of authority – autocratic, democratic or laissez-faire.

Autocratic leadership is where the manager takes all decisions in the business and expects to have their orders followed.

Autocratic leadership

Autocratic leadership exists when managers are in total charge of the business and they expect to have their orders followed without question. They keep themselves separate from the rest of the employees. They make virtually all the decisions and keep important information to themselves. They tell employees only what they need to know. Communication in the business is mainly one-way, that is, downward or top-down, and the employees have little or no opportunity to comment on any work-related issues.

Advantages

» There is quick decision making, for example, during a crisis. A fire or flood at a factory will require rapid decisions to be taken and instructions given out that everyone must follow.
» Autocratic managers have full control over employees as they have given clear orders and will check to see that these have been carried out.
» Unskilled employees may not have the ability or experience needed to make effective decisions at work. Autocratic leadership might be most effective in this case.

Disadvantages
- There is no opportunity for employee input into key decisions which can be demotivating as it reduces job satisfaction.
- Better decisions can often be made if employees are asked for their opinions or are even involved in making some decisions. They have important practical work experience which managers may lack.
- Employees often have creative and innovative ideas but autocratic leaders will never consult them.

Democratic leadership

Democratic leadership is based on the idea that employees may be able to contribute to successful business decisions. When managers use this style, information about future plans is openly discussed with employees before the final decision is made. Communication with employees is frequent and two-way, meaning that employees pass messages back to managers as well as receiving instructions.

> **Definitions to learn**
>
> **Democratic leadership** involves employees in the decision-making process but the final decision is left to the leader.
>
> **Laissez-faire leadership** makes the broad objectives of the business known to employees but then they are left to make their own decisions and organise their own work.

Advantages
- Better decisions can often result from consulting with employees and using their experience and ideas.
- Job satisfaction is increased as employees are being trusted to contribute their ideas. This can increase motivation and business efficiency.
- Employees are likely to work harder to make a business decision successful if they were involved in making it.

Disadvantages
- Unpopular decisions, such as making employees redundant, could not effectively be made using this style of leadership.
- It can be time-consuming to consult with employees on problems and decisions. This style of leadership would not be effective during a crisis, for example.

Laissez-faire leadership

Laissez-faire is French for 'leave to do'. Laissez-faire leaders make the broad objectives of the business known to employees but then leave them to make their own decisions and organise their own work. This is often done within teams of employees, with each team working on separate projects. Communication can be difficult in this type of organisation as clear direction is not given. Once the laissez-faire leader has set clear objectives, they have a limited role to play in decision making.

Advantages
- It encourages employees to show creativity and responsibility. It is often used in business organisations that need creative solutions to problems, for example, in advertising or research into new product ideas.
- Laissez-faire leaders trust team members and give them the power to make decisions independently. This trust can boost team morale and develop a sense of ownership over their work.
- The job satisfaction that can result from laissez-faire leadership may reduce the number of skilled employees leaving the business.

Disadvantages

» This leadership style would not be appropriate in organisations where a consistent and clear decision-making structure is needed, for example, in providing customer service.

» Without strong leadership, teams may lack self-control and focus. These problems can result in missed deadlines, incomplete projects and a disorganised work environment.

> **Extend your skills of analysis**
>
> A question which asks why a democratic style of leadership might be recommended for a specialist manufacturing business could be answered as follows:
>
> A democratic leadership style will encourage employees to be involved in making decisions.
>
> *Extend your analysis by explaining why this is an advantage.*
>
> Employees who have experience of the specialist production process often have good ideas for improving the process or service offered, which managers who do not operate machines might not have thought of.
>
> *Extend your analysis by explaining why this is important to the business.*
>
> When specialist production employees are given the chance to participate in decision making, the final decision might lead to more efficient production because of their experience. Sales and revenue for the business are likely to increase.

How to recommend and justify an appropriate leadership style for a given situation

The best style of leadership for a manager to use can vary depending on the type of employees, as well as the type of work the business does and the situation the business is in. For example, managers may not be autocratic leaders all of the time. It may be appropriate for them to use democratic leadership at times but in other situations they may need to use a more autocratic style.

Therefore, different situations often require different styles of leadership. The most effective leaders use different styles of leadership at different times and in different situations. The way in which a manager leads a business during a particular situation can have a big impact on employees and how they react to the manager. It is important to remember that a good manager will adopt the style of leadership that best suits each situation.

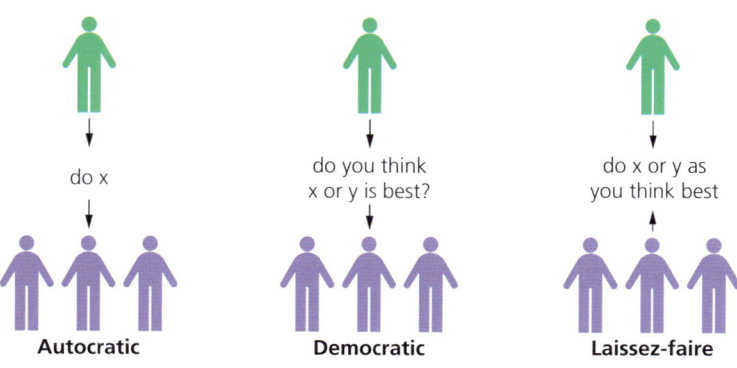

▲ Leadership styles

Study tips
Make sure you know the advantages and disadvantages of the three leadership styles and can apply them to different work situations.

> ### Activity 6.4
> For each of the following situations, choose a suitable leadership style and justify why it is the best one to use and why you have rejected the other two leadership styles.
> a The owner of a small business making wooden toys wants to increase output. She has 5 employees who are all very experienced and skilled in making the wooden toys. She needs to decide on new ways of working to increase efficiency so she does not have to employ any more workers. Which leadership style should she choose?
> b The Managing Director of a large insurance company is reducing the size of the workforce as the business is making large losses. If action is not taken soon, the business could fail. Which leadership style should the manager choose?
> c A medical research company employs many skilled and experienced scientists. They work in small teams to develop new medicines. Each team has its own specialist area of knowledge. What style of leadership is best for the directors of this business to use?

Why reducing the size of the workforce might be necessary

The concept of downsizing

Chapter 2 explained why many businesses grow in size. This usually means increasing the size of the workforce. **Downsizing** is the reverse of this process as it means making the labour force smaller by permanently reducing the number of people employed. This does not necessarily mean that the business, using other measures of size, is getting smaller. For example, buying a new automated machine might lead to 10 employees losing their jobs yet the volume of business output could actually increase.

Definitions to learn

Downsizing a business means permanently reducing the number of people it employs.
Redundancy is when an employee loses their job because the business closes down or the work done by the employee is no longer needed.

Why reducing the size of the workforce might be necessary and the concept of redundancy

Redundancy is where the specific job of an employee is no longer needed by the business. The employee is not being dismissed due to poor work but because the job itself is no longer needed. This can be for a number of reasons, as outlined in the following sections.

Automation

Automated machines that require no or very few employees to operate them often result in many job losses. The employees who used to do the jobs now being done by machines will be made redundant. New jobs might be created in programming or maintaining complex automated machines but, often, the original employees do not have the skills to do this work.

Reduced demand for products

If the demand for the products made by a business is falling, fewer employees will be needed. If the business believes the fall in demand is not a short-term problem, employees will be made redundant as fewer of them will now be needed. Demand for the products of a business could fall because:

» they are becoming less appealing to customers who prefer competitors' products
» the economy is in recession and unemployment reduces customers' incomes.

6 ORGANISATION AND MANAGEMENT

Need to lower costs

If competitors' products are being sold at low prices, a business might have to reduce costs so that it can cut its own prices. One way to cut costs is to encourage employees to do their jobs more efficiently which will mean that the total number of employees required will be less. Some will be made redundant.

How to recommend and justify which employee(s) to make redundant in a given situation

Making employees redundant is a very important decision. Redundancies mean employees lose their incomes and the employees who remain will be very worried about their own jobs too. The following factors help managers decide which employees to make redundant and which to retain:

> **Definitions to learn**
>
> **Redundancy payments** are made to employees by the business when they are made redundant.
> A **trade union** is a group of employees who have joined together to ensure their interests are protected.

- **Length of time employed.** Loyal employees who have stayed with the business for many years may be retained. **Redundancy payments** will be highest for these employees so it is costly to make them redundant.
- **Essential skills.** No business wants to lose key employees who will be difficult to replace. These will not be made redundant unless the situation for the business is very serious.
- **Future potential.** Some of the more qualified employees may be the most productive and creative and be able to cope with change better than employees who find change difficult to accept.
- **Employment record.** Managers will consider whether the employee has good or poor absenteeism and attendance records and whether they receive positive reports from their managers.
- **Voluntary redundancy.** Some employees may have another job they can move to, they may want to retire early or want to start their own business with the redundancy pay.

The role of trade unions

What a trade union is

Trade unions can play an important role in relations between employers and employees. Employees generally all have the same objectives which include:

- higher pay
- better working conditions
- training opportunities
- opportunities to contribute to business decisions
- job security.

Joining a trade union can sometimes help employees achieve these objectives. The key role of a trade union is to represent its members during negotiations with employers on employment issues.

Benefits to employees of being a trade union member

When a person starts work, they may be asked by someone who represents a trade union if they want to join. If the employee decides to join the trade union, they will pay an annual fee or subscription. The most likely benefits to an employee of being a trade union member are:

» **Strength in numbers when negotiating with employers.** A trade union can take industrial action – such as calling for **strike** action – to put pressure on employers. This makes it more likely that employers will accept employee demands for higher pay and better working conditions.
» **Negotiating with employers for improved work environment.** For example, in matters of health and safety, noise levels, heating or air conditioning.
» **Negotiating with employers for improved benefits for members who are not working.** For example, for those who are sick, retired or have been made redundant.
» **Improved job satisfaction by encouraging employers to offer training opportunities.**
» **Advice and/or financial support.** For example, if a member thinks that they have been unfairly dismissed or made redundant, have received unfair treatment or have been asked to do something that is not part of their job.
» **Benefits that have been negotiated or provided for union members.** These include discounts in certain shops and provision of sporting facilities or clubs.

Key info

In 2024 the trade unions representing pilots working for Air India said the new hours of work and rest periods should be reviewed to ensure the health and safety of cabin crew. The unions felt these new rotas were different to those laid out in the regulations set out for the industry by India's Directorate General of Civil Aviation.

Definitions to learn

A **strike** is when a trade union tells its members not to work in order to put pressure on employers to meet trade union demands.

REVISION SUMMARY

Benefits to employees of being a trade union member

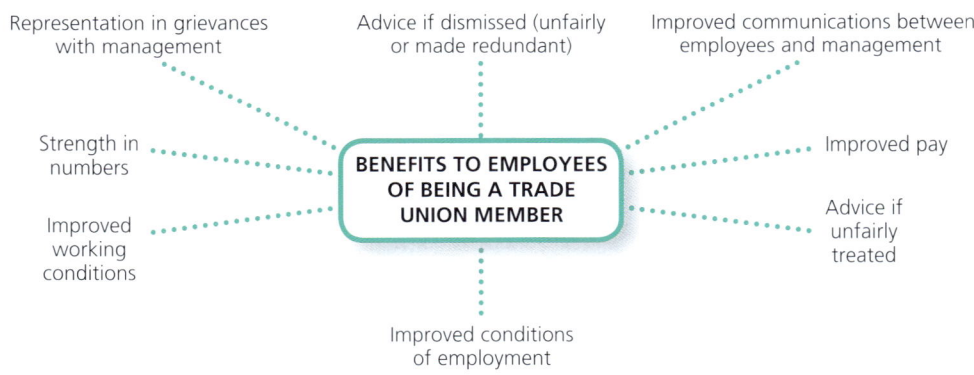

Study tips

Make sure you can explain the benefits of trade union membership from the employees' viewpoint.

Activity 6.5

Shona has just started work as an Administrative Assistant in a government department and has been asked if she wants to join the trade union that represents the employees in that department. She does not know what to do as she knows nothing about trade unions. Write her an email outlining the advantages and disadvantages of joining a trade union. Include a recommendation to Shona as to whether to join the trade union or not.

6 ORGANISATION AND MANAGEMENT

International business in focus

Downsizing Spotify

In 2023 Spotify made about 1500 employees redundant – 17% of its employees. CEO Daniel Ek said slowing economic growth and rising costs were to blame for the job cuts, which he said would make Spotify a more efficient company. He claimed the reduction was needed because the company had too many employees in supporting roles rather than working on the main activities that make a real impact on customers.

Discussion points

- How did Spotify benefit from making 1500 employees redundant?
- What were the likely problems Spotify had in making so many employees redundant?

Chapter review questions: Short answer and data response

1 Sasha owns a business which produces office furniture. She is the Managing Director. The business employs 100 people in the Operations department and 15 people in total in Marketing, Finance and Human Resources. All marketing and HR employees are allowed flexible working. There are 3 supervisors in the Operations department so the span of control is wide. Sasha says that using a democratic leadership style is very important to the success of the business. Very few employees leave each year. The best ideas for new products come from the meetings she has with employees.
   a Define 'span of control'. [2]
   b Outline **two** functions Sasha undertakes as the manager of this business. [4]
   c Explain **two** advantages to the business of allowing flexible working for some employees. [6]
   d Do you think Sasha is right to say that the democratic leadership style is very important to the success of the business? Justify your answer. [8]

2 The organisational chart below is for PPB. It is a private limited company which owns and operates a chain of supermarkets. The organisational chart shows the hierarchical structure of the business. Most employees are given specific tasks to perform and managers are reluctant to delegate. A trade union is trying to encourage supermarket assistants to become members.
   a Define 'hierarchical structure'. [2]
   b Outline **two** benefits to the supermarket assistants of joining a trade union. [4]
   c Explain **two** disadvantages to PPB of having a tall organisational structure. [6]
   d Do you think more delegation would be a good idea for PPB? Justify your answer. [8]

The role of trade unions

Revision checklist

In this chapter you have learned:

- ✔ the main functional areas of a business
- ✔ the meaning of hierarchical structures, span of control and chain of command
- ✔ how to interpret simple organisational charts
- ✔ different ways of flexible working
- ✔ advantages and disadvantages of part-time and full-time employees
- ✔ the functions of management
- ✔ the advantages and disadvantages of delegation
- ✔ the main leadership styles and their advantages and disadvantages
- ✔ how to recommend and justify an appropriate leadership style for a given situation
- ✔ the concept of downsizing and redundancy
- ✔ why reducing the size of the workforce might be necessary
- ✔ how to recommend and justify which employee(s) to make redundant in a given situation
- ✔ what a trade union is
- ✔ the benefits to employees of being a trade union member.

NOW – test your understanding with the revision questions in the Student etextbook and the Workbook.

7 Methods of communication

This chapter will explain:

Why communication is important:

★ why communication is important for a business
★ methods of communication
★ advantages and disadvantages of different methods of communication
★ internal and external communication
★ how to recommend and justify which method of communication to use in a given situation.

Communication barriers:

★ examples of communication barriers
★ reasons for communication barriers
★ problems caused by communication barriers
★ how communication barriers can be reduced or removed.

Why communication is important

Why communication is important for a business

We all communicate with other people every day. We communicate with our families, at school or college, when we go shopping, when chatting with friends or when using social media. **Communication** with others is a natural part of life. Why do we need to study something which comes naturally to us? There is one important reason for this: communication must be effective. This means that the information or **message** being sent is received, understood and acted upon in the way intended. If it is not, it can be annoying for us when, for example, we communicate with our friends. However, for businesses, communication which is ineffective can result in serious consequences.

Businesses need to communicate internally – with managers and other employees – and externally – with customers and suppliers, for example. Both forms of communication are very important to the efficient operation of a business.

Internal communication

Without **internal communication**, employees would be operating as individuals with no links to other employees or managers. The tasks of management in guiding, instructing, warning and encouraging employees would become impossible without good internal communication links.

Here are some examples of common messages internally communicated in businesses. The method used to communicate each message is also shown.

» 'How many hours did you work last week?' (manager speaks to an employee)
» 'There will be a fire drill at 11:00 today.' (notice on a noticeboard)
» 'The cutting machine has broken down. Can you call the engineer as soon as possible?' (telephone call)

> **Definitions to learn**
>
> **Communication** is the transferring of a message from the sender to the receiver, who understands the message.
>
> A **message** is the information or instructions being passed by the sender to the receiver.
>
> **Internal communication** is between members of the same organisation.

- 'Sales last week reached a record level. You will need to increase output so that we do not run out of inventories.' (email to Operations Manager)
- 'Keep this door locked at all times.' (sign on a door)
- 'You have been dismissed because of frequent absences from work. Please acknowledge receipt of this letter.' (letter written to an employee)
- 'Shoplifting is on the increase in our store – we all need to suggest ideas on how the problem can be reduced.' (meeting with all shop employees in a store)

The list could have been very long indeed, but these examples show the wide range of topics which need to be communicated within a business. Can you imagine the serious problems that could occur if these messages were not communicated effectively to the people who needed this information?

> **Key info**
>
> Many businesses now use social media for communications. For example, WhatsApp messages allow a business to send quick communications to employees. If a WhatsApp group has been created for a department, for example, the message function can be used to send out updates to all members of the department.

> **Definitions to learn**
>
> **External communication** is between the organisation and other organisations or individuals.

> **Activity 7.1**
> a Suggest three more examples of communication sent to people within a business or your school or college.
> b For each example, give details of the message to be sent and the method you think should be used to send it.
> c Explain what problems the business could face if each message failed to reach the intended receiver.

External communication

External communication occurs when messages are sent between a business and other businesses or between a business and its customers. Some of the main examples of external communication are:

- orders for goods from suppliers
- informing customers about prices and delivery times
- advertising goods or services
- asking customers to pay invoices on time.

The methods of communication used when communicating externally are similar to those used for internal communication. However, the growth of the internet and social networking has transformed how a business can communicate with the 'outside world'. The main difference between internal and external communication is who is being communicated with.

External communication is very important to the image and efficiency of a business. If a company communicates ineffectively with suppliers, it may be sent the wrong materials. If it sends inaccurate information to customers, they may decide to buy a product from another company.

Here are some more examples of external communication. You can imagine how serious it would be if communication failed in all of these cases.

- A Finance Manager writes a letter to the tax office asking how much tax must be paid this year.
- A Sales Manager records a customer order taken over the internet for 330 items to be delivered by next Wednesday.
- A business must contact thousands of customers who have bought a product which turns out to be dangerous. An email is sent to all customers who bought the product to ask them to return the item for a refund.

7 METHODS OF COMMUNICATION

> ### Activity 7.2
> a Suggest **three** more examples of communication with people outside a business or your school or college.
> b Give details of the message to be sent and the method you think should be used to send it.
> c Explain what problems the business could face if each message failed to reach the intended receiver.

Definitions to learn

Feedback is the reply from the receiver which shows whether the message has arrived, been understood and, if necessary, acted upon.

Effective communication

Effective communication involves the following four features:

» a transmitter or sender of the message – this is the person who wishes to pass on the information to others. This person has to choose the next two features carefully in order to make sure that communication occurs effectively
» a method of communication which is suitable for the message
» a receiver of the information – the person to whom the message should be sent
» **feedback**, where the receiver confirms that the message has been received and responds to it. This requires two-way communication and this often leads to a more effective form of sending a message than one-way communication.

One-way communication occurs when the receiver of a message has no chance to reply or respond to the message. An example would be an instruction to 'take these goods to the customer'. One-way communication does not allow the receiver to contribute to the communication or to provide any feedback.

Two-way communication is when there is a reply or a response from the receiver. This could be just simple confirmation of receipt of the message or it could be a discussion about the message. Both people are therefore involved in the communication process. This could lead to better and clearer information and the receiver feels more motivated as they are directly involved in the communication process.

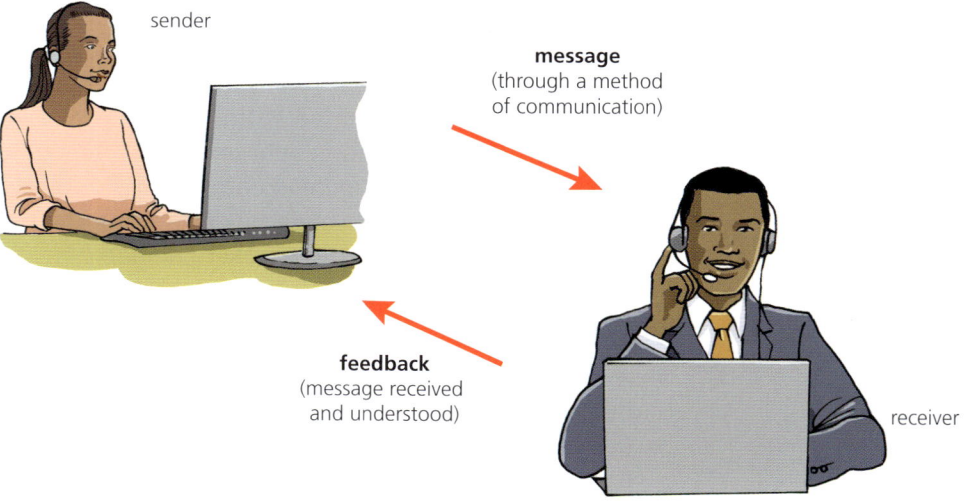

▲ The features of effective communication

Why communication is important

> ### Activity 7.3
>
> Sales were below target at the Cooperative Retail Store. The manager was very concerned about this. They decided to write to every employee, about 30 in all, to warn them of the problem of falling sales and how jobs were now at risk. The letter asked for ideas on how to increase sales. Employees were asked to confirm that they had received the letter and tell the manager if they had any good ideas.
>
> a Identify:
>   i the sender of the message
>   ii the method being used
>   iii the receiver of the message.
> b Did the communication involve feedback?
> c Do you think that the letter sent by the manager to employees was the best way to communicate with them? If not, which method would have been more effective? Explain your answer.

REVISION SUMMARY — **Effective communication**

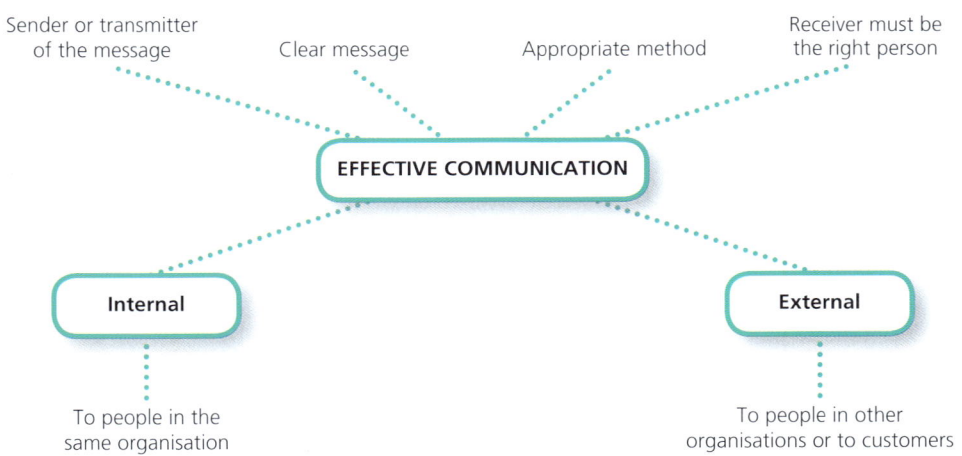

Definitions to learn

A **virtual meeting** is a method of communication that enables people in different physical locations to use their mobile phone or internet-connected device to meet in the same virtual room.

Methods of communication

Information can be sent or transmitted in a number of different ways – these are called the communication methods. They include:

- meetings
- emails
- text messages
- social media
- phone calls
- letters
- posters
- noticeboards.

Meetings

These can be face-to-face meetings which could include one-to-one talks, team briefings or meetings between the sender of the message and several or many people. Also, there can be **virtual meetings**, where groups of people in different locations are able to see and hear each other through a video/internet link. Virtual meetings can be easier to organise and cost less than asking people to travel to physically attend a meeting.

7 METHODS OF COMMUNICATION

Advantages

- Information can be given out quickly. When this happens at big meetings, it is an efficient way of communicating with a large number of people.
- There is opportunity for immediate feedback and two-way communication. Questions can be asked and answers to these will help improve understanding of the message.
- The message can be reinforced by seeing the speaker. The body language of the speaker is referred to as non-verbal communication. It can include how they stand and their facial expressions. These forms of non-verbal communication often help to put the message across effectively.

Disadvantages

- In a big meeting, there is no way of knowing whether everybody is listening or has understood the message.
- It can take longer to gain feedback and in large meetings feedback is difficult, if not impossible.
- A meeting is not suitable when an accurate and permanent record of the message is needed, such as a disciplinary warning to an employee.
- It can be very difficult to gather a large number of working people together at the same time. This problem is made worse by the increased use of flexible working.

Emails

Emails allow rapid electronic communication with a specified list of people who can access the messages online. Printouts of messages can be obtained if a hard copy is required. The internet allows easy and effective email communication with employees, customers and suppliers.

Advantages

- There is usually 'hard' evidence of the message which can be referred to in the future. This should help to reduce disagreements between the sender and the receiver about the contents of the message.
- It is essential for certain messages involving complicated details which might be misunderstood if, for example, a telephone call was made.
- An email can be sent to many people at once. This could be more efficient than telephoning all of those people to give them the same message.
- Email is a quick and cheap way to reach a large number of people.

Disadvantages

- Direct feedback is not always possible, so the sender is unsure whether the email has been received.
- They can lead to too many emails being created and information overload, meaning people are unable to pick out the really important messages from the many that might be received.
- It is not as easy to check that the message has been received and acted upon as it is with verbal messages – although it is possible to set up a 'please acknowledge' function.

> **Definitions to learn**
>
> **Email** is a digital communication tool used for sending messages, documents and other information to specific people or groups.

- The language used can be difficult for some receivers to understand. If the email is too long it may be confusing and lose the interest of the reader.
- There is no opportunity for body language to be used to reinforce the message.

Text messages

Text messages sent on mobile phones are often used to communicate with employees and customers.

Advantages

- They allow for quick and convenient communication with others. Shortened words mean text messages are quick to write and can also be dictated, making them even quicker to send.
- Text messaging allows the sender to communicate with others in situations where a face-to-face or phone conversation is not possible or appropriate.
- A record exists of the communication until this is deleted.

Disadvantages

- Only short messages can be sent using this method and this restricts the amount of information that can be sent.
- If there is no connection to the mobile phone network then the message cannot be sent.
- There is no way of assessing the tone of the message or the mood of the sender and this can cause some failures in communication.
- As with email, the body language of the sender cannot be assessed.

Social media

> **Definitions to learn**
>
> **Social media** refers to online platforms and networks that facilitate social interaction and content sharing with other users.

Social media sites, such as Facebook and Instagram, mean written or visual messages can be sent between all other users of the site. Some social media sites have over 1 billion subscribers. These sites are widely used, especially by the marketing departments of businesses to promote their products to a very large potential market.

Advantages

- Photographs and cartoons can be used to add variety, colour and humour to a message which may increase the chances of the communication being read and understood by the receiver.
- These methods can present information in an appealing and attractive way. People are often more prepared to look at films or posters than to read letters or notices because of the interesting way they communicate messages, leading to increased awareness of the products and increased sales.

Disadvantages

- There may be no feedback and the sender of the message may need to use other forms of communication to check that the message has been understood.
- With so many adverts on social media, potential customers may be put off by the constant viewing of adverts.
- It can be expensive for businesses to post advertisements if expert help is used to create them or if pop-ups are paid for.

7 METHODS OF COMMUNICATION

Phone calls

Telephone conversations can take place on landline telephones or mobile phones.

Advantages

- Information can be given out quickly. It is an efficient way of communicating with an individual employee, supplier or customer.
- There is opportunity for immediate feedback and two-way communication. Questions can be asked to check if the message has been understood.
- It is a suitable method when the message is urgent as the sender will at least know it has been received.

Disadvantages

- A phone call is not suitable when an accurate and permanent record of the message is needed, such as a disciplinary warning to an employee.
- A phone call is not suitable if a large number of people need to be informed. It can take a long time to call many people.
- The message will not be sent if the receiver does not answer the call.

Letters

A letter is a suitable method of communication when a hard copy is required, especially for legal documents.

Advantages

- The hard copy of the message can be referred to in the future. This should help to reduce disagreements between the sender and the receiver about the contents of the message.
- It is essential for certain messages involving complicated details which might be misunderstood if, for example, a text message was sent.
- A letter can be copied and sent to many people at once, saving time.

Disadvantages

- Rapid and direct feedback is not always possible.
- It is difficult to check that the message has been received and acted upon.
- The language or jargon or terminology used in a letter can be difficult for some receivers to understand. If the letter is too long it may be confusing to the reader.
- It is a slow method of communication and is only suitable if the communication is not urgent.

Posters

Posters are large forms of visual communication. They can combine text and images to attract attention. The law in many countries requires safety messages to be written and displayed on posters in business premises, including offices and factories. Posters can be used to communicate internally with employees or externally with customers. Examples include posters in a supermarket promoting a new product for sale.

Advantages

- A poster often combines a written message with visual images to attract attention.
- Posters are cheap to produce.
- They can easily be seen by everyone passing by.

Disadvantages

- A poster is static and cannot be taken away by the reader as a written record of the message, so the content of the message may be easily forgotten.
- A poster can be easily missed if people are not paying attention.

Noticeboards

Noticeboards are used in business to display information which is open to all employees. They can usually hold a large number of written messages.

Advantages

- They are cheap to produce.
- They can easily be seen by everyone passing by in an office or factory.
- They can be placed in the factory or office to remind employees of important instructions to follow, such as safety instructions for the use of a machine.

Disadvantages

- A notice cannot be taken away by the reader as a written record of the message, so the content of the message may be easily forgotten. There will not be a written record of the notice kept by workers.
- Similar to posters, with a noticeboard there is no certainty that the message has been read.
- Information can easily be missed.

> **Key info**
>
> In some cultures, non-verbal communication can be just as important as the words that make up a message. For example, during a face-to-face conversation or in a meeting, Chinese people rely on facial expression, tone of voice and posture to tell them what someone feels.

> **Study tips**
>
> Remember that in some cases it might be essential to use written forms of communication (for example, with legal contracts). In other cases, for example, when raw materials are needed urgently from suppliers, it would be better to use a quicker method, such as a telephone call.

Activity 7.4

Copy out this table of methods of communication. Under the headings of Speed, Written record and Feedback, fill in the main advantages and disadvantages of each method. The first one has been done for you.

	Speed	Written record	Feedback
Meetings with employees	Can be called quickly and workers should be able to attend speedily (unless they are part-time and not working that day)	No	Can be immediate as employees can respond or ask questions during the meeting
Emails			
Text messages			
Social media			
Phone calls			
Letters			
Posters			
Noticeboards			

7 METHODS OF COMMUNICATION

> ### Activity 7.5
>
> Which communication method might be most appropriate for the following messages? Justify your answer in each case.
>
> a There should be no smoking in the staff canteen.
> b The management want to instruct all employees on how the new IT system works.
> c Details of the business's sales figures for the last 4 years are being sent to shareholders.
> d The Finance Manager wants to remind the Operations Manager that they have arranged a meeting for next week.
> e The Product Development Manager wants to inform directors of market research into 3 new product ideas. He hopes that they will agree to launch 1 of these products.
> f The Office Manager wants to obtain views from all office employees on how paper waste could be reduced.
> g A supervisor plans to warn (for the last time) an employee who is always late for work.
> h Next year's holiday dates need to be made available to all employees.
> i The Human Resource Manager wants to invite an applicant for a job to an interview.
> j The Operations Manager wants to send the plans for a new factory to the Managing Director, who is on a business trip overseas.
> k Existing customers of a bank are to be informed about a new type of bank account.
> l A new contract needs to be agreed and signed between a farmer and the cooperative he sells his milk to.
> m The Marketing department of a cosmetics business wants to launch a new perfume aimed at women with above-average incomes.

How to recommend and justify which method of communication to use in a given situation

Which is the best way to communicate a message? There are several factors that the sender of a message should consider:

- **Speed.** Is it important that the receiver gets the information really quickly? For example, a manager from a division of a company based in another country must be told about a cancelled meeting before they catch their flight.
- **Cost.** Is it important to keep costs down or is it more important to communicate effectively, regardless of cost? For example, customers need to be informed about a serious safety problem with a product.
- **Message details.** How detailed is the message? If it contains technical plans, figures and illustrations then written forms of communication are likely to be essential.
- **Leadership style.** Is the leadership style a democratic one? If it is, then two-way methods of communication with employees are much more likely to be used than with an autocratic style.
- **The receiver.** Who is/are the target receiver(s)? If just one person has to be communicated with, and they work in the next office, then a face-to-face conversation/meeting is likely to be used. However, this may be inappropriate if hundreds of employees need to receive a message.
- **Importance of a written record.** If it is essential that a written record can be referred to at some time in the future, then a telephone call would be inappropriate. For example, legal contracts or the receipt of new orders from customers must have written records.

Study tips

The sender of any message needs to be clear about who it is meant for.

» **Importance of feedback.** If it is essential that the sender receives feedback, perhaps very quickly, then a direct method of communication might be most appropriate, such as a face-to-face meeting. For example, has the customer just leaving the shop paid for those goods yet?

> **Extend your skills of analysis**
>
> A question which asks for an advantage of using meetings to communicate with production employees who make bicycles could be answered as follows:
>
> Meetings usually allow for two-way communication.
>
> *Extend your analysis by explaining why this is an advantage to the business.*
>
> By holding meetings with employees who work in the factory, managers can explain a message about new techniques to manufacture bicycles and ask for feedback to make sure that the message was clear and has been understood.
>
> *Extend your analysis by explaining why this is important to the business.*
>
> By providing feedback, employees can be more involved in communication, and being asked for feedback can improve their motivation and therefore increase output of the products.

REVISION SUMMARY How to choose communication methods

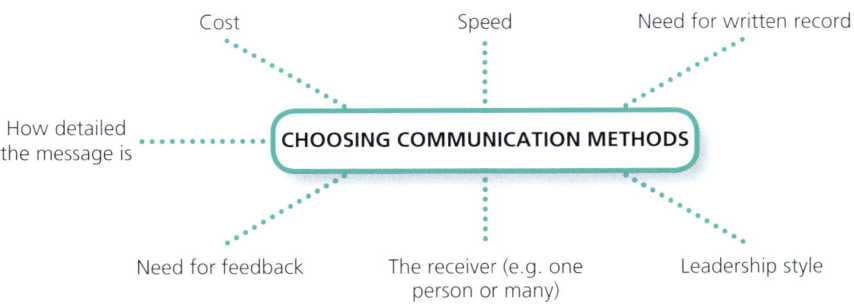

Communication barriers

Reasons for communication barriers and examples of barriers

Definitions to learn

Communication barriers are factors that stop the effective communication of messages.

As we saw on page 102, there are four parts to any successful communication – sender, receiver, method used and feedback. Communication can fail if any one of these four parts does not operate as it should. If one part fails, it is called a **barrier** to effective communication. This can cause a breakdown in communications, which can lead to serious problems for the organisation.

The most common reasons for barriers to effective communication and examples of them are explained in Table 7.1.

7 METHODS OF COMMUNICATION

Table 7.1 Reasons for communication barriers and examples of them

Reason for communication barrier	Examples
Problem with sender	• Difficult language is used that cannot be understood by the receiver. Perhaps jargon or technical language is being used • The sender uses a language spoken in a different country which cannot be understood • The sender speaks too quickly • The sender gives very negative non-verbal signs such as looking bored
Problem with communication method	• The message may be lost, in the mail (post) for example, or IT failure prevents receipt of the message • An unsuitable method has been used, such as a vital safety message being pinned to a noticeboard which many people do not read • No feedback is allowed for so the receiver cannot ask questions to improve understanding • There is no written evidence of the message or the fact that it has been sent, so it cannot be referred back to at a later time
Problem with receiver	• They might be the wrong person/people to receive the message – this is the fault of the sender for not directing the message to the correct receiver • The receiver may not be paying attention or is demotivated so fails to understand the message • There is a lack of trust and understanding between the sender and receiver so there is little attempt to understand the message
Problem with feedback	• The method of communication used does not allow for this, so understanding of the message cannot be shown • The receiver was not aware that feedback was required

Key info

The average office worker receives around 121 emails per day. This number puts pressure on employees as they can find it difficult to identify the really important messages that need quick responses or action to be taken.

Problems caused by communication barriers

The following problems can result from communication barriers:

» There may be low motivation of employees if they feel that they are not communicated with by managers and have no chance of responding to messages. Low motivation will lead to low output per worker.
» There may be poor relations with suppliers as inaccurate messages between the business and suppliers can lead to running out of supplies or delivery of wrong materials. Production may have to be stopped until problems are sorted out.
» There may be low levels of customer loyalty if the business makes no or very poor attempts to communicate with them about special offers, customer loyalty schemes and new products. Customers may switch to other businesses that engage in frequent, lively and informative communication with customers.

How communication barriers can be reduced or removed

Table 7.2 outlines the most important ways to reduce or remove communication barriers.

Table 7.2 Ways to reduce or remove communication barriers

Communication barrier	Ways to reduce or remove barriers
Problem with sender	• Use appropriate language which the receiver will understand • Be aware of non-verbal communication such as body language, which can help to make sure the message is well received • Build trust with the receiver so the message is likely to be received positively
Problem with communication method	• Must be suitable for the message being sent and the person/people receiving it • The best method for the message being sent should be used – see 'How to recommend and justify which method of communication to use in a given situation' on page 108
Problem with receiver	• They must be willing and motivated enough to listen to and respond positively to the message • They must provide feedback when required
Problem with feedback	• Feedback should be requested whenever possible to make clear to the sender of the message that it has been received and understood

Study tips

Questions about communication barriers often ask for examples of barriers and suggestions about how they can be prevented or reduced.

Case study: Reducing communication barriers

Sanchez is a successful business leader. He started his own business, STC, 5 years ago. The business imports tea and coffee and now employs 45 people – 30 in his country and 15 in countries that produce the tea and coffee. As he is very busy, Sanchez holds few meetings with his employees. He emails his managers daily and expects them to pass on his instructions to the employees they are responsible for. In recent weeks, some supplies of tea and coffee have not been to the exact quality and taste that Sanchez demands and he is very angry. He wants to tell his managers and employees how they must improve. He wrote to them all several months ago for new ideas on how to improve the business but he did not get any replies!

Activity 7.6

Read the case study above.

a Identify **four** possible causes of communication barriers within STC.
b Explain to Sanchez how he could overcome the four communication barriers that you identified in a.

7 METHODS OF COMMUNICATION

> **REVISION SUMMARY** — Barriers to effective communication and how they can be overcome

BARRIERS TO EFFECTIVE COMMUNICATION

- **Sender**: Poor attitude/body language wrong; Unclear message; Message too long
- **Method**: Sent to wrong person; Too many people pass on message; Message may be lost; Wrong channel used; Technical breakdown
- **Receiver**: Lack of trust; Poor attitude; Does not listen
- **Feedback**: Not sent; Unclear; Not asked for

International business in focus

Communication technologies

Many global companies use various forms of communication to discuss and provide information for their employees. Here are some examples of the options available to them:

- Microsoft: Outlook for email communication and Teams to discuss projects, share documents and communicate in real time
- Google: Gmail for email communication, Google Drive for document sharing and Google Meet for virtual meetings
- Amazon Web Services: Amazon Chime for online meetings, video conferencing and chat
- Zoom Video Communications: Zoom for video conferencing.

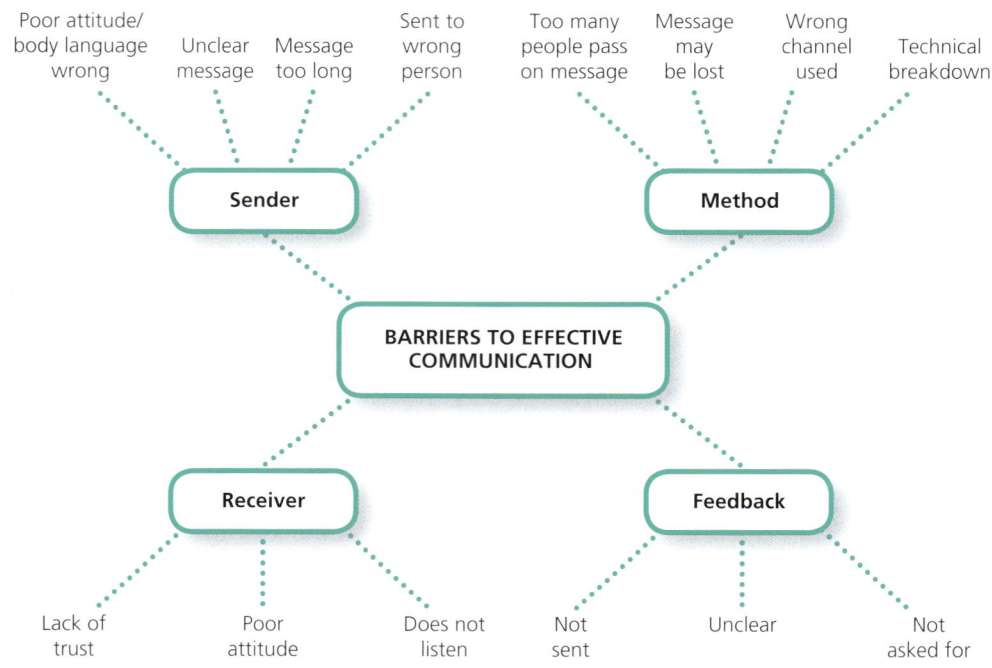

Discussion points

- Explain why effective communication with its employees is important for a business.
- Why do businesses use video conferencing tools such as Zoom when holding meetings with employees based in other countries? Are there any disadvantages to doing this?

Chapter review questions: Short answer and data response

1 Manuel is HRM Manager for a large bank. His responsibilities include internal communication with individual employees and groups of employees. Sometimes he wants to send a message to all 15 000 people employed by the bank. Some employees complain that unless they spend time reading notices or email messages, they do not receive important information. Oscar is a Customer Services Manager at the bank. He is responsible for communicating with the bank's 250 000 customers.
   a Identify **two** disadvantages of using noticeboards for communicating important information to employees. [2]
   b Outline **two** possible barriers to communication within the bank. [4]
   c Explain **two** methods, other than noticeboards, that Manuel could use to communicate with bank employees. [6]
   d Do you think email is the best method for the bank to use to communicate with a large number of its customers? Justify your answer. [8]

2 SEP manufactures electrical appliances such as cookers and heaters. One of Phil's responsibilities as Marketing Manager at SEP is to communicate with thousands of customers in many countries. Some of these customers are wholesalers but many are individual consumers who have purchased products directly from SEP. Phil is worried that communication barriers sometimes prevent his messages being received effectively.
   a Define 'communication barriers'. [2]
   b Outline **two** possible problems with the receiver of a message that could cause poor communication. [4]
   c Explain **two** possible causes of communication barriers between Phil and SEP's customers. [6]
   d SEP has found a major safety problem with one of its products. It needs to communicate with customers quickly. Explain **one** advantage and **one** disadvantage of making a phone call to all of its customers about the safety problem. Do you think telephoning is the best method to use in this situation? Justify your answer. [8]

Revision checklist

In this chapter you have learned:

- ✔ why communication is important for a business
- ✔ methods of communication and their advantages and disadvantages
- ✔ internal and external communication
- ✔ how to recommend and justify the best method of communication to use in a given situation
- ✔ examples of communication barriers and reasons for them
- ✔ problems caused by communication barriers
- ✔ how communication barriers can be reduced or removed.

NOW – test your understanding with the revision questions in the Student etextbook and the Workbook.

8 Motivating employees

This chapter will explain:

The importance of a well-motivated workforce:

★ why people work
★ the benefits of a well-motivated workforce
★ the main motivational theories.

Methods of motivation:

★ financial methods of motivation
★ non-financial methods of motivation
★ how to recommend and justify an appropriate method of motivation for a given situation.

The importance of a well-motivated workforce

Why people work

People work for a variety of reasons. The main reason why most people work is because they need to earn money to buy food and other basic necessities for life. This chapter considers **motivations** for work, how managers can respond to these and the business benefits of a well-motivated workforce.

The reasons why people work are summarised in the diagram below.

> **Definitions to learn**
>
> **Motivation** is the reason why employees want to work hard and work effectively for the business.
> **Labour productivity** is the amount of work done or the number of units produced by a worker in a given time period e.g. one week.

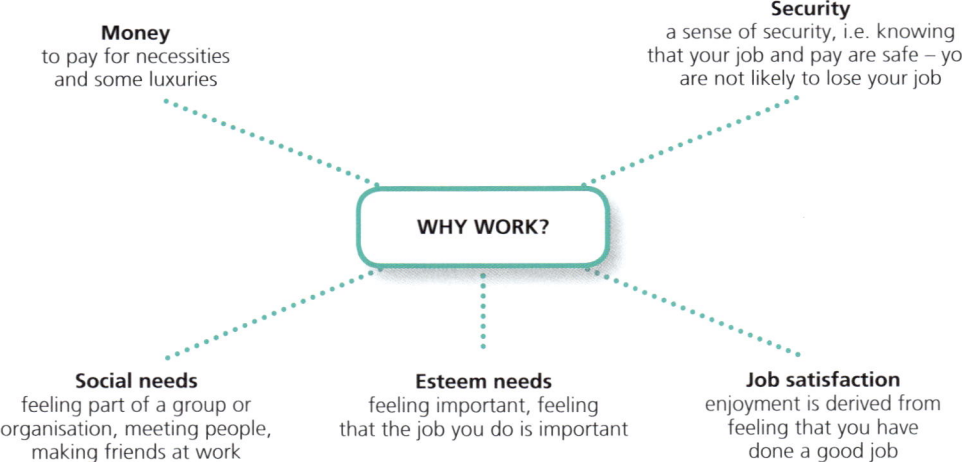

Money – to pay for necessities and some luxuries

Security – a sense of security, i.e. knowing that your job and pay are safe – you are not likely to lose your job

Social needs – feeling part of a group or organisation, meeting people, making friends at work

Esteem needs – feeling important, feeling that the job you do is important

Job satisfaction – enjoyment is derived from feeling that you have done a good job

Benefits of a well-motivated workforce

A well-motivated workforce gives benefits to a business, including:

» improved output per employee. This is also known as **labour productivity**. Higher labour productivity helps to keep business costs low and increase profits
» reduced absenteeism with fewer days off work, helping to reduce disruption in the workplace

- better relationship between employer and employees and this means employees are more likely to make suggestions on how to improve quality and production efficiency
- lower labour turnover – a loyal workforce. This reduces the cost of recruiting employees to replace those who leave, as well as possibly the cost of training these new employees
- greater willingness to accept change, for example, new methods of working.

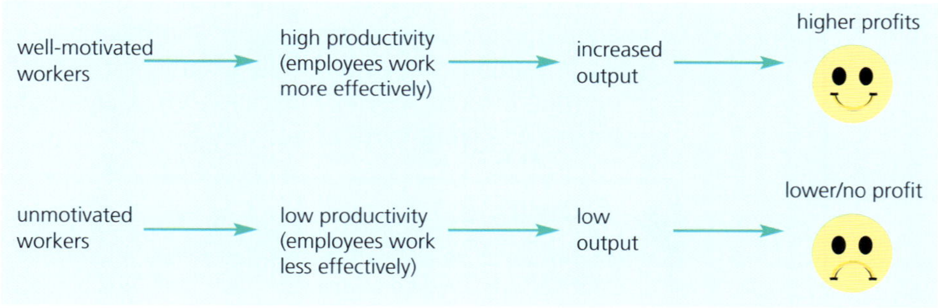
well-motivated workers
high productivity (employees work more effectively)
increased output
higher profits
unmotivated workers
low productivity (employees work less effectively)
low output
lower/no profit

▲ Well-motivated and unmotivated workers

Main motivational theories

Many studies have been undertaken into what needs employees could satisfy through work. These theories often suggest to managers how they could create working conditions for employees to be better motivated. Three of the main theories of motivation are Maslow, Taylor and Herzberg.

Abraham Maslow

Maslow studied employee motivation. He proposed a hierarchy of needs, shown in this diagram.

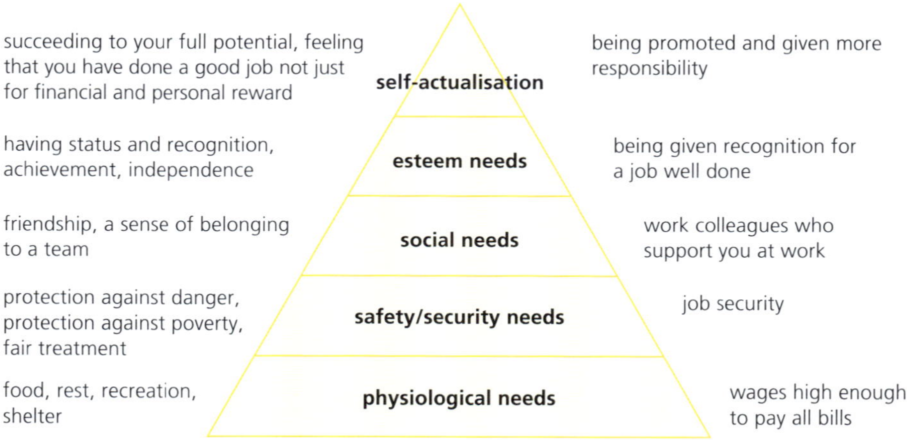
succeeding to your full potential, feeling that you have done a good job not just for financial and personal reward
self-actualisation
being promoted and given more responsibility
having status and recognition, achievement, independence
esteem needs
being given recognition for a job well done
friendship, a sense of belonging to a team
social needs
work colleagues who support you at work
protection against danger, protection against poverty, fair treatment
safety/security needs
job security
food, rest, recreation, shelter
physiological needs
wages high enough to pay all bills

▲ Maslow's hierarchy of needs

- According to Maslow, if employees are going to be motivated to work effectively then the higher levels in the hierarchy must be available to them. Just earning money alone will not be enough for employees to be motivated. Evidence for the levels in the hierarchy can be seen in people who are unemployed. They very often lose their self-respect and self-esteem and may not have the feeling of belonging to society, which often comes from working.

Key info

Nike seems to take Maslow's theory seriously. For example, Nike believes it pays its employees well so they therefore move up 'the hierarchy' to consider 'safety and security' to be an important need. The company offers job security and insurances for health, accidents and disability. There are risk-based safety assessments at Nike's offices and factories. In 2024 over 12 000 employees rated Nike 4.1 out of 5 stars as one of the best places to work (in an anonymous survey).

- » Maslow suggested that each level in the hierarchy must be achieved before an employee can be motivated by the next level. For example, once social needs are met, this will no longer motivate the employee, but the opportunity to gain the respect of fellow employees and self-esteem could motivate the employee to work effectively. If this is true, then managers need to make sure employees can achieve these levels through work.
- » Managers must identify the level of the hierarchy that a particular job provides and then allow employees to strive towards the next level up the hierarchy. For example, employees in agriculture who have temporary employment may have their physiological needs fulfilled, but their security needs will not be met. If they were offered secure, full-time jobs, they might feel more committed to the business and work more effectively for it.

> ### Activity 8.1
> - Miguel works as a farm labourer for a rich landlord. He has a small house on the estate and is allowed to grow his own food on a piece of land next to his house. He grows enough food to feed himself and his family and is paid a small wage, which pays for the other needs of the family, such as clothes, shoes and medicines.
> - Pierre works on the assembly line in a car factory. He works in a team with other employees welding car bodies together. He is also a member of the company football team. He is well paid and his family can afford quite a few luxuries.
> - Anya has a degree in Business Management and professional qualifications in human resources management. She is the Human Resource Manager of a large company. She has her own office with her name on the door and is in charge of the rest of the human resources employees. She works long hours but feels it is worth it if the right employees are recruited to the company.
>
> Identify which of Maslow's needs are being satisfied for each of these employees. Explain the reasons for your choices.

Frederick Taylor

Taylor based his motivation theory on the assumption that all individuals are motivated by money. He believed if they are paid more, they will work more productively. He studied workers employed in factories. He broke down their jobs into simple processes and then calculated how much output they should be able to produce in a day. If they produced this target output, they would be paid more money. Taylor saw employees rather like machines. When they were working hard, their productivity would be high and therefore the labour costs would be low for each unit produced.

Taylor's ideas resulted in big productivity gains at the company where he did his research. Many other businesses adopted his ideas. But there are several criticisms of Taylor's theory:

- » His ideas were too simplistic – employees are motivated by many things and not just money.
- » If employees are unfulfilled by their work in some way, there is likely to be no increased output even if they are paid more.
- » A practical problem arises if you cannot easily measure an employee's output, for example, in a school, where it is difficult to link pay to output.

The importance of a well-motivated workforce

> **Activity 8.2**
> a From the following list of jobs, say what you could measure to find out how effectively the employees are working:
> - car production worker
> - shop assistant
> - waiter
> - teacher
> - police officer
> - soldier
> - baker.
> b Are there any jobs on the list for which output is difficult to measure? If so, explain why it is difficult to measure the output in each case.
> c If you cannot measure employees' output, how can you pay them more money if they work harder or more effectively?
> d Does this present problems for modern economies where the majority of the workforce are employed in service sector jobs?

Frederick Herzberg

Herzberg's motivation theory is based on his study of the work of engineers and accountants in the USA. According to Herzberg, humans have two sets of needs. First, the basic maintenance needs, which he called 'hygiene factors'. Second, humans need to be able to grow psychologically. Herzberg called this 'motivational needs' or 'motivators'. Table 8.1 outlines the hygiene and motivational factors.

Table 8.1 Herzberg's hygiene and motivational factors

Motivators
• Achievement
• Recognition
• Personal growth/development
• Advancement/promotion
• Work itself
Hygiene (maintenance) factors
• Status
• Security
• Work conditions
• Company policies and administration
• Relationship with supervisor
• Relationship with subordinates
• Salary

According to Herzberg, the hygiene needs must be satisfied. If they are not satisfied, they can act as demotivators to the employee. In other words, more pay or more security do not act as long-term motivational factors for employees. Once satisfied, the hygiene needs no longer motivate. Long-term motivation at work is only achieved by satisfying the motivational factors.

8 MOTIVATING EMPLOYEES

> **Case study:** Employee motivation
>
> Company A employs 100 employees taking telephone orders and making calls to potential customers. The company thinks it treats its employees well. The offices they work in are well lit and warm but not too hot. The salary is the same as the pay in other similar jobs. The supervisors are polite and keep checking the work of the employees. The employees are told what to do and have no opportunities for promotion. There is no recognition of employees who have done well in their job. The management is worried because the employees do not seem to be particularly happy and have not increased their productivity. There is high labour turnover, i.e. a high number of employees leave each year.

Study tips

Make sure you can explain the three motivational theories discussed, and explain how knowledge of them can help managers to improve the motivation of their employees.

> **Activity 8.3**
>
> Read the case study above.
>
> a Why do you think the employees might not be happy in their jobs?
> b Suggest ways the management might try to increase the motivation of the employees.

People often say that money is the main motivator but this may not be correct. Surveys show that the other factors discussed on page 114 may be much more important to people than money alone. The lack of these other motivators is often a reason why employees leave a job and seek employment elsewhere.

REVISION SUMMARY   Motivation theories

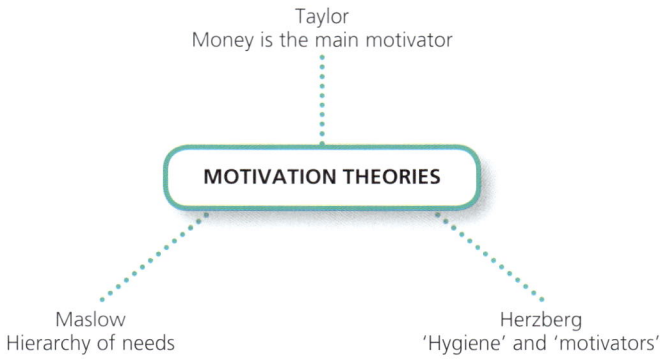

Methods of motivation

Financial methods of motivation

Definitions to learn

A **wage** is payment for work, usually paid weekly.
Time-based rate is the amount paid to an employee for one hour of work.

There are many ways in which businesses can offer financial rewards to their employees.

Wages are paid regularly every week, sometimes in cash and sometimes directly into a bank account. Wages tend to be paid to manual workers, such as those who work in a warehouse or factory. The weekly amount paid in wages can be calculated in two ways.

Time-based wages

Time-based rates are based on an hourly wage rate, agreed in advance with the employer, such as $6.50. The employment contract will include the length of the working week. This could be 40 hours. So an employee paid on a time-based rate in this case would earn 40 hours × $6.50 = $260 per week.

If the employee works longer than their normal hours, they can usually be paid overtime. This is a higher hourly wage rate for the extra hours, such as $8 per hour. This is an incentive to work additional hours when required by the business. If the employee worked 50 hours in one week their total wages would be (40 × $6.50) + (10 × $8) = $340.

Advantages

- Time-based wages are easy to calculate each week. Employees know how much they will receive, depending on the hours worked.
- Time-based wages may have to be paid when it is impossible to directly calculate the output of each employee, for example, a hotel receptionist or a bus driver.

Disadvantages

- An employee paid a time-based wage may be less productive than an employee paid by piece-rate as there is no incentive to produce more.
- Good and bad employees get paid the same amount of money.
- Supervisors may be needed to make sure the employees keep working and producing a good quality product or service. Employing supervisors adds to business costs.
- A clocking-in system may be needed to determine the number of hours worked by the employees.

Piece-rate wages

Piece-rate is where employees are paid based on the number of products made. The more they make, the more they get paid. A basic amount is usually paid, with additional money paid according to how many products have been produced. Piece-rate can be increased when employees produce more than a set output target. Piece-rates can only be used where it is possible to measure the performance of an individual or a team.

Advantages

- Piece-rate motivates employees to work faster and to produce more goods.
- The most productive employees earn the highest wages.

Disadvantages

- Employees may concentrate on making a large number of products and ignore quality. Products may not sell well if they are of a poor quality and the business's reputation may be damaged. A quality-control system may be needed and this adds to costs.
- Employees who are careful in their work will earn lower wages compared to those who rush. This may not be seen as fair. There may be conflicts between employees because some will earn more than others.
- If the machinery breaks down and production is stopped, the employees will earn less money in total even if they are paid a guaranteed minimum wage.

> **Definitions to learn**
>
> **Piece-rate** is an employee payment method that is paid for each unit of output produced.

8 MOTIVATING EMPLOYEES

> **Definitions to learn**
>
> A **salary** is payment for work, usually paid monthly, and is not usually for a specific number of hours worked.
>
> A **bonus** is an additional payment above basic pay as a reward for good work.
>
> **Commission** is a payment linked to the number of sales made, often in addition to a basic wage.

Salary

Salaries are paid monthly into a bank account and are not paid in cash. It is usual for office employees and managers to be paid salaries.

Advantages

- An annual salary is divided into 12 monthly amounts, so it provides income security for employees.
- There may be greater flexibility over hours worked than with wages, as long as the salaried employee has finished their work.

Disadvantages

- Some employees may prefer to be paid weekly and therefore may be less motivated if they only receive payment each month.
- There is usually no overtime payment for extra time worked. Some employees may be reluctant to work longer hours when needed unless it is part of their employment contract.

Bonus

Bonuses do not have to be paid every year or to every employee. They can just be a 'one-off' payment for good work. Businesses can pay a bonus just to an individual employee or to all employees if certain targets have been met or exceeded. A bonus is paid in addition to the standard wage or salary.

Advantages

- Being paid a bonus can have an additional motivating effect on an employee to work hard.
- Employees often consider themselves to be 'recognised' and 'special' if they are paid a bonus.

Disadvantages

- Bonuses can become expected every year. If they are not paid one year then employee disappointment can be difficult to manage.
- If only one or a small number of employees are paid a bonus it can cause bad feelings as other employees may resent this. Demotivation can result.

Commission

Commission is an additional payment often paid to sales employees. The more sales they make, the more money they are paid.

Advantages

- Sales employees are motivated to sell as many products as possible. This should be good for the business as sales and profits may increase.

Disadvantages

- Sales employees may be very persuasive and encourage people to buy goods they do not really want. Sales may increase in the short term and then fall again if the business gets a bad reputation for this.
- It can be stressful for sales employees because they have little income security. If sales fall, so will their pay.

Methods of motivation

» Sales employees might compete with each other to gain commission and not work as a team.

Profit sharing

When employees receive a share of the profits in addition to their basic wage or salary it should motivate them to help make the business a success. This is known as **profit sharing**. The remainder of the profit is either paid to the owners of the business or kept in the business to finance growth.

Advantages

» Increased motivation to make the business successful could lead to employees increasing productivity and making suggestions to increase profitability.
» Relations between managers and other employees should improve as they all benefit from the business being profitable.

Disadvantages

» If a business makes very low profits or even a loss, then no profit share will be possible, leading to employee demotivation.
» The profit share is usually calculated on the basis of an additional percentage of an employee's existing wage or salary. Higher paid employees will receive a higher profit share. This could cause conflict with lower paid employees who consider that they have worked just as hard.

Fringe benefits

In addition to the payment methods already mentioned, businesses may give employees other financial benefits. These usually vary according to the seniority of the job. Factory workers may get discounts on the business's products but they would not be offered a company car. Senior managers may have several **fringe benefits**, such as accommodation, a car and free health care. Examples include:

» company car
» discount on the business's products
» free health care
» children's school fees paid
» free accommodation
» share options (where company shares are given to employees)
» pension paid for by the business.

Advantages

» Fringe benefits help to maintain employee loyalty and reduce the number of employees leaving.
» They offer symbols of status to employees which can improve their self-esteem.
» They can attract skilled or talented employees if the fringe benefits are better than those offered by competitors.

Disadvantages

» Fringe benefits increase the costs of the business, especially if they are offered to most of the workforce.
» Restricting fringe benefits to just a few senior employees can cause conflict within the business.

> **Definitions to learn**
>
> **Profit sharing** is when a proportion of business profits is paid out to employees.
>
> **Fringe benefits** are a form of financial motivation given in addition to an employee's regular form of payment.

8 MOTIVATING EMPLOYEES

> **Key info**
>
> Google is often voted one of the best companies in the world to work for. Its employee benefits are highly original. Comprehensive health plans are provided that include dental and optical/eye care and there are on-site wellness centres. Free healthy food is always available to employees. New parents get extra time off and extra spending money to help them welcome their new baby. Staff are also entitled to four 'work from anywhere' weeks each year. These are to name just a few of the fringe benefits offered by Google.

REVISION SUMMARY — Methods of financial motivation

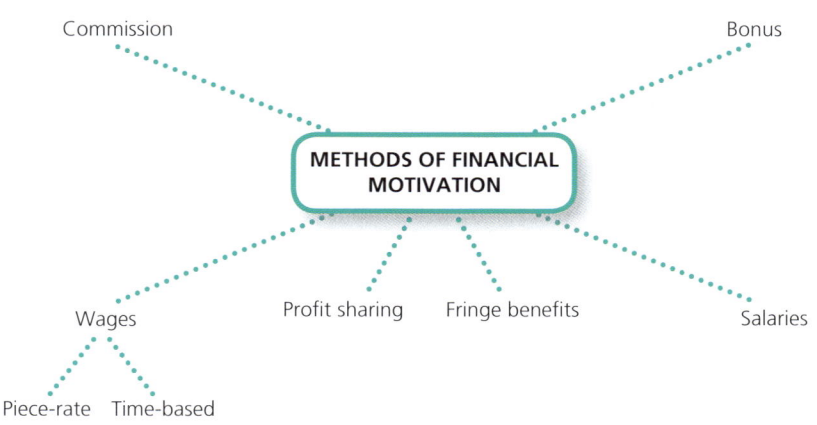

Methods of financial motivation: Commission, Bonus, Wages (Piece-rate, Time-based), Profit sharing, Fringe benefits, Salaries.

Extend your skills of analysis

A question which asks for a disadvantage of using piece-rate to calculate the wages of production employees in a laptop assembly business could be answered as follows:

- Piece-rate means paying employees' wages based on the number of items they produce.

Extend your analysis by explaining what the impact of this might be.

- Employees will be motivated to work harder to increase output of laptops but they may be less focused on high quality.

Extend your analysis by explaining why this would be a disadvantage to the business.

- If the quality of laptops falls, then consumers will switch to other brands and the higher output of this business will not be sold, reducing revenue.

Definitions to learn

Job satisfaction is the enjoyment derived from feeling that you have done a good job.

Non-financial methods of motivation

Pay is not the only way to motivate employees and make them more committed to their job to work more effectively. Many non-financial methods of motivation are focused on increasing the level of **job satisfaction** – the enjoyment from doing a job. However, as Herzberg suggested, there are some factors that will make employees unhappy and these must be changed before the employees can be motivated in a positive way. For example, if the management of the business is autocratic and the employees are dissatisfied, offering them more pay or fringe benefits will not increase motivation.

Methods of motivation

Study tips

Make sure you are able to identify suitable non-financial methods of motivation for different jobs.

Key info

Within the Pakistan State Oil company there is a regular performance appraisal of every employee. Strengths are praised and weaknesses are identified, and training is given to help employees improve their skills and become more effective.

Definitions to learn

Job enrichment involves giving employees work tasks that require more skill and responsibility.

Activity 8.4

Compare a nurse with a machine operator in a factory. What do you think makes their jobs satisfying? Copy out the table below and list your ideas for each.

Nurse	Machine operator

The motivation theories of Maslow and Herzberg suggest that the motivational features of work are that it should give recognition, responsibility and satisfaction. These allow employees to gain a sense of achievement from the work itself. Some jobs may seem dull and boring, but with a little thought and creativity they can be made more interesting and more motivating.

These are the non-financial methods of motivation businesses can use to increase the job satisfaction of its employees:

- job enrichment
- job rotation
- training
- opportunities for promotion
- praise
- employee of the month.

Job enrichment

Job enrichment involves giving employees more interesting and challenging, but rewarding, work tasks. Additional tasks that require extra skills and sometimes extra responsibilities will be added to make the job more demanding and give the employee a greater variety of duties.

Advantages

- If managers can design jobs so that they fulfil higher level human needs, employees will be more motivated, gain more job satisfaction and increase productivity.
- Employees will be more willing to make suggestions for further improvements, possibly raising productivity further.

Disadvantages

- These may require additional skills and responsibilities so additional training may be necessary to enable the employee to take on the extra tasks. This is likely to increase training costs for the business. For example, some employees in a furniture workshop could be given responsibility for the production of complete tables, not just one part of them.
- Some employees may not feel able or be willing to take on tasks that require more skill and they may not carry out the tasks effectively, resulting in lower quality output.

8 MOTIVATING EMPLOYEES

receptionist employed to greet customers

word-processes letters

deals with telephone enquiries
training will be needed – receptionist will need to know about products sold in order to deal with enquiries

takes orders

Job rotation

Employees on a production line may carry out simple tasks that are different to each other. **Job rotation** involves the employees swapping jobs and doing each specific task for a limited time and then rotating jobs again.

Advantages

» This increases the variety of work each employee performs and makes it less boring.
» It also makes it easier for the managers to move employees around the factory if people are absent and their jobs need covering.

Disadvantages

» It does not make the tasks themselves more interesting or challenging.
» Some work is not suitable for tasks to be carried out by other employees, for example, tasks that require a very specialist skill.

> **Definitions to learn**
>
> **Job rotation** involves workers swapping jobs and doing each specific task for only a limited time and then changing jobs again.
> **Training** is the process of improving an employee's skills.

every hour, or every half day, each person moves along and changes jobs

Training

Training to improve an employee's level of skills can have beneficial effects on motivation levels.

Advantages

» Employees can feel a great sense of achievement if they successfully gain and apply new work-based skills.
» They could now be given more challenging and rewarding work to perform. This is the key element of job enrichment.
» Employees who are selected by management for training courses may think that their good work has been recognised.

Disadvantages

» This increases costs for businesses.
» An employee may leave once the training has been completed, especially if the employee gains a recognised qualification that can be used to gain employment elsewhere.

Methods of motivation

> **Definitions to learn**
>
> **Promotion** is the advancement of an employee in an organisation, for example, to a higher job/managerial level.

Opportunities for promotion

Many businesses fill posts of responsibility through internal recruitment and **promotion**. This offers opportunities for advancement to existing employees to become supervisors, team leaders and managers.

Advantages

- Not only does the business benefit from promoting employees who already know how it operates, but it also gains from better-motivated workers.
- Employees who are promoted will feel recognised, have a higher status and will be given more challenging work to perform. All of these benefits are closely linked to the views of both Maslow and Herzberg.

Disadvantages

- Employees who are not promoted may feel jealous and be demotivated, leading to reduced output and efficiency.
- The business may lose out on employing better people from outside the business, so no new ideas come into the business.

Praise

Giving praise to an employee for work well done can both increase their self-confidence and motivate them to achieve even better standards in the future.

Advantages

- Employees who are praised will experience higher levels of job satisfaction.
- They are more likely to stay working at the business, displaying increased loyalty towards it. This will reduce labour turnover and recruitment costs.
- Praise costs the business nothing but it can have long-term benefits.

Disadvantages

- If praise is given out too often then it may lose its effect.
- It may cause demotivation if hard-working employees are ignored and not given praise.

Employee of the month

With this scheme, managers – and sometimes all employees – select one worker to be identified as the person who has made the biggest contribution to the business in the last month. This can give public recognition to that employee and increase their self-esteem. The advantages and disadvantages are similar to giving praise.

Advantages

- It might encourage competition between all employees to gain this title, which will increase overall levels of motivation.

Disadvantages

- Such a scheme will not work well if employees feel that the selection made is unfair.
- If some employees never receive the recognition despite putting in their best effort they can become demotivated.

8 MOTIVATING EMPLOYEES

> **Activity 8.5**
>
> For the following jobs, identify which methods of employee motivation would be most suitable and why. (Remember to consider whether it is easy to measure an employee's output as this may affect how you decide to reward their efforts.)
>
> a Garment production worker
> b Hotel receptionist
> c Teacher
> d Shop assistant
> e Managing director
> f Taxi driver

How to recommend and justify an appropriate method of motivation for a given situation

When recommending an appropriate method of motivation for a business to use it is important to understand that most businesses use more than one method. For example, a large manufacturing business could:

- pay hourly wage rates to some production employees
- use job enrichment for production employees
- pay salaries to office employees and managers
- offer profit sharing to all or some employees in addition to wages/salaries
- offer fringe benefits to senior managers.

For many businesses, the recommendation for motivation methods would be to use a variety of different methods. No single method is likely to be the most appropriate for all employees in all situations. Table 8.2 explains some of the factors a business would consider when selecting appropriate methods of motivation. These are just a few possible business situations.

> **Study tips**
>
> Examination questions will consider a range of different businesses. Make sure that your recommendations are clearly linked to the business in the question.

Table 8.2 Factors a business may consider when selecting appropriate methods of motivation

Factor	Possible appropriate motivation method(s)
Business aims to keep production costs low	• Piece-rate for production employees to maximise output. This should reduce the average cost of each unit produced
Business aims for high-quality production/service	• Salaries paid to employees to increase security and retain experienced employees • Bonus system for high-quality work • Job enrichment to increase employee job satisfaction and employee suggestions for improvements at work
Business operates in research with well-qualified employees	• Salaries to increase security and retain well-qualified employees • Fringe benefits to increase status, self-esteem and retain employees • Profit sharing to encourage a sense of ownership over the success of the business
Business manufactures cars in a fast-changing competitive market	• Time-based wages for production employees – lost output through making product changes will not reduce wages paid • Job enrichment to encourage employee involvement in suggesting improvements • Commission paid to sales employees to try to take sales away from competitors
IT business has recently started up and has good growth prospects	• High salaries to attract well-qualified applicants • Bonus system to add to salaries to attract well-qualified applicants • Profit sharing to encourage employees to make the business profitable as quickly as possible

Methods of motivation

| REVISION SUMMARY | Financial and non-financial methods of motivation |

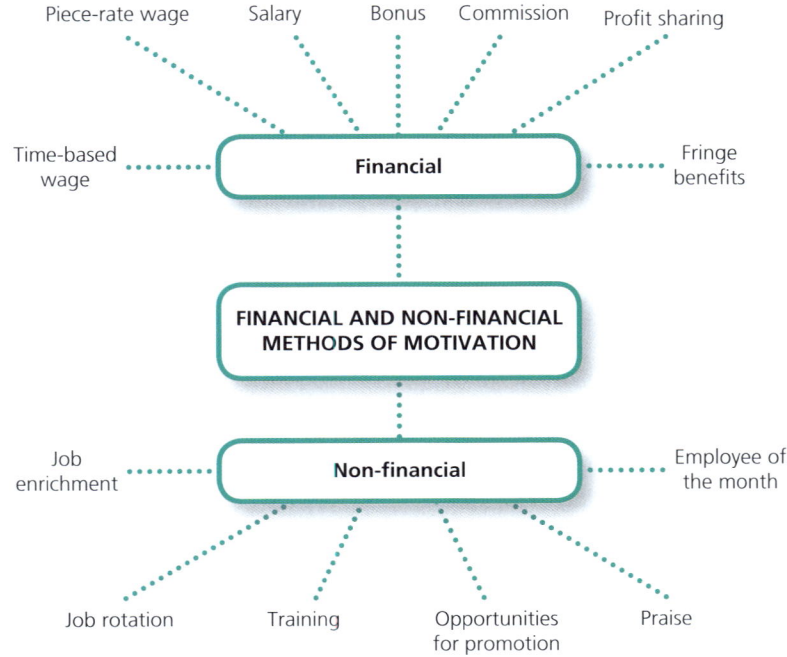

Study tips

Make sure you are able to choose suitable methods of non-financial motivation for employees in different jobs.

Extend your skills of analysis

A question which asks for an advantage of using job enrichment for factory employees to increase motivation could be answered as follows:

Job enrichment aims to make work more interesting, challenging and rewarding, for example, by giving factory workers responsibility for whole units of output.

Extend your analysis by explaining why this could improve motivation.

Motivation of factory employees can be low if they have boring and repetitive work to do. Theories such as those of Maslow and Herzberg suggest that employees will become more motivated if they can satisfy self-esteem needs (or achieve self-actualisation) and have a sense of personal achievement by doing challenging work well.

Extend your analysis by explaining why this is important to the business.

Improving motivation of factory employees through job enrichment may not increase business costs and it could lead to employees being more productively efficient.

Activity 8.6

- Sita works in a clothes shop. She spends her time looking after the changing room, where she checks customers into the changing rooms and returns unwanted garments to the shop's clothes rails. There are several other shop employees: 1 works at the cash till, 1 puts out the clothes on the rails and 1 does the shop displays. Sita gets paid whether customers buy any clothes or not.
- Tim works in a clothing factory. He cuts out the collars for shirts. The rest of the processes for making shirts are carried out by other employees. He has done this job for 2 years now and gets very bored with what he is doing.

These two employees are not happy in their work. Suggest how you would try to improve their job satisfaction. Explain the reasons for your suggestions.

8 MOTIVATING EMPLOYEES

International business in focus

Low levels of job satisfaction among Malaysian nurses

A recent study reported that shortages of nurses in some hospitals in Malaysia are resulting in a high workload and job stress, which have also been linked to low job satisfaction. Financial rewards for the job include salaries, benefits and bonuses. Hospital managers claim that the job of nursing offers personal rewards including status, recognition, and personal and professional development opportunities. Reasons for nurse dissatisfaction appear to include lack of involvement in decision making, a poor relationship with management, low salaries compared to other jobs with a similar level of qualifications, lack of job security and low levels of recognition. Job dissatisfaction is shown when nurses say they wish to leave their job.

Discussion points

- Why do some nurses seem to have a low level of job satisfaction?
- What could hospital managers do to improve motivation?
- Which methods to improve motivation of nurses would be most effective and why?

Chapter review questions: Short answer and data response

1 Joe owns a business which produces high-quality wooden furniture. He employs 20 workers in the Operations department and 3 employees in the office. Joe pays time-based wages to all employees. He is thinking of changing to wages based on piece-rate. He has a high labour turnover from the factory as his employees are not well motivated.
   a Define 'piece-rate'. [2]
   b Outline **two** likely reasons why many employees leave their job at the furniture company. [4]
   c Explain **two** methods of non-financial motivation that Joe could use to improve the job satisfaction of his employees. [6]
   d Do you think a wage calculated by piece-rate is a suitable method of payment for all of Joe's employees? Justify your answer. [8]

2 Sasha is a hotel manager. She has 30 employees who all have full-time employment contracts. They are divided into teams working in the following departments: kitchen, restaurant, hotel reception and housekeeping (room cleaning). Sasha has trained 2 of the hotel receptionists in hotel management. Sasha believes that her employees are well motivated. A modern hotel has recently opened 2 kilometres away. Sasha wants to improve the motivation of all the employees and is thinking of introducing job rotation and an employee bonus scheme.
   a Define 'bonus'. [2]
   b Outline **two** levels in Maslow's hierarchy of needs experienced by the hotel employees. [4]
   c Explain **two** benefits to the hotel of having well-motivated employees. [6]
   d Do you think introducing job rotation is the best way to improve the motivation of the employees at the hotel? Justify your answer. [8]

Revision checklist

In this chapter you have learned:

- ✔ why people work
- ✔ the benefits of a well-motivated workforce
- ✔ the main motivation theories of Maslow, Taylor and Herzberg
- ✔ financial methods of motivation
- ✔ non-financial methods of motivation
- ✔ how to recommend and justify an appropriate method of motivation for a given situation.

NOW – test your understanding with the revision questions in the Student etextbook and the Workbook.

People in business: end-of-section case study

Case study: The Lakeview Restaurant

The Lakeview Restaurant is owned by 2 brothers, Chris and Abdul. They set up the restaurant 10 years ago as a private limited company. It is located on the edge of the city.

The business is split into 2 separate dining areas. 1 area is for families and the other area serves more expensive meals. The family dining area is large and is hired out for weddings and birthday parties. The other area is mainly for business customers.

Both sections of the restaurant are always busy and fully booked on weekdays. Chris and Abdul want to expand the business. The restaurant cannot be expanded on its existing site as it has buildings on one side and it is next to a lake on the other side. New employees for the kitchens and new waiters will need to be recruited.

There are 2 options for the business to expand:

- Option 1: Buy a ship and convert it into a floating restaurant next to the main restaurant to hire out for weddings and birthday parties. The ship will cost $100 000 to buy and convert to a restaurant. The projected profit is $20 000 per year. Unemployment in the area is high.
- Option 2: Close the existing restaurant and relocate to a new building which is much larger and in the centre of the city. The additional cost of buying a new restaurant is $250 000 and the projected profit is $25 000 per year. Unemployment in the city centre is low.

Appendix 1

There are 2 job applications for the post of Restaurant Manager of the Lakeview Restaurant.

Name	Mr J Patel	Mr N Guitano
Qualifications	10 IGCSEs, 3 A levels, BA degree in Business Management	7 IGCSEs, 2 A levels
Management experience	3 years as General Manager of a small cafe	20 years as Restaurant Manager
Interests	Cricket, football, rugby, reading	Reading, watching television, helping to keep the accounts for a local children's charity
Number of restaurants at which they have worked	4 restaurants for 4 weeks each as they were holiday jobs	10 different restaurants in 20 years
Preferred management style	Autocratic – believes the manager knows best	Democratic – believes employees should be asked their opinions

Appendix 2

```
5th March meeting

From: Chris (c-smith@gotmail.co.uk)

Sent: 23 March 2024 23:41:47

To: Abdul (Abdul@gotmail.com)

Hi Abdul

We need to employ a new Restaurant Manager. We had to dismiss the last manager as he failed to
establish good relations with employees which led to low levels of motivation - we do not want
someone like him again.

I want someone who is careful with money and who will give a good service to the customers.
They need to come up with ideas of how to increase the number of customers to the restaurant
on weekends.

What do you think?
```

8 MOTIVATING EMPLOYEES

> ### Practice questions: Case study
>
> 1 a Explain **two** reasons why well-motivated employees are important for the restaurant. [8]
>   b Chris and Abdul have advertised a job vacancy for a Restaurant Manager. Using Appendix 1 and Appendix 2, consider the advantages and disadvantages of the two job applicants. Which applicant should Chris and Abdul choose to employ? Justify your answer. [12]
> 2 a The Lakeview Restaurant is expanding. Explain **two** reasons why an organisational chart would be helpful to the management of the restaurant. [8]
>   b The restaurant needs to communicate with its suppliers to order its weekly food ingredients. Consider the advantages and disadvantages of using email, letters or phone calls. Which is the best method for Chris and Abdul to use for an urgent order from suppliers? Justify your answer. [12]
>
> **Optional question**
> The question below asks you to think about topics covered in earlier sections of this textbook. You can choose not to answer it if you prefer to focus on just the topics covered in this section at this time.
>
> 3 a The Lakeview Restaurant is located near to several restaurants which are competitors. Explain **one** advantage and **one** disadvantage to the business of being located near to competitors. [8]
>   b Consider the advantages and disadvantages of the **two** options for the restaurant business to expand. Which option should Chris and Abdul choose? Justify your answer. [12]

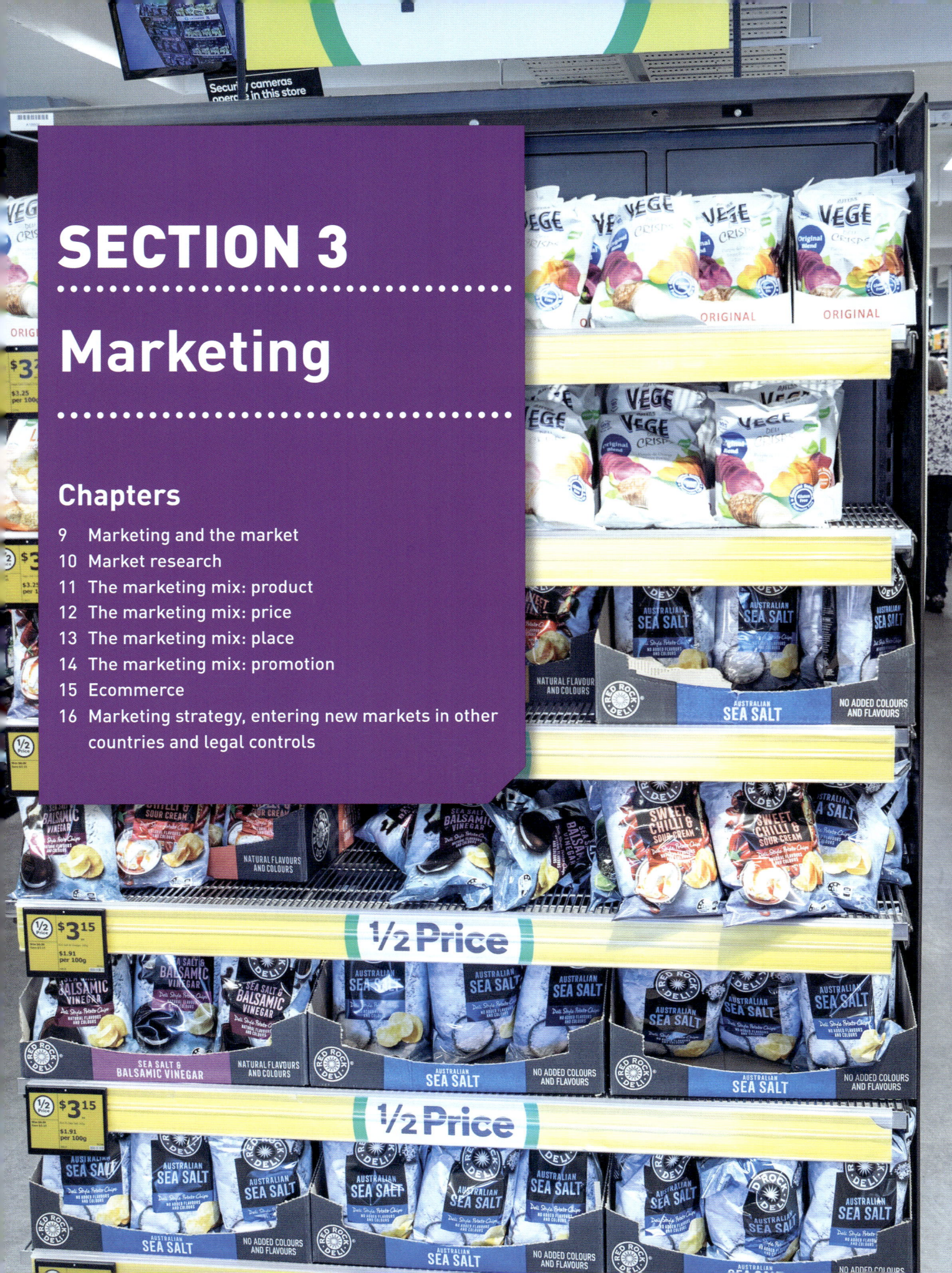

SECTION 3
Marketing

Chapters

9 Marketing and the market
10 Market research
11 The marketing mix: product
12 The marketing mix: price
13 The marketing mix: place
14 The marketing mix: promotion
15 Ecommerce
16 Marketing strategy, entering new markets in other countries and legal controls

9 Marketing and the market

This chapter will explain:

The role of marketing:

★ identifying customer needs
★ satisfying customer needs
★ maintaining customer loyalty
★ building customer relationships
★ anticipating changes in customer needs.

Understanding market changes:

★ why consumer spending patterns may change
★ why some markets are becoming more competitive
★ how businesses can respond to changing spending patterns and increased competition
★ how to calculate market share.

Mass markets and niche markets:

★ the concepts of mass markets and niche markets
★ advantages and disadvantages of mass markets and niche markets.

Market segmentation:

★ how markets can be segmented
★ advantages and disadvantages of market segmentation.

The role of marketing

Most businesses, unless they are very small, will have a **Marketing** department. In a large public limited company, the Marketing Director will have people responsible for market research of new products, promotion (including sales promotions and advertising), distribution, pricing and sales.

Large businesses will have different sections within their Marketing department:

» The **sales team** is responsible for the sales of the product. It will usually have separate sections for each region to which the product is distributed. If the product is exported, there may also be an **export team**.

» The **market research section** is responsible for finding out **customers**' needs, market changes and the impact of competitors' actions. It will report on these to the Marketing Director and this information will be used to help make decisions about research and development of new products, pricing levels, sales strategies and promotion strategies.

» The **promotion section** deals with organising the advertising of products. It arranges for advertisements to be produced. For example, social media posts will need to be designed or the location of billboard advertisements will need to be decided. The department also decides on the types of sales promotion

> **Definitions to learn**
>
> **Marketing** is identifying customer wants and satisfying them profitably. A **customer** is a person or business which buys goods or services from a business.

The role of marketing

that will be included in campaigns. The promotion section will have a budget – a fixed amount of money to spend. It has to decide which types of advertising media will be the most effective to use because there will only be a certain amount to spend; the department cannot spend what it likes!
- **Distribution** transports the products to the market.

Marketing is not just about advertising and selling a good or service. A Marketing department has many functions to perform and actually selling the product is just one of them. The role of marketing includes the following:

Identifying customer needs

It is most important for marketing to be successful to find out what kind of products or services customers want, the prices they are willing to pay, where and how they want to buy the goods or services, and what after-sales services they might want. Businesses usually use market research to carry out this task.

Satisfying customer needs

To sell goods and services profitably, customer needs must be satisfied. Customers want the right product, in the right place and at the right price. Failure to meet these needs, or doing it less well than competitors, will lead to the business facing the risk of closure.

Maintaining customer loyalty

Customer loyalty encourages customers to keep buying from the business rather than from competitors. Keeping close links with customers and finding out if products or services are continuing to meet their needs will help to ensure the success of the business. If customers change their expectations of what they want from a good or service, then the business should respond to meet these new needs. This will be identified by maintaining close customer relationships. It is very important to keep existing customers (customer loyalty) and not just concentrate on attracting new ones. It is much cheaper for a business to try to keep existing customers (for example, with loyalty cards) than to try to gain new customers.

Building customer relationships

Building long-term **relationships** with customers allows information about their buying habits to be analysed. This means that their changing needs can be understood. This is one of the most important roles of the Marketing department in today's globally competitive world. Building a relationship with customers means that market research information can be used to understand why customers buy products and how they use them. This makes for more effective marketing and further increases customer loyalty.

Anticipating changes in customer needs

A business will gain a competitive advantage if it can identify new trends in consumer demand or gaps in the market and market products not currently available. Market research will be used to try to anticipate future customer needs. Keeping ahead of competitors by developing products that satisfy future needs should increase **market share**.

> **Definitions to learn**
>
> **Customer loyalty** is when existing customers continually buy products from the same business.
> **Customer relationships** is about communicating with customers to encourage them to become loyal to the business and its products.
> **Market share** is the percentage of total sales revenue for the whole market held by one brand or business.

9 MARKETING AND THE MARKET

Summary of role of marketing

If the Marketing department is successful in its role, then it should be able to:

- raise customer awareness of a product or service of the business
- increase revenue and profitability
- increase market share
- improve the image of products
- target a new market or market segment
- enter new markets at home or in other countries
- help develop new products or improve existing products.

> **Case study:** Pepsi-Cola
>
>
>
> Pepsi-Cola Products Philippines Inc. manufactures Pepsi, 7-Up, Mirinda, Sting, Mountain Dew, Gatorade, Mug Root Beer, Tropicana, Lipton and Milkis and accounts for a large percentage of the total carbonated and non-carbonated drinks market in the Philippines. It wants to increase its share of the market still further to become the leading drinks company in the Philippines. The Marketing department will be vital in deciding how this can be achieved.
>
> Source: www.pepsiphilippines.com/media/news/view/128

> **Activity 9.1**
>
> Read the case study above.
>
> Suggest ways Pepsi-Cola Products Philippines Inc. could increase its market share. Which way do you think will be most effective? Explain your answer.

Understanding market changes

The world of markets and marketing is constantly changing. It is very unusual if a business does not have to change its goods and services over time to respond to important market changes. Some markets are changing at a rapid pace, such as smartphones, whereas other markets, such as breakfast cereals, do not change very quickly.

Why consumer spending patterns may change

Definitions to learn

A **consumer** buys goods or services for personal use – not to re-sell.

- **Consumer tastes and fashions change.** Fashions may change for clothes and so **consumers** may want different styles of clothes to those they wore the previous year.
- **Changes in technology.** With new products being developed, such as iPads, tablets and smartwatches, sales of desk computers have fallen in many countries. New products mean old versions or alternatives do not have high sales anymore.
- **Change in incomes.** If an economy has high unemployment, incomes will be low and many consumers will buy low-priced products. If the economy then grows and unemployment falls, the sales of more expensive products will increase.

Understanding market changes

> **Key info**
>
> Rapidly changing technology is giving consumers more choice than ever before. The total number of smartphone subscriptions in the world was approximately 7 billion in 2023, and most people use their phones for browsing the internet and making purchases from suppliers all over the world. Increasingly popular 'wearable gadgets', such as smartwatches, allow consumers to track their own health data, including activities and diet. For many consumers, wearable tech is the first step to eating better, reducing stress and adopting a healthier lifestyle.

- **Ageing populations.** The age structure of the population in many countries is changing to have a greater percentage of older people. This has changed the type of products which are increasing in demand, such as anti-ageing face creams and care homes for older people.

If businesses fail to respond to changing customer needs and spending, then they are likely to fail. The 'customer is king' because as their needs change, it is the businesses which research and know what these changes are, and respond to them, that will be most successful.

Why some markets are becoming more competitive

- **Globalisation of markets** has meant that products are increasingly sold all over the world (see Chapter 29). Increased competition from low-cost imports makes it more difficult for local businesses to survive.
- **Transportation improvements** in recent years have meant that it now costs much less to transport products from one part of the world to another. This has led to more competitive imports entering most countries' markets.
- **Internet/ecommerce** has meant that consumers can search for products and buy at low prices from suppliers all over the world. Even some services such as insurance can be bought from businesses based in another country.
- **Increased consumer information**, usually provided by the internet or social media, about products and the national and international businesses that sell them, makes a market much more competitive.

How businesses can respond to changing spending patterns and increased competition

A business will have to take action to maintain its level of sales and market share whenever there are changes to spending patterns or increasing competition. In order to remain successful, a business may need to do the following:

- **Maintain good customer relationships.** This has a key role in continuing to meet customer needs and it also provides market research information about customers. Marketing departments which become experts on customer needs will respond to these needs as and when they change, and this will maintain customer loyalty. It is much cheaper to keep existing customers than gain new ones.
- **Keep improving its existing product.** This is especially true if its competitors improve their products. By making the goods or services it sells very different from those produced by competitors, the business will become well known for differentiated products. Apple and Samsung are good examples of companies that react to increased competition by making even more advanced products.
- **Develop and launch new products.** A business needs to keep customers interested in its own company rather than its competitors'. This will help the business to maintain, or even increase, its market share. An example of this is Microsoft, which keeps on improving and developing its operating systems.
- **Keep costs low.** This should help keep prices low and allow the business to maintain competitiveness.

9 MARKETING AND THE MARKET

> **Case study:** What happens when consumer preferences change?
>
> One of the few things that is certain in this world is change. In a world where technology is advancing at such a rapid pace, change happens even more quickly. It is very important for companies to adapt to change as rapidly as they can.
>
> Take the example of gas (petrol) filling stations in the future. As more people buy electric cars, there will be lower demand for gas (petrol) and these filling stations will have to adapt or will be forced to close.

> **Activity 9.2**
>
> Read the case study above.
>
> a Why will gas (petrol) filling stations get into financial difficulties in the future if they do not change?
> b Explain **two** ways in which a gas (petrol) filling station in your country could try to increase revenue.

How to calculate market share

Market share is an important measure of the success of a business within its own market. If a business has a market share of 25% this year, up from 22% last year, its marketing performance is better than most or all of its competitors.

Market share, in a particular time period, is calculated as shown below.

> **Calculations to learn**
>
> $$\text{Market share (\%)} = \frac{\text{Sales revenue of a business}}{\text{Total sales revenue for the whole market}} \times 100$$

The result is always a percentage.

Worked example

ABC produces e-bikes. In the last 12 months its revenue in Country A was $23 million. The total value of the market for e-bikes sold in Country A in this period was $340 million, so ABC's market share for the last 12 months was:

$$\text{Market share (\%)} = \frac{23}{340} \times 100$$

$$= 6.76\%$$

This result can now be compared with other e-bike producers in Country A and with previous years for ABC.

> **Definitions to learn**
>
> A **mass market** is where a business sells to the largest part of the market, often where standardised products are being sold.
> A **niche market** is a small, usually specialised, segment of a much larger market.

Mass markets and niche markets

A market for a particular product is made up of the total number of customers for, and sellers of, that particular product. These markets can be either **mass markets** or **niche markets**.

Businesses have to decide whether they are aiming at a mass market or a niche market when developing their marketing plans. The decision will have a major impact on the products sold and the ways in which they are priced and promoted.

Mass markets

Many consumer products are sold to a mass market, such as bread, gas (petrol) and soft drinks. Total sales in these markets can be very high but competition between businesses is often fierce.

If a business decides to use mass marketing it will:

» develop products that satisfy the needs of most consumers in a market
» promote the products widely
» price the products so that they can be afforded by most consumers in the market.

Table 9.1 explains the advantages and disadvantages of mass markets.

Table 9.1 Advantages and disadvantages of mass markets

Advantages of mass markets	Disadvantages of mass markets
Sales could reach a high level, leading to high revenue and potential economies of scale (see Chapter 20)	It is often difficult to differentiate a standardised mass market product from similar products sold by other businesses
There are no additional costs of producing different products for different consumer groups	Some customers will not be attracted by the mass market image of the product as it does not meet their specific needs
Promotions that appeal to the whole mass market can be used, keeping costs low	It may be difficult to sell mass market products in some countries and locations unless cultural differences are taken into account in marketing
The name of the business and its brand names will be widely known	Competition can be high, with many businesses competing to sell similar products to a large number of consumers

Niche markets

In contrast to mass markets, some products are sold only to a small number of customers who form a small segment of a much larger market. This is referred to as a niche market. These products are quite often specialised and sold by small businesses that would find it difficult to compete in a mass market. For example, there is a mass market for shops selling essential food products in any country. However, if there is a small group of migrant workers in that country then food shops selling specialised food for this group of people may be set up. Expensive products, such as Rolex watches or Burberry designer clothes, are also aimed at niche markets.

9 MARKETING AND THE MARKET

> **Study tips**
> Make sure you can explain the difference between mass markets and niche markets using examples of goods or services.

> **Key info**
> Some niche markets become mass markets as large businesses start to realise the potential for growth and want a share of the action! Virtual reality headsets and voice-enabled speakers both started out as 'niche products' but as prices have fallen and more choice is available, millions of customers now want these products – making them mass market products.

Table 9.2 explains the advantages and disadvantages of niche markets.

Table 9.2 Advantages and disadvantages of niche markets

Advantages of niche markets	Disadvantages of niche markets
Small businesses may be able to sell successfully in niche markets as larger businesses may not have identified them and are concentrating on the mass markets instead. This will reduce competition in niche markets	Niche markets are usually relatively small and therefore have limited sales potential. This means that small businesses often have an opportunity to operate successfully in these markets. If the business wants to grow, it will need to look outside the niche market to develop products for mass markets
The needs of consumers can be more closely focused on, and therefore targeted, by businesses in a niche market. This may lead to high levels of consumer loyalty and good customer relationships	Often businesses in a niche market will specialise in one product. If the product is no longer in demand the business will fail as it has not spread its risks
Consumers may be prepared to pay higher prices for specifically branded products that are targeted at meeting their particular needs. This should raise business revenue	If niche markets are successful for one business, new competitors will see this and may be attracted to enter the market too

> **Extend your skills of analysis**
>
> A question which asks for an advantage of niche markets for a small business selling specialist climbing clothing could be answered as follows:
>
> Niche markets focus on a small section of a larger market instead of mass markets.
>
> *Extend your analysis by explaining why this is an advantage.*
>
> A small business might not have the resources to enter a mass market for outdoor clothing with many competitors, so niche markets give it a better chance of success.
>
> *Extend your analysis by explaining how this benefits the business.*
>
> By focusing on a niche market for climbing clothing, a small business could produce a specialist product aimed at a small group of consumers who want something different. They might be prepared to pay a high price for a well-designed and branded product, increasing revenue and profit.

Market segmentation

How markets can be segmented

Market segmentation recognises that groups of consumers are not all the same and that what appeals to one set of consumers may not appeal to others.

Market segmentation is when a market is broken down into sub-groups which share similar characteristics. Businesses will then develop products and market them directly at specific consumer groups. For example, chocolates are eaten by young children, teenagers and adults of both sexes. However, different types and brands of chocolates will appeal to these different groups of people. A Marketing department will divide the whole market into different groups and categories; these are called **market segments**.

> **Definitions to learn**
>
> **Market segmentation** is when a business knows that different segments of a market exist and it develops and markets different products to each segment.
> **Market segment** is an identifiable sub-group of a whole market in which consumers have similar characteristics or preferences.

Each segment is researched in great detail. This will help develop products and advertisements that appeal to each market segment. An example might be teenagers buying clothes. Research might involve asking teenagers about which social media platforms they use, which television programmes they watch, which smartphones they have and general questions about what they like. Promotions can then be directed accurately at the targeted market segment.

Businesses can use market segmentation to sell more products. They do this by making different brands of a product and then aiming each brand at a different market segment. As the case study below shows, a business could produce various brands of soap to satisfy most of the market segments.

Case study: Market segmentation

This is an example of how the market for soap may be segmented.

Type of soap	Characteristics of market segment
Beauty soap	People who buy beauty soap will be people who want to keep their skin soft. They will therefore buy soap which contains moisturisers. This is likely to be bought mainly by women
Baby soap	This is mild soap which will not harm a baby's skin. It will be bought mainly by parents or carers for their babies
Medicated soap	Sometimes soap is sold to help fight acne. This tends to be bought mainly by teenagers, both male and female
Non-branded soap	This is a low-priced product which is plain soap with no extra perfume added. This is likely to be bought by people on low incomes

There may be other types of soap you can think of which are aimed at different groups. Sales of soap can be affected by income group, gender and also age.

▲ Which type of soap will each person use?

Activity 9.3

Read the case study above.

a List the different brands of soap sold in your local shops.
b Which segments of the market are each of these brands of soap aimed at?

9 MARKETING AND THE MARKET

> **Study tips**
>
> Remember that consumers can be part of more than one segment. You should be able to explain how and why businesses segment a market and use examples to illustrate this.

The most common ways to segment a market are explained in Table 9.3.

Table 9.3 How markets can be segmented

Age	The products bought by people in different age groups will often be very different. Young people buy very different clothes to people in older age groups. The toys bought for babies will vary from those bought for older children
Income	Incomes vary widely in most countries. For example, the average monthly income in Malaysia is about US$1500 but some people in this country will earn millions of dollars each year. Consumers with high incomes will often demand different types of products to those consumers with low incomes, for example, cars and perfumes. Only someone on a high income could afford a Ferrari, but a person on a much lower income might afford to buy a Tata Tiago. Producing different products for consumers with different incomes is a common way of segmenting markets
Location	In different regions of a country people might buy different products. For example, if there are dry and wet parts of the country then waterproof clothing will be sold in the rainy part of the country but not in the dry part. A food processing business will often change recipes and flavours to meet the cultural and tastes needs of consumers in different countries
Gender	Some products have traditionally only been bought by women, such as beauty products, and others have mainly been bought by men, such as heavy gym weights. This is now changing and more businesses use gender-neutral marketing. However, clothing businesses usually make a clear distinction between designs for women and designs for men
Lifestyle	Different consumers have different ways of living. Some groups spend a lot of spare time playing sport while others are keen on crafts and indoor hobbies. Developing different products and marketing them directly at these different groups is called lifestyle segmentation

Advantages and disadvantages of market segmentation

The advantages and disadvantages of market segmentation are explained in Table 9.4.

Table 9.4 Advantages and disadvantages of market segmentation

Advantages of market segmentation	Disadvantages of market segmentation
The needs of each consumer group can be more completely satisfied by products designed specifically for them. This helps build customer relationships	It might not be profitable to target some market segments that have a small number of consumers
Total sales should increase if different products are accurately directed at different consumer groups	Costs of developing different products for several different consumer groups are high. Extensive and detailed market research will be needed too
Promotion and advertising will use information about each consumer group to appeal to them directly and this makes more effective use of the marketing budget	Storage costs of several different types of products could be high
Revenue should increase as consumers may pay higher prices for products that directly meet their needs	Developing different advertisements and promotions for different products and different consumer groups is costly

Market segmentation

> **Extend your skills of analysis**
>
> A question which asks for an advantage of market segmentation for a holiday business could be answered as follows:
>
> Market segmentation is when a business knows that different segments of a market exist and it develops and markets different products to each segment.
>
> *Extend your analysis by explaining why the holiday market is segmented.*
>
> Not everyone who goes on holiday wants to go to the same destination or take part in the same activities.
>
> *Extend your analysis by explaining how the holiday business will benefit from market segmentation.*
>
> By developing different holiday packages for different groups of consumers, such as families or those interested in mountain climbing, total demand and revenue will be greater than if just one holiday package was offered to all groups of consumers and the business is likely to attract more customers in total.

Activity 9.4

Toyota produces a range of cars aimed at different market segments. It even owns a separate company called Lexus, whose cars are aimed at a particular market segment.

▲ Luxury car

▲ Family car

▲ Hybrid/electric car

▲ 4x4 SUV

a Look at the photographs from the Toyota range of cars and identify what characteristics the consumers of these models are likely to have. The characteristics you identify might include age, income, location, gender or lifestyle.

b Explain the advantages to Toyota of producing a large range of cars aimed at different market segments.

9 MARKETING AND THE MARKET

REVISION SUMMARY — Ways of segmenting markets

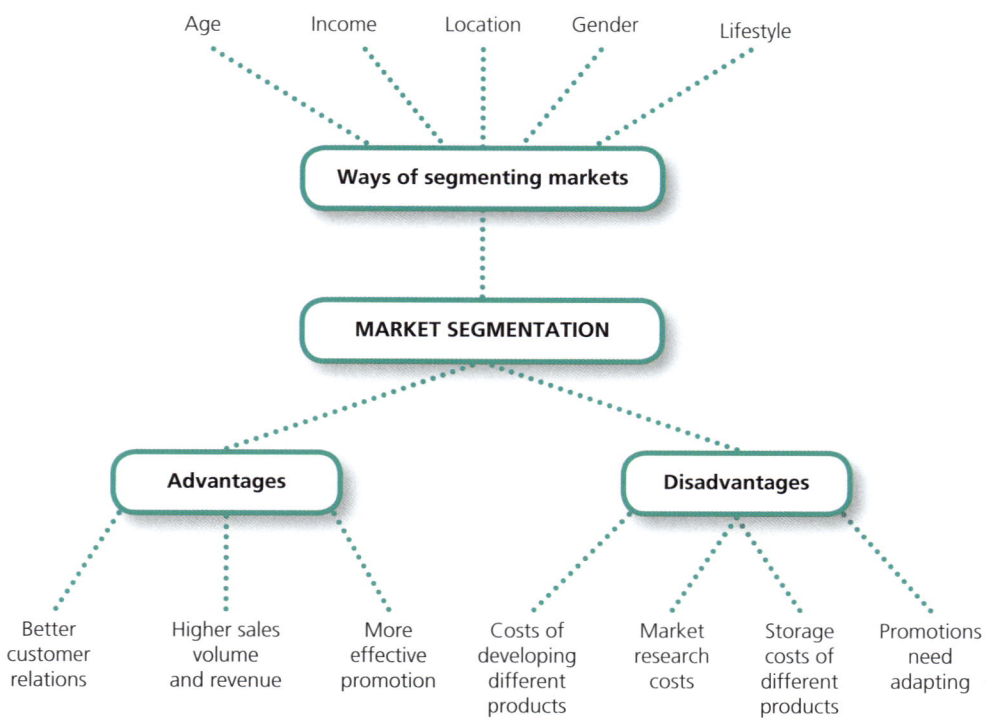

International business in focus

Personal computers and technology

▲ Personal computer and smartphone technology has seen many advances over the last 30 years

The personal computer market has seen many changes over the last few decades. The standard desktop computer is becoming a thing of the past in many offices, where laptops have taken its place. In the home this is also true. However, the introduction of the netbook and then the Apple iPad changed the market again.

Predictions for the future of the personal computer market are that mobile devices will become market leaders in terms of global sales, followed by tablets and netbooks. Home computers are seen as becoming a smaller and smaller share of the global market.

Discussion points
- How has the market for personal computers changed?
- Why have these changes happened?
- How should businesses in the personal computer market respond to these changes?

Chapter review questions: Short answer and data response

1 D&F owns several fruit farms. The fruit is sold to large supermarkets in other countries. D&F also grows coffee which is sold to companies that process and brand the coffee. The branded coffee is also then sold to large supermarkets in other countries. The world price of coffee has recently dropped by 20%. There has been a growing demand for fruit from consumers in developing economies with rising incomes. In high-income countries there has been a growing trend towards 'healthy eating', encouraged by government policies to tackle the obesity problem. Fresh fruit is an important part of a healthy diet.
   a Define 'consumer'. [2]
   b Outline **two** reasons, other than income, why consumer spending patterns can change for food products. [4]
   c Explain **two** likely reasons why the fresh fruit market is becoming more competitive. [6]
   d Do you think D&F should respond to changing consumer spending patterns by stopping the production of coffee and growing more fruit instead? Justify your answer. [8]

2 TGH is a public limited company which makes sports shoes (trainers). The directors want to build strong customer relationships. The business only produces a few shoe designs, all aimed at the mass market. The mass market consumers are young people who want fashionable sports shoes as well as those who play sport. The Directors recently decided to target a niche market. This is a market segment of customers who have a medical problem with their feet and need specially designed sports shoes.
   a Define 'mass market'. [2]
   b Outline **two** ways TGH could build customer relationships. [4]
   c Explain **two** advantages to TGH of segmenting the market for sports shoes. [6]
   d Do you think the Directors of TGH were right to target a niche market or should they only sell sports shoes to the mass market? Justify your answer. [8]

Revision checklist

In this chapter you have learned:

- the role of marketing
- why consumer spending patterns may change
- why some markets are becoming more competitive
- how businesses can respond to changing spending patterns and increased competition
- how to calculate market share
- the concepts of mass markets and niche markets and their advantages and disadvantages
- how markets can be segmented
- the advantages and disadvantages of market segmentation.

NOW – test your understanding with the revision questions in the Student etextbook and the Workbook.

10 Market research

> This chapter will explain:
>
> **Methods of market research:**
>
> ★ why businesses use market research
> ★ primary research methods
> ★ the concept of sampling and why it is useful to businesses
> ★ advantages and disadvantages of primary market research methods
> ★ secondary research methods
> ★ advantages and disadvantages of secondary market research methods
> ★ factors influencing the accuracy of market research data
> ★ how to analyse simple market research data.

Methods of market research

Why businesses use market research

A toy-making business is planning to add a new product to its existing range. Should it use **market research** data to help it plan what type of toy to launch?

» Manager A thinks: 'We have been selling toys for over 30 years. We know what consumers want so market research is unnecessary.'
» Manager B thinks: 'New competitors have entered the market recently with products focused on digital features. We must find out what potential consumers now want in new toys.'

In your opinion, who is right?

Hopefully, you think Manager B is correct! Many times in this book the risks and uncertainties involved in business activity have been explained. Market research aims to reduce these risks as far as possible, especially when taking decisions such as which new products to develop.

The purpose of market research is to try to find out answers to questions such as:

» Why are sales of existing products falling?
» What type of consumers buy our products?
» Would consumers be prepared to buy the new product that we plan to develop?
» What price would consumers be prepared to pay?
» Where would consumers be most likely to buy our product?
» What feature of the new product do consumers most like or dislike?
» What type of promotion would be effective?
» How strong is the competition and who are our main competitors?

> **Definitions to learn**
>
> **Market research** is the process of gathering, analysing and interpreting information about a market.

> **Key info**
>
> Market research is big business. Global business spending on market research is around $84 billion. Obviously, businesses around the world know it is of great importance to find out more about the market and consumer tastes.

Methods of market research

By carrying out market research, a business can:

- Identify consumer needs in a changing and competitive international environment.
- Reduce the risks of new products failing.
- Understand the most significant changes in the market and in competitors' decisions.

Collecting this information and analysing it is essential if a business is to remain competitive in the future.

Research methods

Market research can find out information about the quantity of something, for example, 'How many sports shoes were sold in the month of December?' or 'What percentage of children drink sugar-free cola?' It can also find out information about opinions or judgements, for example, 'What do consumers like about Product X?' or 'Why do more women than men buy our company's products?'

Both types of information can be gathered as a result of:

- **primary market research**
- **secondary market research**.

> **Definitions to learn**
>
> **Primary market research** (also called field research) is the collection and collation of original data via direct contact with potential or existing consumers.
>
> **Secondary market research** (also called desk research) uses information that has already been collected and is available for use by others.

Primary market research

Primary market research is the collection of data from research that has not already been undertaken. It involves direct contact with potential or existing consumers.

Advantages of primary market research

- It is up to date.
- It is relevant to the business undertaking it because it is usually planned and carried out by the people who want to use the data; it is first-hand.
- It is most effective when it is used to gather information which will help the business with a specific problem, for example, to test the market to see if a new product would be likely to succeed.
- It is not available to other businesses (unless they undertake their own research).

Disadvantages of primary market research

- It can be expensive, for example, when individually interviewing many people.
- It is not available immediately – it takes time to collect.

The figure on the next page shows the stages a business will go through to undertake primary research:

10 MARKET RESEARCH

1. What is the purpose of the market research?

What does it want to find out? What information will be needed? What action will be taken as a result of the research? This will affect the type of market research undertaken.

2. Decide on the size of sample needed and who is going to be asked

How big will the sample size need to be to keep costs down but get a sufficiently accurate result? Which different groups of people will need to be included in the survey? Different age groups? Different income groups?

3. Decide on most appropriate method of primary research

Will more than one method be necessary? The cost of the research and the time required will need to be taken into account.

4. Carry out the research

5. Collate the data and analyse the results

The information will need to be put together and the data analysed. What does it seem to show?

6. Produce a report of the findings

A report will need to be produced showing the findings. Included in the report will be a summary of the research findings and conclusions drawn based on these results. Recommendations should be made as to what actions are necessary as a result of the research; these should be based on the conclusions.

▶ The stages of primary research

Primary research methods

Questionnaires or surveys

Questionnaires or surveys form the basis of most primary market research. They may be conducted face-to-face (for example, in the street), by telephone, by mail (post) or on the internet.

Deciding what questions to ask is difficult if you want to be sure of getting accurate results. Some questions may not be very clear and some questions may lead the respondents to answer in a certain way which may not be what they really think. 'Closed' questions often require a Yes/No answer but 'open' questions allow respondents to explain answers in their own words. The researcher also needs to decide who to ask. The advantages and disadvantages of questionnaires are explained in Table 10.1.

> **Definitions to learn**
>
> A **questionnaire** is a set of questions to be answered as a means of collecting data for primary market research.
> **Interviews** involve asking individuals a series of questions, often face-to-face or over the phone.
> A **focus group** is a group of people who are representative of the target market, brought together to discuss opinions about products and promotions.

Methods of market research

Table 10.1 Advantages and disadvantages of questionnaires for primary market research

Advantages of questionnaires	Disadvantages of questionnaires
Detailed information can be gathered about consumers' opinions about the good or service. For example, the reasons for preferring Product A over Product B	No feedback is possible. This means that if questions are confusing or ambiguous, respondents cannot ask for explanations. They also cannot be asked to explain or expand upon their answers if they are unclear
Consumers' opinions about the product or service can be obtained	Postal questionnaires can be expensive and time-consuming and the response rate (percentage of replies to questionnaires sent out) can be very low
They can be sent to consumers online and this reduces costs and can speed up the process	If not undertaken online, collating and analysing the results can be time-consuming.
Online questionnaires can be distributed to consumers worldwide	The emotions or thought processes involved in consumer buying decisions may be unclear.
They can be fast to collect and analyse if online questionnaires are used	Online questionnaires cannot reach potential respondents who do not have access to the internet

Interviews

When **interviews** are used for market research, the interviewer (the person asking the questions) will have ready-prepared questions for the interviewee (the person answering the questions). Interviews can be conducted face-to-face or over the telephone. Table 10.2 explains the advantages and disadvantages of interviews.

Table 10.2 Advantages and disadvantages of interviews for primary market research

Advantages of interviews	Disadvantages of interviews
The interviewer is able to explain any questions that the interviewee does not understand	Whether consciously or subconsciously, the interviewer could lead the interviewee into answering in a certain way, resulting in inaccurate results due to interviewer bias
Feedback is possible so follow-up questions can be asked when a more detailed answer is needed	Interviews are very time-consuming to carry out and this is a higher cost method than questionnaires
A skilled interviewer can build rapport and trust with the interviewee and this will improve accuracy of answers as the interviewee may be more honest.	Sample size may be lower than when using other methods due to the cost of employing an interviewer. This could limit the accuracy of the data
They are useful for studying a sensitive subject, for example, products needed by older age groups, that most people might not answer questions on if using a questionnaire	If the interviewer writes the answers on paper, time-consuming manual data entry is necessary

▲ Focus groups allow consumers to express their opinions

Focus groups

A **focus group** is where a group of people agree to provide information through a group discussion with a researcher present. The group might discuss a specific product or their reaction to an advertising campaign, for example. This helps the business make future marketing decisions. Groups may also test new products and then discuss what they think of them, explaining what they like and what they dislike about them. Table 10.3 explains the advantages and disadvantages of focus groups.

10 MARKET RESEARCH

Table 10.3 Advantages and disadvantages of focus groups for primary market research

Advantages of focus groups	Disadvantages of focus groups
They can provide detailed information about consumers' tastes and preferences	Discussion could be biased if some people in the group are too argumentative or dominate the discussion
Interaction between members of the group can help the business understand the reasons behind consumer behaviour	It can be difficult to form an overall conclusion of a discussion involving several people
Interaction between members of the group can help provide information about how consumers can be influenced by other people's opinions	Shy members of the group may be unwilling to join in and this could lead to a biased discussion
They are quicker and cost less than individual interviews	Group members might not fully represent the target market

Observation

Useful information can be gained by observing consumers as they shop, in a supermarket, for example. Which packaging seems to attract them? Which shelves do they visit first? Are there some parts of the store they do not visit at all? Table 10.4 explains the advantages and disadvantages of **observation** as a market research method.

> **Definitions to learn**
>
> **Observation** is a method of market research that collects data about consumer behaviour by watching them and recording their actions when buying or choosing between products.

Table 10.4 Advantages and disadvantages of observation for primary market research

Advantages of observation	Disadvantages of observation
It is low cost and less time-consuming than face-to-face interviews	As there is no questioning of consumers, the reasons for their actions cannot be identified
It is easy to achieve accurate results as there is little scope for bias	If there are few consumers during the observation period, the necessary sample size might not be reached
Consumers are observed in real-world situations without their knowledge, so they are not trying to please or misinform the data collector	If consumers have to be told that they are being watched (in order to meet legal requirements) they may change their behaviour

> **Extend your skills of analysis**
>
> A question which asks for an advantage of using a focus group to research consumer interest in a new e-scooter could be answered as follows:
>
> The focus group will discuss the opinions of the members of the group about a new product, watched by someone from the business.
>
> **Extend your analysis by explaining why this will provide useful data.**
>
> The group can discuss the features of the e-scooter that they like or dislike or even try it for the first time.
>
> **Extend your analysis by explaining why this will be useful for the business.**
>
> It will be costly to produce and launch the new e-scooter. It is important to find out how the product can be improved before it is launched to better satisfy consumer needs as explained by the group. This should result in a successful launch of the new e-scooter.

Methods of market research

The concept of sampling and why it is useful to businesses

In market research it is impossible to ask for everyone's opinion unless the total number of consumers is quite small. It would be expensive and time-consuming to collect data from the whole consumer population of a market. A **sample** must usually be chosen from the total target market – or population of people – that a business is aiming its products at. Sampling means getting opinions from a number of people chosen from this specific group. The answers from the sample will allow the business to find out the tastes and preferences of the whole group.

The aim of sampling is to try to ensure that the people included in the research are as representative of the whole target market population as possible. If the sample is not representative, then the results from the research will not be accurate.

The most common method of sampling is random sampling. This is when the group of people to be questioned are selected entirely by chance. An alternative is quota sampling, when the group of people to be questioned are selected on the basis of a certain characteristic such as age, gender or income. This requires more information than random sampling to prepare the group to be questioned but usually leads to a more representative sample.

The advantages to a business of effective sampling are:

» It saves time and money as the whole population does not have to be included in the market research survey.
» A carefully selected sample can give a representative coverage of the target population.

> **Definitions to learn**
>
> A **sample** is a group of people who are selected to respond to a primary market research exercise, such as a questionnaire.

> **Study tips**
>
> Make sure you can select a suitable method of primary market research for particular products and explain why it is suitable.

> ### Activity 10.1
>
> Decide which method of primary market research would be the most appropriate to use in each of the situations below and explain why.
>
> a   The possible success of a new chocolate bar.
> b   Whether to introduce a new style of watch which uses fashionable bright colours.
> c   Retail store wants to trial a new store layout to increase sales in some departments.
> d   The feasibility of opening a new restaurant.
> e   Why the sales of a sports shoe are falling.

Secondary market research

Secondary market research is the use of information that has already been collected and is available for use by others. Some information can come from internal sources, such as past sales data for the business.

Advantages of secondary market research

» It is often a lower cost way of gathering information than primary research, as the data collection has already been done by others.
» It can be used to help assess the total size of a market by finding out the size of the population and its age structure. This type of information could not be obtained by primary research.
» It is usually quicker to obtain secondary data than to undertake primary research.

> **Key info**
>
> Information on online marketing of products can provide valuable internal secondary data. For example, the sports retailer JD gathers data from its online ordering records. It analyses which parts of the world it receives many orders from which do not have a JD shop. These are called 'hot spots' and they could make a good location for a new JD store.

Disadvantages of secondary market research

» Data may have been collected several years ago and be out of date.
» Data is available to all businesses – it is not just collected for the sole use of one business.
» Data may not be completely relevant as it was not collected with the needs of one particular business in mind.

Secondary market research methods

Competitor websites

Nearly every business of any size will have a website. This is likely to contain information about product range, pricing levels, promotions offered, potential new product releases and the consumer services offered. Other sections of the website might include financial data about the business. This will particularly be the case with public limited companies that have to publish their financial statements. So, details about revenue and profit levels, comparisons of revenue and profit with previous years and the strength of the statement of financial position will be made available to all stakeholders, including competitors. Table 10.5 explains the advantages and disadvantages of using competitor websites as a source of secondary market research.

Table 10.5 Advantages and disadvantages of competitor websites for secondary market research

Advantages of competitor websites	Disadvantages of competitor websites
They are freely available online	Competitors will not make all data about operations, such as discounts available to major consumers or the profit margin made on each product, available on their websites
A business can compare the data it obtains from competitors with its own internal data. This will allow the business to consider changes to its own strategies if competitors seem to be performing more successfully	Financial data about competitors may be at least 12 months out of date

Government sources

Government sources include size of population (census) data, age distribution of the population, national and regional income levels, unemployment data by region and immigration data. Table 10.6 explains the advantages and disadvantages of using government sources of secondary data.

Table 10.6 Advantages and disadvantages of government sources for secondary market research

Advantages of government sources	Disadvantages of government sources
They are widely available and usually free, for example, from online sites or libraries	They are often out of date, for example, population censuses are usually held every 10 years. This limits the accuracy of the data
They cover not just the whole country but individual regions which could be important for a business that trades in just part of the country	The data is often not specifically about an individual market and hardly ever about an individual product or brand. This limits the relevance of the data

Methods of market research

Market reports

These are detailed reports about individual markets, such as car sales or smartphone sales. They can either be international reports (about the global market for a product) or just focused on one country's market for a product. Market reports are produced by specialist market research agencies. Table 10.7 explains the advantages and disadvantages of market research reports.

Table 10.7 Advantages and disadvantages of market reports for secondary market research

Advantages of market reports	Disadvantages of market reports
They are specifically aimed at markets the business is interested in or already operating in	They are available to all competitors as well, unlike primary data collection
They contain more detailed data than the business is likely to be able to obtain from its own research with its own resources	They are usually not updated every year so will become out of date quickly, especially in fast-changing markets
Wide-ranging research methods allow emerging trends in a market to be identified early	There is a high cost to the business to access these reports – the market research agencies aim to make a profit from the research

Trade magazines

These are magazines, journals or newspapers written for managers whose business operates in a particular industry. In general, a trade magazine will have news, current events information, trends, and interviews with well-known businesspeople in that industry. Unlike market reports, trade magazines do not contain original market research. The focus of them tends to be on current trends and issues. Table 10.8 explains the advantages and disadvantages of trade magazines as a source of secondary data.

> **Study tips**
>
> Make sure you can select a suitable method of secondary market research for particular products and explain why it is suitable.

Table 10.8 Advantages and disadvantages of trade magazines for secondary market research

Advantages of trade magazines	Disadvantages of trade magazines
They provide data specifically about a particular industry	They usually do not use the detailed and verified research methods used by market research agencies. They may not be as accurate or detailed as a market report
They often contain interviews with major figures in the industry, discussing most likely future trends	They often contain industry-related advertising. The articles and opinions of the magazine might be influenced by major advertisers. It may not be reliable data

---

Extend your skills of analysis

A question which asks for a disadvantage of a newly formed cafe using a catering trade magazine to research consumer demand in a small town could be answered as follows:

Trade magazines are a method of secondary market research. They provide articles, opinions and interviews for businesses in that industry.

Extend your analysis by explaining the disadvantages of trade magazines.

One disadvantage is that the trade magazine provides information about the whole catering industry in a country and is not focused on new businesses or particular towns.

Extend your analysis by explaining how the business might be affected by this.

The owner of the new cafe will not gain the local knowledge required about which cafes are popular in this small town and what cafe customer needs are, so they could make poor decisions which could result in low sales.

10 MARKET RESEARCH

Activity 10.2

Which of the following sources of information gathered by a business are primary and which are secondary? Suggest one use of each data source.

Data source	Primary or secondary?	Useful for?
A trade magazine article on a competitor's new product		
An interview with a regular consumer of the product being researched		
A report on a discussion between a group of consumers of a particular brand		
An observation count to see how many consumers stop and read in-store promotional material		
Smartphone questionnaire results researching the impact of a new promotion campaign		
A market report on what consumers like and dislike about the major brands on the market		
Annual government population statistics		
Data on a competitor's revenue over recent years		

Case study: Market research

A company manufactures carbonated drinks. It wants to start selling a new drink in your country. To help it assess the size of the market, you have been asked to find out:

- the size of the total population
- how many people there are in the age groups 1–10, 11–20 and 21–30 in your country
- how many different carbonated drinks are sold in your country (how many competitors there are)
- where these competitors come from – are they local companies or are the drinks imported?

Activity 10.3

Read the case study above.

What other market research would you advise the company to undertake before starting to sell in your country? Explain your answer.

REVISION SUMMARY — Methods of market research

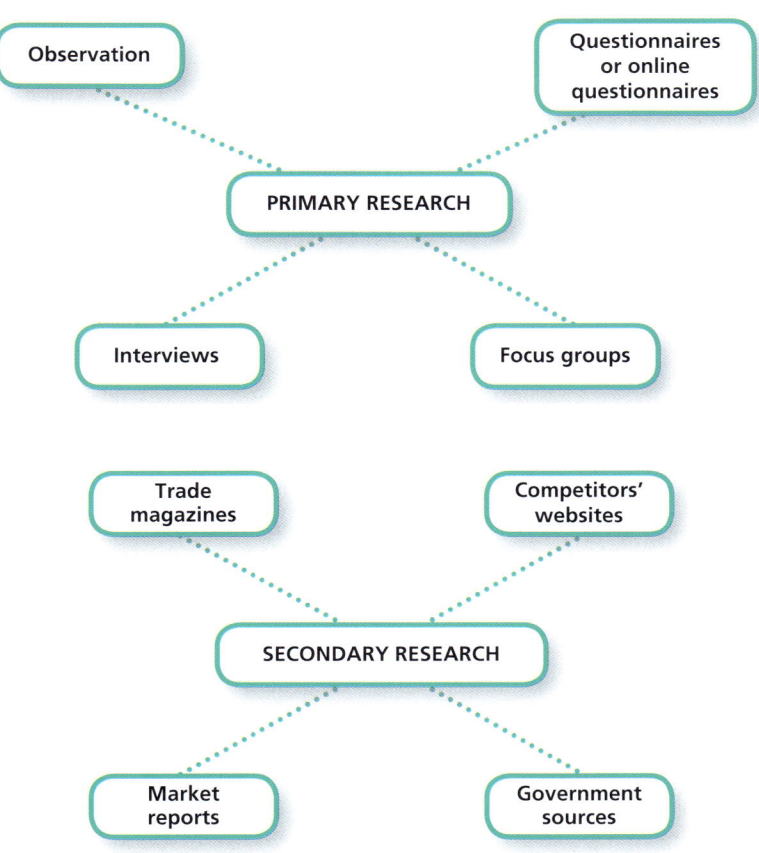

Factors influencing the accuracy of market research data

The reliability or accuracy of the data that has been collected depends largely on:

- **Sample.** How carefully the sample was selected determines how representative the sample is of the total population in that market.
- **Sample size.** The size of the sample is also important. It is not possible to ask everyone in a population, which is why a sample is used. The larger the sample, the more accurate the results are likely to be, but the more expensive the research will be. If only a small sample is surveyed, the results are unlikely to be as accurate. Therefore, the researchers need to decide how many people will give them the accuracy they want and can afford.
- **Question wording.** The wording of the questions can be misleading and lead to inaccurate answers. The questions on a questionnaire could be tested on a small group of people before using them on a large sample to find out if any of the questions could be misunderstood. Any such questions can then be rephrased and the revised questionnaire carried out on the main sample.

» **Source of data.** Secondary market research may not be as accurate as first thought because it was initially carried out for some other purpose and the business would not know how the information was actually gathered.
» **Bias.** Bias can occur for a number of reasons. For example, articles in newspapers sometimes show bias and important data may be deliberately left out, interviewers might select a biased sample, or questionnaire results might be biased in favour of those with more spare time to fill in the questionnaire.
» **Age of the information.** Statistics can quickly become out of date and no longer relate to current trends in consumers' buying habits, instead reflecting what they used to be spending their money on.

These are just some of the reasons why market research data collected from all sources, both primary and secondary, should be used with care. It should never be assumed straightaway that market research data is 100% accurate.

Analysing simple market research data

The analysis of market research data has three stages:

» Present data in an easy to understand form.
» Identify major factors, changes and trends in the data.
» Draw conclusions from the data that might be useful for business decision making.

When information has been gathered as part of market research, it may be difficult to make sense of what it means. The original data will need to be converted into a form which is easy to understand and analyse. The significant points need to be made clear. For example, after conducting a questionnaire, it may not be clear which answer has the greatest number of 'yes' responses.

> ### Activity 10.4
> Analyse the results in the case study at the top of the next page and answer these questions.
>
> a Why is it important that the sample asks people from different age groups?
> b How could this information affect where the business would advertise its restaurant?
> c Why did the questionnaire contain the question 'How often do you eat out?'?
> d How will the responses to questions 2 and 3 be useful to the fast-food restaurant?
> e Suggest **two** additional questions that could have been included in the questionnaire. Explain why the information they could have provided would be useful to the business.
> f Explain why this market research might not be sufficient for the owners of the fast-food restaurant.

Case study: Market research data

Below are some of the results of a questionnaire that was carried out to look into the feasibility of opening a fast-food restaurant in a city centre. 100 people were asked to answer the questionnaire. The aim of the questionnaire was to identify the particular market segment to be targeted in any promotional campaign.

Responses to question 1	Age group (years)	No. of persons
'How old are you?'	10–19	45
	20–29	20
	30–39	20
	40–49	10
	50+	5
Responses to question 2	**Response**	**No. of persons**
'How often do you eat out?'	Never	5
	Occasionally	20
	Once per month	30
	Once per week	20
	More than once per week	25
Responses to question 3	**Response**	**No. of persons**
'Where do you purchase meals most often?'	Hotel	20
	Cafe	20
	Fast-food restaurant	35
	Food stalls (in street)	25
Responses to question 4	**Response**	**No. of persons**
'How far do you usually travel when eating out?'	1 km	30
	2 km	40
	5 km	12
	5–10 km	13
	over 10 km	5

The type of data that has been collected and what it is to be used for will affect the type of presentation used for the data. Market research information can be displayed in different forms:

- tables
- bar charts
- pie charts
- graphs.

Tables

A table, like the one below, can be used to present the actual results of research. This makes it easier to then present the data in a more visual form.

Table 10.9 The products bought in a fast-food cafe over a 5-hour period

Time	Burger	Pizza	Salad	Cake	Drink only
13:00–13:59	10	15	3	8	20
14:00–14:59	15	20	10	5	15
15:00–15:59	20	15	15	5	15
16:00–16:59	30	15	13	15	13
17:00–17:59	38	10	8	25	33

10 MARKET RESEARCH

Bar charts

A bar chart shows the total figures for each piece of data or the proportion of each piece of data in terms of the total number.

For example, the bar chart below shows the data from the fast-food cafe presented more clearly. It can be analysed as follows:

» The sales of all products varied over this 5-hour period.
» Sales of burgers varied the most – from a low point of 10 in the first hour to 38 in the last hour.
» Three products recorded their highest sales in the last hour.

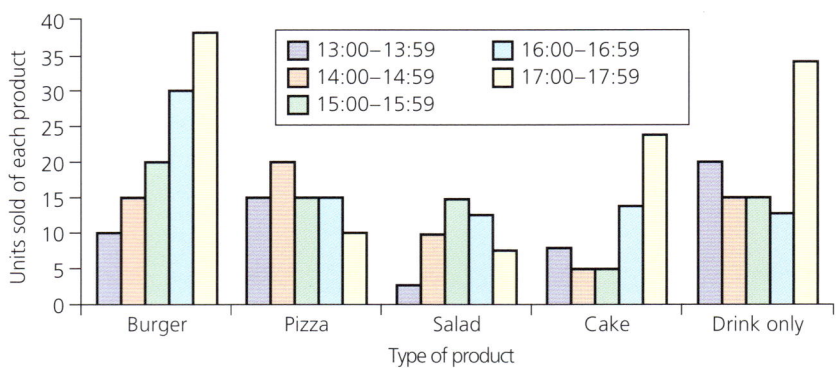

▲ A bar chart of sales data in the fast-food cafe

This data could then be used to help the business decide on:

» staffing levels
» the numbers of products to prepare for each hour
» promotions to be used – for example, to encourage the 'drink only' customers to buy food as well
» whether dynamic pricing (see Chapter 12) should be used during the busy periods for the cafe – for example, offering cakes at a special low price in the first hour.

Pie charts

The pie chart on the left is based on data from a business that sells its products in seven different countries. The relative importance of each market is shown very clearly. It can be analysed as follows:

» The USA is the business's largest market but is this true for its competitors? Further research will be needed.
» Argentina is the business's smallest market. When did the business start selling to this market? If it only started selling last year, then this performance is good.
» Saudi Arabia has a relatively small population. Why is it the business's second-largest market? Is there something the business can use from its marketing in Saudi Arabia and apply it to other markets?

This data is useful – but other information will be needed before business decisions can be taken.

Where company sells its products

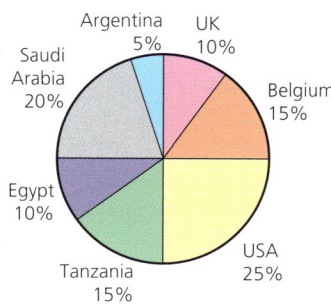

Methods of market research

Graphs

A graph can be used to show the relationship between two sets of data. For example, the line graph below shows how total annual sales have changed over a number of years. The two variables in the graph are 'total annual sales' and 'years'. It can be analysed as follows:

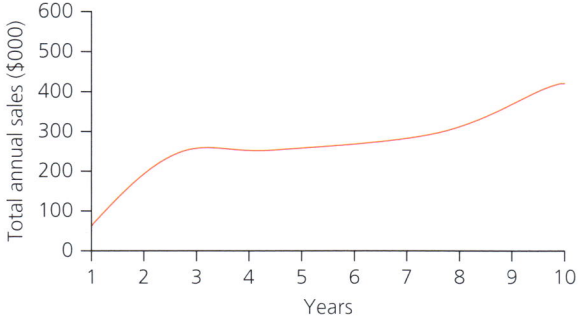

▲ A line graph showing total annual sales over time

» The graph shows clearly that annual sales rose rapidly at first.
» Sales then stayed steady for several years.
» Sales accelerated again in the final two years.
» Over the 10-year period sales have increased almost six times.

The data could be used to help a business decide on the marketing decisions for the next time period – based on the success of its marketing over the last two years.

International business in focus

360-degree cameras – how will market research help?

Whether you are trying to capture a cityscape from a high viewpoint, recreate the experience of an amazing music concert with footage that captures both the crowd and the band, or cover all angles while filming some extreme sport, a 360-degree camera is for you. There are now many businesses producing 360-degree cameras hoping to take a share of this booming market. A good example is Tesseract Imaging, which has developed India's first 360-degree 3D camera, called Methane. The camera is researched, designed and manufactured in India.

A recent report forecasts the global 360-degree camera market to grow at an annual rate of 25%. It suggests that businesses producing 360-degree cameras need to do more market research to find out the following:

- Which type of consumers buy these cameras?
- What are they most used for?

According to the report, one of the main factors driving demand for 360-degree cameras is the increasing popularity of virtual reality (VR) headsets. The gaming market is the highest adopter of VR content. The increased penetration of VR headsets is going to greatly increase the potential market for 360-degree cameras.

Source: www.zionmarketresearch.com/news/global-360-degree-camera-market

Discussion points

- Why would secondary market research have been of little use to the first businesses developing 360-degree cameras?
- Do you think that market research would help a business planning to enter the 360-degree camera market in your country for the first time?

10 MARKET RESEARCH

❓ Chapter review questions: Short answer and data response

1. T&T is a small business which sells many different types of garden tools. It is well known for selling tools of high quality. Sales of its products are growing very quickly. Its Managing Director (MD) feels that market research is not the most important factor contributing to the success of the business. However, the MD does want primary market research to be carried out before developing a new type of lightweight garden tool which is designed to be used by gardeners who are of an older age.
   a. Define 'primary market research'. [2]
   b. Outline **two** primary market research methods that can be used by T&T. [4]
   c. Explain **two** factors which will influence the accuracy of the market research data T&T will collect. [6]
   d. Do you think primary market research is necessary before T&T develops the new product? Justify your answer. [8]

2. H&H is planning to develop a new app for smartphones. It will allow people to control electronic devices in their home when they are not there. The Managing Director, Rita, wants the Marketing department to carry out secondary market research rather than primary market research before launching this new app. Rita thinks that there are very few competitors in the market for this type of app.
   a. Define 'secondary market research'. [2]
   b. Outline **two** methods of secondary market research that H&H could use. [4]
   c. Explain **two** reasons why accurate market research data is important to H&H. [6]
   d. Do you think that Rita is right to want to carry out only secondary market research? Justify your answer. [8]

Revision checklist

In this chapter you have learned:

- ✔ why businesses use market research
- ✔ primary research methods and their advantages and disadvantages
- ✔ the concept of sampling
- ✔ secondary research methods and their advantages and disadvantages
- ✔ factors influencing the accuracy of market research data
- ✔ how to analyse simple market research data.

NOW – test your understanding with the revision questions in the Student etextbook and the Workbook.

11 The marketing mix: product

This chapter will explain:
- ★ the four elements of the marketing mix
- ★ the importance of brand image
- ★ the role of packaging
- ★ the advantages and disadvantages of developing new products
- ★ the main stages of the product life cycle
- ★ how to interpret a product life cycle diagram
- ★ extension strategies a business could use
- ★ advantages and disadvantages of different extension strategies
- ★ how to recommend and justify an extension strategy to use in a given situation.

The marketing mix

The **marketing mix** is a term which is used to describe all the activities which go into marketing products. These activities are often summarised as the 'four Ps'.

The four Ps of the marketing mix

» **Product.** This applies to the good or service itself – its design, features and quality. How does the product compare with competitors' products? Does the packaging of the product help customers identify it? If it is a service being offered, do customers receive a clearly better service than rivals offer?
» **Price.** The price at which the product is sold to the customer is a key part of the marketing mix. A comparison must be made with the prices of competitors' products. Price should, in the long run, cover costs. (See Chapter 12.)
» **Place.** This refers to the channels of distribution that are selected. That is, what method of getting the product to the market and to the customer is to be used? Will the manufacturer sell its product to shops that sell to the public, or to wholesalers, or direct to the customers? (See Chapter 13.)
» **Promotion.** This is how the product is advertised and promoted. What types of advertising methods will be used? It includes discounts that may be offered or any other types of sales promotion, such as competitions or special offers. (See Chapter 14.)

Each part of the marketing mix has to be considered carefully to make sure that it all fits together and one part does not clash with another. For example, a high-priced perfume should be wrapped in expensive-looking packaging and advertised by glamorous people and it should not be sold in small food stores. If it were, the 'place' would not fit in with the other elements of the marketing mix.

> **Definitions to learn**
>
> The **marketing mix** is used to describe all the activities which go into marketing a product or service. These activities are often summarised as the four Ps – product, price, place and promotion.

11 THE MARKETING MIX: PRODUCT

REVISION SUMMARY The marketing mix

Marketing mix – product

The term 'product' refers to the goods and services produced by businesses. Producing the right product is an important part of the marketing mix. What is meant by the 'right' product? These are some of the features a successful product should have:

- It must satisfy consumer wants and needs or it will not sell.
- It needs to be of a satisfactory quality so consumers are willing to pay the price for it.
- It must not be so difficult to make that the costs of production are greater than the price charged for it.
- Design and performance of the product must satisfy all legal controls, such as health regulations for food products.
- It should have a brand image that consumers can relate to and want to be associated with.

The term 'product' refers to the goods and services produced by businesses. These can be split into:

- **Consumer goods and services.** Consumer goods are bought by consumers for their own use. They include food, clothing, cars and furniture. Services bought by consumers include car repairs, hairdressing services and education.
- **Producer goods and services.** Producer goods are produced for other businesses to use and include trucks, machinery and components. Businesses also need services such as accounting, insurance and advertising.

The importance of brand image

Why are Apple smartphones so popular? Why does Nike sell more sports shoes than any other manufacturer? Which company logo is, according to research, the most recognised in the world? (Answer: Coca-Cola!) There are many reasons for the success of these companies' products but the one factor they all have in common is a strong **brand image**.

A brand image is the unique identity that a product has. A strong brand image is quickly recognised by many consumers and this helps to achieve high sales. Consumers often want to be seen with branded goods as it suggests they

> **Key info**
>
> The Apple iPhone has sold over 2.3 billion units worldwide since its launch in 2007. This makes it one of the bestselling consumer products of all time.

> **Definitions to learn**
>
> **Brand image** is an image or identity given to a product which distinguishes it from competitors' brands.

Marketing mix – product

Definitions to learn

A **brand name** is the unique name of a product that distinguishes it from other brands.

Brand loyalty is when consumers keep buying the same brand instead of choosing a competitor's product.

have style and taste – as well as the income that allows them to purchase the products. A brand image can be created by:

» a **brand name**, which is usually protected in law to stop other businesses using it
» a logo with a unique design which becomes easy to recognise – and is also protected from copying by law
» sales promotion and advertising that gives the product a special status in the mind of consumers. This is often achieved by sponsorship of major events or endorsements from celebrities
» a reputation, built up over time, for a consistent level of quality that satisfies consumers.

Advantages of a strong brand image

» The product is recognisable to consumers, sometimes globally, which helps to boost sales.
» It develops **brand loyalty** from consumers even if competitors launch rival products.
» Consumers become less price sensitive – they often continue to buy the product when the price rises.
» The business will receive well-qualified applicants for job vacancies because people want to work for a company that has a well-known brand.

REVISION SUMMARY: Branding

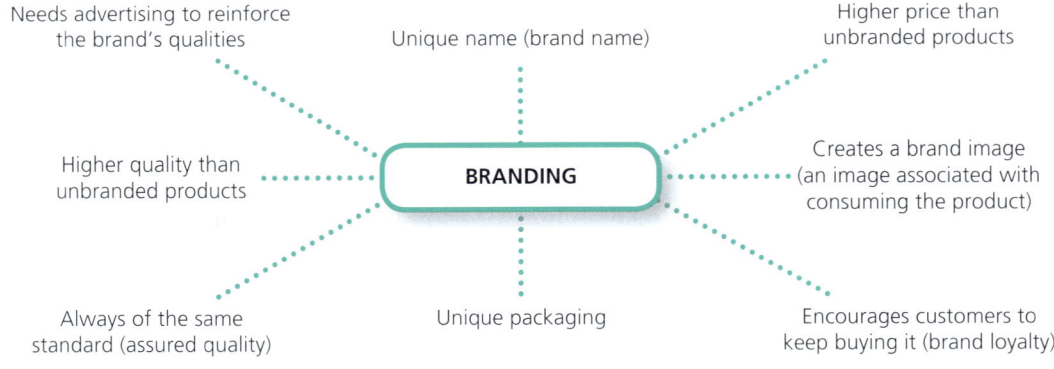

- Needs advertising to reinforce the brand's qualities
- Unique name (brand name)
- Higher price than unbranded products
- Higher quality than unbranded products
- **BRANDING**
- Creates a brand image (an image associated with consuming the product)
- Always of the same standard (assured quality)
- Unique packaging
- Encourages customers to keep buying it (brand loyalty)

Key info

Brand names add value to a business as customers will pay higher prices than for non-branded goods. It has been estimated that the brand name 'Apple' is worth US$880 billion and the brand name 'Google' is worth US$578 billion. These are currently two of the world's most valuable brands.

Case study: Nestlé

Nestlé manufactures chocolate bars. Milkybar (called Galak in Continental Europe and Latin America), which is made of white chocolate and appeals to young children, is 1 of its bestselling bars. An advertising campaign in India shows a mother nudging a child towards a Milkybar. The nudge is supposed to show her child that imagination leads to fun and learning. The advert is intended to be a reminder that a kid's imagination must be encouraged and the best way to do that is with a Milkybar.

11 THE MARKETING MIX: PRODUCT

> ### Activity 11.1
> Refer to the case study on the previous page.
>
> a Which consumers are the target market for Milkybars?
> b Explain how the advert is supposed to attract customers in India.
> c Describe the brand image for Milkybars and explain how the marketing of Milkybars could support this.

The role of packaging

Getting the **packaging** right is an important part of producing a successful product. The packaging of a product has several functions to perform:

Definitions to learn

Packaging is the physical container or wrapping to protect a product and help in promoting it.

» **Product protection.** Packaging has to give protection to the product to prevent damage to it. It also has to allow the product to be used easily. Hair shampoo packaged in a tin which will not allow the liquid to pour out easily will not sell well! The packaging has to be suitable for transporting the product from the factory to the shops, so it must be sufficiently strong or the product could easily get damaged.

» **Product promotion.** Packaging should appeal to the consumer, so the colour and shape of the container is very important. It is the packaging that catches the customer's eye on a shop shelf, not usually the product inside.

» **Support the brand image.** The brand image will be reinforced by the packaging in which the product is sold. An expensive product will have a luxurious-looking container, perhaps using a gold colour. A low-cost product may have basic, simple packaging with plain colours which will cost less to manufacture.

» **Product information.** The labels on some products must, as a legal requirement, carry vital information about the product. For example, most labels on food products sold in supermarkets must explain how to store the item and for how long, and what ingredients it contains, including any allergens.

The most significant recent development in packaging has been the transition towards environmentally friendly packaging materials. Single-use plastic containers are illegal in some countries as they add to the problem of waste and are not biodegradable. Many manufacturers now use recyclable packaging materials and this improves the sustainability of the production process (see Chapter 19).

Study tips

Make sure you can choose suitable packaging for different products to ensure the correct appeal for the brand image/target market.

> ### Activity 11.2
> Select **two** products that have brand names. For each of the products identify:
>
> a who the customers of the product are
> b what it is that attracts them to the product
> c what brand image the manufacturer is trying to create
> d how the name and the packaging of the product help to reinforce the brand image
> e where it is sold.

Marketing mix – product

Case study: Breakfast cereal packaging

Kellogg's manufactures breakfast cereals. The packaging used is bright and colourful and has the brand name clearly printed on the front of the packet in large letters. The outer packet is made of cardboard to keep its shape, so it will stand up on the shelves in shops and prevent the contents from being crushed. The side of the packet contains information about the nutritional qualities of the product. There is also sometimes a special offer printed on the outside of the packet to encourage consumers to buy the cereal. There are sometimes tokens on the packet to be cut out, collected and then sent off to receive a free gift. The cardboard packet has inner packaging to keep the product sealed and fresh until it is purchased and consumed by the customer.

Case study: Drinks packaging

    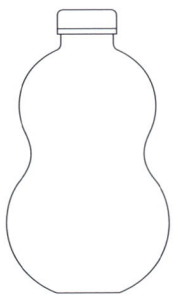

S&B Food Products has decided to produce a new fruit-flavoured milk drink especially for young children. The market segment that it expects to buy the product is parents, for their children. It is a healthy drink which contains vitamins and minerals.

Activity 11.3

Read the second case study above.

a Which of the possible containers shown in the case study would you use for the new fruit-flavoured milk drink? Explain your choice.
b Suggest another container that might be suitable for the new milk drink.
c What colour(s) should the container be? Explain your choice.
d Choose a brand name for the new milk drink. What image does the name give to the product?
e Design a label for the container. Why do you think the design of the label will help the product to sell?
f Explain how the packaging of this drink will influence its marketing success.

11 THE MARKETING MIX: PRODUCT

REVISION SUMMARY Packaging

Advantages and disadvantages of developing new products

Thousands of new products are developed and launched onto the market every year. There are very few businesses that produce exactly the same goods or services every year. Why are new products developed? Here are three reasons:

» Advances in technology are creating new product opportunities.
» Consumers' tastes and needs change and new products are required to satisfy them.
» New businesses are formed by entrepreneurs with unique product ideas.

Table 11.1 explains the advantages and disadvantages of developing new products.

Table 11.1 Advantages and disadvantages of developing new products

Advantages of developing new products	Disadvantages of developing new products
Completely innovative products will create a **Unique Selling Point (USP)**. The business will be first into the market with the new product, giving it a competitive advantage	Developing new products can lead to high costs. These costs will include detailed market research and technical development, sometimes using completely new technology
New products give a business a broader range of products to sell. This is called diversification and reduces the business's reliance on existing products and customers	Not all new ideas can be converted into successful and profitable products. There is always a risk that consumers will not buy the product in sufficient quantities to lead to a profit
New products that respond to the needs of export markets allow the business to become less reliant on the home market	Competitors may quickly develop and launch their own similar products, reducing competitive advantage for the business with the original new product
Businesses can develop a reputation for being innovative and creative with new products, which improves brand image	If a new product performs poorly – for example, if a car developed to drive itself autonomously is involved in several accidents – the reputation of the business could be badly damaged

> **Definitions to learn**
>
> The **Unique Selling Point (USP)** is the special feature of a product that differentiates it from the products of competitors.

Extend your skills of analysis

A question which asks for an advantage of new product development to a bicycle manufacturer could be answered as follows:

New product development means introducing to the market a product that will be new to consumers.

Extend your analysis by explaining why new product development is an advantage.

Consumer tastes and wants change over time and products that do not change will experience falling sales.

Extend your analysis by explaining why this is an advantage to a bicycle manufacturer.

Even though basic bicycles have been produced for many years, existing models will need to be replaced to stay competitive, for example, if other manufacturers are using modern lightweight materials and e-bike technology. A new bicycle with the latest technology will appeal to consumers, give the manufacturer a good brand image and lead to higher sales.

The main stages of the product life cycle

How long are products marketed for before they are withdrawn and replaced by more modern alternatives? This depends greatly on the nature of the product. Some popular food and drink brands have been sold for many years. In the USA, Pillsbury dough (first launched in 1869) and Coca-Cola (1886) are two of the longest-lasting food and drink brands. Other products last for a few months, such as fashion clothes, before they are withdrawn and replaced. The pattern of sales from product launch to being withdrawn is called the **product life cycle**. A typical cycle for a product is as follows.

Definitions to learn

The **product life cycle** is the stages a product will pass through, from its introduction, through its growth to maturity and then finally its decline.

Introduction

After a product has been developed, it is launched onto the market. Sales often grow slowly at first because most consumers are not aware of its existence. Advertising is used until the product becomes known and then establishing a brand identity will be important. Price skimming (see Chapter 12) may be used if the product is a new development and there are no competitors. Profit may be low at this stage as development costs may not yet have been covered.

Growth

If the product appeals to customers, sales start to grow rapidly. The advertising focuses on further developing brand loyalty. Prices could be reduced if new competitors enter the market and try to take some customers. The product should be profitable at this stage if all the development costs have been covered.

Maturity

Sales now increase only slowly and they may reach a peak and stop increasing. Competition becomes intense and pricing strategies are now even more competitive. Building customer relationships is important to maintain customer interest in the brand and receive feedback. Substantial advertising or other promotions might be necessary to maintain sales. The product should still be profitable.

Decline

Sales of the product decline as new products come along or because consumer wants have changed and the product has lost its appeal. The product is usually

11 THE MARKETING MIX: PRODUCT

withdrawn from the market when sales become so low and prices have been reduced so far that it becomes unprofitable to produce the product.

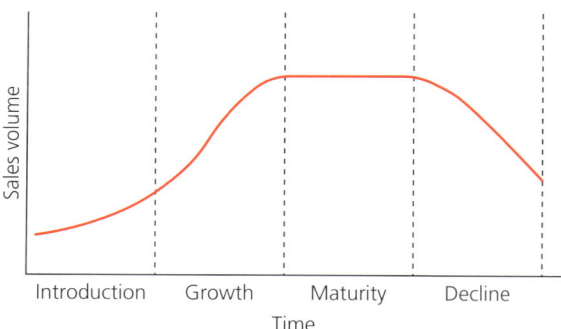

▲ A typical product life cycle

Interpreting a product life cycle diagram

The typical product life cycle cannot predict the actual life span of a product. New developments in technology can make original products rapidly obsolete. The life cycle of the older products will come to a quick end as newly launched products are purchased in preference to old technology. The time span of each stage of the life cycle will also vary between products. A new music download might reach maturity within weeks but a new brand of soft drink might take many months to build up sales before market saturation sets in.

The maturity stage of some well-established products can last for a long time. When the brand image of these products is supported by regular promotions and if **extension strategies** are used effectively, then some products will be marketed successfully for many years.

Definitions to learn

An **extension strategy** is a way of keeping a product at the maturity stage of the life cycle and extending the cycle over a longer period of time.

Key info

Car manufacturers usually replace or largely update their car models every four or five years to remain competitive. However, a few car models have been manufactured largely unchanged for much longer. The Peugeot 405 started production in 1987 and was still made in Azerbaijan in 2024! Its product life cycle has been much longer than that of most car models.

Extend your skills of analysis

A question which asks for an advantage of adapting an existing smartphone model to extend its life cycle could be answered as follows:

Extension strategies aim to keep a product at the maturity stage of its life cycle for longer.

Extend your analysis by explaining why this is an advantage.

Developing brand new products is expensive and adapting existing products is less costly.

Extend your analysis by explaining why adapting an existing model is an advantage to a smartphone manufacturer.

The technology in smartphones is constantly changing. It would be too costly for a manufacturer to develop a new smartphone every few months. Adapting an existing model with one new feature every few months could cost less but still maintain consumer interest and brand loyalty. Sales could remain steady or even increase without the cost of frequently introducing completely new smartphones.

Study tips

Make sure you can identify the stages of the product life cycle for a particular product.

Activity 11.4

Read the case study at the top of the next page.

Draw the product life cycle for the game invented by Compute. Label the diagram with the different stages that the game went through.

Case study: Product life cycle

Compute is a public limited company and it invented a new computer game. The game had been developed over several months before it was finally launched onto the market. Initially it was sold at a high price, being bought by only a few people who wanted to be the first to play the new game. It quickly became successful – a lot of advertising was used to promote the game and sales grew rapidly. Over the next few months, more and more retailers ordered copies of the game and competition between the retailers was fierce. The retailers offered the game at cheaper and cheaper prices to attract customers and prices for the game started to fall. Sales grew steadily now, though not at the fast rates of increase that were first seen. Once most computer users had purchased the game, the market was saturated and sales began to fall, even though prices were now low. The game was making little or no profit for the company and so it decided to withdraw the game from sale and concentrate on other new games that it had introduced.

Extension strategies a business could use

When a product reaches the maturity stage of its product life cycle, a business can attempt to prevent sales falling by adopting extension strategies. These are ways that sales may be given a boost to keep the product on the market for longer. This will reduce new product development costs for a business, although these are likely to become necessary at some point.

Possible extension strategies are described here.

New markets

Exporting the product to other countries would be one way to target new markets.

Advantages

- These new markets might be growing and offer a chance for expanding sales.
- There could be fewer competitors, meaning sales potential might be high.

Disadvantages

- The product might need to be adapted at considerable cost to meet different legal controls.
- Cultural differences might mean existing products need to be changed.

New uses for the product

If a business can find a new use for an existing product, it can sell to the new market segment that would find this useful. Baking soda is an essential cooking ingredient but it can also be used to remove odours from fridges and freezers!

Advantages

- No changes to the product will be necessary which helps to keep costs down.
- The product will already be well known.

Disadvantages

- New advertising and promotions will be needed to inform a new market segment about how the product can also be used.
- Consumers might be reluctant to change their use of a well-known product.

Adapting the product

Many consumer goods are updated during their lives even though the basic design and structure remain the same. Cars might have extra features added

11 THE MARKETING MIX: PRODUCT

or smartphones might be fitted with a more powerful zoom camera. The basic product is the same but the update increases its appeal to customers.

Advantages

- It can help differentiate the product from competitors' products.
- The cost is much lower than developing completely new products more frequently.

Disadvantages

- Consumers are still likely to recognise the product as being the same and may prefer competitors' products.
- The product may not contain the up-to-date features of competitors' new products.

Adapting the packaging

Launching new packaging, perhaps in different sizes than before, may increase the product's appeal and give it a fresh image. This extension strategy is likely to be more effective if the product is adapted too.

Advantages

- New packaging costs are likely to be lower than the cost of adapting the product itself.
- The change may help to develop a new brand image.

Disadvantages

- It is likely to have only a short-term impact on sales if the product itself has not been adapted too.
- Existing consumers may fail to recognise the product in new packaging.

Increased advertising and sales promotion

Spending more on promoting a product is a common extension strategy. This strategy is trying to attract the attention of consumers who may have forgotten about the product or need an extra benefit to be encouraged to buy it – such as vouchers or entry into a competition.

Advantages

- If well designed and attractive, advertising campaigns can recreate interest in an existing product and reinforce its brand image.
- Sales promotions (see Chapter 14) often result in a rapid uplift in sales.

Disadvantages

- Competitors are likely to respond with their own increases in advertising or even more attractive sales promotions.
- If all businesses spend more on promotion there might be no change in market share.

How to recommend and justify an extension strategy to use in a given situation

Marketing managers will weigh up the following factors before deciding on which extension strategy to use:

Marketing mix – product

- » **The cost of the extension strategy compared with the likely impact on sales.** This will require not just cost information but also market research into consumers' likely reaction to the extension strategy.
- » **The number of competitors in the market and whether they are likely to copy the business with their own extension strategies.** The impact of some extension strategies will be much reduced if competitors quickly introduce their own.
- » **The time needed to implement the extension strategy.** New advertising campaigns can be developed quite quickly but adapting a product with new features or preparing it for sale in a new market will take longer.
- » **How long the product has been on the market.** The longer the time since the product's launch, the greater the need to adapt it with up-to-date features to meet consumers' changing wants.
- » **The speed with which a completely new product can be developed and launched.** If this can be done quickly, major and costly adaptations to the existing product are unlikely to be worthwhile and a new sales promotion could be more profitable.

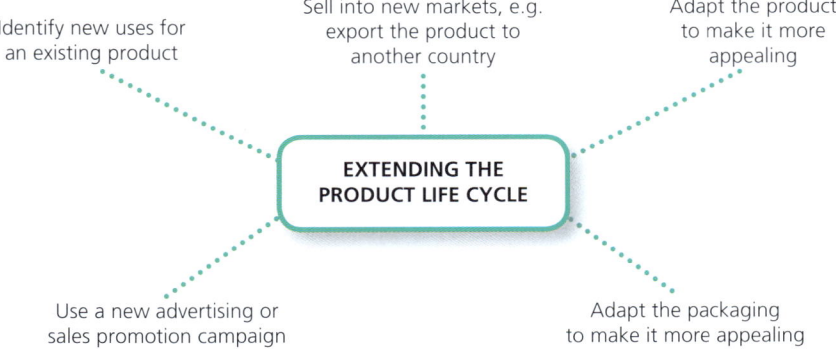

▶ Product life cycle extension strategies

If the extension strategies are effective, the maturity phase of the product life cycle will be prolonged. An example of what might happen is shown in the diagram below.

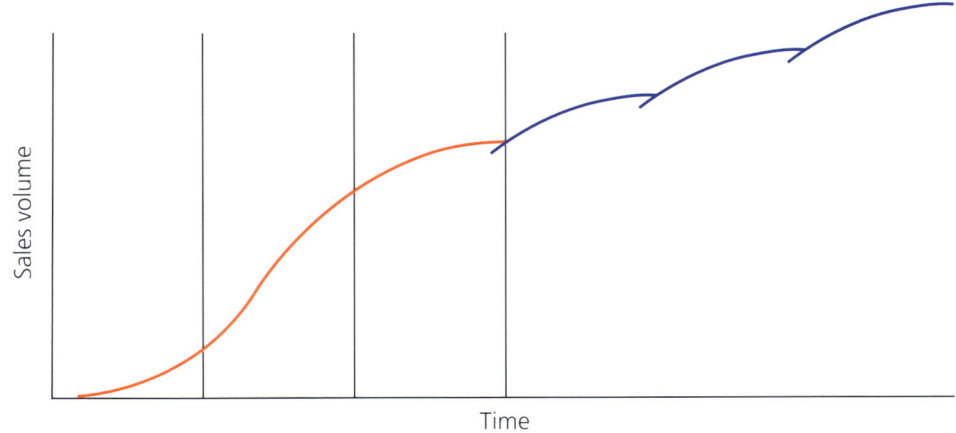

▲ The effect of extension strategies

> **Study tips**
>
> Make sure you can select suitable extension strategies for particular products.

11 THE MARKETING MIX: PRODUCT

> ### Activity 11.5
>
> Suggest possible ways to extend the product life cycle of the products listed below. State which extension strategy you would use for each product and explain why you think it would be successful in boosting sales.
>
> a A chocolate bar which has been sold for many years in the same packaging and has had the same brand image. There are several competitors' brands of chocolate bars also sold in the market and sales have stabilised.
> b A sports shoe that is worn when playing a particular sport. This sport is no longer very popular with young people.
> c The sales of a new model of a car have stopped increasing. The car is only sold in the home country where it is manufactured.
> d A children's toy which is only sold in toy shops. It had steady growth in its sales but now the sales are stable and not increasing any further.

International business in focus

Smartphones

The Apple iPhone, a smartphone, was first launched by Apple in January 2007 in North America and when it went on sale it quickly sold out. The production and sales of the iPhone continued to grow each year and it is now marketed and sold all around the world. The company releases a new model every year and every version has better performance and offers more features than the previous one. There is fierce competition from other smartphone manufacturers such as Samsung, Xiaomi, Oppo and Vivo.

Discussion points

- What stage of the product life cycle do you think the iPhone has reached?
- Why does Apple keep bringing out new versions of the iPhone?

Chapter review questions: Short answer and data response

1. ABC produces garden equipment such as grass mowers and diggers. It has good relationships with customers who provide feedback on the ABC products they buy. The Rovermower has been one of ABC's bestselling products. It can cut grass quicker than most competing products. The Rovermower has experienced a typical product life cycle. After an initial period of rapid sales growth, sales remained steady for several years but have now started to fall. It will cost over $0.5m to develop a replacement product which will cut grass robotically with no one controlling it. If well designed, the new product could help further strengthen the brand image of ABC's products being advanced and of high quality.
   a Define 'product life cycle'. [2]
   b Outline **two** stages of the product life cycle for the Rovermower. [4]
   c Explain **two** advantages to ABC of having a strong brand image for its products. [6]
   d Do you think ABC should develop a new product to replace the Rovermower or use an extension strategy? Justify your answer. [8]

2. XYZ produces popular chocolate bars and sells them to supermarkets. XYZ has many competitors. The business aims to develop and launch a new type of chocolate bar every 2 years. Its bestselling product is ChocDelight which has a strong brand image. It is wrapped in expensive packaging and is sold as a luxury chocolate product. This bestselling chocolate bar has had high and steady sales for the last 5 years. However, over the last 12 months sales of ChocDelight have started to fall. The Marketing Manager of XYZ thinks it has reached the decline stage of the product life cycle and she is planning an extension strategy for it.
   a Define 'brand image'. [2]
   b Outline **two** roles of packaging for chocolate bars. [4]
   c Explain **two** advantages to XYZ of developing new products. [6]
   d Explain **two** extension strategies XYZ could use. Which is the best one to choose? Justify your answer. [8]

Revision checklist

In this chapter you have learned:

- the four elements of the marketing mix
- the importance of brand image
- the role of packaging
- the advantages and disadvantages of developing new products
- the main stages of the product life cycle
- how to interpret a product life cycle diagram
- extension strategies a business could use and their advantages and disadvantages
- how to recommend and justify an extension strategy to use in a given situation.

NOW – test your understanding with the revision questions in the Student etextbook and the Workbook.

12 The marketing mix: price

This chapter will explain:

★ pricing methods
★ advantages and disadvantages of different pricing methods
★ how to recommend and justify an appropriate pricing method for a given situation.

Marketing mix – price

When deciding a price for either an existing product or a new product, a business must be very careful to choose a price which will fit in with the rest of the marketing mix for the product. If a new product is of high quality, aimed at consumers who have high incomes, is wrapped in luxurious packaging but has a low price, consumers will not think it is a good quality product and will not buy it. Some products are sold in very competitive markets and prices have to be set near to their competitors' prices. Other products may be the only ones available in their market and so consumers may be willing to pay a high price for one of these products. Whatever the market situation for a product, the pricing decision is important in determining whether it is successful or not.

Pricing methods

Cost-plus pricing

Cost-plus pricing calculates the cost of making or supplying the product plus the expected profit to be made from it.

This pricing method has four steps:

1 knowing how many units of the product will be produced
2 estimating the total costs of producing this number of units
3 calculating the average cost of producing each unit
4 adding a percentage mark-up for profit.

The formula used to calculate cost-plus price is given below.

> **Definitions to learn**
>
> **Cost-plus pricing** is the cost of manufacturing the product plus a profit mark-up.

Calculations to learn

$$\text{Cost-plus price} = \frac{\text{total cost}}{\text{output}} + \text{percentage mark-up}$$

Worked example

A business estimates it will produce 20 000 bars of chocolate each week.
The total cost of making 20 000 chocolate bars is $20 000.
The business wants to make 50% profit on each bar.
The cost-plus pricing calculation is as follows:

Cost-plus price $= \frac{\$20\,000}{20\,000} +$ percentage mark-up

$\phantom{\text{Cost-plus price }} = \$1 +$ percentage mark-up

Percentage mark-up $= 50\%$ of $\$1 = \$0.50$
Cost-plus price $= \$1 + \$0.50 = \$1.50$

> ### Activity 12.1
> Using the worked example above, calculate the cost-plus price for the following:
>
> a The business now wants to make a 100% profit mark-up on each unit.
> b Total costs of making 20 000 chocolate bars rises to $30 000 and the business wants to make a 50% profit mark-up.
> c Weekly output rises to 30 000 bars and total costs are $45 000. The business wants to make a 20% profit mark-up.

Table 12.1 explains the advantages and disadvantages of cost-plus pricing.

Table 12.1 Advantages and disadvantages of cost-plus pricing

Advantages of cost-plus pricing	Disadvantages of cost-plus pricing
When the output and cost information are available, it is an easy method to calculate	Total profit will only be made if sufficient units are actually sold
Different profit mark-ups can be used in different markets. This allows some flexibility of pricing to suit competitive conditions in the markets	The ability and willingness of consumers to pay a cost-plus price is not considered
Each product contributes to the profit of the business	There is no incentive to reduce costs as any increase in costs is passed on to consumers with higher prices
It is easy to explain to customers if they query the price	The price cannot be changed if market conditions change, for example, new competitors enter the market

> **Study tips**
>
> Remember that cost and price are different things. The price is what is paid for a product by the customer and the costs are payments to make the product.

Extend your skills of analysis

A question which asks for a disadvantage of cost-plus pricing to a hotel could be answered as follows:

Cost-plus pricing adds a mark-up to the unit cost of, in this case, hotel accommodation.

Extend your analysis by explaining why this could be a disadvantage.

When demand is low, for example, outside of the main holiday season, cost-plus pricing might set prices at a level which many consumers are not prepared to pay.

Extend your analysis by explaining how this will impact the hotel.

If many rooms are left empty at certain times of the year because cost-plus prices are too high, the hotel's total costs might not be paid for and a loss could be made.

12 THE MARKETING MIX: PRICE

Competitive pricing

Competitive pricing involves setting prices at the same level as the prices set by competitors for similar products. For example, a company wants to sell a brand of soap powder. It needs to sell it at a similar price to all the other brands available or consumers will buy the competitors' brands. The advantages and disadvantages of competitive pricing are explained in Table 12.2.

Table 12.2 Advantages and disadvantages of competitive pricing

Advantages of competitive pricing	Disadvantages of competitive pricing
By keeping prices close to those of competitors, sales and market share should be maintained	If some competitors have lower average costs, they will be able to charge low prices and remain profitable. Businesses with higher average costs are likely to make a loss by charging the same prices
It is easy to use as there are no calculations required, just a survey of competitors' prices	By keeping prices the same as competitors, there is no price advantage. Businesses will have to use other means of attracting more customers
Setting prices at the same level as competitors can avoid a price war which could lead to all businesses making a loss	If competitors' products have a better image, charging the same prices could lead to sales falling

> **Definitions to learn**
>
> **Competitive pricing** is when the product is priced in line with competitors' prices to try to maintain sales and market share.
>
> **Penetration pricing** is when the price is set lower than competitors' prices in order to be able to enter a new market and gain market share.

▲ Supermarkets often use competitive pricing as it is a very competitive industry

Penetration pricing

Penetration pricing means the price is set lower than competitors' prices in order to 'penetrate' the market. It is often used for newly launched products where the business aim is to build up market share quickly. If the product becomes popular and develops a good brand image, the price will slowly be increased. For example, a company launches a new chocolate bar at a price several cents below the prices of similar chocolate bars already on the market. If this is successful, consumers will try the new bar and become regular customers. Table 12.3 explains the advantages and disadvantages of penetration pricing.

Table 12.3 Advantages and disadvantages of penetration pricing

Advantages of penetration pricing	Disadvantages of penetration pricing
Often used for newly launched products as it can generate sales quickly and build up market share	The low price is likely to mean that profit per unit is low. In the short term at least, a loss could be made on each unit
If a business has low average costs, penetration pricing can still be profitable	Consumers might get used to this low price and stop buying it if the business tries to raise the price
Competitors may find it difficult to reduce their prices if they have higher average costs	A low penetration price might not create the quality brand image that the business is aiming for

Price skimming

Price skimming is often used when a product is newly developed or when there has been an adaptation of an existing product. The business may try to charge a high price for this product, at least initially. This is because a high price might be associated with high quality. In addition, there might have been high development costs for the new product and a high price will help to pay for those costs quickly.

For example, a new computer game is developed. It will be sold in shops at a very high price, much higher than the existing computer games. As it is new and has better graphics than older games, consumers will be willing to pay the high price. This way, the business will earn high profits which will make the research and development costs worthwhile. The price is likely to be reduced from this high level when competitors' develop and start to sell similar or better games. Table 12.4 explains the advantages and disadvantages of price skimming.

> **Definitions to learn**
>
> **Price skimming** is where a high price is set for a new product on the market.
> **Dynamic pricing** is when businesses change the price of a product, usually when selling online, depending on the level of demand.

> **Key info**
>
> Louis Vuitton is a manufacturer of highly fashionable clothing and luxury handbags. It usually adopts price skimming for newly launched product ranges and keeps prices high to give a high profit mark-up.

Table 12.4 Advantages and disadvantages of price skimming

Advantages of price skimming	Disadvantages of price skimming
High prices will lead to high profit on each unit sold	High prices may discourage some consumers from trying the new product. Sales might not reach the expected level
For quality products with a high prestige brand image, a high price will help to reinforce that image	If the product is not different enough from competitors' products, a high price will not achieve the level of sales needed to make a profit
If the costs of developing the new product were high, a skimming price will help to repay those costs quickly	High prices, which can lead to high profits, will encourage competitors to enter the market, launching similar products quickly

Dynamic pricing

Dynamic pricing is a flexible method of setting prices. Its aim is to maximise revenue from the available output or supply of a product. Instead of setting one price for a product, businesses vary the price according to the changing level of demand over time. Airlines regularly use dynamic pricing and charge different prices for flights to the same airport at different times of the day or different times of the year. For example, the price of flights to holiday resorts is much higher during school holidays than during term time.

12 THE MARKETING MIX: PRICE

▲ Dynamic pricing is used for the online sales of air tickets – if tickets for a flight are selling quickly, the price will be increased

Dynamic pricing is often used when products are sold online, to reflect rapid changes in the level of demand. If demand increases then the price will be raised, and at times of low demand the price will be reduced. For example, for American football games, ticket prices often change to reflect the increased demand for tickets to popular games, and when a game is less popular the price is reduced to encourage sales and fill the stadium seats. Hotels often reduce prices substantially for accommodation during the day when it is seen that not all rooms have been booked for that night.

There are ethical issues with some examples of dynamic pricing. Due to new technology, businesses can track the web browsing and buying history of customers and then charge higher prices for products if they have bought them or shown interest in them in the past. This is compared to other customers who are browsing a site for the first time. These customers are charged lower prices for the same product. Table 12.5 explains the advantages and disadvantages of dynamic pricing.

> **Study tips**
>
> Make sure you can select a suitable pricing method for particular products and explain why each is suitable.

Table 12.5 Advantages and disadvantages of dynamic pricing

Advantages of dynamic pricing	Disadvantages of dynamic pricing
By aiming to sell all of the available supply at different prices, revenue is maximised	Consumers may become confused and dissatisfied with constantly changing prices
Some consumers will be able to purchase products at low prices if they, for example, leave purchasing tickets until the last moment. This will increase customer satisfaction	Consumers who pay high prices for a product which is later sold at a lower price may refuse to buy from the business again
There should be no products left unsold so there are fewer costs of storage and wastage	Lowering prices immediately when a competitor lowers theirs could lead to a price war which reduces profits
Dynamic pricing means that rapid changes in price can be made in response to competitors' price decisions	Reducing prices in response to lower demand may mean consumers think the quality of the product has declined

Marketing mix – price

> ### Case study: Coca-Cola pricing
>
>
>
> The Coca-Cola Company manufactures thousands of beverages across more than 200 brands around the world, including waters, soft drinks, teas and coffees. These are sold using different pricing methods depending on the drink itself and the market in which it is sold. It usually sets it prices in line with competitors that produce similar drinks. However, there are times when Coca-Cola uses a lower price to those of competitors in order to increase its sales and its market share.
>
> Its innovation platform, Coca-Cola Creations, develops limited edition products in collaboration with artists, designers and musicians, many of which are designed to appeal to a young market. The products are designed to give consumers flavour experiences rather than have specific tastes. Each product has its own unique design packaging and a clear brand image. As the products are new, fashionable and different, the company can charge a high price for them.
>
> Sources: www.coca-colacompany.com/about-us; www.businesswire.com/news/home/20220218005093/en/Coca-Cola-Launches-Global-Innovation-Platform-Coca-Cola-Creations

Activity 12.2

Read the case study above.

Identify the different pricing methods that Coca-Cola uses and explain when it uses them.

Extend your skills of analysis

A question which asks for an advantage of dynamic pricing to the organiser of a music concert could be answered as follows:

Dynamic pricing is flexible pricing to respond to the strength of demand.

Extend your analysis by explaining how dynamic pricing could be used in this case.

When the tickets are first sold, the prices will be high as demand is expected to be high. As the date of the concert approaches, if some tickets are left unsold they could be offered at much lower prices until none are left.

Extend your analysis by explaining how this benefits the business.

By selling all tickets, revenue is maximised. Profit should therefore be higher than if some tickets were unsold because the business did not reduce prices.

12 THE MARKETING MIX: PRICE

REVISION SUMMARY — Pricing methods

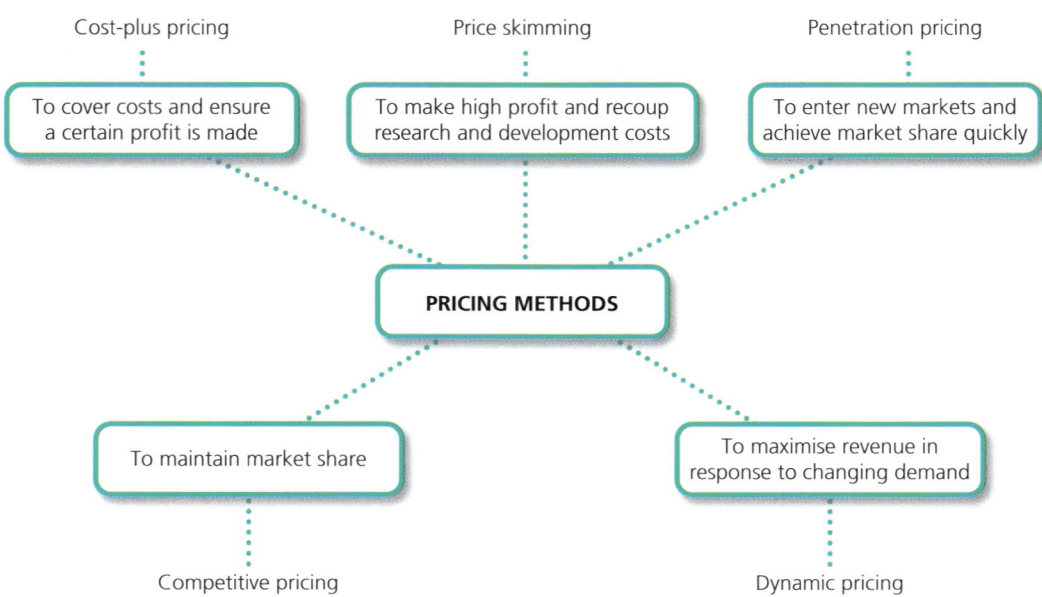

Activity 12.3

What pricing method would most probably be used for the following products? Explain your choice in each case.

a A watch that is very similar to other watches sold in shops.
b A new type of smartphone that has been developed and is a lot higher quality than existing smartphones.
c A shop, which sells food, wants to get its money back on buying the inventory and make an extra 75% as well.
d A new brand of soap powder is launched (there are already many similar brands available).
e A tour operator sells holidays for during the school holidays as well as for other times of the year.

Activity 12.4

Copy out the table and fill in the blank boxes.

Pricing method	Examples of situations when this method would be appropriate	Advantages	Disadvantages
Cost-plus pricing			
Competitive pricing			
Penetration pricing			
Price skimming			
Dynamic pricing			

How to recommend and justify an appropriate pricing method for a given situation

The most appropriate pricing method will depend on four main factors:

- **Business objective.** If the business aims to increase market share then competitive or penetration pricing might be chosen. If the aim is to establish a high-quality brand image then cost-plus with a high profit mark-up or price skimming would be more appropriate. If the business aims to maximise revenue by leaving no products unsold then dynamic pricing would be more effective.
- **Competitors' strength.** If other businesses in the market have a much higher market share then competitive pricing would be appropriate. The exception would be if the business could differentiate its product with a new design or an effective brand image. In this case cost-plus pricing could be more effective.
- **Whether the product is new or established.** A new product, with effective promotion, has a good chance of being noticed by consumers. A *high-quality* product is likely to be launched with price skimming and a *good value* product is likely to be launched with penetration pricing.
- **Product image and the other elements of the marketing mix.** The key message about the marketing mix (see page 172) is the need for consistency between the elements. The pricing method used must be consistent with the type and quality of product, the packaging used, the channel of distribution used and the methods of promotion used.

International business in focus

Big Mac prices

McDonald's is a multinational company with restaurants in 118 countries around the world. Every country has its own customs and cultures that McDonald's recognises and respects. Menu items vary from country to country, but the company's most famous product – the Big Mac – is available in most of its restaurants. (It is called Maharaja Mac in India and is not made from beef.)

When the prices it charges for the Big Mac in all of these countries are converted into US dollars there are some surprising results. Instead of charging the same price in all countries (US$ Big Mac price converted into local currencies), there are some wide variations in prices. At the time of writing, the price in the USA is US$5.69. The most expensive country is Switzerland with a price of US$8.07. In China it is US$3.57 and in India it is US$2.85.

Discussion points

- Why does McDonald's charge different prices in different countries for the same Big Mac product?
- Is the price of the Big Mac (or Maharaja Mac) in your own country higher or lower than the US price? Why do you think there is a difference? (You will have to find out your currency's US$ exchange rate.)

12 THE MARKETING MIX: PRICE

Chapter review questions: Short answer and data response

1. A&B produces a well-known branded breakfast cereal called Oatz which has a reputation for good quality. The cost of producing each box of Oatz is $1.00. The cereal is sold in shops at a price of $2.00 per box. The prices of competitors' cereals range from $1.20 to $2.00 a box. The Marketing Manager says: 'We should change to a more competitive pricing method to increase sales.' The Managing Director thinks that the high price for Oatz helps support its good brand image. A large supermarket has just launched its own brand of breakfast cereal and this is currently sold using penetration pricing.
   a. Define 'penetration pricing'. [2]
   b. Outline **two** reasons why the supermarket did not use price skimming. [4]
   c. Explain **two** factors A&B should take into account when deciding which pricing method to use. [6]
   d. Do you think changing to a competitive pricing method for Oatz is a good idea? Justify your answer. [8]

2. X&Z has recently designed a new game for the Microsoft Xbox, a games console. People in many different countries have been waiting for this new game. Some consumers are willing to pay a high price to be among the first to play the game. 'The business can get back some of the development costs of the new game by using price skimming,' says the Marketing Manager. X&Z has a product range of 20 games, some of which were developed several years ago.
   a. Define 'price skimming'. [2]
   b. Outline **two** reasons why X&Z did not use penetration pricing for its new game. [4]
   c. Explain **two** advantages to X&Z of using price skimming for its new game. [6]
   d. Do you think X&Z should use dynamic pricing to sell its games? Justify your answer. [8]

Revision checklist

In this chapter you have learned:

- ✔ different pricing methods a business can use
- ✔ the advantages and disadvantages of the different pricing methods
- ✔ how to recommend and justify a suitable pricing method for a given situation.

NOW – test your understanding with the revision questions in the Student etextbook and the Workbook.

13 The marketing mix: place

This chapter will explain:
★ different distribution channels
★ advantages and disadvantages of different distribution channels
★ how to recommend and justify an appropriate distribution channel for a given situation.

Marketing mix – place

Products – goods and services – must be available where and when customers want to buy them. How and where customers can buy a product will affect how well it will sell. Think of a local convenience store. Would high-priced luxury chocolates sell well there? If many of the customers who use the shop are on low incomes then not many highly priced chocolates will be sold. If a product is not available to customers in a convenient location then they may give up searching for it and buy a competitor's product. It is very easy for a business to get the place wrong and therefore lose sales.

Different distribution channels

> **Definitions to learn**
>
> A **distribution channel** is the means by which a product is passed from the producer to the customer.

Businesses must decide whether to sell directly to customers or use other businesses to do this. The most appropriate **distribution channel** will depend greatly on the nature of the product and where customers live.

There are several different distribution channels that businesses can use. The diagram below summarises them.

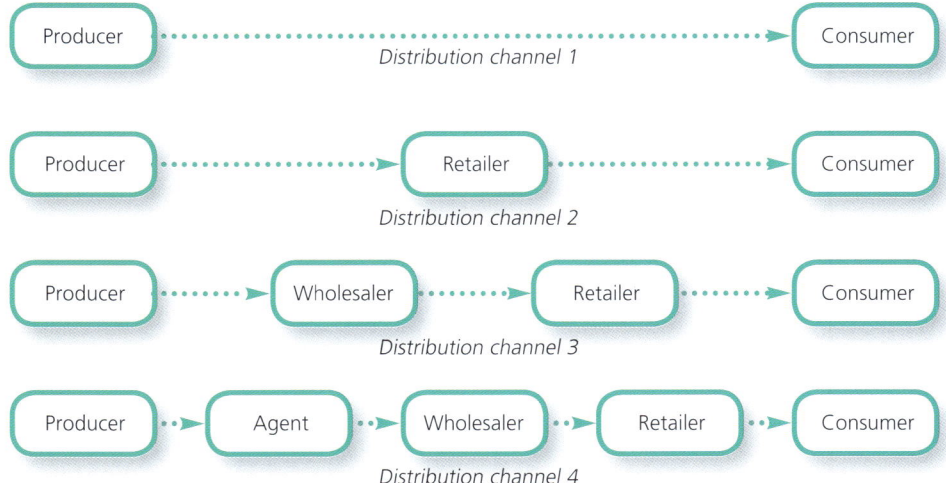

▲ The main distribution channels

13 THE MARKETING MIX: PLACE

Selling direct to customers (Distribution channel 1)

This is called a direct channel of distribution and means manufacturers sell to customers with no intermediary, such as by online selling. This channel is commonly used when selling directly from one manufacturer to another manufacturer. For example, car components are sold directly to the car producer. The advantages and disadvantages of direct selling are explained in Table 13.1.

Table 13.1 Advantages and disadvantages of selling direct to customers

Advantages of selling direct to customers	Disadvantages of selling direct to customers
This distribution channel is direct and low cost. It can be undertaken by mail order, factory shops or manufacturers' websites	It may be impractical for factory shops to sell effectively because most customers probably do not live near to the factory and could not go there to buy the products
It is suitable for products, such as certain types of fresh food products, which are sometimes sold straight from the farm	This method may not be suitable for products which cannot easily be delivered by mail (post) or courier
All the profit is earned by the manufacturer	Delivery by mail (post) or courier can add considerably to the price paid by customers
The manufacturer has full control over how its product is sold and promoted	It is less convenient for customers who want to see or try on a range of products in a retail shop before buying

Selling through retailers (Distribution channel 2)

With this channel the producer sells to retail outlets and then they sell the product to the customer. This is most common where the **retailer** is a big business, such as a supermarket chain of shops, or when the products are highly priced, such as furniture or jewellery. With this distribution channel the retailer is the only intermediary. The advantages and disadvantages of the retailer-only distribution channel are explained in Table 13.2.

Table 13.2 Advantages and disadvantages of retailer-only channel of distribution

Advantages of selling through retailers	Disadvantages of selling through retailers
The producer sells large quantities to retailers, rather than individual items to each customer. This reduces the administration and delivery costs	There is no direct contact between the manufacturer and the customers, which could have provided useful feedback about the products
The producer can focus on manufacturing the product or supplying the service. The marketing, display and pricing are the responsibility of the retailer	The price paid by the customer is often higher than direct selling as the retailer has to cover its costs and make a profit
Customers have more choice of products than if they just buy from a single producer as products from several manufacturers are usually available	The manufacturer will make a lower profit per unit as it will sell to retailers at a lower price than to consumers

Selling through wholesalers (Distribution channel 3)

This distribution channel involves using a **wholesaler** that performs the function of breaking bulk.

Breaking bulk is where wholesalers buy products from manufacturers in large quantities. They then divide these up into much smaller quantities for small retailers to buy. The wholesaler often provides transport to the retailer and may

> **Key info**
>
> There are about 13 million traditional retail stores in India, most of which are small stores. However, the Indian retail market is predicted to see significant growth due to the many developments across its major cities, including Delhi-NCR, Chennai, Bengaluru and Hyderabad.

> **Definitions to learn**
>
> A **retailer** is a business that sells products to customers in relatively small quantities.
> A **wholesaler** is a business that buys in bulk from a manufacturer and then sells to retailers in smaller quantities.

Marketing mix – place

also allow payment on credit from retailers. The advantages and disadvantages of the wholesaler to retailer distribution channel are explained in Table 13.3.

Table 13.3 Advantages and disadvantages of wholesaler to retailer distribution channel

Advantages of selling through wholesalers	Disadvantages of selling through wholesalers
Wholesaler holds most of the inventory so manufacturers gain from reducing the storage space they need and cutting storage costs	It is often more expensive for retailers to buy from wholesalers than directly from the producer
Wholesalers usually hold products from a number of producers and this increases the range of goods available to retailers and, eventually, customers	A second intermediary increases the ordering/buying process in the distribution channel and adds to costs
Buying frequent small quantities from wholesalers allows retailers to maintain the freshness of food products, especially perishable products. This will benefit consumers as well	The customer price is often higher than direct selling as both the wholesaler and retailer have to cover costs and make a profit
Manufacturers have fewer orders to process and fewer delivery journeys to make	Manufacturers lose control over the selling process as wholesalers will decide which retailers to supply and what prices they must pay

▶ Without a wholesaler, a manufacturer has to process many orders from retailers and deliver to them

▶ With a wholesaler, a manufacturer has fewer orders to process and makes fewer delivery journeys

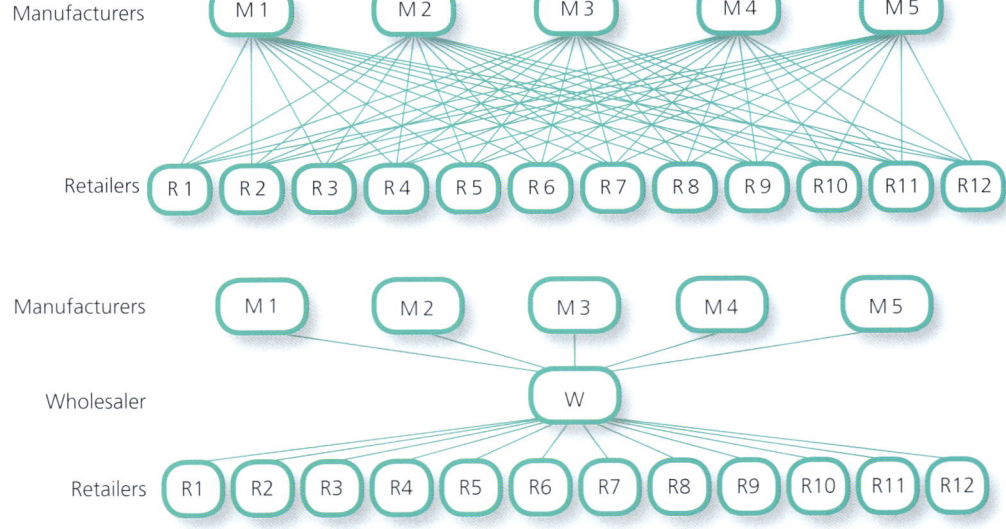

Definitions to learn

An **agent** is an independent person or business that is appointed to deal with the sales and distribution of a product or range of products.

Selling through agents (Distribution channel 4)

When products are exported, the manufacturer sometimes uses an **agent** in the other country. The agent sells the products on behalf of the manufacturer. This can allow the manufacturer to have some control over the way the product is sold to customers. The agent will either put an additional amount on the price to cover their expenses or will receive a commission on sales. The agent may also act as the wholesaler. The advantages and disadvantages of using an agent in the distribution channel are explained in Table 13.4.

13 THE MARKETING MIX: PLACE

Table 13.4 Advantages and disadvantages of using an agent in the distribution channel

Advantages of selling through agents	Disadvantages of selling through agents
All distribution functions are undertaken by the agent, not the producer	The producer has less control over the way the product is marketed and distributed to customers
The agent often has specialist, local knowledge and this should help to make the marketing of the products successful, especially in other countries	Agents will have less detailed knowledge of the producer's goods than the producer itself. Incorrect information could be given to customers
The producer will be able to reduce the number of its own sales employees	Agents' fees and commission may increase the final price paid by customers

Case study: Unilever (Malaysia) Holdings

Unilever (Malaysia) Holdings Sdn Bhd manufactures ice cream and sorbets. It is located in Malaysia.

It is famous for its quality ice cream and sorbets. The company sells ice cream and sorbets directly to local shops because they sell to tourists. Unilever (Malaysia) Holdings Sdn Bhd also sells its ice cream to wholesalers that sell to small shops in other towns and cities. Very large retailers, for example, supermarkets, buy the ice cream and sorbets in bulk and purchase it directly from Unilever (Malaysia) Holdings Sdn Bhd. A variety of channels of distribution are used by the company, depending on the customer and the quantity of ice cream and sorbets purchased.

Activity 13.1

Read the case study above.

Why does Unilever (Malaysia) Holdings Sdn Bhd use several different channels of distribution in Malaysia?

Key info

With total global sales of US$643 billion in 2024, Walmart is the world's biggest retailer. A typical Walmart superstore has 142 000 different product ranges. Compare that with your local convenience store!

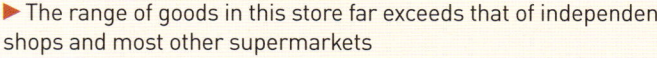 The range of goods in this store far exceeds that of independent shops and most other supermarkets

Study tips

Make sure you can develop an explanation of the advantages and disadvantages of each channel of distribution and not just list them.

Activity 13.2

Choose **six** different products that you or your family buy and find out which distribution channels are used to get the products from the manufacturer to you, the customer.

Are the distribution channels used the ones you would expect? Explain your answer.

Case study: Distribution channels for children's toys

You have been asked by a manufacturer of children's toys whether it should use a wholesaler to sell its products. It originally manufactured just a few different types of toys and sold them to a few large retailers. It has expanded and is now selling many different types of toys to many small retailers.

Marketing mix – place

> ### Activity 13.3
> Read the second case study on the previous page.
>
> Write to the company advising it why you think it might be an advantage to use a wholesaler. It needs persuading that a wholesaler will be beneficial, so give a detailed explanation and examples to support your point of view.

Extend your skills of analysis

A question which asks for an advantage to a clothing manufacturer of selling to retailers and not selling directly through its own factory shop could be answered as follows:

A retailer is a business that sells products to customers in relatively small quantities.

Extend your analysis by explaining why selling through retailers is an advantage.

By selling through retailers, the clothing manufacturer might have much higher sales as the number of customers able to visit the factory shop might be very limited.

Extend your analysis by explaining how this benefits the business.

By selling to retailers, more consumers will be able to see and try on the clothes than could visit a factory shop. This is likely to increase sales and income for the clothing manufacturer. If the cost of transport to retailers is not too high, this extra revenue (income) should increase the manufacturer's profit.

How to recommend and justify an appropriate distribution channel for a given situation

When deciding which distribution channel to use, the Marketing Manager of the producing business has to answer a number of questions. This will help them decide which channel will be the most appropriate for the products. These are the questions that the Marketing Manager must consider:

» **What type of product is it?** Is it sold to other businesses (business-to-business, or B2B) or to customers (business-to-customer, or B2C)? If it is sold to other businesses, for example, robots for factories, then direct selling is much more likely to be used than for most customer products.
» **Is the product very technical?** If it is, it should be sold to the customer by someone with technical knowledge who can explain how it works and what it is capable of doing. Direct selling from the producer may be used, for example, with an aircraft engine. Technical customer products could use a specialist retailer which sources the products, and relevant product training, from the manufacturer.
» **How often is the product purchased?** If it is a product bought every day, it will need to be sold in many retail outlets across the country. An example would be a product like bread or newspapers which are often purchased daily. Producers would be likely to sell to wholesalers which will arrange frequent deliveries to retail outlets.
» **What image would the business like the product to have?** Does it have a quality image which is supported by high prices? If the product is marketed as being exclusive and of high quality, such as an expensive watch, it might only be sold through well-located and well-furnished retail outlets in upmarket shopping malls. These outlets could purchase directly from the manufacturer.
» **How perishable is the product?** If the product goes rotten quickly, such as fruit or meat, then it will need to be distributed from the farms to the customers quickly. Direct selling can be used or large quantities sold and delivered quickly to big supermarket retailers.

13 THE MARKETING MIX: PLACE

» **Where are the customers located?** If most of the customers are in export markets in other countries, then agents with local knowledge could be used by the producer to manage the distribution channel in each country. The internet might also be used for online trading if the product can be mailed (posted) or sent by courier.

» **Why use just one channel of distribution?** To gain the widest possible market coverage, some producers will use more than one channel of distribution. Each channel used may attract different types of customers. A car manufacturer may use its own direct sales team when selling a fleet of cars to a car hire business. Selling individual cars to customers may be through a car retailing business which will hold inventories of several models.

» **Where do competitors sell their products?** The distribution channels that competitors use will need to be considered. If customers expect products to be available in retail shops, then selling direct to them may not be effective. However, if the lower cost of selling directly is passed on to customers with lower prices, this might encourage them to switch from retail shops for some products.

Study tips

Make sure you can select and justify a suitable distribution channel for a particular business or its products.

Activity 13.4

Choose an appropriate distribution channel for each of the following products. Explain your choice in each case.

a Farm tractor
b Children's clothes for export
c Tins of peas
d Made-to-measure suits

REVISION SUMMARY Factors affecting choice of distribution channels

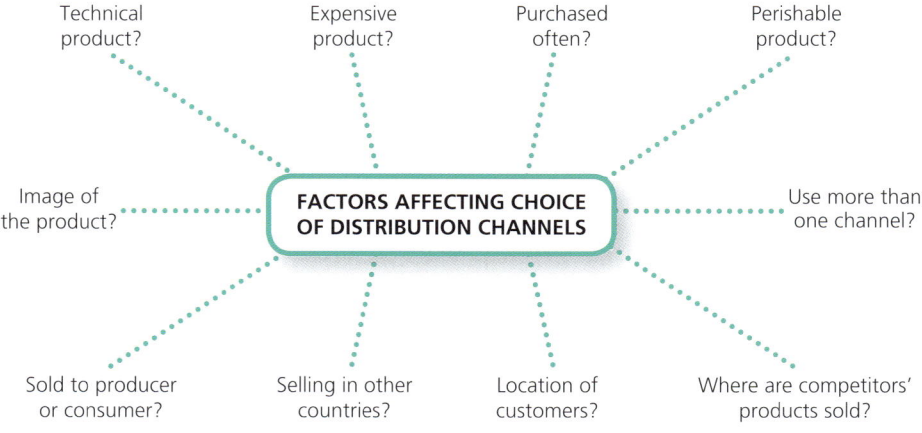

Marketing mix – place

International business in focus

Apple distribution

Less than half of Apple sales are through its own stores. In 2023 only 37% of sales were made this way. Apple has stores in major cities across the world, including New York, London, Tokyo, Beijing, Rome, Sydney, Rio de Janeiro, Mumbai and Dubai. Apple stores aim to display the products themselves and provide technical advice and support to customers. The rest of Apple's sales in 2023, 63%, were from authorised distributors including mobile phone network providers, wholesalers and retailers.

Discussion points

- What are the advantages and disadvantages of Apple having its own stores?
- Why are most of Apple's sales through other distribution channels other than its own stores?

Chapter review questions: Short answer and data response

1 D&D manufactures footballs in Country Y. The footballs are sold in sports shops in Country Y and around the world. The distribution channel D&D uses to sell its footballs in Country Y is through wholesalers to retailers. When selling to other countries, local agents are used. The Managing Director of D&D wants the company to start selling footballs online but the Marketing Director thinks there are too many problems with this distribution channel.
   a Define 'distribution channel'. [2]
   b Outline **two** reasons why 'place' is an important part of the marketing mix for D&D. [4]
   c Explain **two** possible advantages to D&D of selling footballs through agents in other countries. [6]
   d Do you think D&D would be better selling directly to retailers rather than through wholesalers in Country Y? Justify your answer. [8]

2 Pinkor manufactures childrens' clothes. It distributes these through wholesalers. These businesses then sell the clothes to retailers, including specialist childrens' clothes shops. Pinkor's senior managers are worried about falling sales and profit. One manager said, 'If we sold directly to consumers we could sell our products at lower prices than retailers charge and still make a profit.'
   a Define 'wholesaler'. [2]
   b Outline **two** advantages to Pinkor of using wholesalers. [4]
   c Explain **one** advantage and **one** disadvantage to Pinkor of its clothes being sold to consumers through specialist childrens' clothes retailers. [6]
   d Do you think Pinkor should start to sell its products directly to consumers? Justify your answer. [8]

Revision checklist

In this chapter you have learned:

- ✔ different distribution channels between producer and consumer
- ✔ the advantages and disadvantages of different distribution channels
- ✔ how to recommend and justify an appropriate distribution channel for a given situation.

NOW – test your understanding with the revision questions in the Student etextbook and the Workbook

14 The marketing mix: promotion

This chapter will explain:
★ reasons for promotion
★ methods of sales promotion
★ methods of advertising
★ how to recommend and justify which sales promotion to use in a given situation
★ how to recommend and justify which method of advertising to use in a given situation.

Marketing mix – promotion

Promotion gives the consumer information about the rest of the marketing mix – without it, consumers would not know about the product, the price it sells for or the place where the product is sold. Promotion is also important in creating a brand image, especially for consumer goods.

It is often thought that promotion is just about advertising the product but it includes sales promotion, or incentives to buy, as well as advertising.

Promotion as part of the marketing mix refers to the following activities:

» **Sales promotions.** These are often used for short periods of time in order to reinforce the message given out by advertisements. They provide incentives for customers to buy the product. Examples include vouchers, reward schemes, competitions and special offers/discounts.
» **Advertisements.** These are messages to customers or potential customers. They can take different forms, such as social media, direct/targeted emails, leaflets and billboards.

Definitions to learn

Promotion refers to the marketing activities of advertising and sales promotion which aim to raise customer awareness of a product or brand, generate sales and help create brand loyalty.

Reasons for promotion

The overall objective – or reason – of promotion is to increase sales of a product. This is done by raising awareness of the product and encouraging consumers to make a purchase or to buy more of it. The specific reasons of promotion are summarised in the diagram below.

Marketing mix – promotion

Methods of sales promotion

Definitions to learn

Sales promotions are incentives such as special offers or reward schemes aimed at consumers to achieve short-term increases in sales.

Sales promotion is used to support advertising and encourage new or existing consumers to buy the product. It is used in the short term to give a boost to sales, but it is not usually used over long periods of time as its impact on consumers usually declines over time. An example of the use of sales promotion is when a new chocolate bar has been introduced onto the market and is being advertised on billboards. In the shops where the chocolate bars are to be sold, vouchers may be given out to encourage customers to try the new chocolate bar and, if they like it, to become regular buyers.

The aims of sales promotion are to:

» boost sales at times of year when sales are often low
» encourage new customers to try a product
» encourage existing customers to buy more
» increase brand loyalty.

Study tips

Make sure you can select a suitable sales promotion for particular products and explain why it is suitable.

There are several different sales promotion methods that can be used by businesses. The advantages and disadvantages of each method are explained in Table 14.1.

Table 14.1 Advantages and disadvantages of methods of sales promotion

Sales promotion method	Advantages	Disadvantages
Vouchers 	• They increase consumer interest in products as they give them a 'certificate' to buy a product at a discount or even to obtain a free sample • They may help to create sales from consumers who have not tried the product before • They raise awareness of the product and the brand • These factors can lead to increased brand loyalty in future	• They may damage a product's exclusive or luxury image as consumers ask 'Why is the business having to use vouchers to increase sales?' • Profit margin will be lower – will increased sales make up for this? • Consumers may delay buying until the next voucher becomes available and this could make inventory control difficult • The system is open to fraudulent use which would increase costs to the business
Reward schemes – such as customer loyalty cards 	• By offering consumer benefits through a reward programme, customer loyalty is increased and customers keep coming back to make purchases. Sales may be maintained or even increase • New consumers may be attracted to a brand or retail outlet just because of the reward scheme offered • Consumers have to provide information about themselves to register for a reward scheme and this provides much market research data to the business about its customers	• Consumers may belong to many reward schemes, mainly basing buying decisions on the most attractive one. Keeping a reward scheme competitive is therefore essential and costly • An effective IT system may have to be purchased to manage customer rewards and maintain close communication with consumers • If the reward scheme proves to be too costly and is withdrawn, many customers will switch away from the brand/business
Competitions 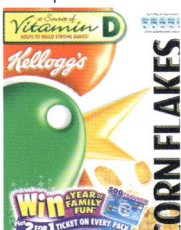	• A competition to attract consumers towards a product can receive good media attention if it is imaginative with original or exceptional prizes • Competitions can raise brand awareness and, if offered through social media, are likely to create viral promotion	• Competitions have to be well costed so that the overall impact of them is to increase profits for the business • Sales could slump after the competition ends if many consumers were attracted to buy only for the competition. Future sales will depend on value of the product to consumers, not on competitions. It is only a short-term boost to sales

14 THE MARKETING MIX: PROMOTION

Sales promotion method	Advantages	Disadvantages
Special offers – such as price discounts and 'buy-one-get-one-free' (BOGOF) 	• A lower price is likely to encourage consumers to try the product for the first time and may develop brand loyalty • They could also encourage existing consumers to purchase more/increase the number of customers • They may improve the image of the brand as being 'good value' • Shops can use special offers to reduce inventories, for example, of goods nearing sell by dates/out of fashion/end of season	• Profit margin per unit sold is reduced – will higher sales make up for this? • Consumers might buy more in the short term to add to their stock of the product but they then need to buy less in future • Consumers may be unwilling to pay the full price in future so overall sales may not increase • They may damage a product's exclusive or luxury image as consumers ask 'Why is this being sold more cheaply?'

> **Extend your skills of analysis**
>
> A question which asks for a disadvantage of vouchers as a sales promotion for an expensive watch brand could be answered as follows:
>
> Vouchers offer a reduction in price for the watch.
>
> **Extend your analysis by explaining why they could be inappropriate in this situation.**
>
> Vouchers are not usually well targeted at specific groups of consumers and they do not create a very high-brand image.
>
> **Extend your analysis by explaining why this is a disadvantage to the business in this situation.**
>
> By apparently promoting the watch brand to the general public with vouchers, an exclusive brand image for the watch is not being created. High-income consumers may not want to be seen wearing these watches and as a result sales will be low.

Activity 14.1

Choose **five** products which you and your friends buy regularly. Collect examples of sales promotions that have been used for these products and explain why these methods of promotion were used.

Activity 14.2

For each of the following five products, decide the best method of sales promotion to use. Explain your choice in each case.

a A new magazine aimed at teenage boys.
b A new type of pen which is very comfortable to use and does not smudge.
c A company making a famous brand of football boots wants to expand sales.
d A new fast-food takeaway opens in a small town.
e A soft toy has been invented that changes colour when hugged and can be dressed in different clothes which also change colour when warmed.

Case study: McDonald's Monopoly promotion

The use of the Monopoly game by McDonald's restaurants as a form of promotion, turning peeling stickers into a high-stakes game, has been one of the most successful sales promotions of all time. There were millions of prizes won, from free food to a top prize of $100 000 in some countries. During the period of the promotion, McDonald's sales increased and some analysts believe that much of this growth was due to the Monopoly promotion.

Activity 14.3

Read the case study above.

Why do you think this method of sales promotion was effective? Explain your answer.

Marketing mix – promotion

Methods of advertising

> **Definitions to learn**
>
> **Advertising** is a paid-for communication with potential customers about a product to encourage them to buy it.

Advertising can be either informative or persuasive. Informative advertising provides information about the product, such as its design, features, price and benefits it has compared with competitors' products. Persuasive advertising focuses more on creating an image for the product that customers will want to identify with by buying the product.

The aims of advertising are to:

» inform potential consumers of a new product
» remind consumers of a brand's existence and key features
» support a new sales promotion campaign
» help build brand image
» increase brand loyalty.

Table 14.2 shows the main advertising methods that businesses can use. It also explains the advantages and disadvantages of each method.

Table 14.2 Advantages and disadvantages of main methods of advertising

Advertising method	Advantages	Disadvantages
Social media 	• It can be directed at a huge population of social media users – 5 billion globally • The average age of social media users is lower than average age of population • It allows two-way communication with social media users, which can encourage them to buy the product • It can lead to an increase in visits to the business advertiser's website • Popular advertisements can go viral which greatly increases number of views • It has less impact on the environment than printed forms of advertising • The business can respond quickly to market changes and information can be updated quickly • It can be cheap if just placing adverts and not using social media marketing specialists • It can be used to target groups that are difficult to reach in other ways	• Using this method means advertisers have to invest resources and time in constant communications with social media users • There is always a danger of negative feedback about the advertisement or the product, which can go viral • It can be very difficult for social media advertisements to stand out from the many thousands which are posted each day • Adverts can become annoying which may put off potential customers from making a purchase • It can be expensive if using pop-ups • Some potential customers may not use social media and so will not see the advert
Direct/targeted emails 	• Emails advertising products are sent to selected subscribers so they are targeted at potential customers • It is cost effective – no printing, advertising fees or media costs • It helps to establish customer relationships which can lead to higher sales and long-term customer loyalty • Adverts can be shared and they could go viral • There is less impact on the environment than printed forms of advertising	• Commercial emails irritate many consumers. If the email messages are not targeted correctly, the recipients may delete emails or unsubscribe • Emails might not be delivered or, if key spam words are used, they could be directed to 'junk' and not be viewed at all • Emails with many images may take too long to download and this risks annoying potential consumers • Resources and time are needed to develop effective emails

14 THE MARKETING MIX: PROMOTION

Advertising method	Advantages	Disadvantages
Leaflets 	• They are a low-cost method of advertising relative to other methods such as television • They can be given out in the street to a wide range of people • Direct mail leaflets could be delivered door-to-door or mailed to a large number of people • Sometimes they contain a money-off voucher to encourage the reader to keep the advert • The adverts are printed and can be kept by consumers for future reference	• They may not be read • Direct mail, also called 'junk mail', can be annoying and put customers off buying the product • They can be viewed as being bad for the environment as so much paper is used in a big leaflet campaign and ends up as garbage
Billboards 	• They are displayed for long periods of time • They have a relatively low cost • They are potentially seen by everyone who passes them. They are able to use large, eye-catching images	• Adverts can easily be missed as people go past them • No detailed information can be included in the advert as people, especially drivers, will not have time to read it
Television 	• The advert could be seen by millions of people • The product can be shown in a very favourable way, making it look attractive • It can reach a specific target by advertising when the programmes the potential buyers are likely to watch are being shown • An advert can appear on sales channels which allows the product to be shown off to its best features. It can use persuasive advertising and will be much longer than normal TV adverts	• It can be a high-cost form of advertising – both preparing the advertisement and paying for TV time • Young people are increasingly downloading films and music and may not watch many television programmes • No printed material about the product is provided
Newspapers (national or local) 	• Printed advertisements can be kept by consumers for future reference • National newspapers are often bought by particular consumer groups, which makes them useful for advertising products to these groups • Local newspapers cost much less to advertise in than national papers. The advertisements can be directed at one region or area • A lot of product information can be put in the advertisement	• Newspaper adverts are often only in black and white and are therefore not very eye-catching. They are not as attention-grabbing as television adverts and may not be noticed by the reader, especially if the advert is small • Many people, especially younger age groups, access news online instead of buying traditional newspapers and these sources may not contain advertising

Marketing mix – promotion

Key info

Total global expenditure by businesses on advertising in 2024 was estimated to be US$1 trillion. Around 59% of this was spent on digital advertising, 23% on TV advertising and 6% on printed media.

Extend your skills of analysis

A question which asks for an advantage of social media advertising for a new sports shoe could be answered as follows:

Social media advertising uses YouTube, Facebook and other platforms to display information and images about a product.

Extend your analysis by explaining how this helps to promote a sports shoe.

Creative and appealing content, perhaps using a well-known sports star, can generate attention and develop brand image for a new sports shoe.

Extend your analysis by explaining why this is an advantage for the business.

Many sports shoes are bought by younger consumers and they use social media extensively. If they share the advert and it goes viral this can be a quicker way for many potential customers to see the advert. It can be a cost-effective way of increasing sales of sports shoes to the target market.

Case study: Advertising financial services

ING is a global company of Dutch origin, offering banking, investments, life insurance and retirement services. As it is a large international business it can afford a large marketing budget. It uses advertising on the internet, television and billboards.

Study tips

Make sure you can select suitable types of advertising for particular products and explain why they are suitable.

Activity 14.4

Read the case study above.

Do you think ING's current methods of advertising are the best methods to use or should it change them? Explain your answer.

Activity 14.5

a Choose **five** products which you and your friends buy regularly. Collect examples of the advertising for them and write down where the products are advertised. Copy out the table below and fill in the blanks when you have all your examples.

Product	Social media	Direct/targeted emails	Leaflets	Billboards	Television

b What can you observe from your completed table?
c Do the places where the adverts are found suggest a particular target audience for the products?
d Is the target population a very large number of people or a relatively small number of people?
e Do the places suggest the product is only sold locally or also nationally?
f Are these findings what you expected? Explain your answer.

14 THE MARKETING MIX: PROMOTION

Study tips

Remember that advertising does not necessarily increase sales and profits. A lot of money can be spent on advertising that is not effective. Advertising may increase sales, but if the costs of advertising are high then profit might not increase.

> ### Activity 14.6
>
> For each of the following products, decide on the best method of advertising to use. Explain your choice in each case.
>
> a Nike, which produces an established brand of sports shoes that is sold to teenagers as a leisure shoe, wants to become more competitive with rival companies. This product is sold in many areas of the country.
> b A new bicycle has been produced which is suitable for using over rough ground and for cycling up mountains.
> c A new computer game has been developed.
> d A new restaurant has opened in a small town.
> e A famous brand of carbonated soft drink wants to expand its sales.
> f A local town is holding a festival.

How to recommend and justify which method of sales promotion to use in a given situation

The range of sales promotion methods available to a Marketing Manager is very large. How do they select the most appropriate methods for the products of their business? Below are some of the most important factors that a Marketing Manager must consider before deciding on the most appropriate methods.

» **Cost.** The cost of sales promotion must be compared with the size of the financial budget available for promotion. If the cost takes a very high proportion of the finance available, the sales promotion method might need to be changed.
» **Expected revenue gain.** The aim of sales promotion must be, in the long term, to increase revenue from sales of the product. The key question is: will the return from the promotion be greater than its cost? Market research can be used to forecast the likely consumer reaction to any new sales promotion.
» **The stage of the product life cycle.** The stage of the product life cycle a product is at will influence whether sales promotions are used and which methods are used. Sales promotions could focus on vouchers to encourage consumers to try a new product in the introduction stage. In the decline stage of a product, sales promotions might be focused on special offers to try to sell the remaining products.
» **The nature of the product.** If the product is a producer good, the methods of sales promotion would be quite different to the methods used with consumer goods. For example, money-off coupons would not be suitable but discounts when goods are purchased in bulk would be appropriate. Businesses would not be influenced by collecting money-off coupons, but they will buy in large quantities and will be influenced by a discount.
» **Target market.** The average age and income level of the consumers targeted by a product have an important impact on sales promotion methods. Competitions that offer activity holidays could appeal to a younger age range. Some sales promotion methods might be viewed as 'cheapening' the product for high-income earners, so care needs to be taken. However, providing free trials of expensive cars to targeted high-income consumers would still be seen as an exclusive offering.

- **Brand image.** Sales promotion for a low-priced value brand of breakfast cereal might aim to encourage consumers away from competitors' brands, so vouchers or special offers would be appropriate. These methods would be unsuitable for exclusive jewellery aimed at the highest income consumers. Hopefully, you can begin to understand why!

How to recommend and justify which method of advertising to use in a given situation

Below are some of the most important factors that a Marketing Manager must consider before deciding on the most appropriate methods of advertising.

- **Cost.** The cost of any advertising must be compared with the size of the financial budget available for promotion. A small business would be most unlikely to have the resources for a nationwide TV advertising campaign. Advertisements focused on social media might be within budget and if the business only has a local market then social media might still be suitable as it can still be a low cost way of advertising. Using billboards in just the local area might be the most cost effective method.
- **Expected increase in revenue.** As with sales promotion, the aim of advertising must be, in the long term, to increase revenue from sales of the product. This is often difficult to forecast. The success, or failure, of previous advertisements would help to make sales forecasts for future advertising campaigns. With past results available, the business should be able to focus its advertising on those products for which the demand responds most to an increase in advertising.
- **Stage of the product life cycle.** Advertising at the introduction stage is likely to focus on informing potential customers about the new product and its features. Social media might be most effective if the new product is aimed at younger consumers. Later stages of the product life cycle might need advertising to combat the entry of competing products or to tell consumers about product life cycle extension strategies. Targeted emails to customers who have purchased the product in the past might be most effective.
- **Nature of the product.** A product sold to other businesses, for example, a machine to package perfume bottles, will not be advertised using the same methods as the perfume itself, which will be bought by consumers. The advertising for the machine could use targeted emails or leaflets to Operations Managers. Advertising the perfume to consumers will be persuasive and may use billboards and social media.
- **Target market.** The average age and income level of the consumers targeted by a product have an important impact on advertising methods. If a product is targeted at the youth market then social media is likely to be the most effective advertising method. Products aimed at top income earners could be advertised using selective and targeted emails using information already gathered about these consumers.
- **Brand image.** Advertisements can have a big impact on the brand image created for a product. The image a business wants to create for a new product will be influenced by the advertising methods used. A regularly purchased food product with a low-priced value brand, such as a breakfast cereal, could be advertised effectively on billboards or leaflets which are not targeted at particular consumer groups.

14 THE MARKETING MIX: PROMOTION

REVISION SUMMARY — Methods of promotion

International business in focus

Ed Sheeran

Ed Sheeran is a British singer and songwriter. He started writing his own songs and releasing them on his own record label in 2005. He became more well known and signed for a main record label in 2011. Ed's first hit single sold almost 58 000 copies in the week it was released and it became a top ten hit in eight countries. Tickets for his world tours often sell out very quickly.

Discussion points

- Discuss the best way for the dates of his concerts to be advertised.
- Choose another singer or group and consider what methods of advertising could be used to promote them and their music.

Chapter review questions: Short answer and data response

1. TP manufactures high-quality, exclusively designed shoes for women. It sells these shoes through its own retail stores. 'Advertising and sales promotion have been important to help us develop our well-known brand image,' the Marketing Director said. TP's Directors want to reduce costs to try to improve profitability. One Director thinks that as TP is a well-known business, spending on expensive methods of advertising is a waste of money.
   a Define 'sales promotion'. [2]
   b Outline **two** methods of sales promotion that TP could use. [4]
   c Explain **two** possible reasons for advertising the existing styles of shoes. [6]
   d Do you think advertising is needed for TP's range of products? Justify your answer. [8]

2. FK manufactures drinking glasses. Customers pay FK to put their own designs or messages on the outside of the glasses as decoration. The glasses are often given as gifts at weddings, birthdays or other special celebrations. FK is planning to also manufacture plain glasses for everyday use. These glasses would be sold in supermarkets but the specially designed glasses can only be ordered online. FK has a small marketing budget so the owners will have to think carefully about the best methods of sales promotion and advertising for them.
   a Define 'advertising'. [2]
   b Outline **two** reasons for promoting the plain glasses. [4]
   c Explain **two** advertising methods FK could use for its existing range of decorated glasses. [6]
   d Explain **two** methods of sales promotion FK could use for its new range of plain glasses. Which method should FK choose? Justify your answer. [8]

Revision checklist

In this chapter you have learned:

- ✔ reasons for promotion
- ✔ the different methods of sales promotion
- ✔ the different methods of advertising
- ✔ how to recommend and justify which method of sales promotion to use in a given situation
- ✔ how to recommend and justify which method of advertising to use in a given situation

NOW – test your understanding with the revision questions in the Student etextbook and the Workbook.

15 Ecommerce

This chapter will explain:
★ the concept of ecommerce and examples of ecommerce
★ advantages and disadvantages of ecommerce for business
★ advantages and disadvantages of ecommerce for customers.

The concept of ecommerce

The very rapid growth of ownership of internet-connected devices means that **ecommerce** is now one of the major ways in which goods and services are traded globally. Ecommerce has greatly changed the way people shop and consume goods and services. Around 3 billion people in the world now turn to their laptops and smart devices to order goods, which can easily be delivered to their homes. Ecommerce has therefore made life much more difficult for high street or bricks and mortar retailers. Amazon, Alibaba and other online selling platforms have taken sales away from traditional distribution channels, forcing retailers to make changes to the way they operate.

Ecommerce operates in all markets. Not only is it used by businesses selling to consumers but also by businesses selling producer goods and services to other businesses. In addition, ecommerce has led to the development of consumer-to-consumer digital marketplaces, such as Ebay and Etsy.

One of the major differences between ecommerce and traditional shopping is the lack of personal contact between customers and sellers. This is a key feature of all three of the examples of ecommerce that follow. This loss of direct contact makes building customer relationships more difficult, especially in those situations where customers look for information, advice or support. Cost savings, efficiency gains and greater sales growth are positives of ecommerce but they need to be weighed against this loss of personal, direct contact with customers.

Examples of ecommerce

Mobile phone/internet banking

In some countries with extensive use of smartphones, more financial transactions are made online than by using bank branches. **Internet banking** has revolutionised the way most people operate their bank accounts, with some customers never visiting branches at all.

In particular, internet banking has had a huge positive impact in low-income countries which never had a branch banking system. By allowing transactions to take place through online payment systems, trade and commerce have increased at a much faster rate than they would have done if only traditional banking systems were in use.

> **Definitions to learn**
>
> **Ecommerce** (or electronic commerce) is the online buying and selling of goods and services using internet-linked devices such as laptops and smartphones.
> **Internet banking** (also known as online banking) is a system of electronic payment that enables customers of a bank to make a range of financial transactions through the bank's website.

> **Activity 15.1**
> Write an email to a friend to explain why they should use internet banking instead of using a physical bank branch. Include the possible problems they might have.

The concept of ecommerce

Online shopping

When was the last time you purchased a product online by computer or smartphone? For some people the answer to this question will be 'Never', but others will say, 'Five minutes ago!' The growth of internet selling has been very rapid in recent years. **Online shopping** only started in the USA in 1992 – yet by 2024 online sales in the USA alone were worth US$1 222 billion.

Consider these two statements by different Marketing Managers:

» Manager A: 'Since my company, which makes components for bicycles, introduced a new website which allows ecommerce, sales have increased by 55%. This includes sales to countries we have never sold to before. We are now thinking about closing some of our retail shops.'

» Manager B: 'My company sells handmade suits for men and women. We offer a personal service and customers visit us several times during the making of their suit to check for size and style. We use the internet only for gaining market research and handling financial transactions.'

How can both managers be so convinced their company has the correct approach to ecommerce? The answer is … they could both be right. Not every good or every service will be successfully sold using ecommerce – but a great many of them are.

> **Definitions to learn**
>
> **Online shopping** is the action or activity of buying goods or services over the internet.
>
> **Online ticketing** is booking a service such as a flight or cinema seat and receiving an online ticket which can either be printed out or stored in a device's memory.

> ### Activity 15.2
>
> You want to purchase the following items. Which ones would you be more likely to buy using online shopping and which ones would you prefer to buy from a physical shop? Give reasons for your choices.
>
> - Fresh fruit
> - Computer game
> - Car
> - New clothes
> - Holiday in another country
> - Smartphone

Online ticketing

Most airlines, train and bus companies and businesses that sell tickets for different types of performances now offer customers **online ticketing** instead of traditional paper tickets. The purchase of an e-ticket is stored in the computer system of the business and when the customer arrives to benefit from the service, a smartphone image or QR code will be sufficient to allow entry.

▲ QR code

15 ECOMMERCE

Advantages and disadvantages of ecommerce

Table 15.1 explains the advantages and disadvantages of all three examples of ecommerce for businesses.

Table 15.1 Advantages and disadvantages of ecommerce for businesses

Advantages to businesses of ecommerce	Disadvantages to businesses of ecommerce
Mobile phone/internet banking	
Banks can reduce the number of branches they need and this cuts the overhead costs of the business	Banks may have IT problems which may result in complete failure of their banking system for a period of time. Customers may lose confidence in the bank and switch to another one
Banks keep all their customers' data in a digital form which is very easy to retrieve and analyse so labour costs will also be reduced	Some bank customers without smart devices may switch their accounts to other finance institutions with traditional branches
If their customers move to another country, they can keep their accounts operating online instead of having to switch to another bank	There is no personal contact with customers which might limit the bank's ability to form customer relationships, so customer loyalty might be low
Online shopping	
Websites can be used to promote the company and its products worldwide at lower cost than other forms of marketing	Operating in a global market increases competition, especially from lower-cost producers in other countries. Businesses will have to remain competitive and websites updated frequently, which can increase costs
Global markets reached through websites should increase sales compared to just using retail shops	Customers may prefer to feel, touch or try on the products and switch to businesses that still have retail shops
Orders can be taken from customers over the internet. They are then sent digitally to the warehouse for dispatch, speeding up the process of selling and distributing goods	Delivery costs of products to each customer's address increases costs – or increases the price paid if customers have to pay these delivery charges
Consumers might be encouraged to purchase more products than intended by giving them easy to follow links to other products on the website that could also be bought	Product returns from customers are much higher because they cannot feel, touch or try on the product until it is delivered to them, increasing costs of processing returned products
Online ticketing	
Customers can place their orders at any time of the day or night (24/7) – there do not have to be sales employees available, so labour costs might be reduced	There is a risk of hackers getting into the IT system. This could lead to its failure to operate and customers will not be able to place orders, meaning sales are lost
No paper tickets are issued, reducing costs and making the process more sustainable	Some customers may not have internet access and will not be able to buy tickets if this is the only method available

Table 15.2 explains the advantages and disadvantages of all three examples of ecommerce for customers.

Table 15.2 Advantages and disadvantages of ecommerce for customers

Advantages to customers of ecommerce	Disadvantages to customers of ecommerce
Mobile phone/internet banking	
It is more convenient for many customers as their nearest bank branch may be many miles away and internet banking can be done at home or work	If they do not have access to a smartphone or other internet device, the closure of bank branches makes it very difficult for customers to make use of banking services, such as paying bills
Customers are able to make payments or check account balances at any time and it may be possible to communicate with businesses through chatbots at any time	Many customers fear having their online accounts hacked and believe that internet banking is less secure than branch banking
In countries with few bank branches, internet banking has stimulated trade for nearly all businesses and reduced costs of banking services for customers	It makes it very difficult to pay cash into bank accounts which could be a serious problem for market stall traders and other businesses that mainly use cash

The concept of ecommerce

Advantages to customers of ecommerce	Disadvantages to customers of ecommerce
Online shopping	
Comparisons between prices and products or services offered can be easily made by surfing from one website to another – or using price comparison websites	Products cannot be seen, touched or tried on (clothing, for example) and returning products because they are unsuitable is often inconvenient and can be costly
Consumers can buy some products for prices much lower than they would be without the competition of ecommerce, for example, books, music and insurance policies	Delivery costs are often added to the purchase price of the products and this is not the case with most goods bought in shops
There is much more consumer choice available online than is available in even the largest shops	There may be some delay between ordering goods and their delivery. This is less likely to be a problem if a shop has the goods in stock
It is easy to pay online with debit/credit cards	There is no personal face-to-face contact with sales staff, so much less advice and information when buying is available compared to in high street shops
Online ticketing	
Customers are able to buy tickets at any time of the day or night (24/7) and it is often easy to choose a seat, in a cinema, for example	Some businesses selling online tickets offer limited customer service. For example, booking a holiday online might be made more difficult if all of the different air route options are not explained
There is no risk of losing a paper ticket and even if a smartphone is lost, the ticket can be retrieved on another device	There are many bogus websites and fake email offers that claim to offer genuine tickets – there may be less consumer security than buying in person

▲ Price comparison sites give consumers help with finding the lowest prices

Case study: Online ticketing

Visitors to the Taj Mahal must purchase an official ticket issued by the Indian government. These tickets can be purchased online through various official ticketing websites.

15 ECOMMERCE

> **Activity 15.3**
> a What are the advantages to the managers responsible for operating the Taj Mahal of using online ticketing for visitors?
> b Are there any disadvantages to the managers responsible for operating the Taj Mahal of using online ticketing for visitors?

Extend your skills of analysis

A question which asks for a disadvantage of online shopping to a shoe retailer could be answered as follows:

Online shopping can encourage many consumers to order products knowing that they can send them back for a full refund if they do not like the style or the fit of them.

Extend your analysis by explaining a disadvantage of this.

When customers return unsuitable shoes the shoe retailer will have increased costs from processing these returned shoes.

Extend your analysis by explaining why this is a problem for the business.

If consumers receive the wrong shoes, the wrong size or if they just do not like the shoes when they try them on, there will be many returns to the shoe retailer which will add to administration and inventory costs of processing these returns, increasing total costs for the business.

Study tips

Make sure you can explain the advantages and disadvantages of ecommerce to a particular business.

Key info

Although traditional markets and local stores are very important forms of distribution in Kenya, ecommerce is growing quickly. This is due to higher incomes, more people using mobile phones, more secure online payment systems and improved roads and other infrastructure. Ecommerce in Kenya is expected to grow at an annual rate of 6.5% up to 2029.

REVISION SUMMARY Ecommerce – advantages and disadvantages to businesses

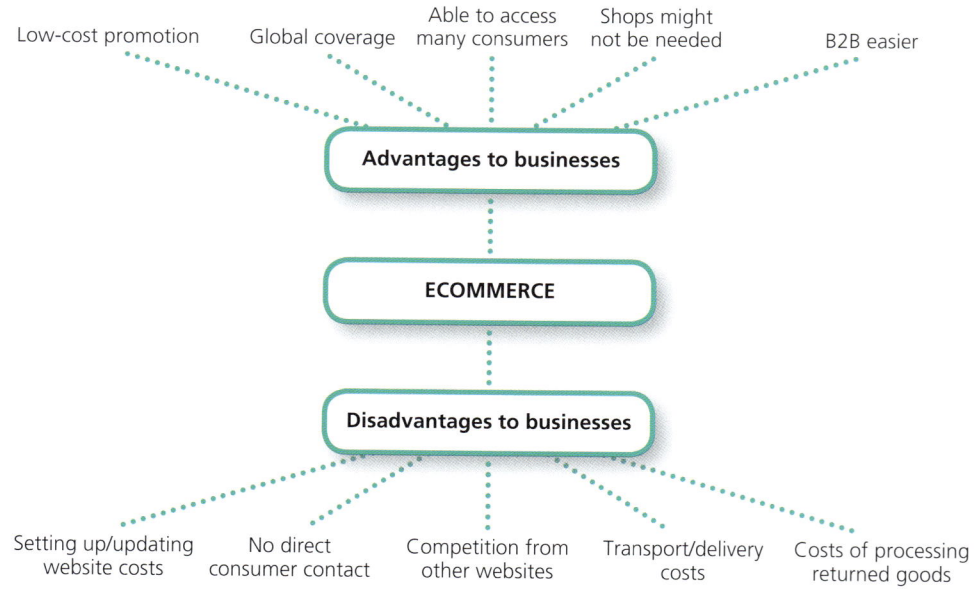

The concept of ecommerce

REVISION SUMMARY — Ecommerce – advantages and disadvantages to customers

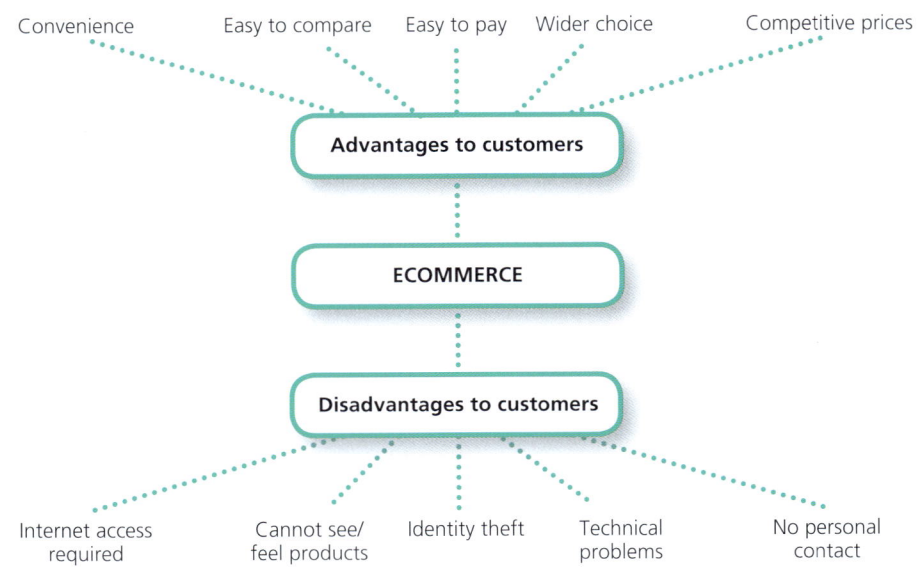

International business in focus

Airbnb

Airbnb allows people to lease or rent short-term accommodation including holiday apartments, rooms or hotel rooms. Airbnb does not own any of the accommodation. It acts as an intermediary and receives a percentage of the fee charged from both guests and owners of the accommodation for every booking. In 2024 the company had over 7.7 million accommodation listings in 100 000 cities across 220 countries. Prices are set by the owners of the accommodation. There were 448 million nights booked through the company in 2023.

Airbnb can be accessed via either the Airbnb website or mobile app. On each booking, Airbnb typically charges a guest services fee of around 14% and charges the owner of the accommodation a host service fee of around 3%.

People can search online based on accommodation type, dates, location and price. Before booking, customers must provide a valid name, email address, telephone number, photo and payment information.

Discussion points
- Could Airbnb exist without the internet?
- How has Airbnb changed the market for accommodation across the world?
- How is Airbnb a disadvantage to local businesses?

15 ECOMMERCE

❓ Chapter review questions: Short answer and data response

1. JJ sells high-priced handmade jewellery. The jewellery items are designed and made to the exact requirements of each customer. JJ successfully advertises its products on social media and the business uses internet banking. However, Jonathan, the owner of JJ, does not want to sell jewellery online. JJ's products are sold through its only shop, in the capital city of Country B. He has been advised by a friend that online shopping is very popular for all goods and services.
   - a Define 'internet banking'. [2]
   - b Outline **two** advantages to JJ of using internet banking. [4]
   - c Explain **two** disadvantages to customers of JJ only accepting online payments. [6]
   - d Do you think JJ should start selling its jewellery online? Justify your answer. [8]

2. PP is a holiday company. It only sells holidays online through its own website. The owner believes that ecommerce is the future for selling holidays and that in time all holiday shops will close.
   - a Define 'ecommerce'. [2]
   - b Outline **two** disadvantages to customers of PP selling only through its own website. [4]
   - c Explain **two** reasons why customers buy holidays from PP rather than going to a shop selling holidays. [6]
   - d Do you think PP is right to sell holidays to customers only using its website? Justify your answer. [8]

Revision checklist

In this chapter you have learned:

- ✔ the concept of ecommerce and examples of ecommerce
- ✔ the advantages and disadvantages of ecommerce for businesses
- ✔ the advantages and disadvantages of ecommerce for customers

NOW – test your understanding with the revision questions in the Student etextbook and the Workbook.

16 Marketing strategy, entering new markets in other countries and legal controls

> This chapter will explain:
>
> Marketing strategy:
>
> ★ the importance of the different elements in the marketing mix
> ★ how to recommend and justify an appropriate marketing mix for a given situation.
>
> Entering new markets in other countries as a method of growth:
>
> ★ advantages of entering new markets in other countries
> ★ disadvantages of entering new markets in other countries.
>
> Legal controls related to marketing:
>
> ★ the purpose of legal controls to protect customers
> ★ the effects of legal controls on marketing.

Marketing strategy

A **marketing strategy** is a plan of action for the Marketing department. The strategy starts with a clear marketing objective. It then gives details of the appropriate marketing mix designed to achieve that objective.

Possible marketing objectives include:

» increasing sales of an existing product by selling to new market(s) or selling more to the existing market(s)
» achieving a target market share with a newly launched product
» increasing market share of an existing product
» maintaining market share if competition is increasing
» improving customer loyalty.

Definitions to learn

A **marketing strategy** is a plan with a marketing objective and details of the marketing mix that aims to achieve it.

Case study: Marketing strategies cannot stand still – Jawbone

Jawbone was a fitness tracker company that faced challenges in keeping up with its marketing strategy. It was once a main business in the wearable fitness tracker market and sold different fitness bands. However, the company had several issues mainly with the 'product' part of its marketing mix due to product reliability, customer service and innovation.

Jawbone was initially successful but then struggled to maintain significant product updates and improvements. Consumers wanted more advanced features, such as heart rate monitoring, GPS tracking and more accurate activity tracking, which competitors like Fitbit and Garmin were offering. The price Jawbone was charging did not match the prices charged by competitors.

This example shows how failure to keep up with consumer demands for a product that matches those products offered by competitors, at a price that consumers are willing to pay, can lead to the decline of a company.

16 MARKETING STRATEGY, ENTERING NEW MARKETS IN OTHER COUNTRIES AND LEGAL CONTROLS

> ### Activity 16.1
> Read the case study on the previous page.
>
> Explain why the marketing strategy Jawbone used for its fitness trackers failed.

Study tips

Make sure you can develop a marketing strategy for a given product/service. The four elements of the marketing mix should all link together in order to be effective in attracting the target market to buy the product/service.

> ### Activity 16.2
> Choose a product which you think will sell well in your country (this could be a new product or an existing product such as bottled water). Create a marketing strategy for this product by including answers to the following questions.
>
> a Who is your target market? What are the characteristics of the consumers you think will buy your product? What is their market segment? Justify your answers.
> b How does your product meet their needs? Why will consumers buy your product rather than a competitor's product? What is your product's Unique Selling Point (USP) that makes it different to your competitors' products? Justify your answers.
> c What price will the target market be willing to pay? What pricing method will you use? Justify your answers.
> d Which method(s) of distribution (place) will you use and will it be suitable for your target market? Justify your answers. Which method(s) of distribution do your competitors use?
> e What methods of promotion will you use? Remember you may have a small budget/small amount of money to spend. Decide both where you will advertise and what sales promotion you might use. Justify your answers.
> f Summarise by explaining why you think your new product will be successful.

Importance of the different elements in the marketing mix

The four elements of the marketing mix are important in influencing consumer decisions. The appropriate combination of the 'four Ps' is essential to the success of a marketing strategy. If the marketing strategy does not combine the elements of the marketing mix correctly then the marketing objective will not be achieved. For example, the marketing objective of increasing sales will not be achieved if:

» a product meets customer needs and is priced at the right level for the target market but potential consumers are not informed about it so the promotion is ineffective

» a product does not meet the needs of consumers in the target market. The product will not sell at any price, even if it is well advertised, because it is unsuitable

» a product is well designed, effectively promoted and sold in suitable distribution channels but it is priced 25% above competitors' products.

These examples show the correct combination of the four Ps is vital to the success of a marketing strategy. If just one of the four Ps is not consistent with the other three, then the marketing strategy will fail.

It is important to remember that marketing strategy – the marketing objective plus the four elements of the marketing mix – will need adapting throughout a product's life cycle (see Chapter 11).

Marketing strategy

Key info

The great success of Nike's sports gear marketing strategy is often explained by the fact that it does not promote itself to the obvious target market of professional athletes but to everyone, no matter what their sporting abilities: 'If you have a body, you are an athlete.' This appeal is summed up by the famous slogan 'Just Do It'.

▲ The marketing strategy must always be focused on the target market

How to recommend and justify an appropriate marketing mix for a given situation

This is one of the most important functions of a Marketing Manager. No business can keep the same marketing mix forever, so changes, some of them substantial, will be necessary. This is especially the case with the launch of a new product when all four Ps may need to be very different from those used for existing products. A Marketing Manager will have to consider carefully the following points before developing a new marketing mix.

» **Marketing objective.** This will have a big impact on the marketing mix decisions. Is the objective to enter a new niche market, for example, or is it to achieve the highest market share possible?
» **How much finance is available.** For example, can TV advertising be afforded or would social media promotion be more cost effective?
» **Target market.** Is the product aimed at high-income consumers or families with young children, for example?
» **Competition.** The number of main competitors will always impact on the marketing mix used by a business. The more competition in the market, the greater the need for innovative products, effective promotion and place decisions and competitive pricing – unless a completely unique product has been developed.
» **Balanced marketing mix.** The four Ps will need to fit together and tell the same story about the product to consumers.

Study tips

If you are asked to recommend and justify an appropriate marketing mix, you will also have to analyse these factors. Make sure you always refer to the situation the business is in when the marketing mix decisions are made.

16 MARKETING STRATEGY, ENTERING NEW MARKETS IN OTHER COUNTRIES AND LEGAL CONTROLS

> **Extend your skills of analysis**
>
> A question which asks for an advantage of having a suitable marketing mix for a new luxury hotel could be answered as follows:
>
> A suitable marketing mix means that all four Ps give the consumer the same image about the product.
>
> *Extend your analysis by explaining why this is important.*
>
> If the hotel has a great brand image, excellent accommodation and high prices, advertising only on roadside billboards may give a very misleading impression to consumers.
>
> *Extend your analysis by explaining why a suitable marketing mix would benefit the hotel.*
>
> By advertising in expensive magazines targeted at consumers with active lifestyles or by using targeted emails to existing customers of famous hotels, the new hotel will create an image of luxury which will fit in with the other three Ps and help to increase the number of guests wanting to stay there.

> **Activity 16.3**
>
> a Identify a product that has recently been introduced in your country.
> b Find out the price of this product and how it compares to the prices of other similar products in the same market. Which pricing method seems to have been used for the new product? Do you think this method is appropriate?
> c Find out how this product is being promoted – try to identify at least **two** different ways. Do you think these methods of promotion are likely to be effective? Explain your answer.
> d Outline **one** way in which the price of the product may change as it passes through its product life cycle.
> e Outline **one** way in which the promotion of the product might change as it passes through its product life cycle.
> f Write up your ideas in a brief report and present it to your group.

Entering new markets in other countries as a method of growth

It is not easy selling products in other countries but there can be huge benefits. Deciding to start selling in other countries is a major change to the marketing strategy of a business. In many cases, big changes will be needed in the marketing mix if the decision is to be successful.

Advantages of entering new markets in other countries

Increase sales

The total market size for a business will increase if it starts selling internationally. This should lead to higher sales and increased business growth as there will be many more potential customers. If the country is a high-income country, then it might be possible to set prices higher than in the domestic/home market. These higher prices would help to increase revenue even further.

With the internet, selling to international markets has been made much easier. There might not be any need to open retail stores or employ agents in other countries. The business could set up an online store and start selling its products to customers anywhere in the world. However, many businesses will need to establish a physical distribution channel for their products in other countries. Selling ice cream, fast food or specialist off-shore rescue boats cannot easily be done online!

Spread risk

Business risks will be high if sales are only made to the home or domestic market. This is because a major problem within that market could cause a big drop in sales. Such problems include a new competitor entering the market with lower prices or a large increase in unemployment which leaves consumers with less money to spend. By selling to markets in other countries, these risks are reduced and spread between different markets. So, if the economy of the home market is in recession, another country's economy could be booming. A fall in sales in the home country could be offset by increased sales in another country.

Disadvantages of entering new markets in other countries

Cultural differences

Cultural differences between countries include religious beliefs, style of dress, lifestyle choices, the role of women in the workforce and approach to education. These and other cultural differences mean that it will be very difficult to market the same products in all countries using the same marketing mix. A business must adapt its marketing mix to match the culture of the market it plans to enter. Here are some examples:

- Some communities do not approve of selling certain products directly to children. The 'place' decision must be appropriate so children do not have access to these products.
- Advertising images must be appropriate for the religious and social norms of a country.
- Prices will have to be adjusted for the additional costs of matching the marketing mix to a particular culture.
- Food products containing certain types of meat or fish are not acceptable to some cultures. The products sold by a food processing business must change to satisfy these cultural differences.

A business that fails to recognise and respond to these cultural differences could find its products rejected by a country's population. The costs of entering these markets will then be greater than any extra revenue gained.

Lack of knowledge

Cultural factors are not the only differences that exist between national markets. Markets in other countries may be very different from the domestic or home market because:

- Average income levels might be higher or lower. Consumers may have more or less money to spend than consumers at home, influencing their demand patterns.
- The average age of the population might be higher or lower. This will affect the type of products they buy and the social media they use.
- There might be more or fewer competitors than in the domestic market. This will affect the prices that can be charged.

16 MARKETING STRATEGY, ENTERING NEW MARKETS IN OTHER COUNTRIES AND LEGAL CONTROLS

> **Key info**
>
> How did Domino's Pizza become so successful? Domino's CEO J. Patrick Doyle says: 'The joy of pizza is that bread, sauce, and cheese works fundamentally everywhere, except perhaps China, where dairy has not been a big part of the diet until lately, and it is easy to just change toppings market to market. In Asia, it is seafood and fish. It is curry in India. But half the toppings are standard offerings around the world.

If businesses lack knowledge about these differences then an unsuitable marketing mix will probably be used. This will mean that entering a market in another country is unlikely to be successful. Gaining knowledge about other markets is costly. For example, detailed market research or employing an agent in the other country will add to the cost of entering the other country's market. However, detailed local knowledge will increase the chances of successful entry into new markets.

Legal requirements

Most governments have passed laws to control some marketing activities. The next section of this chapter explains why this is done and the most common legal controls. Business managers planning to enter markets in other countries must make sure they know what the legal requirements are for the products sold by their business. These may be different to the legal controls used in the home country. For example:

» Certain products are illegal in some countries.
» Advertisement images of people are strictly controlled in some countries.
» Safety requirements for electrical products may be of a higher standard.
» Maximum price limits might exist.

Without detailed knowledge of these legal requirements, a business could make serious marketing errors resulting in a loss being made from the entry into markets in other countries.

> **Key info**
>
> Toyota's target market is diverse in terms of consumer preferences and regional and local market conditions. The company's marketing mix is tailored to respond to these variations. In high-income countries it markets the exclusive Lexus range heavily. In low-income countries it charges competitive prices for rugged vehicles with few extras or special features.

> **Extend your skills of analysis**
>
> A question which asks for a disadvantage for a yoghurt manufacturer entering a new market in another country could be answered as follows:
>
> *Entering new markets in other countries is a way to expand the business but lack of knowledge could be a disadvantage.*
>
> **Extend your analysis by explaining why lack of knowledge is a disadvantage.**
>
> *The yoghurt manufacturer may not know that the other country has no tradition of eating dairy products such as yoghurt.*
>
> **Extend your analysis by explaining how this will impact on the business.**
>
> *If the manufacturer enters the market, then sales are likely to be low and a loss could be made if the product does not meet customer needs.*

> **Study tips**
>
> Make sure you can apply the advantages and disadvantages of entering new markets in other countries to a business in a given situation.

Case study: McDonald's enters markets in other countries

McDonald's has developed a special menu for its restaurants in India. The menu does not have beefburgers but does have chicken burgers, known as Chicken Maharaja Macs, and cheeseburgers, called McSpicy Paneer, on its menu. These products are suitable for the culture of this market as the majority of Indians are Hindus so do not eat beef for religious reasons, but many do eat chicken, fish and cheese.

Activity 16.4

Read the case study above.

a Why did McDonald's change its menu in Indian restaurants?
b Do you think McDonald's should have different menus for every country it operates in? Justify your answer.

Legal controls related to marketing

The purpose of legal controls to protect customers

Consumers can be easily misled. It is quite easy to sell consumers goods that are either unsuitable or that fail to perform as the manufacturer claims. This is not because consumers are unintelligent. It is because products are now so complicated and technical that it is very difficult for a consumer to know how good they are or how they are likely to work. Also, modern promotion methods can be so persuasive that nearly all of us could be sold products, even if they were later discovered to be of poor quality or not as good as the advert claimed.

Most governments agree that consumer protection is important. Without **legal controls** to protect consumers the following problems could exist:

>> Goods might be so badly made that they do not work effectively.
>> Goods could be unsafe for consumers to use.
>> Goods may not last as long as claimed by the manufacturer.
>> Price 'reductions' may not be lower prices at all and may mislead consumers.
>> Businesses might refuse to repay consumers for faulty or dangerous goods.
>> Advertising and sales promotions might make untrue or misleading claims about the product.

To avoid consumers being badly treated in these ways by businesses, most governments have passed consumer protection laws.

Typical examples of legal controls that protect customers

>> **Weights and Measures.** Retailers and producers must not sell underweight goods or use weighing equipment that is inaccurate.
>> **Misleading promotions.** It is illegal to give the consumer deliberately misleading information about or image of a product. For example, it is illegal to state that a pair of trousers is made of wool when they are made of cotton. Advertisements must therefore be truthful.
>> **Product quality.** It is illegal to sell:
   - products which have faults or problems and are not of a satisfactory quality
   - products which are not fit for the purpose intended by the consumer, for example, if the consumer asks for a drill to make holes in walls and is sold one which is only suitable for wood
   - products which do not perform as described on the label or by the retailer, for example, if the label states 'These shoes are completely waterproof' and the shoes leak the first time they are used.

   If a product causes injury to the consumer then the manufacturers and retailers are liable to pay compensation.
>> **Misleading price reductions.** It is illegal to make misleading pricing claims, such as '$40 off for this week only' when the product was being sold for the same price the previous week. This legal control stops consumers from being misled about the true value of a product by untrue price reductions.

> **Definitions to learn**
>
> **Legal controls** on marketing are laws passed by government to protect consumers from faulty goods, unsafe goods and misleading promotion.

16 MARKETING STRATEGY, ENTERING NEW MARKETS IN OTHER COUNTRIES AND LEGAL CONTROLS

▲ It is illegal in many countries to sell items that do not live up to the claims made for them

The effects of legal controls on marketing

Positive effects on business

» Businesses are legally required to produce safe products with no faults. By selling these products, businesses will gain a good reputation and consumers can buy with confidence. Goods and services which always reach a satisfactory level of quality will encourage consumers to buy more from that business. This should lead to business growth.

» By complying with consumer protection laws there will be much less risk of fines and bad publicity. If a business regularly sells faulty goods or uses misleading promotions, negative social media feedback could even lead to the business being forced to close.

> **Extend your skills of analysis**
>
> A question which asks for an advantage to a battery charger manufacturer of observing all legal controls could be answered as follows:
>
> Legal controls over business protect consumers from faulty goods and misleading promotion.
>
> *Extend your analysis by explaining why these controls are important.*
>
> Poorly designed battery chargers, for example, for electric bikes, which do not meet legal standards can explode when charging batteries under certain conditions.
>
> *Extend your analysis by explaining why the controls are a benefit to the business.*
>
> By designing a battery charger to meet all legal standards, the manufacturer greatly reduces the risk of fires or accidents when the charger is used. In this way the business will avoid bad publicity and consumers will have confidence in buying chargers from this manufacturer and sales should increase.

Negative effects on business

» Meeting the legal requirements imposed by governments increases costs to business. New, safer designs of products might have to be introduced. Quality methods will have to improve, such as using more accurate machinery, and this will cost more. Compensation amounts paid to customers who complain about faulty goods or misleading promotion can be high. Increased costs will mean that businesses will have to increase prices to consumers too.

Legal controls related to marketing

Study tips

Make sure you can explain why governments pass laws to protect consumers and what the laws mean for businesses when selling their goods or services. You do not need to know about specific laws.

» Some businesses might try to save costs by ignoring the laws and selling products very cheaply to consumers. Some market traders could do this for one week and then move on to another market. Some online sellers operate for a short period of time before closing their website – but in that time they sell illegal products at low prices. A business which follows all legal requirements may lose many sales to traders that do not meet their legal obligations. This is more likely when the law breakers are not stopped by the authorities.

Is all consumer protection a good idea? Most people would say that the consumer needs to be protected as much as possible. They believe that goods should be as safe and as suitable for the purpose intended as possible. However, some business managers believe that these laws add to the costs of making and selling products and this increases the prices in the shops. What is your view?

> ### Activity 16.5
> Here are 3 situations in which consumers might need some protection:
>
> a 'These shoes are made of the finest leather.' In fact, they are made of plastic.
> b A consumer buys 1 kg of potatoes and re-weighs them at home. In fact, he has only 800 g.
> c A motorist asks for a tow rope 'strong enough for my trailer'. It breaks the first time he tries to use it.
>
> Do you think the consumer needs some legal protection in these cases? Explain your answers.

International business in focus

Yeo's

Yeo's is a food business which was set up in 1901 in China, originally as a small shop making soy sauce. It moved to Singapore in the 1930s and started expanding. The business now makes a variety of food and cooking products including curry sauces, pastes, noodles and drinks. Today the company sells across the world including in Singapore, Malaysia, Indonesia, Hong Kong, China, Canada and the USA.

The Directors of Yeo's expanded sales in the European market. The company conducted 'sampling tours' throughout major UK, French and German Chinese supermarkets to raise awareness of its products. The company did not introduce the full range of its products into the European market.

Discussion points
- Why do you think Yeo's conducted 'sampling tours' across European countries?
- Why did Yeo's not introduce the full range of its products into the European market?
- What possible problems do you think Yeo's might have had in entering the European market?

16 MARKETING STRATEGY, ENTERING NEW MARKETS IN OTHER COUNTRIES AND LEGAL CONTROLS

Chapter review questions: Short answer and data response

1 KKosmetics manufactures make-up for women. The business sells its products in high-income European countries. The Directors of KKosmetics want to start selling to African countries. The Marketing Director says: 'There are a lot of advantages of entering these markets but also some potential disadvantages. We have reached the maturity stage of the product life cycle in the European markets and we need to increase sales in new markets.' The Managing Director suggested that a different marketing mix will probably be needed for the business to sell its products successfully in African countries.
   a Identify **two** ways a new market in another country for KKosmetics might be different to the home market. [2]
   b Outline **two** possible reasons why KKosmetics wants to enter a new market in another country. [4]
   c Explain **two** possible disadvantages for KKosmetics if it tries to enter markets in other countries. [6]
   d Do you think that the marketing mix will have to change for KKosmetics to sell successfully in African countries? Justify your answer. [8]

2 Nish and Dan work together and own 2 businesses. Both are located in a national park that has many tourists. The first business is a cafe which serves fresh food to park visitors. The other business offers rock climbing and zip-wire adventure activities. Nish and Dan believe in following all legal controls. Nish is a qualified chef who recently gained an advanced 'Food Safety' certificate. Dan is an experienced mountain climber. He insists on the strictest safety standards. They have low-priced competition from a cafe that recently failed a health and safety check and mountain adventure leaders who use old safety equipment.
   a Define 'legal controls' on business to protect consumers. [2]
   b Outline **two** types of legal controls that protect consumers of Nish and Dan's businesses. [4]
   c Explain **two** possible disadvantages to the low-priced competitors of not observing legal controls. [6]
   d Do you think Nish and Dan are right to follow all legal controls? Justify your answer. [8]

Revision checklist

In this chapter you have learned:

- ✔ the importance of the different elements in the marketing mix
- ✔ how to recommend and justify an appropriate marketing mix for a given situation
- ✔ the advantages of entering new markets in other countries
- ✔ the disadvantages of entering new markets in other countries
- ✔ the purpose of legal controls to protect consumers
- ✔ the effects of legal controls on marketing.

NOW – test your understanding with the revision questions in the Student etextbook and the Workbook.

Marketing: end-of-section case study

> **Case study:** ChocoCrocs

ChocoCrocs was set up 10 years ago as a private limited company. The business grew slowly as the owners used reinvested profits as the only source of finance for expansion. The company has share capital of $10 million which is owned by 6 members of the Hassan family. ChocoCrocs has 3 main types of products which are:

- large chocolate bars mainly sold to men
- chocolates with praline-filled centres mainly sold to women
- small chocolate bars shaped like a crocodile mainly sold to children.

ChocoCrocs has skilled employees in the Marketing department. This department carries out market research and it also develops new products for the company to market. The Managing Director says this is one of the most important departments in the company. The Directors of ChocoCrocs want to expand the business.

> **Appendix 1:** Sales for the products of ChocoCrocs

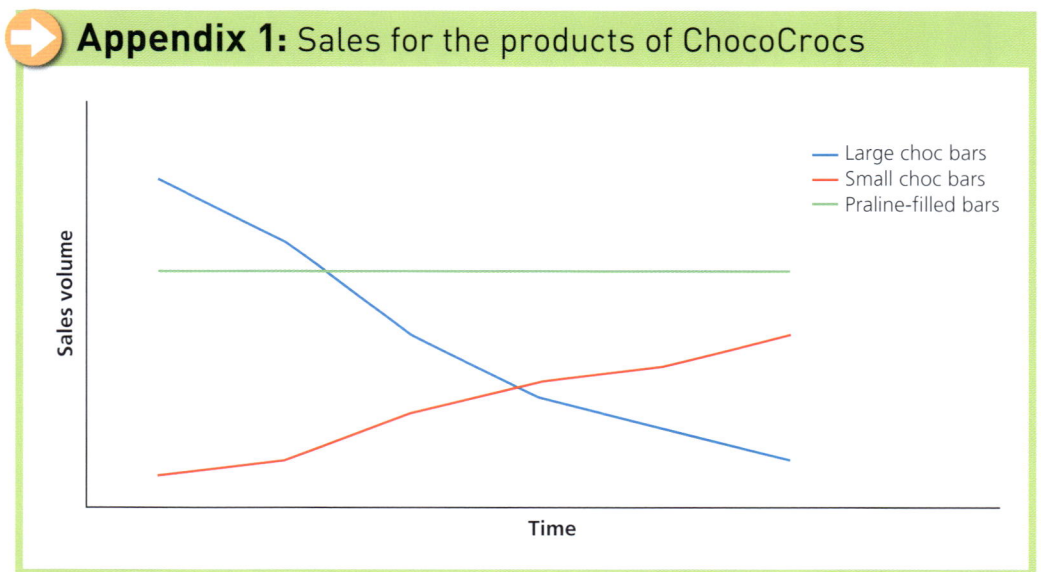

> **Practice questions: Case study**

1   a   Appendix 1 shows sales of ChocoCrocs products. Explain which stage of the product life cycle each of the following ChocoCrocs products are at:
        i   small choc bars   ii   large choc bars. [8]
    b   ChocoCrocs is considering what pricing method to use for the crocodile-shaped children's chocolate bars. Consider the advantages and disadvantages of **two** pricing methods it could use. Which pricing method should ChocoCrocs choose? Justify your answer. [12]

2   a   ChocoCrocs has a website which gives customers information about the products it sells. Explain **two** other ways that ChocoCrocs could find the internet useful to the business in the marketing of its products. [8]
    b   Consider why primary market research and secondary market research are important to the success of ChocoCrocs. Which is more important to ChocoCrocs when developing a new product? Justify your answer. [12]

Optional question
The question below asks you to think about topics covered in earlier sections of this textbook. You can choose not to answer it if you prefer to focus on just the topics covered in this section at this time.

3   a   Explain **four** ways in which the size of the ChocoCrocs business could be measured. [8]
    b   Consider the following **two** ways ChocoCrocs could expand. Which way should ChocoCrocs choose? Justify your answer. [12]
        - Internal growth   • External growth

SECTION 4
Operations management

Chapters

17 Production of goods and services
18 Technology and production of goods and services
19 Sustainable production of goods and services
20 Costs, scale of production and break-even analysis
21 Quality of goods and services
22 Location decisions

17 Production of goods and services

This chapter will explain:

Production processes:

★ how to calculate labour productivity
★ why efficiency is important for a business
★ how to increase efficiency
★ the concept of lean production and how to achieve it
★ advantages and disadvantages of lean production methods
★ why businesses hold inventory
★ factors affecting how much inventory businesses hold.

The main methods of production:

★ job, batch and flow production
★ advantages and disadvantages of job, batch and flow production
★ how to recommend and justify an appropriate production method for a given situation.

Production processes

Production is the provision of a product or a service to satisfy customer wants and needs. The production process applies to service industries as well as manufacturing. In adding value (see Chapter 1), businesses combine the inputs of a business (factors of production: land, labour, capital and enterprise) to produce more valuable outputs (the final good or service). The figure below illustrates this process.

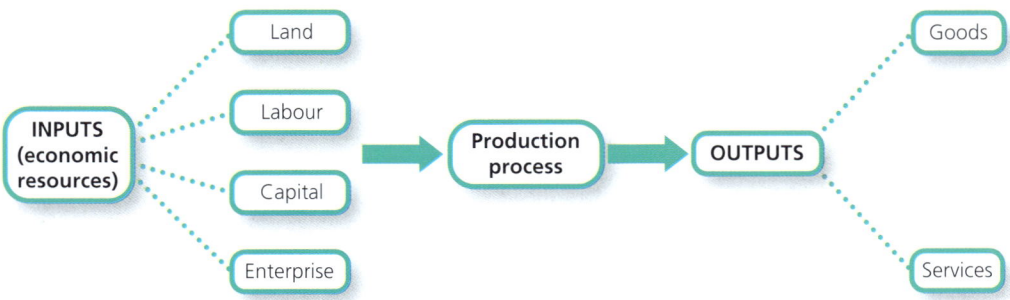

For a business to be competitive it should combine these inputs of resources efficiently so that it makes the best use of resources at its disposal to keep costs low and increase profits. In a developing economy, where wages are low, it may be more efficient to use many employees and few machines to produce goods – this

17 PRODUCTION OF GOODS AND SERVICES

production process is called 'labour intensive'. However, in high-income countries where labour costs are high, production is often 'capital-intensive', where businesses use machines/robots and employ fewer people.

> **Case study:** Adding value
>
> A restaurant combines the 4 factors of production to produce a meal for customers.
>
>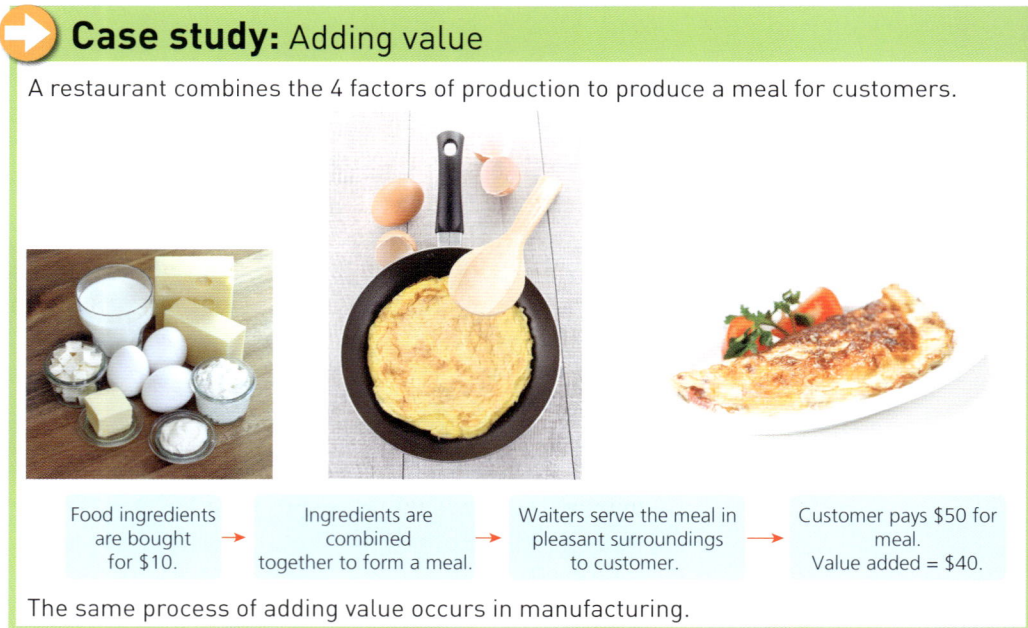
>
> Food ingredients are bought for $10. → Ingredients are combined together to form a meal. → Waiters serve the meal in pleasant surroundings to customer. → Customer pays $50 for meal. Value added = $40.
>
> The same process of adding value occurs in manufacturing.

Calculating labour productivity

The 'level of production' is the total output of a business in a given time period. This is not the same as **productivity**. Productivity is how a business measures its efficiency. The most common measure of productivity is **labour productivity**. This can be measured by the formula given below.

> **Definitions to learn**
>
> **Productivity** is the output measured against the inputs used to create a product or service and is a measure of efficiency.
> **Labour productivity** is the amount of work done or the number of units produced by a worker in a given time period e.g. one week.

Calculations to learn

$$\text{Labour productivity} = \frac{\text{Output per period (units)}}{\text{Number of employees}}$$

Worked example

A pottery business makes 3000 plates each week with five employees.

$$\text{Labour productivity} = \frac{3000}{5} = 600 \text{ plates per employee per week}$$

This is an important measure of the efficiency of a business.

Production processes

> **Study tips**
>
> Make sure you can discuss the effects of increased efficiency on employers and employees. How are the effects different?

> ### Activity 17.1
>
> Better Bakers produces cakes for local supermarkets. It has steadily increased the number of employees and has improved employee training. The owner, Benson, thinks the efficiency of the business has improved.
>
> **a** Do you agree with the owner? Use the information below to justify your answer.
>
> | Year | Output = number of cakes produced | Number of employees | Labour productivity |
> |---|---|---|---|
> | 2023 | 10 000 | 30 | |
> | 2024 | 20 000 | 40 | |
> | 2025 | 30 000 | 50 | |
>
> **b** Outline **one** way Benson could further improve labour productivity.
> **c** Explain **two** advantages to Better Bakers of improved efficiency.

Why efficiency is important for a business

Businesses are always aiming to increase the efficient use of their inputs. Producing higher output with the same level of inputs increases efficiency. There are several benefits to businesses from this:

- Lower average cost per unit produced, increasing profit per unit if prices are unchanged.
- Increased output from the same level of inputs makes it easier to satisfy increasing customer demand.
- In a competitive market, prices could be lowered without reducing profit per unit.
- Higher productivity means that wages can be increased without increasing unit costs. This could raise employee motivation.

How to increase efficiency

There are two important ways to increase efficiency.

Increasing automation and technology

There have been great changes to the level of automation and technology used by most businesses in recent years. New technology such as automated manufacturing machines or chatbots used in customer service have increased labour productivity and efficiency. See Chapter 18 for more details.

Improving labour skills

If employees are trained to make the best use of their time at work, labour productivity can increase substantially. Improving the following labour skills raises efficiency:

- Managing time more effectively by, for example, dealing with the most important work items first.
- Training employees to improve the quality of their work so fewer items are rejected.
- Training employees to use the latest technology at work.

> **Study tips**
>
> Make sure you understand that increased output is not the same as increased efficiency, although increased efficiency is likely to lead to increased output.

17 PRODUCTION OF GOODS AND SERVICES

REVISION SUMMARY Ways to increase efficiency

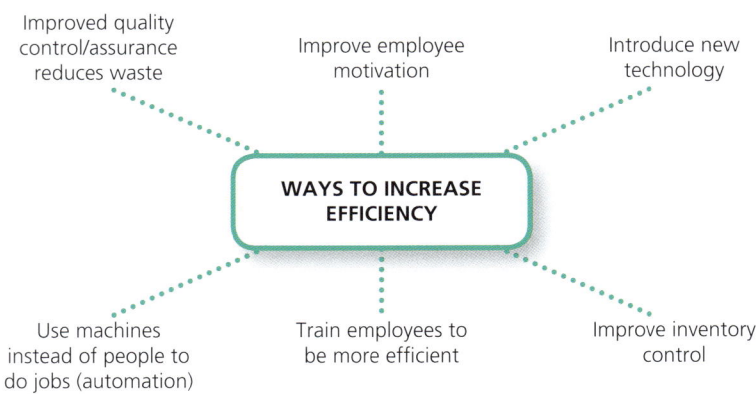

The concept of lean production and how to achieve it

Lean production covers a variety of techniques used by businesses to cut down on waste of resources to increase efficiency. Lean production cuts out any wasteful activities which do not add value for the customer and this applies to services as well.

There are several types of waste that can occur in production:

» **Overproduction.** Producing goods before they have been ordered by customers results in high storage costs.
» **Waiting.** When goods are not moving or being processed in any way, waste is occurring.
» **Transportation.** Moving goods around unnecessarily causes waste and is not adding value to the product. Goods may also be damaged when they are being moved around.
» **High inventory.** Too much inventory takes up space, may get in the way of production and costs money.
» **Motion.** Any actions, including bending or stretching movements of the body of the employee, wastes time. It may also be a health and safety risk for the employees. This also applies to the movement of machines which may not be necessary.
» **Over-processing.** Using complex machinery to perform simple tasks is wasteful. Some activities that take place during production of goods may not be necessary and may be because the design of the product is poor.
» **Defects.** Any faults require the goods to be fixed and time can be wasted inspecting the products.
» **Non-utilised skills.** If an employee is over-trained for the simple tasks they are performing, their skills are being wasted.

> **Definitions to learn**
>
> **Lean production** aims to use fewer inputs, cut down on waste and therefore increase efficiency.
> **Inventory** refers to the raw materials, semi-processed goods and finished goods held by a business at any one time.

Production processes

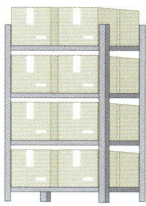
Overproduction

Waiting

Transportation

High inventory

▶ The causes of waste that lean production aims to eliminate

Motion

Over-processing

Defects

Non-utilised skills

> ### Activity 17.2
> Choose a business activity with which you are familiar, for example, a restaurant, cafe or hairdresser, and identify examples of the several types of waste which might occur.
>
> How could these types of waste be eliminated?

The two most widely used ways to achieve lean production are explained in the following sections.

Just-in-time inventory control

Just-in-time (JIT) is a production method which focuses on greatly reducing or virtually eliminating the need to hold inventories of raw materials or components and on reducing work in progress and inventories of the finished product.

If JIT is in operation:

» Raw materials or components are delivered just in time to be used in the production process.
» The making of any parts is undertaken just in time to be used in the next stage of production.
» The finished product is made just in time to be delivered to the customer.

These three efficient JIT operations result in the following advantages:

» The cost of holding inventory is greatly reduced.
» No raw materials and components are ordered to keep in the warehouse just in case they are needed.
» Warehouse space is not needed, again reducing costs.
» The finished product is sold quickly and so money will come back to the business more quickly, helping its cash flow.

Definitions to learn

Just-in-time (JIT) is a production method that involves reducing or virtually eliminating the need to hold inventories of raw materials or unsold inventories of the finished product.

17 PRODUCTION OF GOODS AND SERVICES

Key info

JIT is not just used by manufacturing businesses. Service providers such as hotels and fast-food restaurants can reduce waste and lower costs by only ordering food and other supplies as and when needed – as long as they arrive just in time to provide a good customer service.

To operate just-in-time, inventories of raw materials, work in progress and finished products are run down and no extra inventory is kept. The business therefore needs very reliable suppliers and an efficient system of ordering raw materials or components.

Kaizen

Kaizen means 'continuous improvement' in Japanese and its focus is on the elimination of waste. The improvement does not come from investing in new technology or equipment but through the ideas of the employees themselves. Small groups of workers meet regularly to discuss problems and possible solutions. This has proved effective because no one knows the problems that exist better than the employees who face them all the time, so they are often the best ones to think of ways to overcome them. Employee motivation improves as the views of workers are considered to be very important by managers.

Kaizen eliminates waste by reducing high inventory levels and by reducing the amount of time taken for employees to walk between jobs so that they eliminate unnecessary movements. When Kaizen is introduced, the factory floor is reorganised by repositioning machines tightly together in cells, in order to improve the flow of production through the factory. The floor will be open and marked with colour-coded lines which map out the flow of materials through the production process.

Definitions to learn

Kaizen is a Japanese term meaning 'continuous improvement' through the elimination of waste.

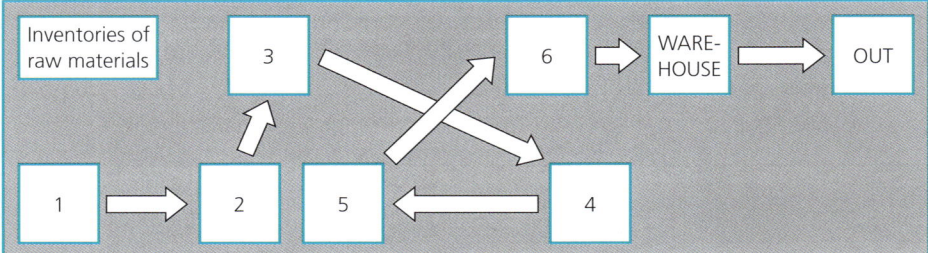

▲ The Kaizen effect: before

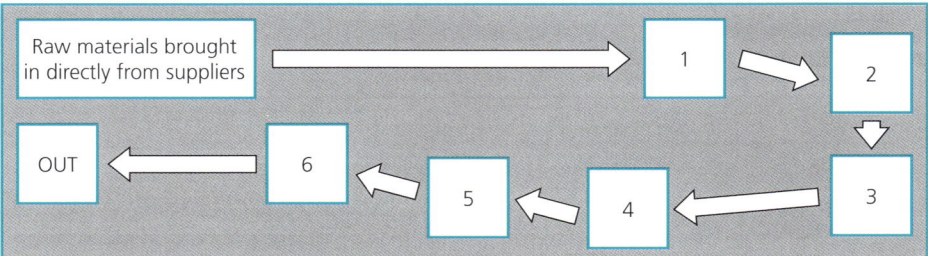

▲ The Kaizen effect: after

Activity 17.3

From the diagrams above, identify the changes that have taken place in the reorganisation of the factory floor using Kaizen principles.

Advantages and disadvantages of lean production methods

Advantages
- Inventory costs of raw materials and components are lower.
- Wastage rates are lower which improves sustainability of operations as well as reducing costs.
- Employees' time is used more effectively because operations are more efficiently planned and organised.
- Active involvement in Kaizen groups increases employee motivation.
- Labour productivity is increased as less time is wasted and production is more efficient.
- Production processes are faster as less wasted time means that production is not delayed by excessive movement of employees or the product in the factory.
- There are no storage costs of finished products as they are delivered to customers just as they are completed.

The overall benefit to businesses from lean production is to reduce unit production costs as efficiency is higher. Lower costs of production for each item make a business more competitive. A very efficient business could possibly lower its prices and become the most competitive business in the market. This will increase sales, revenue and profit.

Disadvantages
- Using JIT increases risks to the business if there is a delay in materials or components from suppliers. Production will have to stop until supplies arrive.
- Unreliable suppliers will cause frequent hold-ups to production.
- Employees might be resistant to some changes if they think that increased efficiency could result in redundancies.
- There will be high initial costs. Investment in a powerful IT system to control JIT inventory orders will be needed.
- Kaizen results in reorganisation of factories which can disrupt production while it takes place.
- Employees will need training to be able to operate new processes efficiently and to be able to contribute effectively to Kaizen groups.

The potential disadvantages of lean production are likely to be mainly short-term. With effective management and training of employees, the long-term advantages of lean production will nearly always be greater than the disadvantages.

Extend your skills of analysis

A question which asks for an advantage to a food processing business of using JIT inventory control could be answered as follows:

Just-in-time inventory control keeps inventories of raw materials, work in progress and finished goods very low – zero if possible.

Extend your analysis by explaining why this is an advantage.

Keeping inventories as low as possible reduces warehouse costs and keeps goods as fresh as possible.

Extend your analysis by explaining how this will benefit the business.

Food processing uses natural raw food ingredients. It is important that these are used in the process as soon as they are delivered to the factory to maintain freshness. This will help improve the brand image of quality fresh products and there should be no customer complaints.

17 PRODUCTION OF GOODS AND SERVICES

Why businesses hold inventory

Have you ever gone into a shop and found it has run out of what you wanted? If so, then the shop might have had higher sales than usual or else its delivery of supplies might have been late. To ensure that there is always enough inventory to satisfy demand, inventory levels must be carefully controlled.

Inventories can take various forms, including raw materials, components, partly finished goods or finished products ready for delivery. It can even include inventory of spare parts for machinery in case of breakdowns.

Businesses hold inventories for several reasons. These are to:

- give consumers a wide choice when they are ready to purchase
- prevent customers from having to wait a long time before the product is available
- avoid not having anything to sell during busy periods
- reduce the risk of running out of materials and components
- be able to benefit from bulk discounts from suppliers if very large orders are placed with them.

Factors affecting how much inventory businesses hold

The factors that affect how much inventory a business can hold are:

- **Cost.** There can be high costs of holding inventory. Warehouses need to be built. Inventory has to be insured. Goods might be damaged while in storage. Finance tied up in inventory might be borrowed at high rates of interest. The higher these costs are, the lower the levels of inventory a business will want to hold.
- **Space available.** This could be the main factor, especially for small businesses with small premises such as convenience shops.
- **Perishability.** If the materials or finished goods are perishable, as with food products, it will be vital to keep inventory levels as low as possible. Throwing away inventory which is unsellable would be a major cause of waste.
- **Technological change.** If the product held in inventory could be made obsolete by a new technological innovation, the value would be greatly reduced. If there is a risk of this a business will want to hold as low a level of inventory as possible.

The main methods of production

There are three main methods of production:

- job production
- batch production
- flow production.

Job production

> **Definitions to learn**
>
> **Job production** is where a single product is made at a time, usually to a customer's specific requirement.

Job production is used when products are made specifically to order, for example, a customer would order a particular piece of furniture and the business would make it. Each order is different and may or may not be repeated. Other examples include specialist machines to perform a particular function, unique IT systems to meet the requirements of one business, bridges, ships, made-to-measure suits and

The main methods of production

individual works of art. Table 17.1 explains the advantages and disadvantages of job production.

Table 17.1 Advantages and disadvantages of job production

Advantages of job production	Disadvantages of job production
Each product meets the exact requirements of the customer	Skilled labour is often required and high wages have to be paid
Each product can be different and this offers employees interesting and challenging work	Costs are also high as the work is labour-intensive with few opportunities for automation
Employee motivation can be high because of the interest in the work they do	Products are specialised and made to order so any errors can be costly to correct
It is a flexible production method allowing for product changes	Production can take a long time
One-off products can often be sold for high prices	Specialist materials might have to be purchased at high cost

Batch production

Batch production is where similar products are made in groups or batches. A certain number of one product is made, then a certain number of another product is made, and so on. Examples of businesses using batch production include a small bakery making batches of bread, several houses built together using the same design, furniture production (a certain number of tables are made, then a certain number of chairs) or clothing (a batch of a particular size of jeans is produced and then a batch of another size). Table 17.2 explains the advantages and disadvantages of batch production.

> **Definitions to learn**
>
> **Batch production** is where a quantity of one product is made, then a quantity of another item will be produced.
>
> **Flow production** is where large quantities of a product are produced in a continuous process.

Table 17.2 Advantages and disadvantages of batch production

Advantages of batch production	Disadvantages of batch production
Production will be higher than job production and average costs are likely to be lower than job production	Machines have to be reset after each batch to start making another product
There may still be some variety in employees' work if several products are made in batches	There are many products at different stages of production so inventory of work in progress will be high
A range of products can be made in batches, offering some consumer choice	More machinery is used than with job production and this can add to costs
There is some flexibility as employees and machines can be switched from one product to another	Employees with several skills are required so that they can switch from one product to another and high wages might have to be paid
Large orders can be met much more quickly than with job production	Partly completed products have to be moved from one stage to the next and this wastes time

Flow production

Flow production is where large quantities of an identical product are produced in a continuous process. It is sometimes referred to as mass production because of the large quantity of a standardised product that is produced.

17 PRODUCTION OF GOODS AND SERVICES

It is called flow production because products move down the production line in a continuous flow. The basic structure of the product is created at the start of the production line and then the product moves down the line for more parts to be added. This continues until the product is finished and packaged ready for sale. Examples of products produced in this way include cars, televisions, packaged foods and drinks; in fact, any mass produced, standardised product which is sold to a mass market will be produced in this way. Table 17.3 explains the advantages and disadvantages of flow production.

Table 17.3 Advantages and disadvantages of flow production

Advantages of flow production	Disadvantages of flow production
There is a high output of a standardised product	The costs of purchasing the equipment needed to construct a flow production line are high
The quality of every product should be consistent	The work can be very boring and repetitive for employees
Average costs of each unit will be lower than with the other two methods because of the higher efficiency of production – each employee becomes skilled and efficient at one task	Boring work can lead to low levels of employee motivation
Lower prices could be charged to customers as a result	The breakdown of one machine on the flow production line can result in all production being stopped
There is huge scope for automation as tasks are repetitive and need to be performed quickly	Consumers are becoming more demanding and often require products that are not standardised or identical
Automated production lines can operate 24 hours a day	If not operated continuously, the average cost can be higher because of the high fixed costs of flow production systems

Case study: Methods of production

Tara wanted to start her own business. She decided to start cooking dishes of Thai food and selling them to local people for dinner parties. She advertised in the local newspaper and used her own kitchen to prepare the food. The food was extremely popular and soon she had to turn down customer orders.

So Tara decided to rent a small factory unit in which she could put large cookers. She took on several employees to help her increase output. The number of orders received continued to grow and shops started to order large quantities of a particular dish and they would sell it to customers in smaller containers as a takeaway dinner which they could heat up at home. Tara would now make a large quantity of a dish and then divide it into large containers ready to be sent out for sale. She would then make a large quantity of another dish, and so on. Still the popularity of the food grew!

After about 2 years Tara decided she could afford to buy much larger premises and invest in new automated machinery to cook the food. The demand was there and the food sold to airlines, hotels and supermarkets, as well as the original shops. The new automated process would produce particular dishes in very large quantities and would produce the same dish continually.

Activity 17.4

Read the case study on the previous page.

a What are the different methods of production that Tara used as her business expanded?
b Why do you think she changed production methods as her business expanded?

Study tips
Make sure you can choose a suitable method of production for different products or a particular business.

Extend your skills of analysis

A question which asks for a disadvantage to a laptop manufacturer of using flow production could be answered as follows:

Flow production involves the use of machinery to produce a continuous flow of identical units.

Extend your analysis by explaining why this might be a disadvantage.

Consumers may not be prepared to buy identical products even if the prices are kept low because production costs are low.

Extend your analysis by explaining how this might affect the laptop manufacturer.

If the market for laptops is changing towards more specialised and personalised units then large-scale production of identical products could lead to overproduction. If these laptops remain unsold, the prices of them might have to be cut substantially as consumers prefer laptops with different and varied features.

How to recommend and justify an appropriate production method for a given situation

These are the factors that a business will consider when choosing the most appropriate production method:

Key info
Flow production can achieve very high levels of output. One of the world's largest car factories is in South Korea. The Hyundai factory aims to produce one new car every 10 seconds – 1.53 million each year. This would be impossible using any other method of production.

» **The nature of the product.** If a fairly unique product or an individual service is required (in fact many services are individual to the customer and will be specifically tailored to their requirements), job production will be used. If the product can be mass produced using an automated production line, then flow production could be used.
» **The size of the market.** If demand is higher and more products can be sold but not in very large quantities, batch production will be used. The product will be produced in a certain quantity to meet the particular order. Small local markets or niche markets will be served by businesses using job or batch production. International markets for standardised products are served by businesses using flow production.
» **The nature of consumer demand.** If there is a large and fairly steady demand for the product, such as soap powder, it becomes economical to set up a production line and continuously produce the product (flow production). If demand is less frequent, such as for furniture, then job or batch production are more likely to be used.
» **The size of the business.** If the business is small and does not have access to large amounts of capital, then it will not produce on a large scale using automated production lines. Only large businesses can operate on this scale. Small businesses are more likely to use job or batch production methods.

17 PRODUCTION OF GOODS AND SERVICES

Activity 17.5

a What method of production is used by each of the following businesses? Explain the reasons for your choice.
   - Wall's manufactures well-known brands of ice cream. The ice creams are sold in many different shops and other outlets, and millions are sold every year.
   - Alexander is a hairdresser. He styles men's hair and has a number of regular customers.

b Hudson's is a private limited company and has been in business for 10 years manufacturing components for cars. It sells to several large car producers. Hudson's wants to expand and manufacture components for aircraft engines. It has decided to build a new factory in another country, near to where aircraft engines are manufactured. Some of the new components it plans to produce will be designed for only 1 type of engine, whereas most of the other components will be standardised and used in several different models of engine. Hudson's has chosen the new site for the factory but has not decided on the method of production to use. You have been asked to advise it on what to use. Justify your choice of the method(s) of production it should use.

International business in focus

Toyota was the first company to start using just-in-time (JIT) in the early 1970s. Since then many businesses have adopted the technique, from retailers, restaurants and on-demand publishers to tech and vehicle manufacturers. Toyota, McDonald's, Apple and Dell are just some of the global businesses that use JIT today. However, one of the main challenges of JIT production is that it requires high dependence on suppliers who can deliver the right materials, at the right time, in the right place and of the right quality. Disruptions caused by the global health crisis in 2020 affected the supply chain for a large number of businesses, particularly automotive businesses, such as Toyota, which experienced delays with the delivery of chips. This caused problems to the production flow of many consumer goods businesses and affected customer satisfaction as products were not available to order.

Discussion points
- Why have so many businesses adopted JIT after Toyota first started using the technique in the early 1970s?
- Will the problems caused to supplies during the global health crisis mean that businesses will no longer use JIT?

Chapter review questions: Short answer and data response

1 Carlos owns a private limited company called BettaBakers. It produces bread loaves and a variety of cakes which are sold in local shops. The method of production used for these products is batch production. Carlos is worried about the low level of labour productivity in the wedding cake section. This makes one-off wedding cakes to customers' own designs. He also wants to increase output in other sections of the bakery. He said: 'I have been told that a flow production method in the bakery for the standard bread loaves would help me increase profits.'
   a Define 'labour productivity'. [2]
   b Outline **two** advantages to BettaBakers of using job production for wedding cakes. [4]
   c Explain **two** disadvantages to Carlos of using batch production. [6]
   d Do you think Carlos should change to flow production for the standard loaves of bread? Justify your answer. [8]

2 Mr Patel owns a business which manufactures wooden chairs. He uses flow production in the factory. Employees use machines to help them measure, cut and shape the wood needed for each type of chair. These parts are then assembled by workers who are at different stages of the production line. Many resources are wasted in the factory and inventories are high. Mr Patel is worried about the level of efficiency in his factory and wants to improve it. He is thinking of introducing lean production methods.
   a Define 'flow production'. [2]
   b Outline **two** reasons for Mr Patel to hold inventory in his factory. [4]
   c Explain **two** disadvantages of low levels of efficiency in this factory. [6]
   d Do you think Mr Patel should introduce lean production methods into his factory? Justify your answer. [8]

The main methods of production

> **Revision checklist**
>
> In this chapter you have learned:
>
> ✔ how to calculate labour productivity
> ✔ why efficiency is important for a business
> ✔ how to increase efficiency
> ✔ the concept of lean production and how to achieve it
> ✔ the advantages and disadvantages of lean production methods
> ✔ why businesses hold inventory and factors affecting how much inventory businesses hold
> ✔ the main methods of production: job, batch and flow production
> ✔ the advantages and disadvantages of each method of production
> ✔ how to recommend and justify an appropriate production method for a given situation.

NOW – test your understanding with the revision questions in the Student etextbook and the Workbook.

18 Technology and production of goods and services

> This chapter will explain:
>
> The use of technology in the production of goods and services:
> ★ how technology is changing production methods through automation and mechanisation
> ★ how technology is improving productivity in the service sector
> ★ advantages and disadvantages of changes in technology for businesses and employees.

Definitions to learn

Mechanisation is the introduction of machines into production methods.
Automation is the use of advanced technology to make a production method work automatically without employee control.
Computer-aided manufacturing (CAM) is the use of software and computer-controlled machinery to automate a manufacturing process.
Computer-aided design (CAD) is the use of IT to help create, modify and improve designs.

The use of technology in the production of goods and services

How technology is changing production methods through automation and mechanisation

Technological advances have allowed the **mechanisation** and **automation** of production methods in many industries. Mechanisation has transformed industry over the last 300 years. Flow production lines, with employees working at just one stage of production, would not have been possible without mechanisation. Machines are vital to these production processes but they are often controlled by employees.

Automation is a much more recent advance which has accelerated with cheap computer processing power. Automated machines have replaced most employees on flow production line systems. The use of automation, robotics and **computer-aided manufacturing (CAM)** keeps businesses ahead of the competition, keeps average costs falling, reduces prices and improves the products manufactured.

Computer-aided manufacturing

Automation is very widely used in manufacturing industries. The equipment is robotically controlled by computers. Human input is required to program the computers and maintain machinery but no employees are needed for the production process. These automated machines can operate 24 hours a day, 7 days a week. The quality of work produced is often much higher than when there is employee input. There is no human error – assuming the computer has been correctly programmed! This type of automation is referred to as computer-aided manufacturing (CAM). A good example of it in operation is in car manufacturing. All of the welds needed to hold a car body together are done by robots with big welding heads and multi-swivel capability. They can complete the welds needed in much less time than humans – and with much greater accuracy.

Computer-aided design

Computer-aided design (CAD) is computer software that draws items being designed more quickly and allows them to be rotated to see the item from all sides instead of having to draw the item several times. It is used to design new products or to re-style existing products. It is particularly useful for detailed technical drawings of buildings used in architecture.

CAD and CAM can be combined together so that the design of products can be linked directly to the computers in the manufacturing process.

3D printing

Definitions to learn

3D printing is producing a physical three-dimensional object from a digital design.

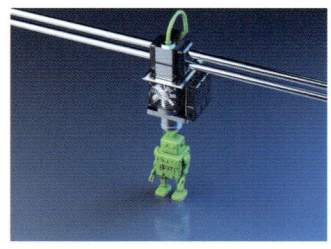

3D printing allows a designer to produce a physical three-dimensional object from a digital design. This process can be used to develop prototypes of new products at a much lower cost than building them in the material that will eventually be used. No skilled labour is needed (in fact, no labour at all is needed) to make these physical objects. Architects can produce a 3D image of a new house design for a client. Designers of sports shoes can print out a new design of shoe and test it much more quickly than producing it using traditional methods. In the future it is predicted that some 3D printers will be able to print components required in the manufacture of goods, saving transport costs. 3D printers which use chocolate, dough or pureed fruit instead of ink can even produce food products.

 Case study: 3D printing

Sportsmaster is a sports retailer of footwear, clothing and equipment. In order to remain competitive it uses 3D printers to produce prototypes so they can be tested and have minor adjustments made if necessary. This is a much faster process as before, Sportsmaster used to create designs of new products and then these would be manufactured into prototypes. If an error was found or something needed adjusting then the prototype would have to be made all over again. This would take weeks to complete. Now that Sportsmaster uses 3D printers to create prototypes it takes 40% less time for new products to be created and it reduces costs by 30%.

Activity 18.1

a Research examples of products that can be printed using 3D printers.
b Outline **two** advantages of 3D printing.
c How could 3D printers affect the location decisions of businesses in the future?

How technology is improving productivity in the service sector

The application of technology and automation is also transforming productivity in the service sector. Here are some examples:

Contactless payments

This is increasingly being used in many countries. It is a fast, easy and secure way to pay for purchases. Large transactions can be made when a passcode, fingerprint or some other method is used to ensure the purchase is authorised by the account holder. Pre-paid debit, charge and credit cards, key fobs, wearable devices such as watches and wristbands, and mobile devices such as smartphones and tablets, can be used to make contactless payments. When a device is close to or touches a contactless terminal, it securely transmits information about the purchase.

Contactless payments improve convenience for the customer as well as raising security levels and speed of operation. Any process that increases speed of service sector operation will reduce operating costs.

18 TECHNOLOGY AND PRODUCTION OF GOODS AND SERVICES

EPOS (electronic point of sale)

This is used at checkouts in shops where the operator scans the barcode of each item individually. The price and description of the item is displayed on the checkout monitor and printed on the till receipt. The inventory record is automatically changed to show one item has been sold and if inventory is low and needs reordering then more inventory can be automatically ordered.

Artificial intelligence

Artificial intelligence (AI), such as chatbots, is widely used by businesses when providing customer service. These AI chatbots are programmed with large amounts of data to provide a wide range of non-scripted, conversational responses to customers' text or voice input. This type of technology speeds up responses to customer enquiries as well as greatly reducing the number of employees providing telephone services to customers.

> **Study tips**
> Keep up to date with changes in technology, including how AI is changing the jobs that employees do. Understand which tasks AI is replacing and which tasks AI is creating.

> **Activity 18.2**
> Research contactless payment methods used by retailers.
> a What are the advantages and disadvantages of using this method of payment for the business?
> b What are the advantages and disadvantages of using this method of payment for the customer?

The advantages and disadvantages of changes in technology for businesses

Advantages

- Productivity is increased as more efficient production methods are used, leading to reduced average costs. This will increase business competitiveness.
- Employee costs are reduced as many unskilled jobs will no longer be needed.
- Better quality products are produced owing to more accurate production methods. This improves the quality image of the business and reduces waste.
- New 'high-tech' products are introduced as new technology makes completely new products available.
- New information technologies (IT) allow for quicker communication and reduced paperwork, leading to increased profitability.
- Constant 24/7 operation increases output from existing factories so there is less need to expand them or build new ones as capacity utilisation is increased.
- The safety record in factories is improved as many dangerous tasks are now done automatically by machinery. This reduces the cost of health and safety provision and there are fewer accidents.
- It leads to faster customer service when paying or contacting the business.

Disadvantages

- The initial costs of buying new technology equipment are high. If loans are used to buy the machines, then interest costs will be higher.
- Automated machinery cannot be afforded by smaller businesses so they become less competitive.

The use of technology in the production of goods and services

- » Businesses will need to pay to train more employees to program and maintain advanced equipment. They may offer training to existing employees but it might take time for them to reach the necessary skill level.
- » The use of automation in the service sector can reduce the quality of consumer service if there is no personal, human communication at all. This could be a particular problem for older or disabled consumers. The 'caring' image of the business could be damaged.
- » Any failure of automated equipment will bring the whole production process to a halt instantly. This increased reliance on technology can then prove to be a problem.
- » Redundancies resulting from using automated machines can lead to poor relations with employees. Many employees will suffer a loss of security, reducing overall motivation.
- » The use of automated machines is likely to be inappropriate in craft-based businesses where the focus is on handmade, unique items of work.
- » Redundancy payments will need to be made to employees losing their jobs. There is a legal requirement in many countries to make redundancy payments.

Overall, despite these disadvantages, most businesses are adopting mechanisation and automation to some degree. Many industries are now dominated by businesses that use the latest technology because of the substantial competitive benefits that it offers.

REVISION SUMMARY — **Advantages and disadvantages of changing technology for businesses**

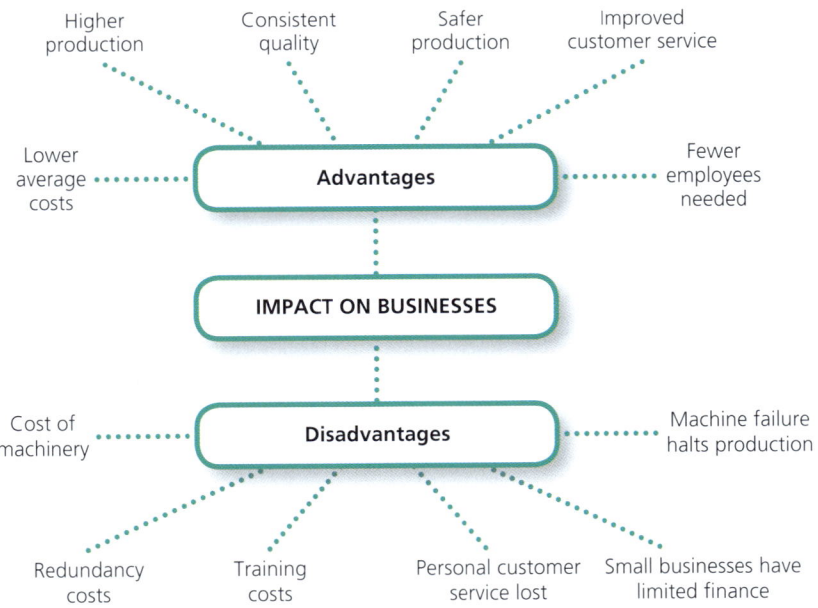

18 TECHNOLOGY AND PRODUCTION OF GOODS AND SERVICES

> **Extend your skills of analysis**
>
> A question which asks for an advantage of using automation in a steelmaking factory could be answered as follows:
>
> *Automation uses machinery which is controlled by computers, not humans.*
>
> **Extend your analysis by explaining why this is an advantage.**
>
> *Employees no longer have to perform repetitive, boring and possibly dangerous jobs.*
>
> **Extend your analysis by explaining why this is an advantage to the steelmaking business.**
>
> *Making steel is very dangerous with hot, heavy materials being transported around the factory. Many employees are likely to be injured if they did this work. Automation makes the production method safer and reduces injuries, therefore reducing the health and safety costs of the business.*

The advantages and disadvantages of changes in technology for employees

Advantages

- Employees losing their jobs will be offered redundancy pay. This could be a very large sum of money.
- There is greater job satisfaction for workers who remain employed, as routine and boring jobs are now done by machines. This gives them time to use high-order skills and be more creative.
- Wages might be increased if employees demand this because labour productivity increases. This could improve motivation for these employees.
- There may be more opportunities for training in high-technology skills of programming and maintenance.

Disadvantages

- Job losses – redundancies – will affect unskilled workers most but all employees may fear a loss of job security. This may reduce their motivation levels.
- There may be fear of change as not all employees want jobs in new technology. Any loss of security through fear of change will reduce employee job satisfaction and motivation.
- If employees are not capable of being trained or lack flexible skills, then there is a great risk of long-term unemployment.

The use of technology in the production of goods and services

REVISION SUMMARY — Advantages and disadvantages of changing technology for employees

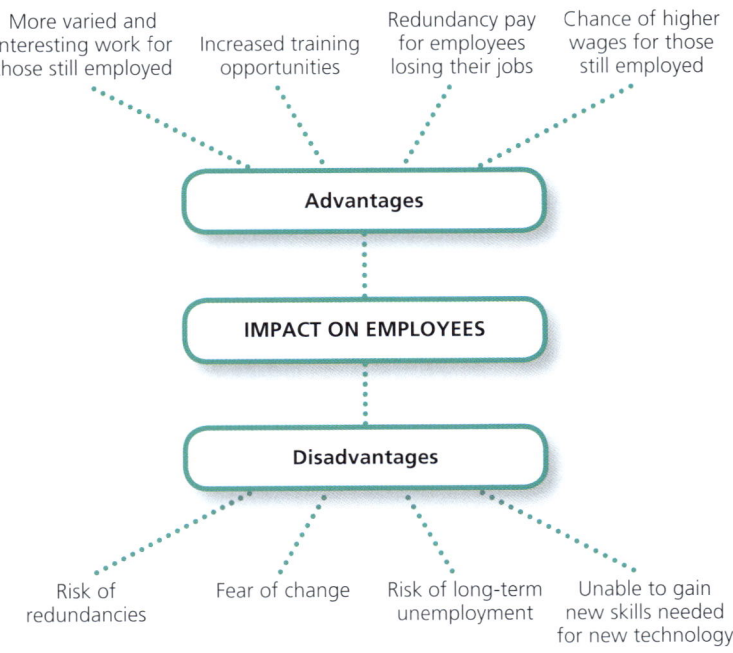

Key info

The increase in artificial intelligence and machine learning technology has been accompanied by a decline in traditional manual jobs. In the USA it is estimated that half of workers' time is spent doing tasks that could be automated and that 39 million jobs could be lost due to automation by 2030.

Study tips

Make sure you can discuss the effects of new technology on businesses and employees. How are the effects different?

Activity 18.3

A friend of yours owns a business producing football boots using old equipment and production techniques. The friend has asked you to provide advice on the following points:

a **Two** types of changes in technology that would make the business more efficient
b The advantages and disadvantages of these changes
c The impact they could have on: employees, product quality and profit

Activity 18.4

A friend of yours owns a business which designs and draws up the plans of new buildings for customers. The friend has asked you to provide advice on the following points:

a **One** type of change in technology that would make the business more efficient
b The advantages and disadvantages of this change
c The impact it could have on customer service and profit

18 TECHNOLOGY AND PRODUCTION OF GOODS AND SERVICES

International business in focus

Technology in banking

Nigerian banks, for example, Access Bank, United Bank for Africa, Zenith Bank and Fidelity Bank, have found that most Nigerians are gradually losing the desire to carry cash around. Most customers prefer banks with efficient online banking facilities as they do not like to queue in branch banks. Increasing profits and increasing the number of customers is a major incentive to change the way banks provide banking services.

The impact of technology in banking is leading to fewer branch banks with face-to-face services and new channels of accessing banking services such as automated teller machines (ATMs), internet banking, point of sale (POS) terminals and mobile (cell) phone banking. Using these technologies allows banks to achieve economies of scale, reducing the average cost of performing each transaction as well as responding to customers' preferences.

Discussion points

- Why have Nigerian banks been changing the way they provide bank services?
- How has technology changed the way banks provide their services to customers?
- What benefits do the banks gain from introducing more technology into their business?

Chapter review questions: Short answer and data response

1 ATZ is a supermarket business with many shops. It owns a factory that processes some of the food products sold in the shops. These include soups, curries and desserts. Until several years ago these food products were made by a production method where employees had tasks of preparing, cooking, finishing and packaging the products. The products had a good reputation for being 'handmade'. Now, a production line using automation undertakes all these tasks. Production has increased by 50%. ATZ offers consumers contactless payment and a chatbot service if they have any queries or complaints.
   a Define the term 'automation'. [2]
   b Outline **one** advantage and **one** disadvantage of automation to factory employees at ATZ. [4]
   c Explain **one** advantage and **one** disadvantage to the business of using technological methods to improve customer service. [6]
   d Do you think ATZ was right to introduce automation in its factory? Justify your answer. [8]

2 Engineers working for RDZ Aero Engines use 3D printing to manufacture some important engine parts. The business has set up training programmes for its employees in this new technology. RDZ engineers can now produce new parts with less weight and less waste than traditional techniques. Some RDZ engineers, because of their high skills, have taken very high-paid jobs with other employers. RDZ also uses computer-aided manufacturing (CAM) to help keep production costs low.
   a Define '3D printing'. [2]
   b Outline **two** advantages to RDZ of using 3D printing. [4]
   c Explain **one** advantage to employees and **one** disadvantage to the business of RDZ's training of its engineers. [6]
   d Do you think RDZ has benefited from changes in technology? Justify your answer. [8]

Revision checklist

In this chapter you have learned:

✔ how technology is changing production methods through automation and mechanisation
✔ how technology is improving productivity in the service sector
✔ about the advantages and disadvantages of changes in technology for businesses and employees.

NOW – test your understanding with the revision questions in the Student etextbook and the Workbook.

19 Sustainable production of goods and services

This chapter will explain:

Methods of sustainable production:
★ how businesses can be more sustainable
★ advantages and disadvantages of businesses becoming more sustainable.

Methods of sustainable production of goods and services

> **Definitions to learn**
>
> **Sustainable production** needs businesses to minimise the use of natural resources and dangerous materials and to reduce waste and pollution.
> **Renewable energy** is power obtained from sources that are not used up in energy production, such as solar and wind power.

Have you heard of global warming and climate change? Are you worried about levels of pollution and the amount of waste we create? Do you think we should recycle more of what we buy? If you answer YES to all three questions then you have started to understand why businesses are under pressure to use **sustainable production** methods.

How businesses can be more sustainable

These are the most important ways in which a business can become more sustainable:

Using renewable energy

Businesses that use coal, oil, gas or electricity made from these resources are contributing to global warming and climate change. This is because burning these resources gives off pollutants such as carbon dioxide, which contributes to global warming. Also, once the resources have been burnt they cannot be reused. Only **renewable energy** sources such as wind, solar or hydropower are fully sustainable. If the sun is used today to generate electricity, it will not stop the sun shining tomorrow.

Many businesses have made large investments in solar panels to generate electricity and storage batteries to allow the electricity to be used at any time. Other businesses have built wind turbines on their premises or only use energy that has been produced from renewable sources.

▶ Solar panels cover the roof of this factory

19 SUSTAINABLE PRODUCTION OF GOODS AND SERVICES

Using fewer resources

There is a limited supply of natural resources and once used they cannot be used again. If we use up much of this supply, less will be available for future generations. This is not sustainable. Businesses can reduce this problem by using fewer resources during production. One way to do this is to redesign products so that fewer materials are needed. The steel panels on electric appliances are thinner than they were, say, 20 years ago. This makes them lighter but new designs means they are not less strong. Less iron ore and coal are needed to make the steel used for each appliance.

Creating less waste

Waste means resources have been used unnecessarily. By improving the accuracy of production methods and reducing the need to rework faulty products, less waste will be created. For example, more accurate machines for cutting material used in clothing reduces waste.

Reusing

The consumer led 'throw-away' society was created when resources were plentiful and climate change was not an issue. Businesses often adopted the same approach – using machines and furniture and replacing it before it became worn out or obsolete. This is not sustainable. **Reusing** happens when a business offers waste materials, pre-used products, out-of-date products and ageing equipment to other organisations which can use them without alteration. Glass bottles are a good example of a product that can be relatively easily reused and at low cost. They can be cleaned, refilled and new labels added. This can happen a number of times.

Recycling

Many products and materials used in their production can be **recycled**. This means that they can be sorted, cleaned, reprocessed and turned into other, different products. Reject car tyres from a production line can be reprocessed and converted into construction materials or sound deadening materials. They will not look like car tyres – they are not being reused – but the materials in them are being recycled. BMW claims that 85% of the materials used in its cars can be recycled and turned into other products after the cars are scrapped.

Developing environmentally friendly products

Do you like the idea of sitting in a car seat with material made from plastic bottles? Ford was among the first car manufacturers to use a new material made from recycled plastic. The material is used for the fabric of its car seats. It is called Repreve and is a polyester fibre made from recycled materials, including plastic bottles. Other car manufacturers now use similar seat materials. Other examples of **environmentally friendly products** are solar powered ovens, bamboo chopsticks and rice husk lunch boxes – the last two products were designed to replace the plastic versions.

> **Definitions to learn**
>
> **Reusing** means not throwing items away after one use but using them again or using them for another purpose.
> **Recycling** takes previously used products and materials and reprocesses them so they can be used again.
> **Environmentally friendly products** do not cause damage to the environment when they are produced.

Using environmentally friendly packaging

Plastic is one of the most difficult packaging materials to reuse or recycle. Discarded plastic containers are a substantial waste hazard in most countries. Using packaging materials which can be recycled or which are biodegradable is much more sustainable. Bamboo packaging is not just biodegradable but is also made from a renewable resource – doubly sustainable!

> **Key info**
>
> The Global 100 ranks the most sustainable companies in the world based on whether their revenue comes from sustainable sources and whether they use sustainable investment opportunities. The companies in the 2024 list used sustainable investment opportunities for more than half of their investments, compared to less than 20% for corporations with revenues above US$1 billion.

> **Activity 19.1**
>
> Choose **five** products that have packaging made from plastic.
>
> a Could the packaging be made of different materials that are more sustainable?
> b Are there other ways that the plastic packaging could be made more sustainable, i.e. be made less harmful to the environment?

Advantages and disadvantages of businesses becoming more sustainable

Advantages

- **Better brand image and customer loyalty.** The trend towards consumers preferring environmentally friendly products means that they will show loyalty towards genuinely sustainable businesses. An improved brand image through sustainability can be used in promotions and will create goodwill towards the business.
- **Lower costs.** After the initial investments in renewable energy and recycling methods, the costs of making each unit should be lower. Solar energy is free – once the panels have been paid for. Recycled materials might be obtainable at lower cost than natural raw materials which are limited in supply.
- **Less waste.** As materials and machines are being reused or recycled there will be much less waste. Improved production methods will also reduce waste of faulty products.
- **Higher profit.** The combination of high levels of consumer demand, lower average/unit costs and less waste could combine to increase business profits.
- **Improved employee recruitment and retention.** Sustainable businesses are popular with employees. There is often a great sense of pride among employees when they work for a business which is environmentally friendly in all of its operations. This will make it easier to recruit highly skilled/well-qualified employees and to retain them in future.
- **Meeting all legal controls.** Governments are making laws to force businesses to operate more sustainably. By introducing the methods which have been explained, businesses will avoid any problems associated with breaking these legal controls.

19 SUSTAINABLE PRODUCTION OF GOODS AND SERVICES

> **Study tips**
> When justifying a business decision to become more sustainable, it is often true that there will be short-term costs – such as fitting solar panels – but long-term cost reductions – such as free electricity!

Disadvantages

- **Takes time to change.** A business cannot become sustainable overnight. It might take years of planning and development to switch energy sources, develop environmentally friendly products and use more sustainable materials and production methods.
- **Initial costs are high.** Researching and developing sustainable products using recycled materials can be very costly. Solar panels and storage batteries are also high-cost, although these costs are falling. Small businesses, or large ones making low profits, may find it difficult to raise the finance for these sustainable improvements.
- **Competitors which pollute.** Some businesses in countries with few legal controls may be able to produce at a lower cost than sustainable businesses. They might not pay for the pollution and waste that they cause. They could pass these lower costs onto those consumers who are only interested in low prices. Sustainable businesses which act responsibly might experience lower sales.
- **Employee training.** This will be essential if a business is to become sustainable. Employees must be co-operative in achieving this objective and old habits and production methods have to be recognised by employees as being wrong. This will take training but could be helped by the use of well-focused Kaizen groups (see Chapter 17).
- **New suppliers might be needed.** A business does not operate in isolation. It cannot be called a sustainable business unless it can be absolutely sure that all of its supplies come from renewable, environmentally friendly sources. Old established and reliable suppliers might have to be replaced by those that follow much more sustainable practices.

REVISION SUMMARY

Sustainable production

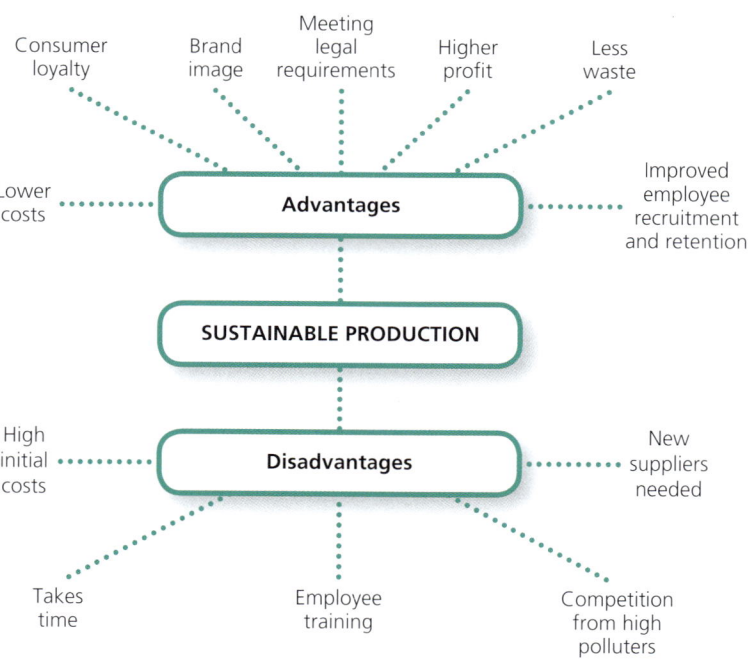

Methods of sustainable production of goods and services

Extend your skills of analysis

A question which asks for an advantage to a toy business of producing environmentally friendly products could be answered as follows:

Environmentally friendly products use materials that do not damage the environment.

Extend your analysis by explaining why this is an advantage.

Environmentally friendly materials that can be recycled could replace plastic, which is still commonly used in toys. Environmentally friendly toys would use renewable resources and materials that could be recycled, causing less waste and pollution.

Extend your analysis by explaining how the toy manufacturer would benefit from this.

The brand image of the toy business would improve and environmentally aware parents would prefer to buy these toys for their children than plastic ones. Sales, consumer loyalty and profit could increase.

Case study: Tunweni Drinks, Namibia

This company was the first in Namibia to adopt the country's Zero Emissions Research Initiative. Examples of sustainable production initiatives at the Tunweni site include:

- Fibres from grain used in the production process are recycled and used in cultivating mushrooms.
- Methane gas is produced from waste using a biodigester – the gas is used as energy within the plant.
- Wastewater is reused to farm fish in a specially constructed pond.

'This makes our business much more sustainable and gives us a competitive edge,' said the Chief Executive of Tunweni Drinks.

Activity 19.2

Read the case study above.

a What is meant by 'sustainable production'?
b Explain why the **three** initiatives taken by Tunweni Drinks make the business 'more sustainable'.
c Explain why the Chief Executive believes that the business now has a 'competitive edge'.

Activity 19.3

Choose a business that is using more sustainable methods of producing and selling its products.

a What has it done to become more sustainable?
b How has the business benefited from changing its production methods?
c Are there any disadvantages for this business from the changes to become more sustainable?
d Are there other changes it could make to become even more sustainable?

19 SUSTAINABLE PRODUCTION OF GOODS AND SERVICES

International business in focus

Sustainable Packaging at Kraft Heinz

Kraft Heinz is focused on increasing the amount of recycled and recyclable materials it uses in its packaging. It has achieved its aim of producing a 100% recycled tomato ketchup bottle and has also worked with Pulpex to develop a paper-based recyclable bottle. The company is on track for all of its packaging to be able to be re-used, recycled or composted by 2025 and it wants to reduce the amount of brand-new plastic that it uses by 20% by 2030.

Source: www.kraftheinzcompany.com/esg/sustainable-packaging.html

Discussion points

- How is the packaging used by Heinz becoming more sustainable?
- What benefits does Heinz hope to gain from using this packaging?
- Will these changes make Heinz products more competitive in global markets?

▲ One day, perhaps, containers such as these could be made of paper

Chapter review questions: Short answer and data response

1 Rishi is the new Managing Director of the Redgate washing machine manufacturing business. The production process uses a lot of electricity, steel sheets and plastic components that cannot be recycled and copper for the electric motors. Rishi said: 'I want to make this the most sustainable washing machine factory in the world.' He has plans to fit solar panels, use recycled copper, reuse water by filtering it and develop more environmentally friendly washing machines that use less steel to make and less energy to operate.
   a Define 'environmentally friendly products'. [2]
   b Outline **two** ways in which more sustainable production at Redgate could benefit the environment. [4]
   c Explain **two** advantages to Redgate of installing solar panels. [6]
   d Do you think Rishi is right to want to make Redgate the most sustainable washing machine manufacturer in the world? Justify your answer. [8]

2 KKQ is a very large online retailer. It mainly sells its own branded products such as clothes, shoes and toys. Recent social media reports have suggested that consumers should boycott KKQ. There is much evidence that its products are not made using sustainable materials and that there is a lot of waste in its factories. A new Managing Director has decided that KKQ should only use sustainable production and environmentally friendly packaging. This will take time to achieve and costs are likely to be affected.
   a Define 'sustainable production'. [2]
   b Outline **two** ways in which KKQ's packaging could be made more environmentally friendly. [4]
   c Explain **two** other ways, apart from packaging, in which KKQ could become more sustainable. [6]
   d Is the new Managing Director right to try to make KKQ more sustainable? Justify your answer. [8]

Revision checklist

In this chapter you have learned:

✔ how businesses can become more sustainable
✔ about the advantages and disadvantages of businesses becoming more sustainable.

NOW – test your understanding with the revision questions in the Student etextbook and the Workbook.

20 Costs, scale of production and break-even analysis

This chapter will explain:

How to identify and classify costs:

★ classify and calculate costs using examples
★ how to use cost data to help make simple decisions.

Economies and diseconomies of scale:

★ the concept of economies of scale
★ the concept of diseconomies of scale.

Break-even analysis:

★ the concept of break-even
★ how to complete or amend a simple break-even chart
★ how to interpret a break-even chart
★ how to calculate break-even output
★ how to define, calculate and interpret the margin of safety
★ how to use break-even analysis to help make decisions
★ limitations of break-even analysis.

Identify and classify costs

Classify and calculate costs

All business activities involve costs. These costs cannot be ignored. For example, the manager of a business is planning to open a new factory making sports shoes. Why does the manager need to think about costs? Some of the reasons are explained below.

» The costs of operating the factory can be compared with the revenue from the sale of the sports shoes. The manager can then calculate whether or not the factory will make a profit or loss.
» The costs of two different locations for the new factory can be compared. This would help the manager make the best decision about which location to choose.
» Knowing the manufacturing costs would help the manager decide what price should be charged for a pair of sports shoes.

Accurate cost information is therefore very important for managers.

> ### Activity 20.1
> These are some of the costs involved in opening and operating a new sports shoe factory:
>
> - rent of the factory
> - insurance of the factory
> - bank charges
> - raw materials used
> - management salaries.
>
> Add **six** other costs to this list that the owner would have to pay.

20 COSTS, SCALE OF PRODUCTION AND BREAK-EVEN ANALYSIS

> **Definitions to learn**
>
> **Fixed costs** are costs which do not vary in the short run with the number of items sold or produced.
> **Variable costs** are costs which vary with the number of items sold or produced.
> **Total fixed costs** are the addition of all of the fixed costs of a business.
> **Variable cost per unit** is the addition of all variable costs of producing one unit of output.
> **Total variable costs** are the addition of all variable costs at a certain level of output.
> **Total costs** are the addition of all fixed and variable costs of a business in a given time period.
> **Average costs** can be calculated by dividing total costs by the number of units produced. Sometimes called cost per unit.

> **Study tips**
>
> Avoid making this mistake: 'Fixed costs do not vary over time.' This is not true because a business might expand by building a new shop, factory or offices. Fixed costs are those that do not vary with the output of the business at the existing factory, shop or office buildings.

Fixed costs

When calculating the costs of the business it is important to understand the difference between different types of costs. Costs can be classified as either **fixed costs** or **variable costs**. Fixed costs have to be paid whether the business is making any output or not. Examples of fixed costs include management salaries and rent paid for business premises. Even if output was zero, these costs would still have to be paid. By adding together all of the costs that do not vary with output, a business can calculate its **total fixed costs**.

Variable costs

Variable costs are costs that vary with the level of output. These costs increase as the level of output rises and fall if the level of output declines. Examples of variable costs include raw material costs and piece-rate labour costs.

Variable cost per unit and total variable costs

The **variable cost per unit** can be used to calculate the **total variable costs** at a given output level using the formula given below.

> **Calculations to learn**
>
> $$\text{Variable cost per unit} = \frac{\text{Total variable costs}}{\text{Number of units}}$$
>
> $$\text{Total variable costs} = \text{Variable cost per unit} \times \text{Number of units}$$

Worked example

If the variable material cost of one pizza is $2 and the variable labour cost is $1, then the variable cost per pizza is $3 (assuming no other variable costs). If 1000 pizzas are produced each week:

$$\text{Total variable cost} = \$3 \times 1000$$
$$= \$3000$$

Total costs and average costs

The **total costs** of a business during a time period, such as one year, can be compared with total revenue and the profit or loss of the business can be calculated. It is also useful to know the **average cost** of each unit and this can be compared with the selling price. Average cost is calculated by the formula given below.

> **Calculations to learn**
>
> $$\text{Total cost} = \text{Fixed costs} + \text{Total variable costs}$$
>
> $$\text{Average cost} = \frac{\text{Total costs}}{\text{Number of units}}$$
>
> The number of units is the output level during the period of time.
>
> The formula can be rearranged to calculate total costs for a certain time period:
>
> $$\text{Total costs} = \text{Average cost} \times \text{Number of units}$$

Identify and classify costs

Worked example

A sports shoe manufacturer produces 30 000 pairs of shoes each year. It has annual fixed costs of $50 000 and total variable costs of $100 000:

$$\text{Total costs of production} = \text{Fixed costs} + \text{Total variable costs}$$
$$= \$50\,000 + \$100\,000$$
$$= \$150\,000$$

$$\text{Average cost} = \frac{\text{Total costs}}{\text{Number of units}}$$
$$= \frac{\$150\,000}{30\,000} = \$5 \text{ per pair of shoes}$$

Activity 20.2

Separate the costs listed in Activity 20.1 on page 243 and the additional costs on your list into two lists: fixed costs and variable costs. Explain why you have put each cost under either 'fixed costs' or 'variable costs'.

Activity 20.3

A car manufacturer produces 3 models, X, Y and Z. It has calculated the annual total costs of each of these 3 car models:

	Model X	Model Y	Model Z
Total variable material costs ($ m)	5	10	8
Total variable labour costs ($ m)	10	14	6
Total fixed costs per year ($ m)	9	12	6
Annual output of vehicles	4 000	12 000	5 000

Total variable cost of manufacturing Model X = $15 million

Total cost of manufacturing Model X = $15 million + $9 million = $24 million

Average cost of Model X $= \dfrac{24\,000\,000}{4\,000} = \$6\,000$ *per car*

a Calculate the total variable cost of manufacturing vehicle Models Y and Z.
b Calculate the total cost of manufacturing Models Y and Z.
c Calculate the average cost of manufacturing Models Y and Z.
d Explain **two** possible uses of these results to managers of the car manufacturer.

20 COSTS, SCALE OF PRODUCTION AND BREAK-EVEN ANALYSIS

REVISION SUMMARY   Business costs

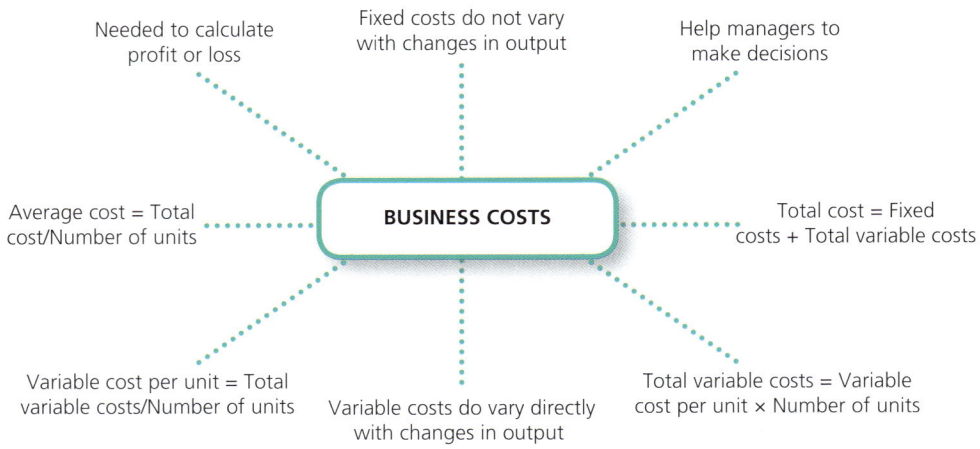

Definitions to learn

Revenue is the income of a business from the sale of goods or services during a period of time.

Use cost data to help make simple decisions

Once a business has classified all costs into either fixed or variable, this information can be used when making business decisions. Table 20.1 explains four uses of cost data to help make decisions.

Table 20.1 Uses of cost data in making decisions

Use of cost data	Example	Explanation

Which product to produce? A business must choose between producing A or B.	• Product A will have variable costs per unit of $9 and a selling price of $18
	• Product B will have variable costs per unit of $12 and a selling price of $20
	• The fixed costs will be the same: $10 000 per year
	• Sales of both products will be 5000 units per year
		• Profit for A = $90 000 − ($10 000 + $45 000)
		             = $35 000
		• Profit for B = $100 000 − ($10 000 + $60 000)
		             = $30 000
		• Product A should make $5000 more profit per year than Product B
		• Product A should be chosen because the annual profit is likely to be higher

Whether to continue or stop production? Should the business stop producing this product?	• Product C has variable costs per unit of $25. Each unit sells for $50 • Fixed costs of producing Product C each year are $76 000 • 2000 units are sold each year	• **Revenue** = $100 000 • Total costs = $126 000 • The business should stop producing Product C • Total costs are greater than total revenue. The product makes a loss of $26 000 each year
What price to set?	• Average costs of making a pizza = $3 • If the business wants to make $1 profit on each pizza sold, it will charge a price of $4	• If the price charged is less than the average cost per unit, then the business will make a loss • Prices should be set to at least pay for average costs
Which supplier to choose?	• Supplier X has agreed to supply an important component for $5 per unit • Supplier Y has agreed to supply a similar component for $4 per unit	Supplier Y should be chosen IF: • The quality of the component is at least as good as units from Supplier X • Supplier Y can supply on time and in sufficient quantities

Economies and diseconomies of scale

> **Extend your skills of analysis**
>
> A question which asks for an advantage of using cost data by an entrepreneur setting up a beauty salon could be answered as follows:
>
> Cost data could be used to help decide which treatments to offer customers.
>
> *Extend your analysis by explaining how cost data would help the entrepreneur.*
>
> The entrepreneur would calculate forecast total costs and revenue for Treatment A and compare with the forecast total costs and revenue for Treatment B. The entrepreneur could decide to offer the treatment that makes the larger profit even with a lower number of customers.
>
> *Extend your analysis by explaining why this is an advantage to the entrepreneur.*
>
> Finance is likely to be in short supply for a newly set-up business. The more profit earned by a treatment option, the quicker the entrepreneur can start to repay loans and reduce interest costs.

Economies and diseconomies of scale

> **Case study:** Cost of making bricks
>
> Consider the average cost and total output of the following 2 businesses, which both make bricks.
>
> | | Brickmaker A | Brickmaker B |
> | --- | --- | --- |
> | Total output per year | 10 million | 1 million |
> | Average cost per brick | 50 cents | 75 cents |

> **Activity 20.4**
>
> Read the case study above.
>
> Explain **three** possible reasons why the average cost of making bricks is lower for Brickmaker A than for Brickmaker B.

Definitions to learn

Economies of scale are the factors that lead to a reduction in average costs as a business increases in size.

The bigger business has much lower average costs than the smaller one. This cost advantage results from the economies of being a large business. These are called **economies of scale**. As businesses expand, the average cost of production can fall.

The concept of economies of scale

There are five economies of scale.

Purchasing economies

When businesses buy large numbers of components, materials or spare parts they can gain discounts for buying in bulk. This reduces the average or unit cost of each item bought and gives bigger businesses a cost advantage over smaller businesses which buy in small quantities.

Marketing economies

There are several of these such as:

» A large business could afford to purchase its own vehicles to distribute goods rather than depending on transport businesses.
» Transport costs per unit carried can be reduced by using larger vehicles.
» Advertising costs per unit of sales can be lower for a large business than for one with a lower level of sales. Having access to the most effective advertising methods, despite high overall cost, should allow a large business to lower the cost of advertising per unit sold.

» The business will not need twice as many sales employees to sell 10 product lines as a smaller business needs to sell 5.

Financial economies

Larger businesses are often able to raise capital at a lower cost than smaller ones. Banks often consider that lending to large organisations is less risky than lending to small ones. A lower rate of interest is therefore often charged, which makes the cost of borrowing relatively cheaper per $ borrowed for large businesses.

Managerial economies

Large businesses employ specialist managers for each department. They should increase the efficiency of the business compared to general managers in a small business, and therefore average costs will fall. An entrepreneur operating a very small business may perform all management functions. They cannot be specialised in all of them.

Technical economies

There are several of these such as:

» Large manufacturing firms often use flow production methods (see Chapter 17). Specialist machines are used to produce items in a continuous flow, with employees responsible for just one stage of production. Small businesses cannot usually afford this expensive equipment. It could also be that they sell their products in small quantities and flow production could not be justified. The use of flow production and the latest equipment will reduce the average costs for large manufacturing businesses.

» Small businesses cannot afford to buy many new advanced items of technology equipment. For example, robots in car factories can cost from around $100 000 each and many robots will be needed in the production process. The equipment can greatly reduce the average costs of production.

» Many machines have a high output capacity. For example, an automatic welding machine can do 100 welds a minute. A small business could not keep the machine working all day because sales and output are quite low. This means the average cost of goods produced by the machine would be high. This is because the machinery is not 'divisible' into smaller capacity machines, so it stays unused for much of the day.

The concept of diseconomies of scale

Is it possible for a business to become so large that it becomes less and less efficient? Is there a limit to economies of scale? Some research suggests that very large businesses may become less efficient than smaller ones. This could lead to higher average costs for large-scale businesses.

There are four main **diseconomies of scale**.

Poor communication

The larger the organisation, the more difficult it becomes to send and receive accurate messages. If there is slow or inaccurate communication within a large workforce then serious mistakes can occur which lead to lower efficiency and higher average costs.

Lack of commitment or loyalty from employees

The largest businesses employ many thousands of workers. It is possible that some employees will never see senior managers. Employees may feel that they

> **Key info**
>
> The oil industry is dominated by a few large companies. One reason is the economies of scale achieved by large oil tankers. Very large oil tankers can carry 2 million barrels of oil whereas ultra large tankers can carry more than 3 million barrels. A tanker twice the length, height and width of a smaller tanker can carry eight times as much oil. Therefore, the cost to transport each barrel of oil is a lot lower for these very large and ultra large tankers.

> **Study tips**
>
> Economies of scale can result in lower *average* costs, not lower *total* costs. A large business is likely to have higher total costs than a small one – but lower average costs. Make sure you can explain this.

> **Definitions to learn**
>
> **Diseconomies of scale** are the factors that lead to an increase in average costs as a business grows beyond a certain size.

are unimportant and not valued by managers. In small businesses it is possible to establish close relationships between employees and managers. The lack of these relationships in a large business can lead to a lack of commitment and low levels of loyalty. These problems will result in lower levels of employee motivation, which can reduce efficiency. This will then increase average costs.

Weak co-ordination

It often takes longer for decisions made by managers to reach all parts of a large business and different groups of employees. This could make it difficult to co-ordinate the work and decisions of all departments and divisions of the business. It will be difficult to ensure that they are working towards the same objectives. For example, the Marketing department may advertise a new product before the Operations department has been able to manufacture the product in sufficient quantities to satisfy demand if the advertising campaign is successful. This may mean advertising costs have been wasted.

Lack of control

It is difficult to control the work being done by thousands of employees. Issues over lack of effort or poor quality work are more difficult to manage in a large business. As a result, more supervisors and quality inspectors may have to be employed by big businesses. This raises costs and could lead to higher average costs.

REVISION SUMMARY — **Economies and diseconomies of scale**

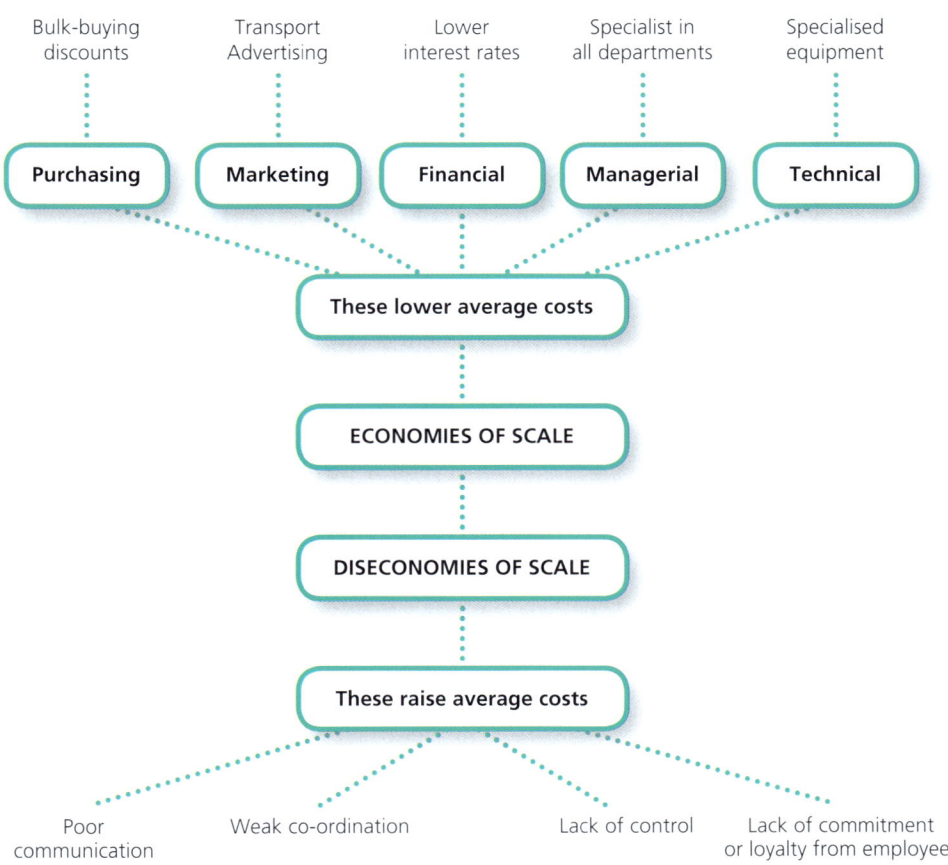

20 COSTS, SCALE OF PRODUCTION AND BREAK-EVEN ANALYSIS

> ### Activity 20.5
> The following cost data has been collected from 2 shoe manufacturing companies.
>
> | | Company A | Company B |
> | --- | --- | --- |
> | Annual output (pairs of shoes) | 20 000 | 700 000 |
> | Variable cost per pair of shoes | $4 | $2.50 |
> | Annual fixed costs | $120 000 | $2.1m |
>
> a Calculate the total annual cost of manufacturing shoes for both businesses.
> b Calculate the average cost of making each pair of shoes for both businesses.
> c Explain **three** reasons why the average cost (cost per unit) for Company B is lower than for Company A.
> d Explain **two** advantages gained by Company B as a result of lower average cost.

> **Definitions to learn**
>
> **Break-even output** is the quantity that must be produced or sold for total revenue to equal total costs.
> The **break-even point** is the level of output and sales at which total costs = total revenue.
> **Break-even charts** show how costs and revenue of a business change with sales and indicate break-even output.

Break-even analysis

The concept of break-even

'Break-even' is a very important idea for any business. It means that at this output level total costs are equal to total revenue. Although no profit is made, no loss is made either. The **break-even output** indicates to business managers the minimum level of output that must be sold so that total costs are covered. The quicker a newly set-up business can reach break-even output, the more likely it is to survive – and go on to make a profit. If a business never reaches **break-even point** then it will always make a loss.

The break-even output can be obtained in two ways – by drawing a **break-even chart**, as shown on the following page, and by calculation, as shown on page 252.

Completing a simple break-even chart

In order to complete a break-even chart we need information about the fixed costs, variable costs and revenue of a business. For example, in a pizza making business:

» fixed costs are $5000 per week
» the variable cost of each pizza is $3
» the selling price of each pizza is $8
» the factory can produce a maximum output of 2000 pizzas per week.

> ### Calculations to learn
>
> *Revenue = Selling price per unit × Number of units sold*

The data in Table 20.2 will be useful when constructing the break-even chart.

Table 20.2 Data to construct a break-even chart

	Output = 0 units	Output = 500 units	Output = 2000 units
Fixed costs per week ($)	5000	5000	5000
Total variable costs ($)	0	1500	6000
Total costs ($)	5000	6500	11 000
Revenue ($)	0	4000	16 000

Now we can plot the data on the chart. Note the following points:

» The y-axis (the vertical axis) measures money amounts – costs and revenue.
» The x-axis (the horizontal axis) shows the output level or number of units produced and sold.
» The fixed costs do not change at any level of output.
» The total cost line is the addition of variable costs and fixed costs for each level of output.

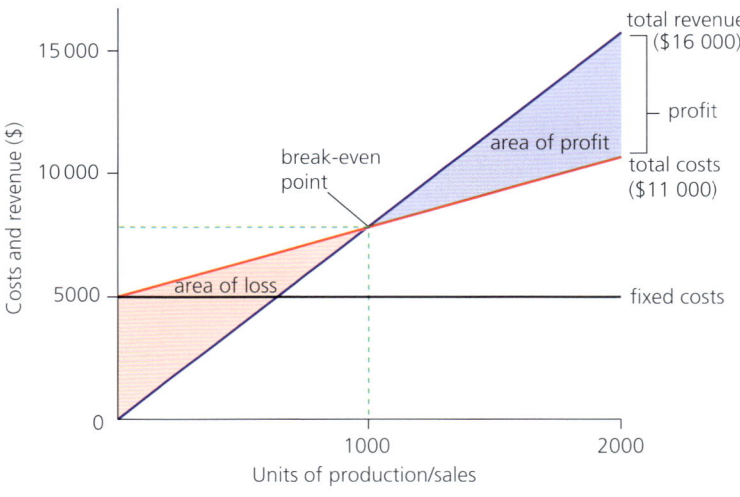

Interpret a break-even chart

What does a break-even chart show?

» The break-even point is the level of output/sales at which total costs equals total revenue.
» In the example above, the business must therefore produce 1000 pizzas in order to avoid making a loss.
» At production below the break-even output, the business is making a loss, i.e. total costs are greater than total revenue.
» At production above the break-even output, the business is making a profit, i.e. total revenue is greater than total costs.
» Maximum profit is made when maximum output is reached and this is a profit level of $5000 per week.

20 COSTS, SCALE OF PRODUCTION AND BREAK-EVEN ANALYSIS

Amend a simple break-even chart

If costs or selling prices change then the break-even chart will need to be amended.

For example, if the selling price of a pizza was increased to $9, the slope of the revenue line would increase as shown below:

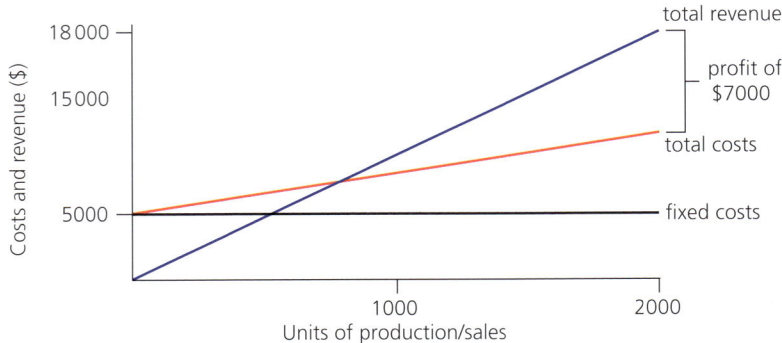

Maximum revenue now rises to $18 000. The break-even point of production falls to 833 units and maximum profit rises to $7000. It seems like a wise decision! However, the manager needs to consider competitors' prices too, and the business may not be able to sell all 2000 pizzas at $9 each.

Calculate break-even output

It is not always necessary to draw a break-even chart in order to know the break-even point of production. Using the **contribution per unit**, it is possible to calculate the break-even level using the formula given below.

> **Definitions to learn**
>
> The **contribution per unit** of a product is its selling price per unit minus variable costs per unit.

Calculations to learn

$$\text{Contribution per unit} = \text{Selling price per unit} - \text{Variable cost per unit}$$

$$\text{Break-even output} = \frac{\text{Fixed costs}}{\text{Contribution per unit}}$$

Worked example

Cape Designs makes wooden desks. The selling price of each desk is $50. The variable costs of materials and production labour are $20 per unit. The weekly fixed costs are $6000. What is the break-even level of production/sales? It is necessary to calculate the contribution of each desk to fixed costs.

Contribution of each desk = Selling price − Variable costs
= $50 − $20 = $30

Each desk gives a contribution to fixed costs of $30. In order to break even each week, the business must make enough desks, contributing $30 each, to cover the fixed costs of $6000. Using the break-even formula:

$$\text{Break-even level of output} = \frac{\text{Fixed costs}}{\text{Contribution per unit}}$$

$$= \frac{\$6000}{\$30} = 200 \text{ units per week}$$

If the business produces and sells less than 200 units it makes a loss as fixed costs are not covered. An output greater than 200 units results in a profit.

Break-even analysis

Case study: Is Namib Tyres breaking even?

Namib Tyres produces motorcycle tyres. The following information about the business has been obtained:

- Fixed costs are $30 000 per year.
- Variable costs are $5 per unit/tyre.
- Each tyre is sold for a price of $10.
- Maximum output is 10 000 tyres per year.

Study tips

Remember that a lower break-even point is better than a higher one! This is because it means that fewer units have to be sold before the business starts to make a profit.

Activity 20.6

Read the case study above.

a Copy out this table and fill in the missing figures.

	Output = 0	Maximum output = 10 000
Fixed costs	x	$30 000
Total variable costs	0	a
Total costs	y	b
Revenue	z	$100 000

b Complete a break-even chart from the information in the table.
c From your break-even chart identify:
   - the break-even level of output/sales
   - the level of profit at maximum output.
d How many more tyres are sold above the break-even level of sales at maximum output?

Activity 20.7

A fast-food restaurant sells meals for $6 each. The variable costs of preparing and serving each meal are $2. The monthly fixed costs of the restaurant amount to $3600.

a Calculate how many meals must be sold each month for the restaurant to break even.
b If the restaurant sold 1500 meals in one month, calculate the profit made in that month.
c If the cost of the food ingredients rose by $1 per meal, calculate the new break-even level of output.

Define, calculate and interpret the margin of safety

Break-even analysis can show the **margin of safety** on a chart or it can be calculated. The margin of safety is the number of units by which current sales exceed the break-even point. A margin of safety means that the level of sales could fall before the break-even point is reached. The higher the margin of safety, the better. This allows a business to still make a profit even if sales fall. The margin of safety can be calculated by the following formula.

Definitions to learn

Margin of safety is the amount by which the current level of output or sales is greater than the break-even level of sales/output.

Calculations to learn

Margin of safety = Actual output − Break-even output

Margin of safety = Actual number of sales − Break-even number of sales

Worked example

In the example which starts on page 250, if the business sells 1000 units with a break-even point of 833 units, then the margin of safety is:

Margin of safety = Actual sales (output) − Break-even output (or sales)
= 1000 − 833
= 167 units

If sales rise to 2000 units then the margin of safety rises to 1167.

Use break-even analysis to help make decisions

Table 20.3 explains how break-even analysis can help managers make important decisions.

Table 20.3 Using break-even analysis to help make decisions

Decision	Using break-even analysis	Other factors to consider before making the decision
Effect of changes in price	• A higher price will reduce the break-even output and increase the margin of safety • A lower price will increase the break-even point and reduce the margin of safety	• Competitors' prices • Reaction of customers – will they buy fewer products if price rises? • Will they buy more if price is reduced?
Effect of changes in fixed costs e.g. by buying a new machine	• If fixed costs increase this will increase the break-even level of output and reduce the margin of safety • The reverse happens if fixed costs fall	• However, if the new machine is much more efficient, variable costs per unit might fall. • Lower variable costs could increase profit even with higher fixed costs
Effect of changes in variable costs e.g. by buying higher or lower cost materials	• Lower variable costs per unit will reduce total costs. Break-even point will be reduced and the margin of safety will increase • The reverse happens if variable costs per unit are higher	• If lower-cost materials are used, will customers notice lower quality? Will demand fall? • Could better materials and higher quality allow the business to raise selling price?

> **Extend your skills of analysis**
>
> **A question which asks for an advantage of using break-even analysis by a cafe manager planning to change prices could be answered as follows:**
>
> Break-even analysis provides data on break-even output, margin of safety and profit at all output levels above the break-even point.
>
> **Extend your analysis by explaining why break-even analysis is useful in making pricing decisions.**
>
> Different price options can be added to a break-even chart or be used to recalculate the break-even output/sales. These changes would show the new break-even output, margin of safety and profit.
>
> **Extend your analysis by explaining why this is an advantage to the cafe manager.**
>
> A lower price for a cup of coffee might indicate that the increase in break-even output is so great that a profit is unlikely to be made. The lower margin of safety might indicate that the chance of earning a profit is much reduced. Profit at maximum output will be lower. These results could be compared with those for other products and help the manager set new price levels.

Activity 20.8

Refer to the data about pizzas on pages 251 and 252.

a Complete a new break-even chart to show a reduction in variable costs to $2 per pizza as a result of the manager buying cheaper materials. (Assume that the manager keeps the price at $8 per pizza.)

b Compare your break-even chart with the one showing the increase in selling price. Would you advise the manager to raise the price of pizzas or to use cheaper raw materials? Justify your answer.

Limitations of break-even analysis

Break-even analysis is useful to managers but the technique does have some limitations:

» Break-even analysis assumes that all goods produced by the business are actually sold. The analysis does not consider the possibility that inventories may build up if not all goods are sold.
» Fixed costs only remain constant if the scale of production does not change. For example, a decision to double output capacity may increase fixed costs. In the case of the pizza business, an increase in output above 2000 will need a larger factory and more machinery.
» The break-even analysis and charts used in this section have assumed that variable costs per unit and selling price remain unchanged. This is often not the case. For example, increasing output to the capacity of a factory may involve paying overtime wage rates to production employees. This will increase variable costs per unit. On a break-even chart this will make the variable cost line steeper and the total cost line steeper.
» It is also assumed that costs and revenues can be drawn with straight lines. This will not often be the case; for example, increased purchases of materials as output increases could lead to lower variable costs per unit.

Activity 20.9

a Copy out this break-even chart and complete it with the following information:
  • Fixed costs = $6000
  • Variable costs per unit = $1
  • Selling price = $2
b Identify from your chart:
  i the break-even level of output
  ii the margin of safety
  iii the level of profit at an output level of 9000.
c Explain what would happen to profit and the break-even point at an output of 9000 units if the selling price was increased to $3.
d Explain why the business might decide not to increase the price to $3.

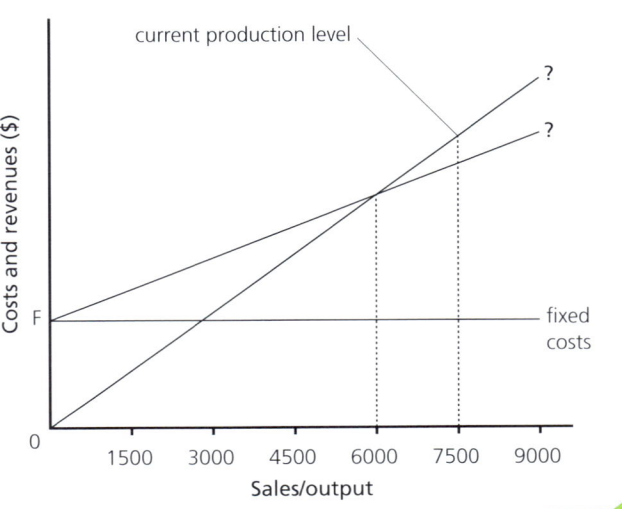

20 COSTS, SCALE OF PRODUCTION AND BREAK-EVEN ANALYSIS

REVISION SUMMARY — Uses and limitations of break-even analysis for decision making

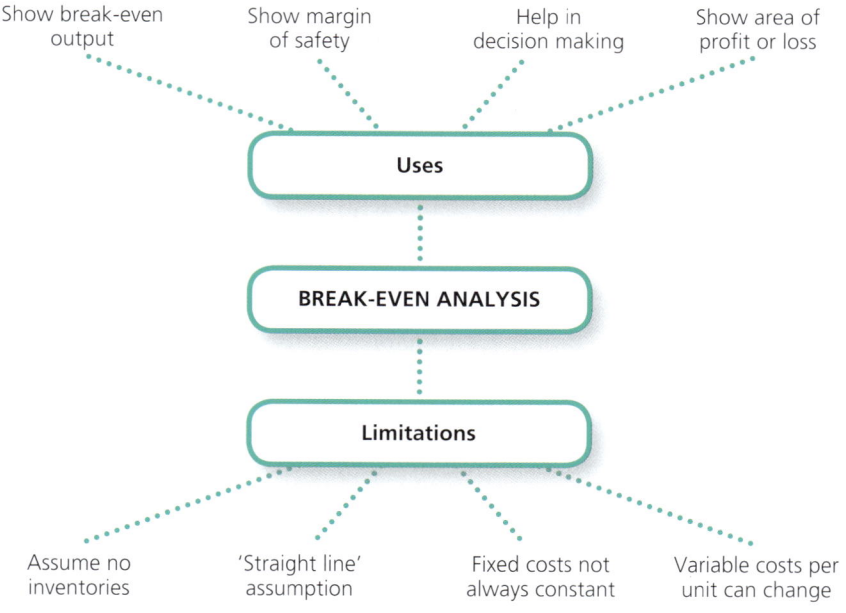

Uses:
- Show break-even output
- Show margin of safety
- Help in decision making
- Show area of profit or loss

BREAK-EVEN ANALYSIS

Limitations:
- Assume no inventories
- 'Straight line' assumption
- Fixed costs not always constant
- Variable costs per unit can change

🔍 International business in focus

Tesla Motors – economies of scale

Tesla Motors had five gigafactories – three in the USA, one in China and one in Germany – by 2024. These factories are up to 1.9 million square metres in size, making them some of the largest buildings in the world. It has been claimed that a gigafactory will produce batteries and electric vehicles for significantly lower average costs using economies of scale, reduction of waste and the simple process of locating the manufacturing process under one roof. By producing the electric vehicles and batteries in these volumes, Tesla estimates that it can make significant reductions in costs.

Tesla is planning to increase the production capacity of its assembly plant in Germany by 100%. This decision would make it the largest car plant in Europe. In contrast, German-owned carmakers are struggling to stay competitive in the transition to electric vehicles.

Discussion points

- Discuss why a Tesla gigafactory will have lower average costs for making electric batteries and vehicles than existing factories.
- Discuss whether a low break-even point for the German factory will ensure it operates profitably.

Chapter review questions: Short answer and data response

1 Sasha rents a market stall selling jewellery. She makes most of the jewellery herself but she also buys in some items from large manufacturers. Her only variable costs are materials and the wages of her sales assistant, who receives a small payment for each item she sells. The business made a small profit last year. Sasha wants to expand her business. She has found out that there is an empty shop in the city centre. The fixed costs of the shop are 3 times greater than those of the market stall.
  a Define 'variable costs'. [2]
  b Outline **two** ways in which Sasha could reduce the break-even level of output from her market stall. [4]
  c Explain **two** reasons why large jewellery manufacturers can produce jewellery at a lower average cost than Sasha can. [6]
  d Explain **two** ways break-even analysis can help Sasha decide whether to open a shop. Which way is most helpful to Sasha when making this decision? Justify your answer. [8]

2 Popsquash is one of the world's largest producers of soft drinks. Sales have risen in recent years. However, profits have not increased because of changes in fixed costs and variable costs. The Managing Director recently said: 'Perhaps the business is just too big and is experiencing diseconomies of scale.' The Finance Manager thinks they should try to reduce the break-even output of the business's most popular soft drink.
  a Define 'fixed costs'. [2]
  b Outline **two** reasons for the costs of Popsquash increasing. [4]
  c Explain **two** possible diseconomies of scale for Popsquash. [6]
  d Explain **two** ways in which Popsquash could try to reduce its break-even level of output. Which way should Popsquash use? Justify your answer. [8]

Revision checklist

In this chapter you have learned:

- ✔ how to classify and calculate costs
- ✔ how to use cost data to help make simple decisions
- ✔ the concepts of economies of scale and diseconomies of scale
- ✔ the concept of break-even
- ✔ how to complete or amend a simple break-even chart
- ✔ how to interpret a break-even chart
- ✔ how to calculate break-even output
- ✔ how to define, calculate and interpret the margin of safety
- ✔ how to use break-even analysis to help make decisions
- ✔ the limitations of break-even analysis.

NOW – test your understanding with the revision questions in the Student etextbook and the Workbook.

21 Quality of goods and services

> This chapter will explain:
>
> Why quality is important and how quality may be achieved:
>
> ★ what quality means and why it is important for businesses
> ★ the concept of quality control
> ★ the concept of quality assurance
> ★ advantages and disadvantages of quality control and quality assurance
> ★ how to recommend and justify whether to use quality control or quality assurance in a given situation.

Why quality is important and how quality may be achieved

What quality means and why it is important for businesses

What does quality mean? Ask yourself this question – if you buy a low-priced rain jacket would you expect it to last for ten years? The answer will probably be no. Consumers' expectations of quality will be much higher for a high-priced product than for one sold at a lower price. However, consumers do expect the low-priced product to be 'fit for purpose', to work effectively and to meet their expectations. So, a **quality product** does not necessarily mean an excellent product or service but it does mean one that meets customer expectations.

> **Definitions to learn**
>
> **Quality products** are of a standard which meets customer expectations.

Assume the rain jacket did not keep out the rain the first time you used it. You would not be a satisfied customer! You would take the jacket back to the shop and expect a replacement. If the shop refused to replace the jacket you would

Why quality is important and how quality may be achieved

feel this was unfair. You could share your dissatisfaction on social media – what impact would that have for the shop and the manufacturer of the jacket? A business should try to ensure that all the products it sells are free of defects and meet the expectations of its customers.

Quality is important for a business because it helps:

- establish a brand image
- build brand loyalty
- maintain a good reputation
- increase sales
- attract new customers
- reduce customer complaints and costs of replacement products.

But if quality is not maintained and customers' expectations are not met then businesses will:

- lose customers to other brands
- have to replace faulty products or offer to repeat a service to customers which raises business costs
- receive negative feedback on social media, damaging its reputation, leading to lower sales and profits.

> **Study tips**
>
> Remember that 'quality' does not necessarily mean producing an excellent, high-priced product. Quality means meeting customers' expectations.

Activity 21.1

What do you, as a customer, expect from the following products or services?

- A meal at McDonald's
- A meal at the 7-star Burj Al Arab hotel in Dubai
- A Ferrari car
- One of the cheapest new cars in the world, the Citroën Ami One
- Football lessons from a coach at a local football club
- Football lessons from the coach at Barcelona FC.

21 QUALITY OF GOODS AND SERVICES

The concept of quality control

Quality control is one method for trying to ensure that goods and services meet quality standards. It focuses on the quality of the finished product. Quality-control departments employ quality inspectors. Their job is to either test every finished product or take samples and test these. If defects are found then that product, or even an entire batch of production, might have to be scrapped as waste or reworked. Reworking means revising the product until it is of satisfactory quality. The inspectors from the Quality-control department are therefore responsible for checking on quality before the product reaches the customer. A service sector business can adopt a similar technique. For example, it could employ an anonymous 'mystery customer' to test out the service provided to check if customers are experiencing the quality service that they expect.

To be absolutely sure that only quality products reach the customer, *every* finished product should be tested. This is not always possible either because it is too costly or because testing the product makes it unsellable, for example, fireworks!

Advantages and disadvantages of quality control

Table 21.1 explains the advantages and disadvantages of quality control.

Table 21.1 The advantages and disadvantages of quality control

Advantages of quality control	Disadvantages of quality control
Testing of final products should ensure that faulty items do not reach the customer	It is a high-cost method as specialist inspectors have to be employed to test quality at the end of the production process
Specialist quality inspectors have experience of testing and identifying faulty products	It can identify faulty products but the process that causes the fault is not necessarily identified and corrected. Therefore, the quality problem will not always be solved
Employees can focus on the production tasks knowing that quality of the final product will be tested by inspectors	There are high costs of scrapping or reworking faulty products
Other employees do not have to be trained to check for quality defects	Not every product can be tested in some cases

The concept of quality assurance

Quality assurance takes a different approach to quality. Quality control checks the finished product. Quality assurance checks that quality standards are reached at each stage of the production process.

To implement a quality assurance system, all stages of production must be given quality standards to meet. For example, when assembling a car:

» Supplies of components must be checked that they meet quality standards.
» Welding and assembly at each stage must meet pre-set levels of quality.
» Painting the car and fitting the interior must all be completed to standards agreed by the Operations Manager and employees.

The key difference between quality assurance and quality control is that with quality assurance all employees must support the use of quality standards at all stages of the production process and always work towards meeting these standards. Employees must check that their own work meets the quality standards or they must identify why this is not happening. If this is done, the finished product should have no defects and require no reworking.

> **Definitions to learn**
>
> **Quality control** is checking for quality of a good or service at the end of the production process.
> **Quality assurance** is setting quality standards throughout the production process and checking these are reached at each stage of the process.

> **Key info**
>
> Researchers at Purdue University have developed a tool to test lithium-ion batteries (used in electric cars) for faults. 'This technique represents a practical quality-control method for lithium-ion batteries,' said Douglas Adams, one of the researchers responsible for the new tool. 'The ultimate aim is to improve the reliability and quality of these batteries.'

Advantages and disadvantages of quality assurance

Table 21.2 explains the advantages and disadvantages of an effective quality assurance system.

Table 21.2 Advantages and disadvantages of quality assurance

Advantages of quality assurance	Disadvantages of quality assurance
All employees work towards agreed quality standards at every stage of production	It is expensive to train all employees to meet and keep a check on quality standards
Quality becomes important at each stage of production. It tries to eliminate faults or errors at all stages of the production process before passing on to the next stage – not just at the finished product stage	Production may be held up if faulty work in an early stage of production takes time to resolve
There will be reduced scrappage costs and reduced reworking costs/the costs of repeating the customer service	It relies on employees being committed to maintaining the quality standards set. This links to the need for the HRM department to maintain high motivation levels
Fewer customer complaints will be received and there is less chance of negative social media feedback	Production may slow down when quality standards are checked at each stage

How to recommend and justify whether to use quality control or quality assurance in a given situation

These are the factors that will influence which method of achieving quality a business will use:

» **Cost.** The quality method used must not be so costly that a loss is made on every product. If quality assurance is too costly to use, quality control could be recommended.
» **Type of product and importance of safety.** If safety is a priority, for example, with methods of transport, then quality assurance can be justified despite the high training costs. In some cases, final quality-control checks will also be necessary. If testing final products makes them unsellable then quality assurance is preferable.
» **Customer expectations.** When these are very high, perhaps because of the high price charged for the product, quality assurance at every stage will be important.
» **The cost of scrapping or reworking the finished product.** If there is a very high cost to scrap a faulty product it is much better to use quality assurance. If the fault can be found at an early stage of production, then it can be fixed without the final product having to be scrapped or reworked.

> **Study tips**
>
> Make sure you can discuss the difference between quality control and quality assurance and select an appropriate method in a given situation.

Extend your skills of analysis

A question which asks for an advantage of using quality assurance for a high-priced restaurant could be answered as follows:

Quality assurance means setting standards at each stage of production – food ingredient supplies, preparation, cooking and presentation.

Extend your analysis by explaining why this is an advantage.

Not every meal can be tasted by the chef before the customer receives it, so setting standards for each stage should make sure the finished meal meets consumer expectations.

Extend your analysis by explaining why this is important.

Consumers will expect a high-quality meal as the price is high. A consistently high-quality meal produced with good ingredients, cooked to a set recipe and presented in a certain way will meet customer expectations and help maintain the top-class excellent image.

21 QUALITY OF GOODS AND SERVICES

REVISION SUMMARY — Advantages of quality

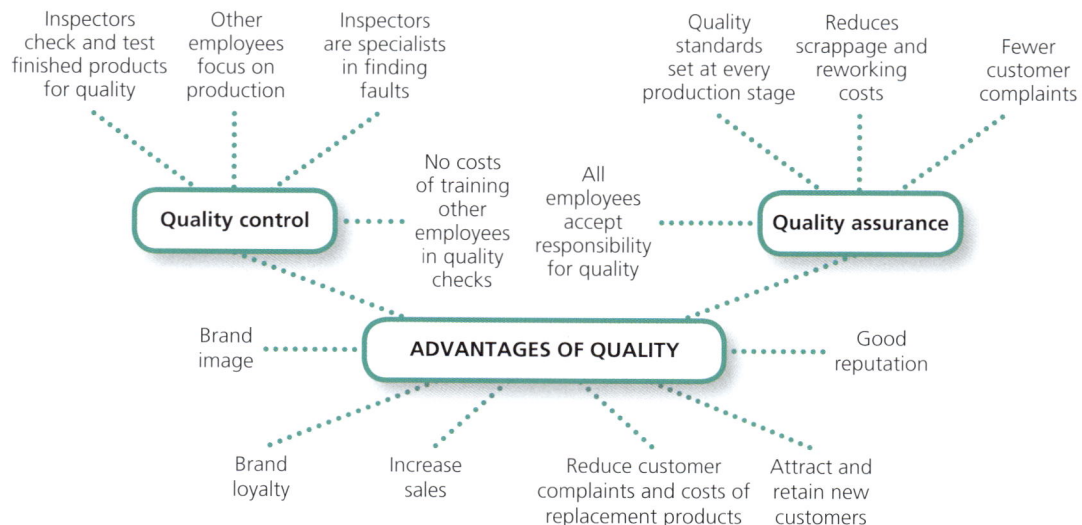

Case study: Rolls-Royce

Rolls-Royce manufactures aircraft engines for international airlines such as Emirates and Turkish Airlines. The engines are produced individually using quality assurance methods. New engines are checked at every stage of the production process and additional inspections are carried out at various stages in the process. Rolls-Royce uses quality assurance where every employee is responsible for ensuring quality in their section. In addition, each completed engine is tested for several hours to be certain of no defects.

Activity 21.2

Read the case study above.

a Why is producing a high-quality product important to Rolls-Royce?
b Do you think quality control of the finished product would be a suitable method for ensuring quality at Rolls-Royce? Justify your answer.

Why quality is important and how quality may be achieved

International business in focus

Quality at McDonald's

McDonald's restaurants have a checklist for employees to follow when serving customers. This is to ensure that a customer is always served to the standard expected by the business. McDonald's has found that ensuring the same quality standard is achieved by training employees to follow the set of rules in preparation of food as well as the service of customers.

Discussion points

- Identify which type of quality checking system McDonald's is using.
- Discuss whether this is the best method for McDonald's to use.
- Consider why McDonald's wants to ensure a quality service in its restaurants.

Chapter review questions: Short answer and data response

1 DR manufactures low-priced flip-flop shoes. It sells its flip-flop shoes through supermarkets in towns and cities across the country. 'We need to employ inspectors who use quality control when we manufacture the flip-flops to make sure they are good quality or our customers will not be happy,' said the Operations Manager.
   a Define 'quality control'. [2]
   b Outline **two** disadvantages to DR if there are faults with some of its products. [4]
   c Explain **two** possible disadvantages to DR of using quality control. [6]
   d Do you think the owners of DR should adopt quality assurance? Justify your answer. [8]

2 LK is a private limited company and it owns and operates 3 cafes in a city centre. Customers expect the cafes to provide a good quality service and also to offer value for money. There has been an increasing number of customer complaints about long waiting times to be served and the coffee and sandwiches being low quality. The owners of LK are planning to introduce quality assurance into their business. There are also cafes in the city centre which have a brand image of high-quality service but these cafes charge high prices.
   a Define 'quality assurance'. [2]
   b Outline **two** possible advantages for LK if it can improve quality and meet customers' expectations. [4]
   c Explain **two** reasons why the owners of LK want to introduce quality assurance. [6]
   d Do you think the owners of LK should use quality-control inspections to improve quality? Justify your answer. [8]

Revision checklist

In this chapter you have learned:

- ✔ what quality means and why it is important for businesses
- ✔ the concept of quality control and how businesses can implement quality control
- ✔ the concept of quality assurance and how businesses can implement quality assurance
- ✔ the advantages and disadvantages of quality control and quality assurance
- ✔ how to recommend and justify whether to use quality control or quality assurance in a given situation.

NOW – test your understanding with the revision questions in the Student etextbook and the Workbook.

22 Location decisions

> This chapter will explain:
>
> The main factors which influence location decisions:
>
> ★ factors which influence the location decisions of a manufacturing business
> ★ factors which influence the location decisions of a service business
> ★ factors that a business could consider when deciding which country to locate its operations in
> ★ how to recommend and justify an appropriate location for a business in a given situation.

Main factors which influence location decisions

Factors which influence the location decisions of a manufacturing business

Where to locate a business is one of the most important decisions of operations management. The location of a business will have a big impact on its profitability. The main factors affecting where a manufacturing business chooses to locate are explained in the following sections.

Costs

Costs play an essential role in location decisions for all businesses. However, they can be of particular significance to manufacturers if large areas of land are needed. Rental costs or purchase prices of land will be lower in remote areas but any benefits might be cancelled out by higher costs of transporting both materials and finished goods.

Production methods used

The type of production methods used in a manufacturing business has a significant influence on the location decision.

» If job production is used, the business is likely to be on a small scale and so the influence of the local availability of components or a large labour force, for example, will be of less importance to the business than if flow production is used.
» If flow production is used on a large scale, the location of component suppliers and transport links will be important. Also, flow production often needs large areas of flat land and the availability of extensive water and electricity supplies.

▲ An example of flow production

Market

Locating a factory near to the market for its products might be important when the product increases in weight during production. For example, a soft-drinks manufacturer might use bottles and ingredients which are lighter than the filled bottles as the finished product contains so much water. So the factory may be located near to the main markets for the product to keep transport costs low.

If the product perishes quickly and needs to be fresh when delivered to the market, such as milk, bread or cakes, the factory might be located close to its retail outlets. However, ways of preserving food for longer have reduced the importance of this factor.

Raw materials/components

Raw materials may be heavier and more expensive to transport than the finished product. When a metal is processed from the ore, the pure metal will weigh less than the ore. The difference in weight is the waste created by processing the ore. It is therefore a lower cost to locate the ore-processing factory near to the mining site than to transport the ore long distances.

If the raw material needs to be processed quickly while still fresh, locating near to the raw material source is still important. An example is frozen vegetables or tinned fruits, which need to be processed quickly, so processing businesses are located near where the products are grown.

▲ Raw materials can be heavy and expensive to transport

Supporting businesses

In addition to component suppliers, businesses which support manufacturers in other ways might need to be located nearby. Support businesses which install, maintain and repair equipment or specialist training centres are two examples of support services that would benefit the business by being nearby. Local education establishments, such as universities, might have research departments that work with the business on developing new products. Being in close contact with them may help the business to be more effective.

Availability of labour

Some employees will be needed in the manufacturing process even if advanced machinery is used. If labour with a particular set of skills is needed, it may be easier to recruit suitable employees if the business sets up in an area where people with the relevant skills live, or close to training colleges or universities that provide the relevant courses. If the manufacturer requires a large number of unskilled employees, an area where there is high unemployment may be more suitable. Also, the wage rates paid to employees might vary and an area where wages are lower might be preferable.

> **Key info**
>
> The midlands area of the UK is where several Formula One racing car teams are located. They are all able to draw on the support of many specialist businesses in the area such as engine suppliers, wind tunnel facilities and test tracks.

Government controls and incentives

When a government wants to create jobs in a particular area because of high unemployment, it can offer state-funded grants to encourage businesses to move there. Governments can also prevent manufacturing businesses locating in certain areas. They might do this because they want to preserve natural beauty or because of pollution risks. An example is where the business produces a harmful waste product during the manufacturing process. The government will not want the waste product, for example, nuclear waste, to potentially poison the surrounding area if it has a high population.

Transport and communications

Manufacturing businesses usually need to be near to a good transport system. Resources used in production and the finished products will require transportation. Cost of transportation is affected by distance from suppliers, distance to the market and the method of transport available. The total costs of manufacturing and delivering products that are very heavy or bulky but relatively low value will be increased greatly if efficient transport links are not available.

A reliable telecommunication network is crucial, especially for businesses relying heavily on technology to order supplies, manage inventories and communicate with customers.

Room for future expansion

A small, low-cost factory site might become a long-term disadvantage for a manufacturer if it wants to expand. Relocating to a completely new location can result in higher costs than expanding the existing site. By choosing a site with the possibility for future expansion, the cost of relocation can be avoided.

Personal preference of the owners

Owners of start-up manufacturing businesses can influence where to locate the business. They often locate their business near to where they live.

> **Study tips**
>
> Make sure you can choose which location factors are the most important for a particular manufacturing business.

Main factors which influence location decisions

REVISION SUMMARY   Factors affecting the location of manufacturing businesses

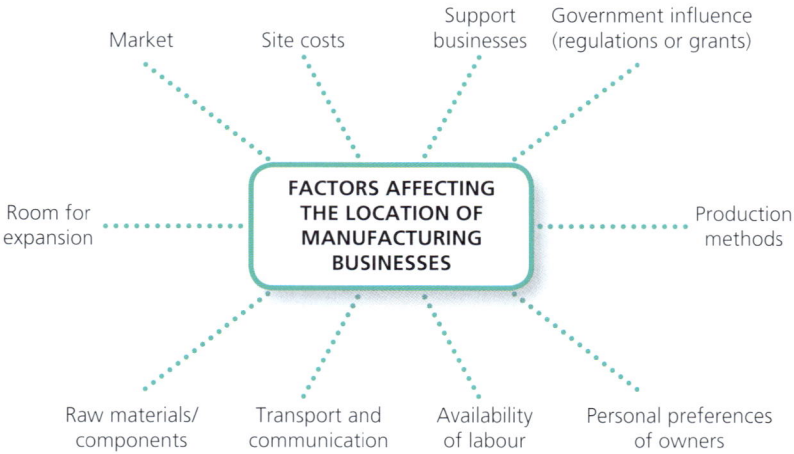

Case study: Location factors

B&B is a public limited company that manufactures food products. It wants to set up a factory to make a new flavoured ice cream. The new ice cream uses fresh ingredients – mainly freshly picked fruit – to maintain the flavour. The fruit used comes from 1 particular region of the country. This region is quite a long way from the main cities where most of the country's population lives. The production process is mainly automated and requires only a few skilled employees to supervise the equipment. The new ice cream will be sold to domestic customers through supermarkets and other food stores. It is not sold in other countries.

Activity 22.1

Read the case study above.

a Which factors affecting the location of the factory will be most important to this business when deciding where to locate? Explain why you think they will be important.
b Which do you think will be the most important factor and why?

Factors which influence the location decisions of a service business

Market

Locating a service business near its customers will be very important for certain types of services, such as retail stores. Many service businesses need direct contact with the customer. Hairdressing cannot be offered online! If a quick response time is needed to serve the customers, as with plumbers or electricians, then the business needs to be located nearby. Other examples of personal services that need to be convenient for customers to use are beauticians, caterers, restaurants, cafes, gardeners, builders and post offices.

Some services do not need to be located near to customers. Direct personal contact is not necessary if the service can be provided by telephone, mail (post) or online. Online customer support services or online banking businesses can therefore be located in different parts of the country or even in different countries to where customers live. With the increasing use of IT and the internet, more service businesses, including online retailing, are becoming free from the need to locate near to their customers.

Availability of labour

If a service business requires a large number of employees then it cannot locate in a remote area. It will need to locate near to a large town or city. If a particular type of skilled labour is required then it may also have to locate near to where this labour is found. If wage costs are a high proportion of total costs, an area with high unemployment could mean that wage rates are lower. This could be an important factor for service businesses that do not need to locate close to the market, such as online banking services.

Costs

The more central the location of the premises in a city or town, usually the higher the rent and local taxes will be. If a retail area is popular, there will be a high demand for sites in this area. Therefore, the cost of renting these sites will be higher. If the area is less popular, such as on the edge of a city or town, the demand and therefore the rents will be lower.

If the service does not need to be on the main streets in a town or city centre, for example, online customer services, dentists or accountants, then these businesses could locate on the outskirts of town to benefit from lower rents and taxes.

Competitors

Would it be good or bad for a service business to choose a location close to competitors? For example, if the business operates clothes shops, then being located near to many other clothes shops encourages people to visit the area as there is so much choice. This could actually increase sales for all similar shops in the area. If the clothes shop is in a position where there are no other similar shops nearby, it may not attract people to visit the shop as there will be limited choice. However, as suggested previously, an area that is popular with customers and other retail businesses might be a high-cost location.

Business image

If a service business is targeting high-income consumers looking for a luxury service, then location can help to reinforce the image of the business. Exclusive shopping districts, with very high rents, are still popular locations for beauty clinics, dressmakers, jewellery stores and other businesses that need to create a special image for consumers to be associated with.

Transport and accessibility

Good transport links and access for delivery vehicles might be a consideration if the service business requires regular deliveries. This is likely to be the case with many retail shops. Access for customers, especially those with limited mobility, is another consideration. If the service business is difficult to get to, only accessed up stairs and has no car parking available, it should not expect many visits from customers!

> **Key info**
>
> According to McDonald's, the company's managers look at a number of elements when selecting a location for a brand new restaurant, including the population of the area, existing restaurants in the area and whether there are shopping centres or retail parks nearby.

▲ The location of a jewellery store can reinforce the luxury image of the business

Security

High rates of crimes such as theft and vandalism may deter a service business from locating in a particular area. Insurance companies may not want to insure the business if it is in an area of high crime. A shopping area which is patrolled by guards might prove preferable, even though it will be more expensive to rent the premises.

Climate

Climate will affect some businesses, particularly if they are linked to tourism in some way. Hotels often need to locate themselves near to a beach where the climate is good.

> **Study tips**
>
> Make sure you can choose which location factors are the most important for a particular service sector business such as a retailer.

> **Extend your skills of analysis**
>
> A question which asks for an explanation of why the labour market is an important factor when making the location decision for a private fee-paying school (not boarding) could be answered as follows:
>
> The customers of fee-paying schools are the parents of school-age children who can afford to pay the fees charged for their children to attend the school.
>
> *Extend your analysis by explaining where is a good location for a fee-paying school.*
>
> An accessible site near residential areas with higher than average house prices would be a good location.
>
> *Extend your analysis by explaining why this would benefit the school.*
>
> The location must be accessible by car and public transport so that pupils can attend school promptly. Parents do not want to drive too far every morning to drop their children off at school, so they would prefer to send their children to a school that is close to where they live. This would potentially increase the number of parents who may send their children to the school.

Activity 22.2

For each of the services listed below:

a Identify **four** factors that you think are likely to affect its location.
b Explain how you think each of those factors will influence the location decision.
  - An electrician (sole trader) serving domestic customers
  - A software business which writes computer games that are sold all over the world
  - A small business that trains people to scuba dive and hires out scuba-diving equipment.

22 LOCATION DECISIONS

> **Case study:** Retail location decision
>
> B&C is a private limited company that is going to open a new shop selling fashion shoes. The shoes are good quality and are aimed at young women. B&C has narrowed down the choice of where to locate the new shop to two nearby towns.
>
> | | Town Y | Town Z |
> |---|---|---|
> | Population | 30 000 | 10 000 |
> | % in age group: | | |
> | 0–9 | 15 | 20 |
> | 10–25 | 30 | 35 |
> | 26–40 | 30 | 30 |
> | 41–65 | 20 | 10 |
> | 66+ | 5 | 5 |
> | Unemployment | Low | High |
> | Crime rate | Low | Low |
> | Shopping centre | Large – about 100 shops | Small – about 40 shops |
> | Parking facilities | Large parking lots but queues build up at busy times | Plenty of parking available – no problems at busy times |
> | Types of shops in the shopping centre | Clothes shops, shoe shops, banks, household goods, food shops | Food shops, household goods, clothes shops, post office, banks |

Activity 22.3

Read the case study above.

a Read the information on the two towns and then select which one will be the best location for the new shop. Justify your choice and justify why the other town was rejected.

b What other information is needed to help make the final decision? Explain why the information is needed.

REVISION SUMMARY Factors affecting the location decisions of a service business

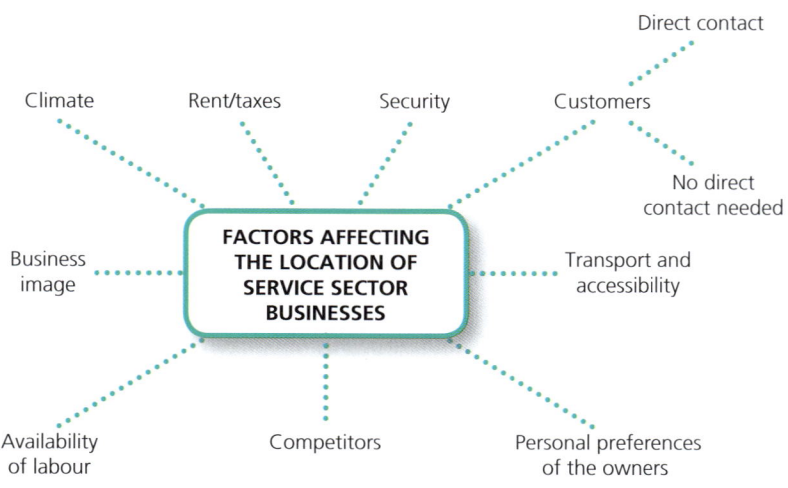

Main factors which influence location decisions

Factors that a business could consider when deciding which country to locate its operations in

Many businesses have operations in more than one country. They are called multinational companies. It can be very costly to start operating in a completely different country with possible transport problems and language and cultural differences. The countries to expand operations in must be chosen carefully. Many of the factors involved in this location decision are the same as locating within the same country – costs, labour availability and transport links, for example. Below are the additional factors that a business should consider when choosing another country to locate in.

Wage costs

These vary greatly between countries. In 2024 the minimum wage in the Netherlands was set at US$2319 per month, yet in Bangladesh the minimum wage was about US$105 per month.

A business which has many employees will consider wage cost differences between countries carefully when making international location decisions.

Political stability

The country with the lowest costs to operate in might not have the most stable political system. If there are frequent riots or violent political demonstrations in a country then a business from another country is unlikely to risk investing in a location there.

Environmental and ethical issues

If a country has serious environmental problems with few legal controls over pollution, it might be unwise to invest in a business location there. It could lead to a poor international image which would damage total sales. Similarly, if corruption is very common, a business may be unwilling to risk its image and reputation by locating in a country where this type of unethical behaviour is normal practice.

Tariffs and quotas

These restrictions on free trade (see page 348) are another important location factor. A country may have high import tariffs on materials and components and it might not belong to any free trade agreements. Setting up operations there could greatly reduce the ability of a business to trade with other countries from this location.

Size of country's market

A manufacturing business is more likely to set up operations in a country with a big market for the products it makes. Tesla has a large factory making its electric vehicles in China. One reason for this is that people in China buy more electric vehicles each year than any other country. Although the benefits of this for Tesla are clear, there are also a growing number of Chinese-owned car manufacturers, such as BYD, competing in this large market.

> **Key info**
>
> Apple has started producing AirPods in Vietnam. The advantages of manufacturing moving to Vietnam include a large labour force, low labour costs and political stability.

22 LOCATION DECISIONS

> **Study tips**
> Make sure you can choose which location factors are the most important for a particular business deciding which country to locate its operations in.

Source of raw materials

Businesses that process raw materials may have problems with buying supplies from other countries. One solution is to locate to a new site in a country which has supplies of these raw materials. This is particularly true of mineral sources such as oil wells – these need to be in the country where the oil is found. Also, it might be lower cost to process the raw materials at their source rather than transport them to another country to process.

REVISION SUMMARY

Additional factors affecting decisions to locate in other countries

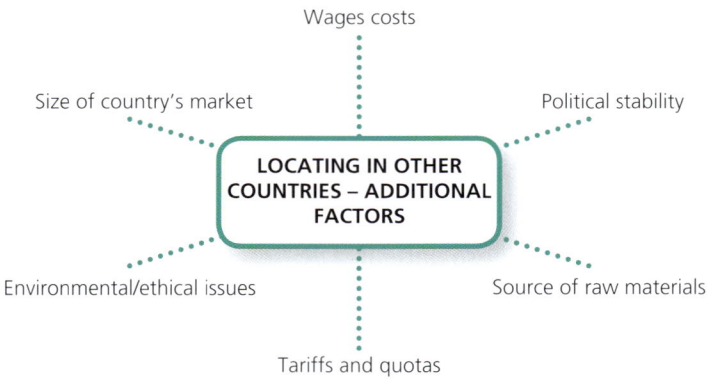

> **Extend your skills of analysis**
>
> A question which asks for an important factor for a manufacturer of low-priced 'value' clothing to consider before deciding which country to locate in could be answered as follows:
>
> Wage costs are likely to be a high proportion of total costs for making clothes.
> *Extend your analysis by explaining what impact wage costs will have.*
> Wage costs vary greatly between different countries and low minimum wages would mean that a clothing manufacturer could make clothes at a lower average cost.
> *Extend your analysis by explaining why this is important to the business.*
> The low-priced 'value' clothing market segment is very competitive. Despite some consumers preferring ethically sourced clothing, more consumers might prefer very low-priced clothing even if this has been made by employees earning low wages and so sales will be higher.

How to recommend and justify an appropriate location for a business in a given situation

The most important factor to consider when recommending and justifying a location is: *What does the business do?* Then you should ask yourself: *What are the most important location factors for this particular business?*

Location decisions should *always* be applied to the business and the situation it is in. Here are three examples. They illustrate how the location decision was influenced by *what the business actually does*.

Example 1: Online retailing business selling toys to customers in many countries

Location decision: An area with a good supply of labour to work in the warehouse and close to several main road and rail links for distribution to consumers in many countries.

Example 2: Exclusive retailer of designer fashion clothes
Location decision: A well-known shopping area that has many shops selling luxury brands in a capital city to help create a luxury brand image and support the reputation of the business.

Example 3: Small convenience shop selling everyday food, drinks and confectionery (candy)
Location decision: A low-cost site to allow prices to be competitive and near to a residential area on a busy road to attract customers passing by the shop. There should also be some parking for accessibility for suppliers and customers.

Justification for a location decision can also include why other location options are less desirable. For example, in the third example above, the business owner might have rejected a larger shop, closer to the town centre if it did *not* have any car parking at all.

> ### Case study: Factory location decision
>
> MT Furniture is a private limited company and plans to expand. Currently it is located in a small factory in the old part of the city. New markets are opening up in other countries and MT has experienced a steady increase in sales for the last 5 years. There is no room to extend the existing factory and none of the nearby factories are for sale. The business has been forced to look for another site if it wants to grow.
>
> Because more and more of its sales are exported, it is considering whether to build a factory in another country or whether to build a larger factory in its home country. The following information has been gathered about 2 sites, 1 near MT's existing factory and 1 in the country where most of MT's products are exported.
>
> | | Location A – on the edge of the city near to existing factory in home country | Location B – in the main export market in another country |
> |---|---|---|
> | **Market** | Large local market | Large export market and growing |
> | **Communications** | Good communications – main roads connect to all parts of the country and the main port, which is several kilometres away | Good communications – main roads connect to all parts of the country and ports are very close to the site |
> | **Raw materials/components** | Raw materials and components are close to the site – easily available | Raw materials and components are not close to the site – not easily available. Some will need to be imported |
> | **Wage rates** | High | Low |
> | **Skilled labour** | Skilled workers employed at the present site which is not too far from this potential site. Additional skilled workers are available in the area | Very few skilled workers are available |
> | **Unemployment** | Low | High |
> | **Rents/land taxes** | High | Low |
> | **Government grants** | No grants available | Grants paid towards capital investment when a new company is setting up in the country |

> ### Activity 22.4
> Read the case study above.
>
> Study the information provided and then write a report to the Board of Directors of MT Furniture advising them of the advantages and disadvantages of each of the locations. Include a recommendation of which you think is the best location to choose. Remember to give reasons for your choice and explain why you rejected the other location.

International business in focus

Relocating from coastal to inland areas of China

To promote development of the inland provinces, the Chinese government is actively encouraging manufacturing firms in coastal areas of China to relocate or move part of their production inland. As well as the initiatives by the central government, regional authorities in inland areas have also introduced a range of policies to attract manufacturing firms to relocate in their areas. These include subsidies, tax incentives, straightforward approval processes, a good labour supply and other cost reduction measures. The low wages in these regions reduce production costs for businesses, making them more competitive in the global market. These regions also have well-developed infrastructure including efficient transportation, reliable telecommunications and stable power supply.

Source: Extracted from https://amro-asia.org/chinese-companies-are-on-the-move-inland-and-to-southeast-asia by Hongyan Zhao

Discussion points

- Why might the Chinese government encourage businesses to move from coastal to inland areas of China?
- How do you think businesses might benefit from this relocation?

Chapter review questions: Short answer and data response

1 ABC produces fruit juice drinks in a factory located just 20 km from the capital city. The fruit to produce the drinks is grown locally on nearby farms. The fruit can also be imported at a lower cost but the quality is not as good. When producing the fruit drink there is a lot of waste from the parts of the fruit which are not used to make the drinks. Land near to the factory is available at a low price and the company wants to buy this land to expand rather than relocate the factory to another country. There is a big market for fruit drinks both at home and in other countries.
   a Identify **two** reasons why ABC buys its fruit from nearby farms. [2]
   b Outline **two** factors which influenced the location decision of ABC when choosing its original site. [4]
   c Explain **two** reasons why ABC might want to buy land near to its existing factory to expand rather than relocate to another country. [6]
   d The government is offering grants to relocate to an area of the country with high unemployment. Do you think the managers of ABC should take advantage of these grants? Justify your answer. [8]

2 SalesRUs is a chain of clothes shops. The owners are looking for a location for a big new shop. It could either be located in the city centre or in a small town which has good transport links. The company's existing shops sell a range of clothes for men and women at low prices and are all located in busy shopping malls. There is a lot of competition from similar shops. The Managing Director thinks the new shop should not be located near to competitors. The Marketing Director has decided that SalesRUs should start selling clothes online and distributing clothes to consumers by delivering them from a large new warehouse.
   a Identify **two** advantages of the new shop being located in the small town rather than the city centre. [2]
   b Outline **two** ways in which the location chosen for the new shop might affect its profitability. [4]
   c Explain **two** factors that could influence the decision of where to locate the large new warehouse. [6]
   d Do you think the Managing Director is right in not wanting to locate the new shop near to its competitors' shops? Justify your answer. [8]

Revision checklist

In this chapter you have learned:

- ✔ factors which influence the location decisions of a manufacturing business
- ✔ factors which influence the location decisions of a service business
- ✔ factors that a business could consider when deciding which country to locate its operations in
- ✔ how to recommend and justify an appropriate location for a business in a given situation.

NOW – test your understanding with the revision questions in the Student etextbook and the Workbook.

22 LOCATION DECISIONS

Operations management: end-of-section case study

Case study: Premium Suits

Sally owns a business called Premium Suits. It is a private limited company. The business makes suits for men using batch production and the production employees are paid an hourly wage. Sally employs 100 people who work on the production of suits. She has 5 employees who help her in the office but she only has 1 manager, who is responsible for finance. Sally carries out all the other management functions for the business.

The business has grown quickly and profits have also grown rapidly over the last 2 years. Sally wants to continue to expand the business and increase the sales of different suits to add to her current range of medium-priced suits. There is a lot of competition for medium-priced suits and the market is not growing. She has identified 2 other markets for suits, both of which have increasing demand. However, she is unsure which option to choose.

- Option 1: She can start selling expensive suits that are handmade and of high-quality material. These suits would be made-to-measure for each customer and individually designed. The market for these suits is a niche market. She would need to increase the number of skilled employees.
- Option 2: She can start selling low-priced suits to the mass market. However, to enter this market Sally will need to invest in either new technology or buy more of the business's existing machinery to produce suits on a large scale. She could gain from economies of scale which would be an advantage.

Sally currently uses batch production. However, if she chooses Option 1 she will use job production and if she chooses Option 2 she will use flow production.

Appendix 1: Added value for Premium Suits

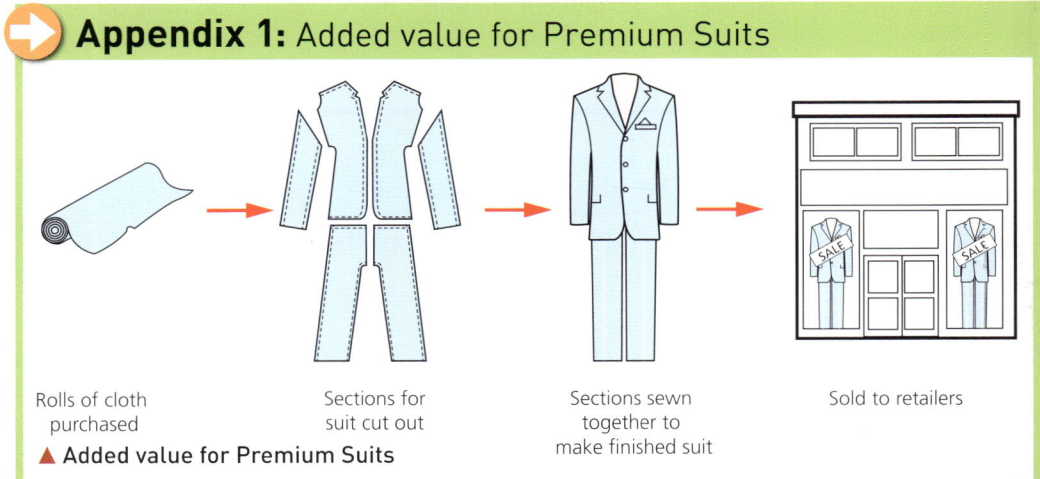

Rolls of cloth purchased → Sections for suit cut out → Sections sewn together to make finished suit → Sold to retailers

▲ Added value for Premium Suits

Practice questions: Case study

1. a Explain **two** economies of scale Premium Suits might benefit from as it grows. [8]
   b Quality is important to Sally. Consider the advantages and disadvantages of quality control and quality assurance. Which method should Sally use to ensure quality suits are produced? Justify your answer. [12]
2. a Explain **two** advantages of using job production for Option 1 and **two** advantages of using flow production for Option 2. [8]
   b Consider the advantages and disadvantages of purchasing new technology or buying more of the business's existing machinery to increase output. Which do you think Sally should choose? Justify your answer. [12]

Optional question

The question below asks you to think about topics covered in earlier sections of this textbook. You can choose not to answer it if you prefer to focus on just the topics covered in this section at this time.

3. a Appendix 1 shows added value for Sally's business. Explain **two** ways Sally could increase the added value for her suits. [8]
   b Consider how the following **three** elements of the marketing mix will be different for Option 1 and Option 2. If Sally chooses Option 1, which element will be most important to the success of this decision? Justify your answer. [12]
   - Price
   - Promotion
   - Place

SECTION 5

Financial information and decisions

Chapters

23 Business finance
24 Cash flow forecast
25 Profit and loss
26 Statement of financial position
27 Analysis of accounts

23 Business finance

This chapter will explain:

The need for business finance:

★ the main reasons why businesses need finance
★ the short-term and long-term finance needs of a business
★ the concept and importance of working capital.

The main sources of finance:

★ internal sources of finance
★ external sources of finance
★ advantages and disadvantages of internal and external sources of finance
★ the main factors to consider when selecting a source of finance
★ how to recommend and justify an appropriate source of finance for a given situation.

The need for business finance

The main reasons why businesses need finance

We all need **finance** or money to purchase the goods and services we require every day, like food, and also more expensive items such as a house or car. Businesses need finance too and this is often called 'capital'. Without finance, businesses could not pay wages, buy materials or pay for buildings or machinery.

Here are five reasons why businesses need finance or capital:

» starting up a business
» expansion/growth of an existing business
» replacing existing non-current assets
» investing in new technology
» working capital.

Start-up capital

When an entrepreneur plans to start their own business, they should think about all the buildings, land and equipment they will need to buy in order to start trading. These are usually called **non-current assets** (see Chapter 26). Nearly all new businesses will need to purchase some of these. In addition, the owner of the business will need to obtain finance to purchase other assets, such as inventories, before goods can be sold to the first customers. The finance needed to launch a new business is often called **start-up capital**.

> **Definitions to learn**
>
> **Finance** is money or capital needed to pay for expenditure.
>
> **Non-current assets** are property, machinery and other assets owned by a business which will not be turned into cash within one year.
>
> **Start-up capital** is the finance needed by a new business to pay for essential non-current assets and current assets before it can begin trading.

The need for business finance

> **Key info**
>
> One of the most common reasons for new business start-ups failing is not a lack of finance for buildings or equipment, but a lack of finance for meeting regular expenses – especially before cash starts to flow into the business from sales to customers. This is a shortage of working capital.

Capital for expansion/growth

The owners of a successful business will often take a decision to expand it in order to increase revenue and profit. Expansion could be achieved by:

» buying additional non-current assets – such as larger buildings and more machinery
» taking over another business
» developing new products, using research and development, to reach new markets.

Replacing existing non-current assets

Business premises, machinery, trucks and other non-current assets can become outdated or worn out. To maintain output levels, it will be necessary to obtain finance to replace these assets over time. The purchase of non-current assets is called capital expenditure. These assets will be expected to last longer than one year.

Investing in new technology

There are very few businesses that do not use at least some new technology such as computers, robots, artificial intelligence (AI) or smartphones. New technologies have the capacity to greatly increase the efficiency and productivity of a business. However, investing in new technology will often require large amounts of finance. For small businesses in particular, this finance can be difficult to obtain.

Working capital

Working capital is often described as the lifeblood of a business. It is finance that is constantly needed by businesses to pay for all their day-to-day activities. These include paying wages, raw material suppliers and energy bills. Working capital is explained in more detail in the following sections.

REVISION SUMMARY — **Reasons why businesses need finance**

23 BUSINESS FINANCE

> ### Activity 23.1
> Look at the list of expenses for a sports centre below. Copy out the table and tick whether you consider each to be capital expenditure or spending on day-to-day expenses.
>
> | | Capital expenditure | Day-to-day expenses |
> |---|---|---|
> | Purchase of building | | |
> | Water bills | | |
> | Employee wages | | |
> | Office computer equipment | | |
> | Gym equipment | | |
> | Maintenance of equipment | | |

> ### Activity 23.2
> Paul has decided to leave his job to set up his own taxi business.
>
> a Explain to Paul why he will need finance for his new business.
> b Make a list of the likely start-up costs of this business for its first month of operation.
> c Indicate which of these costs are day-to-day expenses and which are examples of capital expenditure. Explain your answer.

Short-term and long-term finance needs of a business

This is an important distinction. **Short-term finance** needs include paying a large bill from a supplier or paying for higher inventories before a major festival or event. This short-term need would be financed by a short-term source of finance, such as an overdraft.

Long-term needs for finance include expansion and takeovers. These needs require **long-term finance**, lasting for much longer than one year, such as the sale of shares or a long-term loan.

The concept and importance of working capital

Businesses need to pay for their day-to-day expenses, such as:

- production employees' wages
- suppliers' bills or invoices
- costs of holding goods in inventories
- payment of rent and insurance.

A business will often not receive cash from producing finished goods immediately – the products have to be sold and then customers may be given time to pay.
The main **current assets** of the business are the total value of:

- cash
- inventory of materials
- goods still being made
- inventory of finished goods
- trade debtors, who are customers owing money for products purchased.

Definitions to learn

Short-term finance provides the working capital needed by businesses for day-to-day operations and is repaid within one year.

Long-term finance provides capital which can be repaid over a period of time longer than one year.

Current assets are owned by a business and converted into cash within one year.

> **Definitions to learn**
>
> **Working capital** is the finance needed by a business to pay its day-to-day expenses.
> **Current liabilities** are short-term debts that must be paid within one year.
> **Internal finance** is obtained from within the business itself or from owners, if it is an unincorporated business.
> **External finance** is obtained from sources outside of and separate to the business.

These current assets must be financed before cash is received from customers. The longer it takes to make and sell finished goods and receive cash from customers, the greater the amount of **working capital** needed.

Some of the finance required will be sourced from **current liabilities** – by not paying suppliers' bills immediately, for example. So, the working capital that will still need to be financed is current assets *less* current liabilities.

If a business cannot finance its working capital, it is likely to cease trading. This is why knowing the working capital needed by a business is so important. If it cannot pay employees or suppliers and if it cannot afford to keep inventories of materials and finished goods, closure of the business may be inevitable.

The main sources of finance

It is common to classify sources of finance into **internal** and **external** sources.

Internal sources of finance

The most common examples of internal finance are as follows.

Owners' investment

A sole trader or partners in a partnership can put more of their savings into the unincorporated business. The owners of these businesses are not separate from their businesses and therefore this finance is internal finance.

Advantages

- It should be available to the business quickly.
- No interest is paid as the owners share the profits.
- There is no change in ownership.
- The capital cannot be withdrawn at short notice by an external provider of finance.

Disadvantages

- Owners' savings may be too low and the business might need more than the investment they can afford to make.
- It increases the risk taken by the owners as they have unlimited liability.
- By not using external finance, newly formed businesses would lose the opportunity to receive valuable advice from external finance providers.

Retained profit

This is profit kept in the business after the owners have taken their share of profits. Retained profit can be a source of finance for any type of business organisation.

Advantages

- Retained profit does not have to be repaid, unlike a loan.
- There is no interest to pay as there is with a loan.
- Using retained profit may mean that the business does not need to use external finance.

Disadvantages

- A new business will not have any retained profits.
- Many small businesses make profits which are too low to finance the expansion needed.

» Keeping more profit in the business reduces payments to owners, for example, dividends to shareholders. They might decide to invest in other businesses instead.

Sale of unwanted assets

Existing assets that could be sold are those items of value which are no longer required by the business, for example, unused buildings or surplus equipment.

Advantages

» This makes better use of the capital tied up in the business.
» It does not increase the debts of the business.
» No interest has to be paid.

Disadvantages

» It may take some time to sell these assets and the amount raised is never certain until the asset is sold.
» This source of finance is not available for new businesses as they have no unwanted assets to sell.

Working capital

Finance can be gained from asking trade debtors (receivables) to pay more quickly but they might decide to purchase products from another business. Cash can also be gained by selling inventories for cash and reducing inventory levels. This also has advantages and disadvantages.

Advantage

» This reduces the opportunity cost and storage cost of high inventory levels.

Disadvantages

» It must be done carefully to avoid disappointing customers if not enough goods are kept as inventory.
» If the cash is needed quickly, the inventories might have to be sold off at less than the cost of producing them.

REVISION SUMMARY

Internal sources of finance

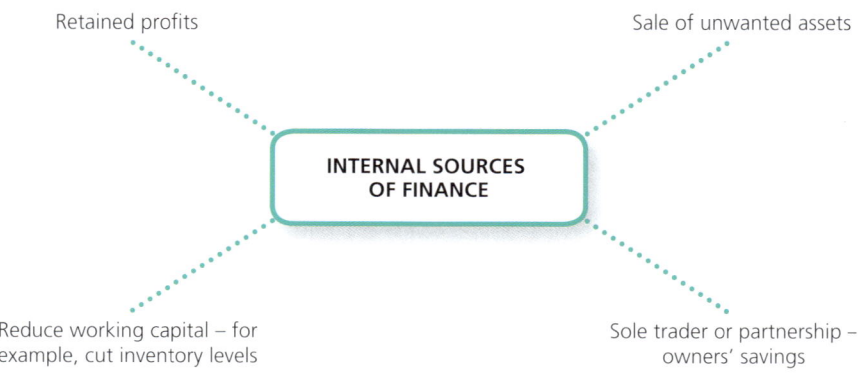

> **Activity 23.3**
>
> Paul needs advice on sources of finance before going ahead with his business plan (see Activity 23.2). Explain the following to him:
>
> a Retained profits are not, to start with, a possible source of finance.
> b His savings will likely be an important source of funds.
> c Selling off inventories is never likely to be an available source of finance to his taxi business.

External sources of finance

The most important examples of external finance are as follows.

Share capital or issuing shares

The issuing of additional shares is a source of finance that is only possible for limited companies, either private or public. Share capital raised by issuing shares is a major source of external finance for nearly all limited companies.

Advantages

» This is a permanent source of capital which would not have to be repaid to shareholders.
» No interest, which can add substantially to business costs, has to be paid, especially if interest rates are high.

Disadvantages

» Dividends to shareholders are paid after tax, whereas interest on loans is paid before tax is deducted.
» Dividends may be expected by the shareholders and these will reduce retained profit.
» The ownership of the company could change hands if many shares are sold. The original shareholders might lose control of the business.

Venture capital

Start-up companies and small businesses operating in risky new technology fields often find it difficult to raise finance. Venture capitalists are big investment organisations that could provide the capital these businesses need, known as **venture capital**.

Advantages

» Provides capital for businesses operating in risky markets which have problems raising finance from traditional sources.
» Venture capitalists are experienced investors and will often provide much advice and support to the small businesses they provide finance to.

Disadvantages

» Venture capitalists expect a share in the ownership in the company and this could be large.
» Management control might be lost to the venture capitalist if the business does not grow as expected.

Study tips

Remember that only limited companies can raise capital by selling shares – and that only public limited companies can offer shares for sale to the public.

Definitions to learn

Venture capital is provided by investors who are prepared to take risks by offering finance to start-up companies or small companies that have good growth potential.

23 BUSINESS FINANCE

> **Definitions to learn**
>
> **Bank overdrafts** are a short-term source of flexible finance which allow more money to be drawn out of the bank account than there is money in the account.
>
> **Leasing** allows a business to pay a regular leasing charge to use the asset without buying it.
>
> **Hire purchase** allows a business to buy a non-current asset over a long period of time with monthly payments which include an interest charge.

Bank overdrafts

This is when the bank gives the business the right to 'overdraw' its bank account, that is, to spend more money than is currently in the account. **Overdrafts** are a widely used source of short-term business finance.

Advantages

- The business could use this finance to pay wages or suppliers but, obviously, it cannot do this indefinitely – the amount will be up to an agreed limit set by the bank.
- The overdraft will vary each month with the needs of the business – it is said to be a 'flexible' form of borrowing. This could benefit a business with a seasonal pattern of sales.
- Interest will be paid only on the amount overdrawn. If the business does not need to overdraw its account then no interest will be charged.
- Overdrafts can cost less than short-term loans of a fixed sum of money as interest is only paid if the account is overdrawn.

Disadvantages

- Interest rates are variable, unlike most loans which have fixed interest rates.
- The bank can ask for the overdraft to be repaid at very short notice. This might occur if the bank is worried that the business has weak finances and could fail.

Leasing

Leasing an asset allows the business to use the asset without having to purchase it. Monthly leasing payments are made. The business could decide to purchase the asset at the end of the leasing period. Some businesses decide to sell off some non-current assets for cash and lease them back from a leasing company. This is called sale and leaseback.

Advantages

- The business does not have to finance a large cash sum to purchase the asset to start with.
- The care and maintenance of the asset are carried out by the leasing company.

Disadvantages

- The total cost of the leasing charges over time will be higher than purchasing the asset.
- If the asset is no longer required it is expensive to end a leasing contract early.

Hire purchase

Hire purchase is often used to obtain items of capital equipment.

Advantages

- The business does not have to finance a large cash sum to purchase the asset.
- It is useful for a business with limited resources or when banks are unwilling to lend.
- The asset is owned by the business when the last payment has been made.

The main sources of finance

Disadvantages

» A cash deposit is paid at the start of the period.
» Interest payments can be quite high.

Bank loans

Long-term bank loans are an important source of capital for expanding businesses.

> **Definitions to learn**
>
> A **bank loan** is a sum of money obtained from a bank which must be repaid and on which interest is payable.
> A **long-term bank loan** is repayable with interest over more than one year.
> **Trade credit** is when a business is allowed to pay a supplier some time after materials have been purchased.
> A **government grant** is a sum of money awarded to a business by the government which does not have to be paid back.

Advantages

» These are usually quick to arrange.
» They can be for varying lengths of time.
» Large companies are often offered low rates of interest by banks if they borrow large sums.
» Interest on bank loans is tax deductable, unlike dividends, so reduces the amount of profit tax to be paid.

Disadvantages

» A bank loan will have to be repaid eventually.
» Interest must be paid every year and this is a business cost. Borrowing money when interest rates are high is a high-cost source of finance.
» Security or collateral is usually required. This means the bank may insist that it has the right to sell some of the property of the business if it fails to pay the interest or does not repay the loan. A sole trader may have to put their own house up as security on a bank loan.

Trade credit

When a business delays paying its suppliers it leaves the business in a better cash position. When **trade credit** is agreed, the supplier becomes a creditor of the business as it gives the business some time to pay after the materials have been purchased.

Advantages

» It is, in effect, an interest-free loan to the business for the length of time that payment is delayed for.
» It reduces the working capital required by the business.

Disadvantages

» The supplier may refuse to give discounts if payment is not made quickly.
» Some suppliers may refuse to supply materials to businesses that do not pay on time.

Government grants

Governments may provide **grants** to businesses that:

» start up in areas of high unemployment
» operate in businesses important to national security
» agree to use sustainable production methods.

Advantages

» These grants do not have to be repaid.
» No interest is payable.

Disadvantages

» They are often given with strict conditions, for example, the business must remain located in a particular area.
» There may be a time-consuming application process before the grant is given.

Crowdfunding

This idea of raising finance for new business start-ups by encouraging a large number of people to each invest small amounts has been used for many years. However, it has only become very popular since the widespread use of the internet. This allows entrepreneurs to contact millions of potential investors around the globe, usually by using **crowdfunding** platforms such as Kickstarter, Indiegogo and Fundable. It is a source which is not suitable for raising very small sums – an invitation to global investors is not worthwhile if only $1000 is required!

> **Definitions to learn**
>
> **Crowdfunding** is funding a business venture by raising money from a large number of people who each contribute a relatively small amount, typically via the internet.

▲ This Mexican business used crowdfunding

Advantages

» No initial fees are payable to the crowdfunding platform. Instead, if the finance required is raised, the platform will charge a percentage fee of this amount.
» It allows the public's reaction to the new business venture to be tested. If people are not prepared to invest, it probably is not a very good business idea.
» It can be a fast way to raise substantial sums.
» It is often used by entrepreneurs when other traditional sources of finance are not available.

Disadvantages

» Crowdfunding platforms may reject an entrepreneur's proposal if it is not well thought out.
» If the total amount required is not raised, the finance that has been promised from investors will have to be repaid.
» Media interest and publicity need to be generated to increase the chance of success.
» Publicising the new business idea or product on the crowdfunding platform could allow competitors to steal the idea and reach the market first with a similar product.

> **Key info**
>
> Crowdfunding is now the fastest-growing source of finance for business start-ups. Globally, US$1.17 billion was raised in this way in 2023. The forecast for 2029 is US$1.27 billion. One of the biggest crowdfunded projects was for a video game called Star Citizen which raised over US$500 million by 2023.

REVISION SUMMARY   External sources of finance

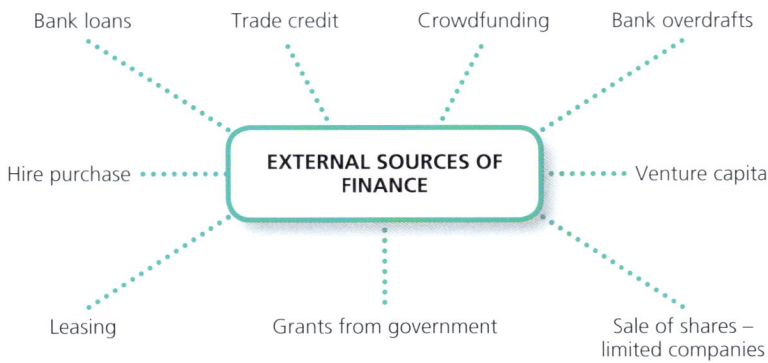

> ### Activity 23.4
> Paul's taxi business has now been operating for 2 years. He wants to expand by buying another taxi and employing 2 drivers on a shift system.
>
> a Explain to Paul the advantages of using the business profits to buy the taxi rather than taking out a bank loan.
> b When would you advise Paul to take out a bank loan to expand his business?

> ### Activity 23.5
> Consider the sources of finance listed in the table below. Are they short-term or long-term sources of finance? Copy out the table and tick the relevant column for each source.
>
> | Source of finance | Short-term | Long-term |
> | --- | --- | --- |
> | Overdraft | | |
> | Leasing | | |
> | Issuing of shares | | |
> | Four-year bank loan | | |
> | Trade credit | | |
> | Hire purchase | | |

Main factors to consider when selecting a source of finance

The finance decision is a crucial one for all businesses. These are the factors senior business managers will consider before deciding on the most suitable source of finance.

Size of business

Small businesses, particularly business start-ups, may find it difficult to obtain bank loans. Owners' savings, venture capital or crowdfunding are more likely to be used by small businesses because of the problems they might have in sourcing finance from traditional banking institutions.

Legal form of business

Companies, especially public limited companies, have a greater choice of sources of finance. Issuing shares is not an option for sole traders and partnerships. These businesses, if they have plans to expand, may have to depend on the savings of their owners and retained profit as sources of finance. They could obtain bank loans if they have a satisfactory trading record. However, they are likely to have the disadvantage of being forced to pay higher interest rates to banks for loans than large and well-established companies. Many companies, especially public limited companies, would issue new shares if they needed to raise substantial sums of long-term finance.

Amount required

Different sources will be used depending on the amount of money needed. A company would not go to the expense of arranging a new share issue if only $5000 of capital was needed. Trade credit, bank overdrafts or bank loans are much more likely to be used if the amount required is quite small.

▲ The purchase of a second-hand business vehicle would not be financed by an issue of shares

Length of time

The purpose to which the finance is to be put is closely linked to the time period it will be needed for. For example, to build a new factory or head office will require a very substantial sum of finance for a long period of time. In contrast, finance to pay for higher inventories during a busy festival period will be required for a short period of time.

The general rule with finance is to match the sources of it with the purpose to which it is to be put, which impact on the time period too.

» If the use is long-term, for example, the purchase of a non-current asset, the source should be long-term. If only short-term finance is used, it will need to be rearranged before the non-current asset has been paid for.
» If the use is short-term, for example, the purchase of additional inventories to cover a busy period, the source should be short-term. If a long-term loan is used to pay for obtaining a replacement machine while an existing one is being repaired, the debt would still exist once the short-term replacement had been returned.

Existing loans

If a business already has high loans compared to its total capital it might be very risky to borrow more. This is because total interest costs will be high and these have to be paid whether the business is making a profit or not. Also, the loans will all have to be repaid eventually and this could be very difficult to do. Banks are always unwilling to lend more finance to businesses that are already financed greatly by loans.

Cost

Obtaining finance is never without cost. It might be in the form of interest costs or the administrative cost of issuing more shares. Delaying payment to suppliers might have the cost of reduced discounts from these supplying businesses. Selling inventories for cash could mean that customers buy from another business if their needs cannot be met immediately. Finance managers must weigh up the cost of each source of finance against its benefits – bearing in mind what the purpose of the finance is.

Purpose

As explained earlier, this is very closely linked to the time period the finance is needed for. Another factor about purpose is risk. If the finance is needed for a long-term research and development project which has some risk of not being profitable, banks are unlikely to be willing to lend. Share issues, government grants or venture capital might be suitable sources of finance in this case.

> **Study tips**
>
> 'Which is the best source of finance for this business?' is a very common question. Be prepared to analyse the advantages and disadvantages of the main sources of finance – and give a justified recommendation.

Extend your skills of analysis

A question which asks for an advantage to a company of issuing shares for the financing of a new factory could be answered as follows:

A share issue raises permanent capital which *does not have an annual rate of interest.*

Extend your analysis by explaining why this is an advantage.

Unlike loans, which have to be repaid and which require annual interest to be paid to the bank, shareholders buy shares but expect an annual dividend. This does not have to be paid when, for example, the business is not making a profit.

Extend your analysis by explaining why this would be a benefit to this company.

It could take several years for the factory to be built and start making products which will earn profit. During this time, no interest has to be paid on the finance raised, which reduces the company's costs, unlike loan capital.

Case study: Choosing the right source of finance

Company A sells fashion clothing. It needs $15 000 to decorate its shop. A new issue of shares would be the wrong choice. This is because the issuing of shares is complicated, expensive to arrange and would take a long time – the business wants the shop decorated now!

Company B owns 3 restaurants. It plans to take over another restaurant company and offers $5 million. Company B already has a large bank loan.

Activity 23.6

Read the case study above.

a Advise Company A on the sources of finance that would be suitable.
b Advise Company B on the sources of finance that would be suitable.
c In each case, which source of finance would be the most suitable to use? Explain why you would choose this source rather than the other sources.
d In each case, explain what other information would have been useful before giving your advice.

Case study: Important decisions about sources of finance

- A sole trader could take on a partner to bring in extra capital – but could that partner start to take important decisions without consulting the original owner?
- The Directors of a private limited company could decide to change to a public limited company and sell shares to the public. This could raise very large sums of money for the business but would the new shareholders own a controlling interest in the business?
- An existing public limited company could arrange a new issue of shares but could these be bought by just 1 or 2 other companies that may put in a takeover bid?

These problems could all be overcome by using loan finance instead.

23 BUSINESS FINANCE

> ### Activity 23.7
> Read the second case study on the previous page.
>
> **a** Would you advise each of these three businesses to use loan capital instead of using the sources of finance outlined? Explain your answers.
>
> **b** Consider all the following reasons for a private limited company needing finance. Copy out the table below and, for each type of need, fill in the gaps with:
>   i what you consider could be the most suitable source of finance
>   ii the reason for your choice.
>
> | Need for finance | Most suitable source of finance | Reason for choice |
> |---|---|---|
> | Planned takeover of another business | | |
> | Temporary increase in inventories over the summer | | |
> | Purchase of new car for the Managing Director | | |
> | Research and development of a new product – to be on the market in four years' time | | |
> | Finance for building a modern factory requiring much less land than the present one | | |

REVISION SUMMARY   Selecting sources of finance – factors involved in the decision

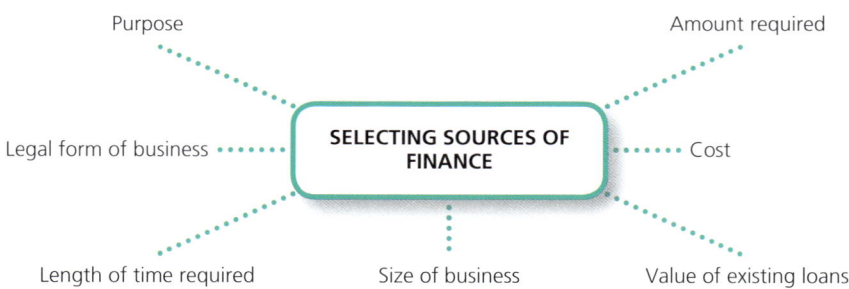

How to recommend and justify an appropriate source of finance in a given situation

The most effective way to approach this type of business decision is to ask the questions shown in Table 23.1 and follow the reasoning used in the second column.

Table 23.1 Recommending a source of finance in different situations

Question	Impact on recommended source of finance
Is the business a limited company?	Yes: Issuing shares possible IF purpose is long-term, such as purchase of non-current assets
	No: Issuing shares not possible unless business converts to a limited company
Is short-term or long-term finance needed?	Short-term: Companies would not use share issuing; all businesses could consider trade credit, overdrafts
	Long-term: Companies could consider issuing shares OR long-term bank loans; other forms of business could consider long-term loans, venture capital, crowdfunding, government grants or leasing of equipment
Does the business already have a high value of loans compared to all of its capital?	Yes: Companies will consider a share issue as banks may be unwilling to lend more to the business
	Yes: Other businesses would consider more capital from owners/partners; venture capital; government grants
	No: Long-term loans can be considered as a potential source of finance
Do the owners want to keep control of the business?	Yes: Companies must be careful that if new shares are issued this does not result in existing shareholders losing control of the company
	Yes: Other businesses must be cautious about taking on partners (or more partners in an existing partnership). Venture capital could lead to loss of control too
	No: In a few situations, perhaps when they plan to retire, business owners may be prepared to lose control by raising finance from investors
Are interest rates very high?	Yes: Companies could consider issuing shares and not long-term loans
	Yes: Other businesses might consider more owners' capital or venture capital to avoid higher long-term borrowing
	No: Loans may be a good option for additional finance

Once these issues have been considered in the context of the given business situation, it is always advisable to:

» Justify the choice of finance by explaining why you have chosen the source you are recommending.
» Explain why you have not chosen a possible alternative source of finance.

International business in focus

CapitaLand

CapitaLand is a leading Asian property business with its headquarters in Singapore. In June 2022 CapitaLand announced plans to raise around $3 billion by issuing shares. The company aimed to use this capital to finance its growth strategies, including property development projects across Asia and other property investments.

CapitaLand has a significant presence in various Asian markets, including Singapore, China, Vietnam and India. The decision to raise capital through share sales reflected the company's confidence in its growth prospects and its commitment to expanding its real-estate portfolio.

CapitaLand's successful share issue in 2022 highlighted the attractiveness of the Asian property sector to investors seeking growth opportunities in real estate.

Discussion points

- Explain whether CapitaLand raised internal finance or external finance from the share issue.
- Why do you think shareholders were so keen to buy these new shares?
- Explain why the company might have preferred to raise finance by issuing shares rather than taking out bank loans.

23 BUSINESS FINANCE

❓ Chapter review questions: Short answer and data response

1. Michelle wanted to start her own business designing and making clothes after she was made redundant from a sugar factory. She prepared several dress designs which she thinks are better than anything else on the market. All the main banks refused Michelle's request for a $5000 loan to finance working capital. Michelle decided to use crowdfunding. After 3 years of successful operation, she has employed 3 other people and sales are rising. She financed further expansion from retained profit.
   a. Define 'working capital'. [2]
   b. Outline **two** reasons why Michelle decided to raise the finance by using crowdfunding. [4]
   c. Explain **two** advantages of Michelle using retained profit to expand her business further. [6]
   d. Ten years after setting up her business, Michelle converted the business into a private limited company to raise finance for business expansion by issuing shares. Do you think issuing shares was the best source of finance for the expansion? Justify your answer. [8]

2. Akram holds the majority of shares in a private limited company which owns a small farm. The revenue of the business varies greatly during the year. The farm makes a small profit but Akram is ambitious. He wants to take over a neighbour's farm and increase the range of crops he sells. He is unsure which type of long-term finance would be best to finance the takeover. He has recently leased a new tractor.
   a. Define 'long-term finance'. [2]
   b. Outline **two** types of external finance Akram could use when farm revenue is low. [4]
   c. Explain **one** advantage and **one** disadvantage of Akram leasing the new tractor. [6]
   d. Explain **two** sources of finance which Akram could use for the takeover. Which source should be used? Justify your answer. [8]

Revision checklist

In this chapter you have learned:

- ✔ the main reasons why businesses need finance
- ✔ the short-term and long-term finance needs of a business
- ✔ the concept and importance of working capital
- ✔ about internal and external sources of finance
- ✔ the advantages and disadvantages of internal and external sources of finance
- ✔ the main factors to consider when selecting a source of finance
- ✔ how to recommend and justify an appropriate source of finance for a given situation.

NOW – test your understanding with the revision questions in the Student etextbook and the Workbook.

24 Cash flow forecast

This chapter will explain:

The importance of cash and cash flow forecasts:

★ why cash is important to a business
★ what a cash flow forecast is and why it is important
★ the main features of a cash flow forecast
★ how to amend or complete a simple cash flow forecast
★ how to interpret a simple cash flow forecast
★ how a short-term cash flow problem may be overcome.

The importance of cash and cash flow forecasts

Why cash is important to a business

Cash is immediately available for spending on goods and services. It can be in the form of notes and coins or bank accounts. All businesses need cash to pay day-to-day expenses, bills and suppliers' invoices.

If a business has too little cash – or even none at all – it will face major problems, such as:

» being unable to pay employees, suppliers, landlord, government
» production of goods and services will stop – employees will not work for no pay and suppliers will not supply goods if they are not paid
» being forced into liquidation – having to sell off everything it owns to pay its debts (see Chapter 27).

What is meant by cash flow?

It is important to understand the key difference between **cash outflows** and **cash inflows** when preparing a **cash flow** forecast.

Cash inflows

Here are five of the most common ways that cash can flow into a business:

» sale of products for cash
» payments made by debtors (trade receivables – see Chapter 26). These are customers who have already purchased products from the business but did not pay for them at the time
» borrowing money from an external source. This leads to cash flowing into the business (it will have to be repaid eventually)
» sale of unwanted non-current assets
» owners or shareholders investing more money into the business.

Cash outflows

Here are five of the most common ways that cash can flow out of a business:

» purchasing goods or materials for cash
» paying wages, salaries and other day-to-day expenses in cash

> **Definitions to learn**
>
> **Cash outflows** are the sums of money paid out by a business during a period of time.
> **Cash inflows** are the sums of money received by a business during a period of time.
> The **cash flow** of a business is the cash inflows and outflows over a period of time.

24 CASH FLOW FORECAST

- purchasing non-current assets
- repaying loans
- paying creditors of the business (trade payables – see Chapter 26). These are other businesses which supplied items to the business but were not paid immediately.

> ### Activity 24.1
> Copy out the table below. For each of the transactions, tick the correct column to indicate whether it represents a cash inflow or a cash outflow for a business.
>
> | Transaction | Cash inflow | Cash outflow |
> |---|---|---|
> | Purchase of new IT systems for cash | | |
> | Sale of goods to customers – no credit given | | |
> | Interest paid on bank loan | | |
> | Wages paid to employees | | |
> | Debtors pay their bills/invoices | | |
> | Additional shares sold to shareholders | | |
> | Creditors/suppliers paid | | |
> | Bank overdraft paid off | | |

Cash flow cycle

The following diagram will help to explain the link between some of the inflows and outflows that have been mentioned. It is called a cash flow cycle. It explains why cash paid out is not returned immediately to the business.

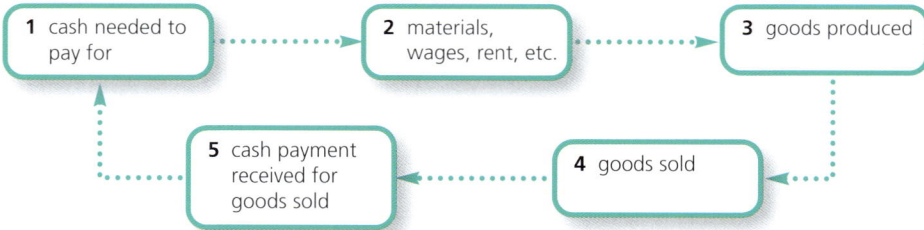

▲ The cash flow cycle

The diagram shows why cash is needed (1) to pay for essential materials and other costs (2) required to produce the product. Time is needed to produce the products (3) before they can be sold to customers (4). If these customers receive credit, they will not have to pay straightaway. When they do pay for the goods in cash (5), this money will be needed (1) to pay for buying further materials, etc. (2), and so the cycle continues. The longer the time taken to complete these stages, the greater will be the business's need for working capital (see page 280).

The diagram also helps us to understand the importance of planning for cash flows. What would happen in the following situations?

- If a business did not have enough cash at stage 1: Not enough materials and other requirements could be purchased, so output and sales would fall.

The importance of cash and cash flow forecasts

» If a business insisted on its customer paying cash at stage 4 because the business was short of money: It might lose the customer to a competitor that could offer credit (allow the customer time to pay for the goods or services).
» If a business had insufficient cash to pay its bills such as rent and electricity: It would be in a liquidity crisis and it might be forced out of business by its creditors.

These three examples illustrate the need for managers to plan ahead for their cash needs so that the business is not put at risk in these ways.

What cash flow is not!

Cash flow is not the same as **profit**. This is an important distinction.

> **Definitions to learn**
> **Profit** is the surplus after total costs have been subtracted from total revenue.

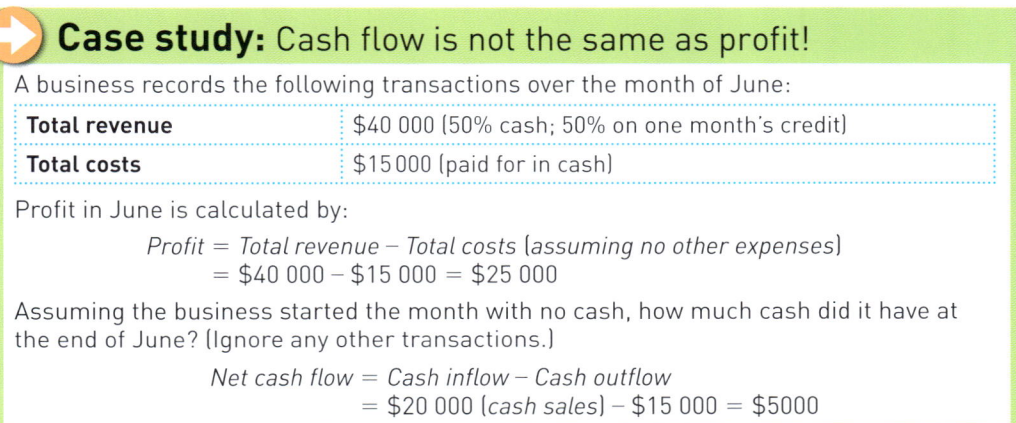

Case study: Cash flow is not the same as profit!

A business records the following transactions over the month of June:

Total revenue	$40 000 (50% cash; 50% on one month's credit)
Total costs	$15 000 (paid for in cash)

Profit in June is calculated by:

  Profit = Total revenue − Total costs (*assuming no other expenses*)
   = $40 000 − $15 000 = $25 000

Assuming the business started the month with no cash, how much cash did it have at the end of June? (Ignore any other transactions.)

  Net cash flow = Cash inflow − Cash outflow
   = $20 000 (*cash sales*) − $15 000 = $5000

There is a clear difference between the profit made by the business and the cash flow over the same period in the case study above.

Q: Why is the cash figure lower than the profit?
A: Because, although all goods have been sold, cash payment has been received for only half of them. The customers buying the goods on credit will pay in later months.

This important example leads to further questions:
Q: Can profitable businesses run out of cash?
A: Yes – and this is a major reason for businesses failing.
Q: How is this possible?
A: By:

» allowing customers too long a credit period, perhaps to encourage sales
» purchasing too many non-current assets at once
» expanding too quickly and keeping a high inventory level. This means that cash is used to pay for higher inventory levels.

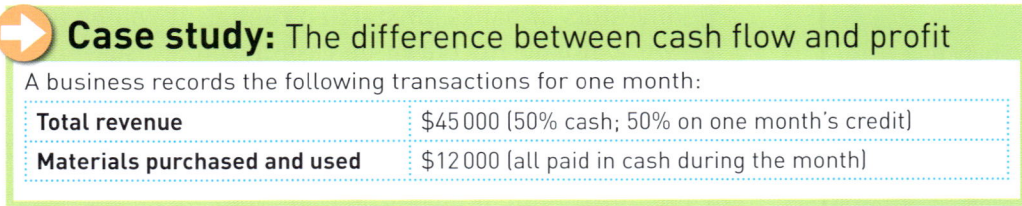

Case study: The difference between cash flow and profit

A business records the following transactions for one month:

Total revenue	$45 000 (50% cash; 50% on one month's credit)
Materials purchased and used	$12 000 (all paid in cash during the month)

24 CASH FLOW FORECAST

> **Activity 24.2**
> Read the second case study on the previous page.
> a Calculate the profit made by the business in this month.
> b Calculate the cash held by the business at the end of this month (assume it had no cash at the start of the month).
> c Explain why the answers to a and b are different.

REVISION SUMMARY Cash flow

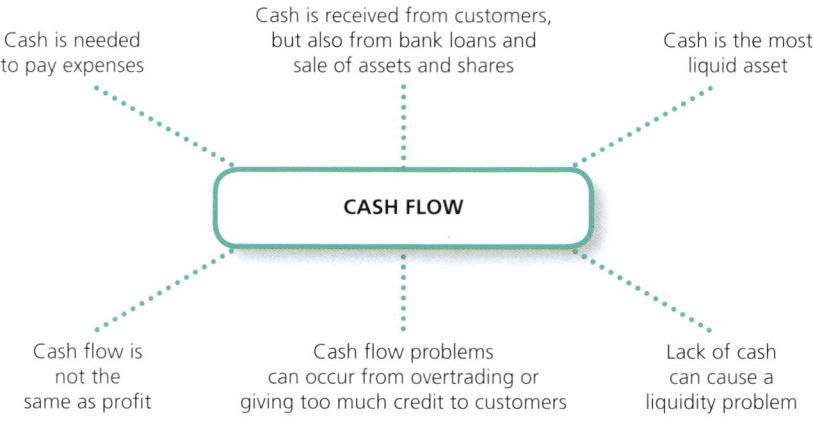

Definitions to learn

A **cash flow forecast** is an estimate of future cash inflows and outflows of a business, usually on a month-by-month basis, showing the expected cash balance at the end of each month.

Key info

An estimated 25 158 companies entered insolvency (meaning they ran out of cash) in 2023 in the UK. Keeping control of cash flow is very important for a business to continue to trade.

Study tips

There can be slight variations in the way businesses lay out their cash flow forecasts. The examples used in this chapter cover what you need to know.

What a cash flow forecast is and why it is important

A **cash flow forecast** is an estimate of future cash inflows and outflows of a business, usually on a month-by-month basis, showing the expected cash balance at the end of each month.

Managers use cash flow forecasts to help them find out the future cash position of their business. They help managers decide what action to take to ensure the business always has enough cash. All businesses need to draw up and regularly update a cash flow forecast. They can help managers answer the following points:

» how much cash is likely to be available for paying bills, repaying loans or for buying fixed assets
» how much cash might need to be injected into the business. This could be done by, for example, the bank agreeing to an overdraft or short-term loan so the business does not run out of cash
» whether the business is holding too much cash which could be put to a more profitable use.

These cash flow forecasts are essential for entrepreneurs when they approach investors or banks for start-up capital. It will be impossible to gain initial capital without a clearly drawn-up cash flow forecast.

Uses of cash flow forecasts

Cash flow forecasts are useful in the following situations:

» **Starting up a business.** Many start-up businesses fail because entrepreneurs fail to realise how much cash is needed in the first few crucial months of operating a new business. A cash flow forecast should help to avoid this problem.

296

- **Operating an existing business.** All businesses need to replace worn out capital equipment at some time or they may experience seasonal changes in sales. Planning ahead for these finance needs through cash flow forecasting will make it easier to obtain money at the right time from the most suitable sources.
- **Keeping the bank manager informed.** Banks will always expect to see a cash flow forecast for a business that is asking for a loan. The bank will need to see how big the loan or overdraft request is, the chances of it being repaid and the net cash flow of the business during the loan period.
- **Managing cash flow.** Cash flow forecasts can indicate when too much cash is likely to be held in the bank account. This cash could be put to better use than just remaining in the account, such as repaying a loan early. Managing cash flows to the best advantage of the business is one of the most important uses of cash flow forecasts.

Main features of a cash flow forecast

A cash flow forecast shows all the forecasted cash inflows and cash outflows in the business's bank account. By taking the cash outflows away from the cash inflows, the **net cash flow** for the month will be shown. If there is a positive net cash flow, the amount in the bank account will increase (or a negative bank balance will be reduced). A negative net cash flow will do the opposite by reducing the amount in the bank account at the end of the month or making a negative figure larger.

The **opening balance** will show how much cash the business has at the start of each month. The **closing balance** will show how much money it will have left at the end of each month. The closing balance at the end of one month becomes the opening balance at the start of the next month.

The example in Table 24.1 shows the main features of a cash flow forecast. Any negative figures are shown in brackets.

> **Definitions to learn**
>
> **Net cash flow** is the difference between cash inflows and cash outflows during each period of time, usually one month.
> The **opening balance** is the cash held by the business at the start of each period of time.
> The **closing balance** is the cash held by the business at the end of each period of time.

Table 24.1 Cash flow, January to March 2025 ($)

	January	February	March
Cash inflows (A)	35 000	45 000	50 000
Cash outflows (B)	30 000	65 000	40 000
Net cash flow (C) = (A − B)	5 000	(20 000)	10 000
Opening balance (D)	10 000	15 000	(5 000)
Closing balance (C + D)	15 000	(5 000)	5 000

Note the following points:

- A positive net cash flow will increase the closing balance.
- A negative net cash flow (as in February) will reduce the closing balance.
- Each closing balance becomes the opening balance for the next month.
- The bank account of this business will become negative, or overdrawn, in February.

24 CASH FLOW FORECAST

> **Extend your skills of analysis**
>
> A question which asks for an advantage of a cash flow forecast to an entrepreneur when planning a start-up business could be answered as follows:
>
> *A cash flow forecast shows the net cash flow expected in future time periods and the opening and closing balances.*
>
> **Extend your analysis by explaining why this is an advantage.**
>
> *The cash flow forecast will indicate whether a business needs to take measures to improve net cash flow to prevent it running out of cash over the next few months.*
>
> **Extend your analysis by explaining why this is important to an entrepreneur planning a start-up business.**
>
> *The entrepreneur will not only benefit from planning the finances of the business but it will also be important to show the cash flow forecast to the bank. The bank will only lend finance to a start-up business if the cash flow forecast shows that net cash flows are under control and the business seems likely to be able to pay interest on the loan and, in time, pay it back.*

Amending or completing a simple cash flow forecast

The skills of amending or completing a cash flow forecast are best developed by working through the following activities. Key points to remember are:

» Use brackets to show a negative net cash flow and negative opening or negative closing balance.
» Do not forget that changing the closing balance of a month will change the opening balance for the next month – and so on.

Activity 24.3

Cash flow forecast for Sierra Promotions, January to April 2025 ($). Negative figures in brackets

	January	February	March	April
Cash inflows:				
Cash sales	15 000	15 000	20 000	25 000
Payments from debtors	5 000	5 000	7 000	8 000
Total cash inflow	20 000	20 000	27 000	33 000
Cash outflows:				
Materials and wages	3 000	3 000	5 000	7 000
Rent and other expenses	15 000	15 000	25 000	15 000
Total cash outflow	18 000	18 000	30 000	Z
Net cash flow	2 000	X	(3 000)	11 000
Opening balance	3 000	5 000	7 000	4 000
Closing balance	5 000	7 000	Y	15 000

a Calculate values for X, Y and Z.
b Suggest **one** reason why 'materials and wages' are forecast to be so much higher in March and April than in the previous months.
c In April, cash sales are now expected to be 10% higher than shown. Materials and wages are expected to be 20% higher than forecast. Amend the cash flow forecast for April and calculate the new closing balance.

The importance of cash and cash flow forecasts

Key info

The Body Shop UK called in administrators in February 2024. It was struggling to sell its products and maintain cash inflows. It had run up high debt levels and closed 75 stores in the UK to reduce costs and reduce cash outflows. It had found it difficult to respond to increasing online sales from competitors. It was trying to get store rents reduced to reduce cash ouflows but it had a major cash flow problem. The Body Shop's German, US and Canadian operations have also filed for bankruptcy.

Case study: Cash flow forecast

The Manager of Capri Motors wants to plan the cash flows of the business over the next 4 months. She asks for your help in making a cash flow forecast. She provides you with the following information:

- Forecasted sales: January $22 000; February $25 000; March $20 000; April $22 000.
- Customers always pay cash.
- Materials are purchased each month and are paid for in cash. The materials used each month are 50% of revenue for that month.
- Other cash expenses (wages, rent, insurance and so on) are forecast to be: January $4000; February $13 000; March $15 000; April $15 000.
- The opening balance in January is $2000.

Activity 24.4

Read the case study above.

a Explain to the Manager the importance of a cash flow forecast.
b Using the same structure as in Activity 24.3, draw up a cash flow forecast for this business over the four months from January to April.
c What do you notice about the closing balance in April? What action could the manager of Capri Motors take now that she is aware of this problem?

REVISION SUMMARY   **Cash flow forecasts**

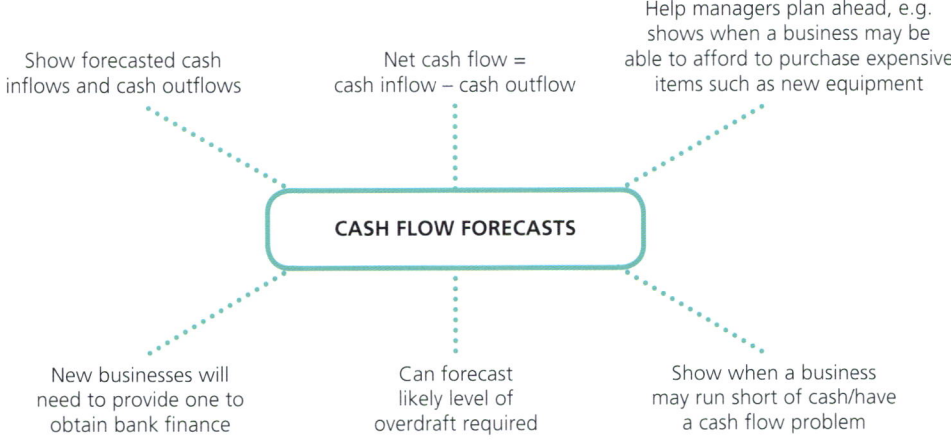

Interpreting a simple cash flow forecast

Table 24.2 shows a simple cash flow forecast with some information that has so far been provided.

Table 24.2 Overtown Fashions cash flow forecast for next six months. Negative figures in brackets

	July ($000)	August ($000)	September ($000)	October ($000)	November ($000)	December ($000)
Cash inflows						
Owner's capital	–	–	50	–	–	–
Cash sales	15	24	35	30	45	50
Sale of unwanted van	–	5	–	–	–	–
Total cash inflow	15	29	85	30	45	50
Cash outflows						
Payments to suppliers	6	18	20	21	25	30
Wages	5	5	8	5	6	6
Rent and other expenses	12	12	30	14	15	12
Total cash outflow	23	35	58	40	46	48
Net cash flow	(8)	(6)	27	(10)	(1)	2
Opening balance	15	7	1	28	18	17
Closing balance	7	1	28	18	17	19

What do you think the cash flow forecast shows about the business?

Interpreting Overtown Fashions cash flow forecast

Here are the observations you could have made:

» The business does not require any additional bank loans or a bank overdraft during the period shown.
» Forecasted cash inflows and cash outflows vary over these months.
» Cash from sales is steadily increasing, apart from October.
» Payments to suppliers are increasing too – this is to be expected as product sales are rising.
» A big increase in expenses in September is forecast – this could be to pay for the repair of equipment. As the owner has forecast this, they are able to plan for it.
» A one-off cash inflow from the sale of the unwanted van leads to a useful cash inflow.
» The owner can see, from the cash flow forecast, that without an injection of cash in September there is likely to be a big negative cash balance for this month. This would need a bank overdraft or bank loan.
» The owner has decided to avoid the need to do this by injecting more of their own savings into the business.
» Future cash flow problems might be avoided if the business increases cash sales more quickly than cash outflows.

The importance of cash and cash flow forecasts

Activity 24.5

Read the case study on the right.

a Why is cash flow forecasting important to Manuel?
b Who else, apart from Manuel, is likely to be interested in a cash flow forecast for Gardener's Green? Give reasons for your answer.
c Why do wage costs stay the same and materials vary each month?
d Explain **two** ways Manuel could improve the cash flow forecast for Gardener's Green.

Case study: Gardener's Green

Manuel Guitano set up Gardener's Green as a sole trader 9 years ago. Manuel designs and looks after the gardens of hotels and large private houses. Customers pay in cash. He is busy for most of the year but not busy in winter months. He has 6 full-time employees.

You have been asked by Manuel to make recommendations as to how he can solve his cash flow problem.

Cash flow forecast for Gardener's Green. Negative figures in brackets

	Jan ($000)	Feb ($000)	Mar ($000)	Apr ($000)	May ($000)	Jun ($000)
Cash inflows						
Cash sales	1	1	30	60	70	70
Total cash inflow	1	1	30	60	70	70
Cash outflows						
Wages	10	10	10	10	10	10
Materials	10	10	30	30	30	30
Total cash outflow	20	20	40	40	40	40
Net cash flow	(19)	(19)	(10)	20	30	30
Opening balance	22	3	(16)	(26)	(6)	24
Closing balance	3	(16)	(26)	(6)	24	54

How a short-term cash flow problem might be overcome

There are several ways in which a short-term cash flow problem could be overcome. These are explained below – and the possible disadvantages of each way are outlined too.

Table 24.3 Methods of overcoming short-term cash flow problems

Method of overcoming cash flow problem	How it works	Possible disadvantages
Overdraft	A bank overdraft allows the business to borrow money when it is needed by spending more cash than is in the bank account	Interest must be paid – this is a cash outflow and will increase expenses, possibly leading to lower profits The overdraft will have to be repaid eventually – a cash outflow
Delaying supplier payments	Cash outflows will decrease in the short term. This will reduce any negative net cash flows	Suppliers could refuse to supply the products if delays in payment are too long Suppliers could offer lower discounts if payments are late
Asking customers (debtors) to pay more quickly – or insisting on only 'cash sales'	Cash inflows will increase in the short term	Customers may purchase from another business that still offers them time to pay (trade credit) – so sales may be lower in the future
Delaying or cancelling purchases of non-current assets	Cash outflows for purchase of equipment will decrease	The long-term efficiency of the business could decrease without up-to-date equipment The price of equipment might be higher in the future

24 CASH FLOW FORECAST

Extend your skills of analysis

A question which asks for a disadvantage to a smartphone retailer of asking customers to pay for all purchases in cash, and not allowing credit, could be answered as follows:

Giving customers credit, or time to pay for purchases, reduces short-term cash inflows.

Extend your analysis by explaining why refusing to give credit is likely to impact on customer decisions.

Smartphone retailing is a very competitive market. Customers might be looking for both the right phone and credit. One factor in their purchasing decision might be whether they can pay for the phone over a period of time rather than pay immediately with cash.

Extend your analysis by explaining why refusing credit is a disadvantage.

Although cash flow from each sale will improve, total sales of smartphones might be lower if customers are offered credit by competing retailers. This means the sales and revenue of the business could fall.

International business in focus

Dealing with cash flow issues in different ways

Kodak – formerly the world's biggest supplier of camera film – cut its workforce by a huge amount as demand for traditional film collapsed as a result of the digital revolution. It sold off many assets, such as company cars and underused premises. Its cash flow problems led to Kodak filing for bankruptcy in 2012. However, Kodak now still manufactures film but not digital cameras. It also produces print systems, inkjet systems, 3D printing and packaging, as well as software for printing, thereby increasing cash inflows from alternative products.

▲ Traditional camera film

Kier Group is a huge construction company based in Europe. The end of a property boom meant that construction companies had less work and were having to wait longer for payment from customers. Kier managed its operations to minimise cash outflows. The company holds no or very low inventories and demands that all of its suppliers deliver goods and equipment as they are needed – or very shortly before. This means that valuable cash is not held up in inventories that will not be used for weeks. It has also reduced its debt and ensures prompt payment from customers when projects are completed.

▲ A Kier construction site

Discussion points

- Explain how technological change had an impact on cash flow for Kodak.
- Explain how the end of a property boom had an impact on cash flow for Kier Group.
- Explain the different ways these businesses tried to resolve a potential cash flow problem.

Chapter review questions: Short answer and data response

1. Bruno manages a hotel. Most of the hotel bedrooms are occupied during the main tourist season, which lasts for 7 months. During the off-peak months around 50% of rooms are occupied. The hotel's main cash outflows are the same each month but food costs and some employee costs increase when there are more tourists. Bruno plans to have the hotel redecorated but he does not know whether the cost of this will mean the hotel exceeds its overdraft limit. The hotel's bank account is overdrawn during the off-peak months of each year.

   a. Define 'cash outflows'. [2]
   b. Outline **two** effects on Bruno's hotel if he offers hotel guests credit of one month if they stay in the hotel in the off-peak months. [4]
   c. Explain **two** advantages to Bruno of producing a cash flow forecast. [6]
   d. Explain **two** ways in which Bruno could improve the cash flow position of the hotel. Which way would you advise him to use? Justify your answer. [8]

2. Abbas Manufacturing produces wheels for cars. It sells them to large car manufacturers that pay 3 months after delivery. It holds high inventory levels so that one-off orders from major car manufacturers can be satisfied quickly. Abbas Manufacturing has prepared the following cash flow forecast for the next 3 months:

	July ($000)	August ($000)	September ($000)
Cash inflows			
Cash from debtors' payments (Trade receivables)	550	475	595
Total cash inflow	550	475	595
Cash outflows			
Materials purchased	160	175	170
Other expenses	340	455	325
Total cash outflow	500	630	495
Net cash flow	50	(155)	X
Opening balance	(75)	(25)	(180)
Closing balance	(25)	(180)	Y

   a. Calculate the values for X and Y in the cash flow forecast. [2]
   b. Outline **two** ways the cash flow forecast could be used by Abbas Manufacturing. [4]
   c. Explain **two** effects on the cash flow forecast for September from material costs increasing by 10% more than originally forecast. [6]
   d. Do you think Abbas Manufacturing should overcome its cash flow problem by reducing its high inventory levels? Justify your answer. [8]

Revision checklist

In this chapter you have learned:

- why cash is important to a business
- what a cash flow forecast is and why it is important
- the main features of a cash flow forecast
- how to amend or complete a simple cash flow forecast
- how to interpret a simple cash flow forecast
- how a short-term cash flow problem may be overcome.

NOW – test your understanding with the revision questions in the Student etextbook and the Workbook.

25 Profit and loss

> This chapter will explain:
>
> What profit is and why it is important:
>
> ★ what profit is
> ★ the importance of profit to private sector businesses.
>
> Statement of profit or loss:
>
> ★ the main features of a statement of profit or loss
> ★ how to make simple calculations based on a statement of profit or loss
> ★ how to make decisions based on simple statements of profit or loss.

What profit is and why it is important

What profit is

Profit is an objective for most businesses. In simple terms, profit made by a business is calculated by the formula given below.

> **Calculations to learn**
>
> Profit = Total revenue − Total costs

This simple formula introduces the idea that profit is a surplus that remains after all business costs have been subtracted. If these costs are greater than **revenue**, then the business has made a loss. The profit formula also suggests that this surplus can be increased by:

1. increasing revenue by more than any increase in costs
2. reducing the costs of the business
3. a combination of 1 and 2.

Importance of profit to private sector businesses

Businesses in the private sector need profit to survive, to provide funds for expansion and to reward people who have invested in them. Profit is important to private sector businesses for several reasons, as outlined in Table 25.1.

Definitions to learn

Profit is the surplus after total costs have been subtracted from total revenue.
Revenue is the income of a business during a period of time from the sale of goods or services.

Statement of profit or loss

Table 25.1 Importance of profit to private sector businesses

Why profit is important	Explanation
Reward for risk-taking	Entrepreneurs and other investors take considerable risks when they provide capital to a business. They may not get their capital back if the business fails. Profits reward them for taking these risks by allowing payments to be made to business owners, for example, dividends to shareholders
Source of finance	Profits after payments to the owners are retained profits (see Chapter 23). These are a very important source of finance for businesses. This finance can be used to pay for expanding the business or purchasing new technology machinery
Measure of success	Profit levels of different businesses can indicate which are more successful than others. When some businesses are very profitable, this signals to other businesses or entrepreneurs that investment in producing similar products would be profitable. If all businesses in an industry are making losses, this would not be a good signal to set up in that industry
Attract investors	Individuals and professional investing institutions will only invest capital into a business if it is either profitable or has a great chance of becoming profitable. A loss-making business with few prospects of making profit will find it very difficult to obtain capital from investors

> **Extend your skills of analysis**
>
> A question which asks why profit is important for a private limited company planning a big expansion could be answered as follows:
>
> Profit kept in a business after all costs and dividends have been paid is an important source of internal finance.
>
> *Extend your analysis by explaining why using profit as a source of finance is an advantage.*
>
> Using retained profit will allow the company to obtain finance without increasing loans and interest costs. Loans will need to be repaid and interest costs will reduce profit.
>
> *Extend your analysis by explaining why profit is so important to the private limited company in this case.*
>
> This private limited company could decide to change to a public limited company and sell shares to the public. As well as being a source of finance, high profit levels indicate to potential shareholders that this business is a good investment and might make them more likely to buy shares in it. So the business will be able to finance the expansion without increasing the amount of company debt.

Statement of profit or loss

Main features of a statement of profit or loss

All businesses should keep accurate accounts. These record all financial transactions with customers, suppliers, investors and government (for the payment of tax). If these accounts are not recorded or if they are inaccurate, businesses managers will not be able to calculate profit or loss accurately.

Statements of profit or loss are one of the most important accounts recorded by businesses. They indicate to managers, business owners and other account users whether the business has made a profit or loss over a period of time. This time period is usually one year but statements of profit or loss could be constructed monthly too. The statement of profit or loss is part of the published accounts of a public limited company. Other types of business organisation, including private limited companies, will also produce an end of year statement of profit or loss. This document looks back on the past year and shows how successful the business has been.

> **Definitions to learn**
>
> A **statement of profit or loss** is a financial account that records the income of a business and all costs incurred to earn that income over a period of time, for example, one year.

25 PROFIT AND LOSS

If the business is making a profit, managers will use the statement of profit or loss to help answer the following questions:

- Is profit higher or lower than last year?
- If lower, why is profit falling?
- Is profit higher or lower than other similar businesses?
- If lower, what can we do to become as profitable as other businesses?

If the business is making a loss, managers will use the statement of profit or loss to help answer the following questions:

- Is this a short-term or long-term problem?
- Are other similar businesses also making losses?
- What decisions can we take to turn losses into profits?

You can now begin to understand why a statement of profit or loss is so important.

Revenue

Revenue is the value of sales made by a business. It is calculated by the formula given below.

> **Calculations to learn**
>
> *Revenue = Selling price per unit × Number of units sold*

Worked example

For example, if the price is $10 and 1000 products are sold in one year:

Revenue = Selling price per unit × Number of units sold
= $10 × 1000 = $10 000

Cost of sales

Cost of sales is the variable cost of production for the goods or services sold by a business. This includes the cost of the materials used in creating the good plus the direct labour costs of producing the good. In a retail business it will be the cost of buying the products sold by the shop. Cost of sales excludes fixed cost **expenses** such as distribution costs, rent and management salaries.

Gross profit

Gross profit is revenue less the cost of sales, as shown by the formula given below. Fixed costs are not subtracted.

> **Calculations to learn**
>
> *Gross profit = Revenue − Cost of sales*

Worked example

If a business bought $270 000 worth of goods during the year and sold them for $450 000 then:

Gross profit = Revenue − Cost of sales
= $450 000 − $270 000 = $180 000

Definitions to learn

The **cost of sales** is the cost of producing or buying in the goods actually sold by the business during a time period.
Expenses are the fixed costs of the business during a period of time.
Gross profit is made when revenue is greater than the cost of sales.

It is important to note the following:

- Gross profit does not make any allowance for fixed costs/expenses.
- Cost of sales is not necessarily the same as the total value of products bought by the business. Some products might have been purchased from suppliers but not sold – so these are added to inventory (and are shown on the statement of financial position – see Chapter 26).

Expenses

These are the fixed costs of the business. They are not included in cost of sales. Expenses may include such costs as rent, leasing charges, management salaries, repairs to equipment and insurance on business buildings. The total value of expenses must be subtracted from gross profit to calculate the profit.

Profit

Depending on the information provided, profit can be calculated in two ways, as shown by the formulae below.

> **Calculations to learn**
>
> Profit = Total revenue − Total costs
>
> Profit = Gross profit − Expenses

How is this information presented on a statement of profit or loss?

Table 25.2 shows a simple example of a statement of profit or loss with some notes to explain each item.

Table 25.2 A simple statement of profit or loss

	($000)	Notes
Statement of profit or loss for XYZ Coat Company		The business/company name should be shown clearly
For the year ending 31/10/25		The time period covered by the statement of profit or loss must be shown
Revenue	450	This is the income to the business from the sale of products during the year. For example, 9000 items at $50 each
Cost of sales	270	This is the variable cost (materials and costs of production labour, for example) of making the goods sold. For example, 9000 items costing $30 each
Gross profit	180	This is gross profit made before expenses are deducted = $450 000 − $270 000
Expenses	50	These are the fixed costs of the business paid during the year
Profit	130	This is the profit after **total costs** have been subtracted from revenue

Study tips

You should be able to make suggestions on how a business might increase its gross profit or profit – do not get these two terms confused.

Definitions to learn

Total costs are the addition of all fixed and variable costs of a business in a given time period.

Making simple calculations based on a statement of profit or loss

Here are some examples of calculations, and activities requiring calculations, based on simple statements of profit or loss.

25 PROFIT AND LOSS

> **Case study: City Cafe**
>
> City Cafe buys cans of drink from a wholesaler for $1 each. It sells them for $2 each. City Cafe started the year with 200 cans in stock. It bought in 1500 cans. At the end of the year it had 300 left. Annual expenses are $1000.
>
> 1. How many cans did the business sell during the year?
> 2. What was the cost of sales during this period?
> 3. What was the gross profit?
> 4. What was the profit figure if expenses of $1000 were paid during the year?
>
> **Answers**
>
> 1. Add together the opening inventory and the cans bought during the year: 200 + 1500 = 1700 cans.
>   The business could have sold 1700 cans during the year. We know that it did not sell this many. How? Because there were inventories of 300 left at the end of the year. Therefore, the business must have sold 1400 cans during the year.
> 2. As the goods were all bought by the business for $1 each, the cost of sales was $1400.
> 3. Remember:
>
>   *Gross profit = Revenue − Cost of sales*
>   *Revenue = $2 × 1400 = $2800*
>   *Gross profit = $2800 − $1400 = $1400*
> 4. Remember:
>
>   *Profit = Gross profit − Expenses*
>   = $1400 − $1000 = $400

Activity 25.1

Copy and complete the following table.

Revenue	Cost of sales	Gross profit
$3 000	$1 500	$ a
$25 000	$16 000	$ b
$80 000	$ c	$20 000
$ d	$25 000	$50 000

Activity 25.2

This is an example of a typical statement of profit or loss.

Statement of profit or loss for ABC for year ending 31/3/2025

Revenue	$55 000
Cost of sales	$23 000
Gross profit	$32 000
Expenses	$12 000
Profit	$20 000

a. Calculate the gross profit for the following year if revenue increased by $4000 and cost of sales increased by $3000.
b. Use your answer to a to calculate the profit for the following year if expenses were $10 000.

> **Key info**
>
> Boeing, the giant US aircraft manufacturer, reported that revenue increased to $77.79 billion in 2023, an increase of about 17% from 2022. However, due to problems with its 737 Max plane coming under more scrutiny about its safety, revenue was expected to fall in 2024. That said, Boeing often makes a high gross profit but due to its high fixed costs it does not always make a profit because it does not sell enough of its commercial airplanes.

Statement of profit or loss

> **Activity 25.3**
>
> Newtown Garden Nursery statement of profit or loss for year ending 31/3/2025
>
> | Revenue | $92 000 |
> |---|---|
> | Cost of sales | $45 000 |
> | Gross profit | x |
> | Expenses: | |
> | Management salaries | $15 000 |
> | Electricity | $6 000 |
> | Rent | $5 000 |
> | Selling and advertising expenses | $5 000 |
> | Total expenses | y |
> | Profit | z |
>
> a Calculate the value of x – Gross profit.
> b Calculate the value of y – Total expenses.
> c Calculate the value of z – Profit.

Retained profit

This term was defined and explained in Chapter 23 as a source of internal finance. The figure below illustrates how retained profit is calculated – it is the profit left in the business after all costs, expenses, tax and dividends have been subtracted from revenue.

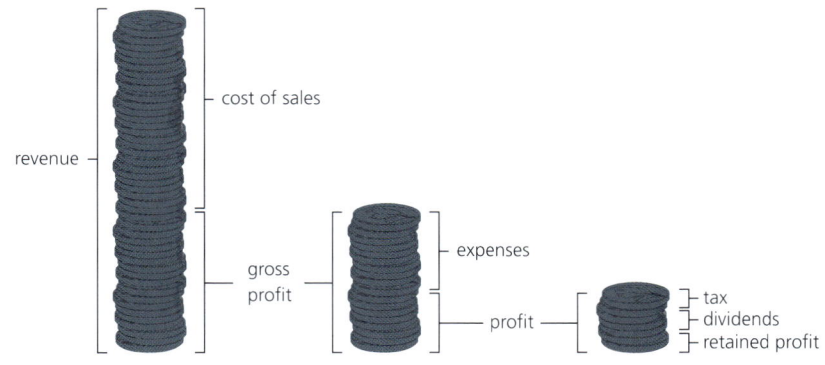

▲ How retained profit is calculated

REVISION SUMMARY

Statements of profit or loss

- Gross profit = revenue less cost of sales
- Profit = gross profit less expenses
- Retained profit = profit less tax and dividends

STATEMENTS OF PROFIT OR LOSS

- Shows profit/loss not cash flow
- Used by managers to compare business performance
- Important part of a company's published accounts

309

25 PROFIT AND LOSS

Making decisions based on simple statements of profit or loss

Managers can use the information on statements of profit or loss to help them in making decisions. If a manager has to choose which one of two new products to launch, one way of making this decision is to construct two forecasted statements of profit or loss. Similarly, if a decision has to be made between two locations for a new shop, two forecasted statements of profit or loss can be compared.

The following case studies and activities are excellent examples of decisions that can be made, mainly based on simple statements of profit or loss.

> **Activity 25.4**
>
> Read the case study on the right.
>
> Do you think Asif made the right decision? Justify your answer using the statements of profit or loss and other information.

Case study: Decision based on statement of profit or loss

Asif has to decide which location, A or B, would be best for a new shop. He has undertaken market research and forecasted the costs of the 2 locations. The information he has collected is shown below:

Forecasted information for next year	Location A	Location B
Revenue	$40 000	$60 000
Cost of sales	$16 000	$24 000
Gross profit	$24 000	$36 000
Rent	$10 000	$16 000
Other expenses	$5 000	$8 000
Profit	$9 000	$12 000

Asif also considered other factors before making the final decision:

- Annual rent at Location B is fixed for 5 years but for only 2 years at Location A.
- A new housing estate is planned to be built just 6 kilometres away from Location B.
- A potential competitor has just closed a shop near Location A.

Asif finally selected Location B for the new shop.

> **Key info**
>
> The decision to retain profit for prospective profitable investment projects rather than pay higher dividends to shareholders is unlikely to affect the company share price. However, if lower profits are predicted this is likely to lead to a lower share price.

Case study: Decision based on statement of profit or loss

Joe is the New Product Manager at a chain of takeaway food stores. He is planning to introduce a new type of 'fast food' – a pizza or a curry. There are 2 product options but the business can only afford to buy the equipment and advertising material needed for 1 of the options.

Joe has undertaken some market research and forecasted the main costs for the 2 product options. He has asked you to help him complete the following statements of profit or loss:

Forecasts for one year	Pizza option	Curry option
Revenue	(50 000 units at $3)	(40 000 units at $5)
Cost of sales	(Unit cost of $1 each)	(Unit cost of $2 each)
Gross profit		
Annual equipment costs	$13 000	$12 000
Annual advertising costs	$15 000	$20 000
Other expenses	$13 000	$15 000
Profit		

Study tips

Business managers often have to use calculations as part of their job – do not be afraid of business calculations! This book explains a number of calculations – practise all of the examples. Take a calculator with you into examinations!

Activity 25.5

Read the case study at the bottom of the previous page.

a Copy out and complete the two statements of profit or loss. Fill in the totals for revenue and cost of sales.
b Calculate the gross profit and profit of each product option.
c Explain **two** other factors Joe should consider before making this decision.
d Joe finally decides on the curry option. After one year, he finds that profit from this product is much lower than expected. Recommend **two** ways Joe could try to increase profits from this product. Justify your recommendations.

International business in focus

Sunlife, revenue and profit up

In 2023 Sunlife hotel group, the large leisure group operating in Mauritius and the Maldives, announced that its profits increased to Rs 1.5 billion in 2023. This was a dramatic increase on 2019's pre-COVID profit of Rs 172 million. Revenue increased by 30% from Rs 6216 million in 2019 to Rs 8133 million in 2023.

The company underwent a rebranding in 2022, changing from Sun Resorts to Sunlife, which was accompanied by promotions and advertising to expand its market presence. It also focused on controlling its costs to offset the challenges from soaring inflation in operational expenses and keep profits increasing.

Source: www.yoursunlife.com/media/xwaicahk/sun-limited-ar23.pdf

Discussion points

- Why are profits important to a large hotel group such as Sunlife?
- Explain why the company increased its profits in 2023.

25 PROFIT AND LOSS

❓ Chapter review questions: Short answer and data response

1. Ikram is a hairdresser. His revenue was 10% higher this year than last year. He earned revenue of $50 000 last year. The average price for each customer this year was $5 and he had 11 000 customers. He buys in materials such as shampoo and hairspray and has calculated that the cost of sales is an average of $2 for each customer.

   a Define 'revenue'. [2]

   b i Calculate Ikram's revenue this year. Show your working. [2]

   ii Calculate Ikram's gross profit this year (using your result from b i). Show your working. [2]

   c Explain **two** possible reasons why revenue was 10% higher this year. [6]

   d Do you think Ikram will increase his profit next year if he increases average prices to $6 per customer? Justify your answer. [8]

2. Sue has a successful business selling computer games online. She has developed 2 new computer games but she only has the capital to launch 1 of these.
   - Game A is aimed at young children of around 6–10 years.
   - Game B is targeted at teenagers of around 13–18 years.

   She has forecast the following financial information:

Forecasts for next year	Game A	Game B
Revenue	(3000 units at $5)	(2000 units at $10)
Cost of sales	($1.50 per unit)	($3 per unit)
Expenses	$4000	$9000

   a Define 'cost of sales'. [2]

   b Outline **two** ways in which Sue could try to increase revenue for any one of her existing games. [4]

   c Explain **two** other pieces of information that Sue would find useful before making a choice between Game A and Game B. [6]

   d Which game should Sue launch? Justify your answer using suitable calculations. [8]

Revision checklist

In this chapter you have learned:

✔ what profit is
✔ the importance of profit to private sector businesses
✔ the main features of a statement of profit or loss
✔ how to make simple calculations based on a statement of profit or loss
✔ how to make decisions based on simple statements of profit or loss.

NOW – test your understanding with the revision questions in the Student etextbook and the Workbook.

26 Statement of financial position

> This chapter will explain:
>
> The main elements of a statement of financial position:
> ★ non-current assets
> ★ current assets
> ★ non-current liabilities
> ★ current liabilities
> ★ the concept of capital employed
> ★ how to make simple calculations based on statements of financial position
> ★ how to make decisions based on simple statements of financial position.

The main elements of a statement of financial position

Chapter 25 explained how a manager can calculate whether a business is making a profit or a loss. The statement of profit or loss contains this information. Knowing that the business is making a profit or loss is clearly of great importance. However, the statement of profit or loss does not tell managers or investors how much the business is worth. Business owners would be very interested to know the value of their business. This information is given on the **statement of financial position**.

A statement of financial position is very different from the statement of profit or loss, which records the revenue and expenses of a business and the profit or loss it makes over a period of time – usually one year. The statement of financial position records the value or worth of a business at one moment in time, usually at the end of the financial year.

A personal statement of financial position example will help to introduce the basic concept of this account.

> **Definitions to learn**
>
> A **statement of financial position** shows the value of a business's assets and liabilities at a particular time.

Case study: A personal statement of financial position

Sanchez plans to start his own business. A government business adviser asked him 'How much money can you put into the business?' and Sanchez had to admit he did not really know!

The adviser asked him for an approximate value of everything he owned, including any bank accounts – as well as any debts or loans that he had.

Together they made these 2 lists:

All items owned by Sanchez	All debts owed by Sanchez
House $50 000	Loan on house (mortgage) $18 000
Car $4500	Bank loan on car $3000
Savings $3000	Owes brother $1500
Bank account $500	
Total $58 000	Total $22 500

The adviser told Sanchez: 'The total value of what you own is $35 500 more than the value of what you owe. This difference is called "wealth or equity" and means that you could, theoretically, invest this much of your own capital into your new business. Unfortunately, it is not all in cash!'

> **Study tips**
>
> A statement of financial position is useful to many stakeholder groups to help analyse the performance and financial strength of a business.

26 STATEMENT OF FINANCIAL POSITION

> **Definitions to learn**
>
> **Assets** are items of value owned by a business.
> **Liabilities** are amounts owed by a business to be paid at a future date.
> **Non-current assets** are property, machinery and other assets owned by a business which will not be turned into cash within one year.
> **Current assets** are owned by a business and converted into cash within one year.
> **Trade receivables** are amounts owed to the business by customers who purchased products on credit.
> **Non-current liabilities** are long-term debts owed by the business, repaid over more than one year.
> **Current liabilities** are short-term debts that must be paid within one year.
> **Total liabilities** equal non-current liabilities plus current liabilities.
> **Total assets** equal non-current assets plus current assets.

Business statements of financial position follow exactly the same principles. They list and give a value to all the **assets** and **liabilities** of the business, as outlined below. This allows the value of the business to be assessed.

Non-current assets

Non-current assets are items of value which are owned by the business for more than one year. Property (land and buildings), machinery, equipment and vehicles are examples of non-current assets. Most non-current assets, apart from land, depreciate (lose value) over time so the value of these may fall on the statement of financial position from one year to the next. Most businesses could not operate without some non-current assets.

Current assets

Current assets are held by a business for less than one year. Cash (usually held in a bank account), inventory (components, part-finished and finished products) and **trade receivables** (owed to the business by customers) are only held for short periods of time. For example, inventories are likely to be sold for cash within one year.

Non-current liabilities

Non-current liabilities are long-term debts, for example, bank loans which do not have to be repaid within one year. They are sources of long-term finance for the business.

Current liabilities

Current liabilities are amounts owed by the business which must be repaid within one year, for example, bank overdraft and trade payables, which are amounts owed to suppliers.

Shareholders' equity

In the personal statement of financial position for Sanchez on the previous page, his wealth or equity was calculated by subtracting all that he *owed* from the value of all that he *owned*. This is true for any business as well. For a sole trader or partnership it is called 'owners' equity' but for a company it is called 'shareholders' equity'. This is the value of the company owned by shareholders after subtracting **total liabilities** from **total assets**. Shareholders will expect the value of their equity to increase each year and this will usually be the case if the company uses retained profits for further expansion.

> **Study tips**
>
> You should take every chance to apply your answers to statement of financial position questions to the business in the case. For example, if asked for 'two non-current assets of a shop' avoid suggesting 'factory' or 'flow production line machines'. In this case, shop premises and delivery vehicles are much more appropriate answers.

The main elements of a statement of financial position

Study tips

To help you analyse data and financial information from more than one year, the earlier year is shown first.

Case study: Company statement of financial position

Below is a typical statement of financial position. It is for Ace Machines. The previous year's figures are also usually shown to allow for easy comparison.

Extract from statement of financial position for Ace Machines, 31/3/2025

	2024 ($000)	2025 ($000)
ASSETS		
Non-current assets		
Land and buildings	440	450
Machinery	600	700
	1040	1150
Current assets		
Inventories	50	80
Trade receivables	60	50
Cash	15	10
	125	140
TOTAL ASSETS	**1165**	**1290**
LIABILITIES		
Current liabilities		
Trade payables	40	65
Bank overdraft	60	65
	100	130
Non-current (long-term) liabilities		
Long-term bank loan	245	300
TOTAL LIABILITIES	345	430
TOTAL ASSETS – TOTAL LIABILITIES	**820**	**860**
TOTAL SHAREHOLDERS' EQUITY	**820**	**860**

Points to note:

» The value of non-current assets has increased, suggesting that the company has used finance to purchase more buildings and machinery.
» Inventories have increased significantly. Does this indicate that the business is finding it difficult to sell all it produces?
» Trade payables have increased as well. Is the company finding it difficult to pay its suppliers on time?
» The long-term bank loan has increased, perhaps to help finance the increase in non-current assets.
» Shareholders' equity has risen so the value of the company owned by the shareholders has increased over the year.

You can now see how much information can be obtained from analysing a statement of financial position. This is why, together with the statement of profit or loss, it is one of the key accounts produced by a business each year.

26 STATEMENT OF FINANCIAL POSITION

> ### Activity 26.1
> A Managing Director of a company is trying to write out the statement of financial position for the business. The following items have been listed. You have been asked to help the Managing Director by putting them all under their correct heading. Copy out the table and tick the correct box for each item.
>
> | | Current assets | Non-current assets | Current liabilities | Non-current liabilities | Shareholders' equity |
> |---|---|---|---|---|---|
> | Company vehicles | | | | | |
> | Cash | | | | | |
> | Ten-year bank loan | | | | | |
> | Share capital | | | | | |
> | Money owed by customers (trade receivables) | | | | | |
> | Unsold inventory | | | | | |
> | Factory building | | | | | |
> | Retained profit | | | | | |
> | Amounts owed to suppliers (trade payables) | | | | | |

The concept of capital employed

Capital employed is the total amount of capital invested in a business for the purpose of generating profits. The term was introduced in Chapter 2 as a method of measuring business size. Large businesses will, obviously, have more capital invested than smaller ones. Capital employed is the total of non-current liabilities and shareholders' equity.

Definitions to learn

Capital employed is the total amount of capital invested in a business for the purpose of generating profits.

> ### Case study: Capital employed
> Coca-Cola is a growing and profitable company. In 2020 its capital employed was equal to $66.1 billion. This rose to $73.6 billion by the end of 2023. This means that, over this period, more capital was invested in making the business profitable.

> ### Extend your skills of analysis
> A question which asks for one way in which a public limited company can increase its capital employed could be answered as follows:
>
> Capital employed is used in a business to operate and become profitable.
>
> *Extend your analysis by explaining how a public limited company can increase the capital available to it.*
>
> If the public limited company issued more shares, more capital would be available to invest in non-current assets.
>
> *Extend your analysis by explaining how this would increase capital employed.*
>
> By using the finance provided by share capital to buy non-current assets such as new technology equipment, the value of non-current assets would increase. This would have the effect of increasing capital employed available for the business to generate profit.

The main elements of a statement of financial position

Making simple calculations based on statements of financial position

To help analyse the financial strength of a business it is often useful to make some simple calculations based on its statement of financial position. Table 26.1 shows ABC's statements of financial position for 2024 and 2025.

Table 26.1 ABC's statements of financial position (incomplete)

	2024 ($000)	2025 ($000)
Non-current assets		
Buildings	30	34
Machinery	9	12
Total non-current assets	39	46
Current assets		
Inventory	4	6
Trade receivables	7	7
Cash	1	2
Total current assets	W	A
Total assets	X	B
Current liabilities		
Overdraft	3	5
Trade payables	6	9
Total current liabilities	9	14
Non-current liabilities		
Long-term bank loan	22	25
Total liabilities	Y	C
Total assets – total liabilities	Z	D
Shareholders' equity	20	22

The following calculations can be made for 2025:

A Total current assets = $15 000
B Total assets = Non-current assets + Current assets = $46 000 + $15 000
   = $61 000
C Total liabilities = Non-current liabilities + Current liabilities = $25 000 + $14 000 = $39 000
D Total assets − Total liabilities = $61 000 − $39 000 = $22 000

Total assets − Total liabilities must *always* equal the figure for shareholders' equity.

> ### Calculations to learn
>
> *Working capital = Current assets − Current liabilities*

Working capital = Current assets − Current liabilities = $15 000 − $14 000
   = $1000

> ### Activity 26.2
> Look at Table 26.1 above.
>
> a Calculate values for W, X, Y and Z in 2024.
> b Calculate working capital in 2024.
> c Comment on the major changes that have occurred to ABC's statement of financial position between the two years.

26 STATEMENT OF FINANCIAL POSITION

REVISION SUMMARY — Statement of financial position

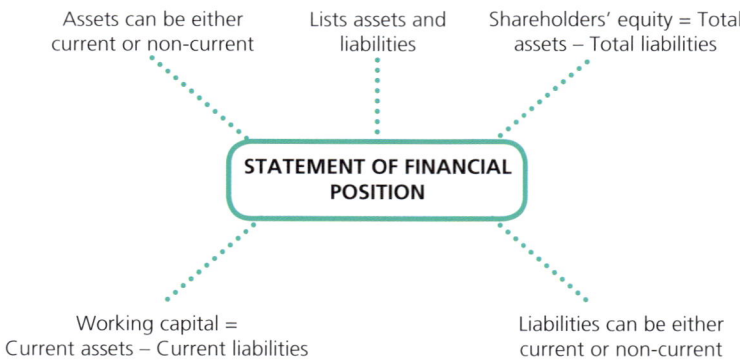

> ### Activity 26.3
> Refer to Ace Machines' statement of financial position on page 315.
>
> a Calculate the change in working capital between the two years shown.
> b Comment on your result.
> c Do you think that this business should reduce the value of its inventories? Explain your answer.
> d Do you think the shareholders of Ace Machines should be pleased with the statement of financial position data? Explain your answer.

> ### Activity 26.4
> KL and HK are 2 private limited companies that manufacture gifts bought by tourists – such as pottery and wooden carvings. The following table contains a summary of the 2 companies' statements of financial position for the year ending 31/10/25.
>
> | | KL ($000) | HK ($000) |
> |---|---|---|
> | Non-current assets | 50 | 120 |
> | **Current assets** | | |
> | Inventories | 12 | 50 |
> | Trade receivables | 8 | 16 |
> | Cash | 1 | 4 |
> | **Total assets** | X | 190 |
> | **Current liabilities** | 18 | 70 |
> | Non-current liabilities | 20 | 30 |
> | **Total liabilities** | 38 | Z |
> | **Total assets – Total liabilities** | Y | 90 |
> | **Shareholders' equity** | 33 | 90 |
>
> a Calculate the values for X, Y and Z.
> b Identify **two** types of non-current assets that these businesses are likely to own.
> c Identify **three** items that are likely to be held as inventories by these businesses.
> d Calculate the working capital of both companies.
> e Which company seems to be in a stronger financial position? Use the data above to support your answer.

Making decisions based on simple statements of financial position

Table 26.2 outlines some of the business decisions that can be made based on statements of financial position.

Table 26.2 Decisions based on statements of financial position

Business decision	How the statement of financial position helps
Increase long-term loans	• What is the current level of long-term liabilities? • If loans were increased further, would the bank be putting in more capital than shareholders? • Are there any non-current assets that have been held for a long time and which are no longer required? Could these be sold off?
Issue more shares to raise capital	• Is shareholders' equity increasing over time? • If not, will shareholders be willing to put more capital into a business that is not increasing in value?
Reduce working capital by selling inventories or reducing trade receivables	• Is the inventory level increasing over time? • Is it higher than that of similar businesses of the same size? (This will require competitors' financial accounts too.) • Is the business offering much longer credit periods than competitors?

> **Study tips**
>
> A statement of financial position can be compared with statements of financial position from previous years or other businesses. See Chapter 27 for more detail of how business accounts can be analysed.

It is important to note that these decisions will nearly always need:

» past years' statements of financial position
» competitors' statements of financial position
» both of these additional sources of data.

This is not unusual. The analysis of accounting data from just one year of business for making business decisions is never sufficient. The next chapter explains in more detail how financial accounts can be analysed and used by managers for decision making.

International business in focus

Hayleys statement of financial position

Hayleys is one of Sri Lanka's largest public limited companies. It is a very diversified business with divisions operating in agriculture, transport, consumer products and energy. A summary of Hayleys' statement of financial position is shown in the table. All figures are in billions of Sri Lankan Rupees (LKR).

	2023 (Rs bn)	2024 (Rs bn)
Non-current assets	175.16	184.72
Current assets	237.58	261.62
Total assets	412.74	446.34
Non-current liabilities	94.93	90.85
Current liabilities	195.11	229.96
Total liabilities	290.04	320.81

Source: https://www.hayleys.com/wp-content/uploads/2024/06/Hayleys-Annual-Report-2024-Quick-Read-.pdf

Discussion points

- Suggest two non-current assets that the transport division of Hayleys is likely to own.
- Suggest why the company reduced non-current liabilities (long-term loans) in the period shown in the table.
- Do you think that the shareholders of Hayleys would have been pleased with the financial position in 2024 compared with 2023? Explain your answer.

Chapter review questions: Short answer and data response

1 An extract from Acme Builders' latest statement of financial position is shown below. During the period shown, the government increased interest rates (the cost of borrowing money). A competitor's business is for sale. The owners have asked the directors of Acme Builders if they wish to buy the business for $4 million.

	31/3/2024 ($m)	31/3/2025 ($m)
Non-current assets	58	67
Current assets	15	23
Current liabilities	12	15
Non-current liabilities	6	12

   a Define 'non-current assets'. [2]
   b Outline **two** ways in which the increase in non-current liabilities might have been used by the company. [4]
   c Explain **two** possible reasons why the company's working capital has increased. [6]
   d Do you think Acme Builders is in a good position to take over the other business for $4 million? Justify your answer using the statement of financial position. [8]

2 Penang Garages is a public limited company. An extract from Penang Garages' latest statement of financial position is shown below. The garage company sells cars and repairs old vehicles. It has many competitors.

	31/12/24 ($m)	31/12/25 ($m)
Non-current assets	90	96
Current assets	25	23
Current liabilities	25	28
Non-current liabilities	40	35

   a Identify **two** current assets. [2]
   b Outline **two** possible reasons why the value of current assets has fallen during the period shown. [4]
   c Explain **two** reasons why current liabilities may have increased. [6]
   d Do you think that the shareholders of Penang Garages would be pleased with the information shown above? Justify your answer. [8]

Revision checklist

In this chapter you have learned:

- ✔ the main elements of a statement of financial position
- ✔ what non-current assets, current assets, non-current liabilities and current liabilities are
- ✔ the concept of capital employed
- ✔ how to make simple calculations based on statements of financial position
- ✔ how to make decisions based on simple statements of financial position.

NOW – test your understanding with the revision questions in the Student etextbook and the Workbook.

27 Analysis of accounts

This chapter will explain:

Profitability:

★ the concept of profitability
★ how to calculate and interpret the three profitability ratios.

Liquidity:

★ the concept of liquidity
★ how to calculate and interpret the two liquidity ratios.

Users of accounts:

★ internal users of accounts and ratio analysis
★ external users of accounts and ratio analysis
★ how users of accounts might use financial information to help make decisions
★ limitations of using accounts and ratio analysis.

Profitability

The concept of profitability

The meaning and importance of profit was explained in Chapter 25. Table 27.1 gives the profit figures of two food retailing businesses.

Table 27.1 Profit figures for two food retailing businesses

	Freshfood	Foodstore
Profit (2025)	$300 000	$30 000

Definitions to learn

Profitability measures the profit of a business in comparison to its revenue or capital employed.

How useful are these figures? The only definite conclusion that can be drawn is that Freshfood made 10 times the profit of Foodstore in 2025. What we cannot claim is that Freshfood 'has a much higher level of profitability than Foodstore'. This is because profitability is a relative measure of business performance. This means that profit results must be compared with another measure before **profitability** can be assessed. For example:

» If Freshfood actually sold 20 times the value of food that Foodstore did in 2025, which business had higher profitability?
» If Freshfood has capital employed of $12m but Foodstore has capital employed of just $1m, which business had higher profitability?
» The answer in both cases is Foodstore. This is because its profit figure is relatively higher than Freshfood, when revenue and capital employed are also being measured.

This example shows how important it is to use more than one figure from accounts when trying to assess how a business is performing. Comparing two figures from accounts in this way is called ratio analysis. This is a very important way of analysing published accounts.

27 ANALYSIS OF ACCOUNTS

There are many ratios which can be calculated from a set of business accounts. This chapter concentrates on five of the most commonly used ratios. These are used to measure and compare the profitability and liquidity of a business.

▲ It is impossible to tell which of these businesses is operating at a higher level of profitability without analysing their accounts using ratios

Calculating profitability ratios

The three main profitability ratios are outlined below.

Gross profit margin

This is calculated by the formula given below.

> **Calculations to learn**
>
> $$\text{Gross profit margin (\%)} = \frac{\text{Gross profit}}{\text{Revenue}} \times 100$$

> **Case study and worked example:** Gross profit margin
>
> ABC Computing made a gross profit in 2025 of $400 million. Revenue was $1300 million.
>
> $$\text{Gross profit margin (\%)} = \frac{\text{Gross profit}}{\text{Revenue}} \times 100$$
>
> $$= \frac{\$400\text{ m}}{\$1300\text{ m}} \times 100 = 30.8\%$$
>
> This means that for every $1 worth of goods sold, the company made, on average, 30.8 cents gross profit. Do not forget that this is before other expenses have been deducted and is not the final profit of the business. This result needs to be compared with other years and other companies before profitability can be judged.
>
> If this percentage increases next year it would suggest that 1 of the following has happened:
>
> - Prices have been increased by more than the cost of sales.
> - Cost of sales has been reduced. Possibly a new supplier is being used or managers have negotiated lower cost prices.

Profit margin

This is calculated by the formula given below.

> **Calculations to learn**
>
> $$\text{Profit margin (\%)} = \frac{\text{Profit}}{\text{Revenue}} \times 100$$

Case study and worked example: Profit margin

ABC Computing made a profit of $280 million in 2025.

$$\text{Profit margin (\%)} = \frac{\text{Profit}}{\text{Revenue}} \times 100$$

$$= \frac{\$280 \text{ m}}{\$1300 \text{ m}} \times 100 = 21.5\%$$

The company made 21.5 cents profit on each $1 worth of sales. This is lower than the gross profit margin because all other expenses have been deducted from gross profit to give the profit figure. The higher this result, the more successful the managers are in making profit from sales. What could this result be compared with? To make useful statements about profitability it should be compared with results from other years and other companies.

Return on capital employed (ROCE)

This is calculated by the formulae given below.

> **Calculations to learn**
>
> $$\text{ROCE} = \frac{\text{Profit}}{\text{Capital employed}} \times 100$$

Case study and worked example: Return on capital employed

ABC Computing made a profit of $280 million in 2025 and its capital employed was $2065 million. Its return on capital employed (ROCE) in 2025 was:

$$\text{ROCE} = \frac{\text{Profit}}{\text{Capital employed}} \times 100$$

$$= \frac{\$280 \text{ m}}{\$2065 \text{ m}} \times 100 = 13.6\%$$

This means that in 2025, the company made a return on the capital employed in the business of 13.6%. Each $1 of capital earned a profit of 13.6 cents. The higher this result, the more successful the managers are in earning profit from capital. If this percentage increases next year, it means that profitability is rising and the managers are operating the business more efficiently. Profit from each dollar invested in the business is higher.

This result should always be compared with other years and other companies to see if the managers are operating the business more profitably or not.

27 ANALYSIS OF ACCOUNTS

Interpreting profitability ratios

One profitability ratio result is not very useful. When a ratio result is compared with others, then some effective analysis can be done and conclusions made. Table 27.2 explains how profitability ratio results can be interpreted and analysed. The results are taken from ABC Computing again.

Table 27.2 Interpreting profitability ratio results

Ratio results	Interpretation	Analysis
Gross profit margin: 2024: 29% 2025: 30.8%	This means that the gross profit on each $1 of revenue has increased	The business is more successful at converting revenue into gross profit in 2025 than 2024. Either the price of goods has increased (by more than costs) or the cost of sales has fallen with prices unchanged. Using this measure, profitability has risen
Profit margin: 2024: 23% 2025: 21.5%	This means that the profit on each $1 of revenue has fallen – even though gross profit margin has increased	The business is less successful at converting revenue into profit in 2025 than in 2024. The expenses/fixed costs of the business must have increased significantly during the year. This has reduced the company's profit compared to revenue. Using this measure, profitability has fallen
Return on capital employed: 2024: 15% 2025: 13.6%	The profit made for each $1 invested in the business has fallen	This must be because either profit has fallen or capital employed has increased more than profit. If capital employed has increased, this could mean that the managers of the business have invested more, hoping to make higher profit in future

Activity 27.1

Summary of statement of financial position, 2025	$m
Revenue	1200
Gross profit	450
Profit	220
Capital employed	965

a Using the 2025 financial information for XYZ Computing, shown in the table above, calculate:
  i gross profit margin
  ii profit margin
  iii return on capital employed.
b Refer to your results and the 2025 ratio results for ABC Computing shown in Table 27.2. Which company do you think had the better performance in 2025? Give reasons for your answer.

Liquidity

The concept of liquidity

Definitions to learn

Liquidity is the ability of a business to pay back its short-term debts.

Liquidity is the ability of a business to pay back its short-term debts. A liquid asset is either cash or an asset that can be quickly converted into cash, such as trade receivables or inventory. If a business cannot pay its suppliers for materials that are important to production, or if the business cannot repay an overdraft when required to, it is said to be 'illiquid'. The businesses and banks it owes money to may force it to stop trading and sell its assets so that the debts are repaid.

Calculating liquidity ratios

The two liquidity ratios are outlined below.

Current ratio

This is calculated by the formulae given below.

> **Calculations to learn**
>
> $$\text{Current ratio} = \frac{\text{Current assets}}{\text{Current liabilities}}$$
>
> Current ratio = Current assets : Current liabilities

Case study: Current ratio

ABC Computing had current assets valued at $125 million and current liabilities of $100 million at the end of 2025.

$$\text{Current ratio} = \frac{\text{Current assets}}{\text{Current liabilities}}$$

$$= \frac{\$125\text{ m}}{\$100\text{ m}} = 1.25 \text{ or } 1.25:1$$

This result means that the business could only just pay off all of its short-term debts from current assets. A current ratio of 1.25 (or 1.25:1) is an acceptable result but a really 'safe' current ratio would be between 1.5 and 2 (1.5:1 and 2:1). If the current ratio is less than 1 (1:1), it would mean that the business could not pay off its short-term debts from current assets. This leads to risks of suppliers refusing to deliver any more supplies or the bank refusing to lend more.

More effective analysis of liquidity is possible if results for previous years and other similar businesses are available. If the current ratio is very high, say over 2 (or 2:1), it could mean that too much working capital is tied up in unprofitable current assets.

The current ratio is useful but it assumes that all current assets could be turned into cash quickly. This is not always the case. For example, it might be very difficult to sell all inventories in a short period of time. For this reason, a second liquidity ratio is used which does not include the value of inventory.

Acid test ratio

This is calculated by the formulae given below.

> **Calculations to learn**
>
> $$\text{Acid test ratio} = \frac{\text{Current assets} - \text{Inventories}}{\text{Current liabilities}}$$
>
> Acid test ratio = Current assets − Inventories : Current liabilities

Case study: Acid test ratio

ABC Computing had $50 million of inventory at the end of 2025. This should be subtracted from current assets. This figure is used to calculate the acid test ratio.

$$\text{Acid test ratio} = \frac{\text{Current assets} - \text{Inventories}}{\text{Current liabilities}}$$

$$= \frac{\$125\text{ m} - \$50\text{ m}}{\$100\text{ m}} = 0.75 \text{ or } 0.75:1$$

A result of 1 (or 1:1) would mean that the company could pay off its short-term debts from its most liquid assets. This is usually considered to be an acceptable acid test result. This result of 0.75 (or 0.75:1) means that ABC Computing cannot do this. This might be worrying for the management and steps may have to be taken to improve the liquidity of the business. One way would be to reduce the level of inventory by selling some for cash and holding less inventories.

27 ANALYSIS OF ACCOUNTS

> **Study tips**
>
> You should be able to explain why just one ratio result is of limited use in analysing the profitability or liquidity of a business.

> **Key info**
>
> Mari Petroleum (MPCL) is one of the largest petroleum exploration and production companies in Pakistan. MPCL made a significant new oil discovery at an exploration well in 2024. Liquidity is very important to an oil and gas exploration company as there will be large cash outflows during exploration and no cash inflows until much later when the oil or gas becomes available for sale.

Interpreting liquidity ratios

One liquidity ratio result is not very useful. When a ratio result is compared with others, then some effective analysis can be done. Table 27.3 explains how liquidity results can be interpreted and analysed. The results are taken from ABC Computing again.

Table 27.3 Interpreting liquidity ratio results

Ratio results	Interpretation	Analysis
Current ratio: 2024: 1.5 (1.5:1) 2025: 1.25 (1.25:1)	The current ratio has fallen between 2024 and 2025. Using this ratio, the business is less liquid	This could be because the business has bought and used many more supplies, but not yet paid for them – it has higher trade payables. It could also be because the business has used cash to pay for non-current assets The business has low liquidity and needs to increase current assets or reduce current liabilities
Acid test ratio: 2024: 0.8 (0.8:1) 2025: 0.75 (0.75:1)	The acid test ratio has also fallen but by much less than the current ratio This suggests inventory has fallen but that cash and trade receivables have not fallen so much	The acid test ratio might be too low. The business might be at risk of not being able to pay its short-term debts from its cash and trade receivables The difference between the two current ratio and acid test ratio results is because of a relatively high level of inventories

> **Activity 27.2**
>
> | Extract from statement of financial position of XYZ Computing 2025 | $m |
> |---|---|
> | Current assets | 135 |
> | Inventories | 70 |
> | Current liabilities | 95 |
>
> a Using the information above for XYZ Computing, calculate the following ratios for 2025:
>   i current ratio
>   ii acid test ratio.
> b Do you think the management of XYZ Computing should be satisfied with the liquidity of the company? Justify your answer using your results and comparing them with those for ABC Computing for 2025.

Users of accounts

Users of accounts and ratio analysis

Internal users

Who uses the accounts of a business? Which groups would analyse the accounts of a business, such as by calculating ratios and why? Table 27.4 explains how the internal users of accounts would find financial information useful.

Users of accounts

Table 27.4 Internal users of accounts and ratio analysis

Internal users	What questions are they asking?	What they use the accounts for
Owners, such as sole trader, partners or shareholders	• Should I invest in this business? • Should I buy shares in this business? • Should I sell my shares in this business? • Should the business stop trading?	• Owners, shareholders and potential investors want to know the profit or loss the business is making. The profitability ratio results will be compared with recent years' results. The higher the profitability ratio results are, the more likely shareholders will be to invest by buying more shares in the company • The statement of financial position will show whether the business is worth more at the end of the year than it was at the beginning. Owners will also assess the liquidity of the business as they will not want to invest in a company with serious cash or liquidity problems

Managers – they will have access to all financial information	• Is the business performing well?
	• How can we improve the business?
	• How well am I doing my job – have I made good decisions?
		• Managers will use the accounts to check on and control the performance of each product or division. Managers will be able to identify which parts of the business are performing well or poorly
		• Financial statements will help in decision making, for example, whether to expand the business, change price levels or close down a product or division that is not doing well
		• Ratios are a useful way for managers to compare their company's profitability and liquidity. It is important to compare accounting ratios as one ratio result on its own means very little. Ratio results may be compared with:
		  • other years
		  • other businesses

Employees	• Should I ask for a wage increase? • Is my job secure or should I be looking for another job?	• Employees will want to assess whether the future of the company is secure or not. This will affect job security. Also, if managers are saying that they cannot afford to give employees a pay rise it would be useful for employees (or their trade unions) to analyse whether profitability of the business is increasing or not

External users

Table 27.5 explains how external users will benefit from using accounts.

Table 27.5 External users of accounts and ratio results

External users	What questions are they asking?	What they use the accounts for
Suppliers	• Should trade credit be given to this business? • Will the business pay for supplies on time?	• The statement of financial position will indicate to suppliers the total value of 'trade payables' that the business has to pay back • Liquidity ratios, especially when compared with the previous year, will indicate the ability of the business to pay back all of its suppliers on time • If these results suggest the business has a liquidity problem, suppliers may refuse to supply goods on credit
Government	• Is the business making a profit and therefore is tax on profit due to be paid? • How successful is the business?	• The government and the tax office will check on the profit tax paid by the business. If the business has declining profitability or is making a loss, the government will be worried about the impact of this on the country's economy. This is especially the case if employees could be made redundant
Lenders/banks	• Will the business be able to pay back a loan on time? • Can the business afford the repayment of a loan/overdraft?	• They will use the financial information to find out the total value of current and non-current liabilities. If the business seems to be at risk of not being able to pay its debts – both to suppliers and long-term loans – it is unlikely that a bank will be willing to lend more

27 ANALYSIS OF ACCOUNTS

> **Key info**
>
> One hundred and forty years of Glasgow Rangers Football club was brought to an end due to a lack of liquidity. It could not pay its debts of more than £55 million, most of which was unpaid taxes owed to the UK Government. The old football club had to be wound up. The assets were sold, a few of the debts were paid and a new Rangers Football club started up under different ownership.

REVISION SUMMARY — Users of accounts and ratio analysis

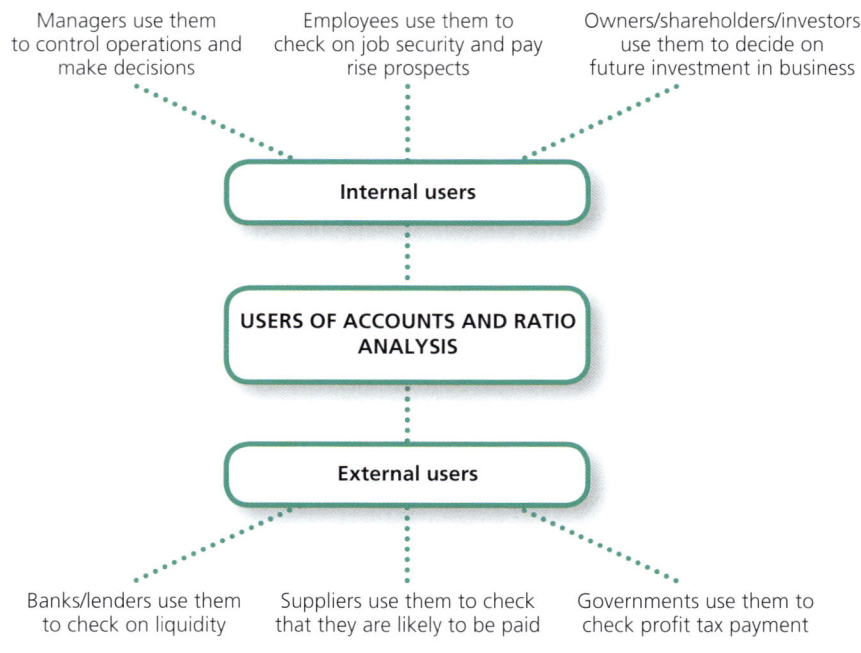

How users of accounts might use financial information to help make decisions

Study tips

Be prepared to explain why different stakeholder groups will find information from a business's published accounts useful – and why ratios will help in the analysis of these accounts.

The users of accounts and ratio results might want to make important decisions based on them. Here are some examples:

- **Banks.** Whether to lend more to the business – banks would be less likely to lend to the business if profitability is falling and liquidity is low. These measures would indicate that the business could find it difficult to pay interest on loans or to pay loans back.
- **Investors.** Whether to buy shares in the company – investors will be interested in rising profitability ratios of the business they are planning to invest in. These would suggest that future dividends will rise and the share price too. They could compare profitability ratios between different companies. They could decide to invest in the business that is performing most profitably.
- **Managers.** How to improve low profitability and liquidity – managers will need to focus on whether gross profit or profit margin is falling – or both – when deciding on how to improve profitability. Falling gross profit margin suggests that prices should rise or efforts be made to reduce cost of sales. Falling profit margin, if gross profit margin is not falling, means that expenses are rising faster than revenue. Fixed costs need to be reduced to restore profitability.

Users of accounts

Activity 27.3

Read the case study below on the right.

a Do you think the management of Gloria Hotels should be satisfied with the profitability of the company? Justify your answer.

b Explain why comparing these ratio results with those of other hotel companies would be useful for Gloria Hotels' management.

c Do you think that Gloria Hotels' bank would be willing to lend more to the company? Use liquidity ratio results to justify your answer.

d Explain **two** ways in which the management of Gloria Hotels could increase the profitability of the company. Which way would you recommend and why?

e Would you advise an investor to buy shares in Gloria Hotels, based on the accounting information provided? Justify your answer.

The two liquidity ratios, over time, will show whether the problem of low liquidity is short-term or long-term. If the current ratio is high but the acid test ratio is low, this suggests that managers should take action to reduce inventories.

Extend your skills of analysis

A question which asks for an advantage to a potential shareholder of analysing a company's accounts could be answered as follows:

Ratio analysis is the most common way to analyse business accounts.

Extend your analysis by explaining why ratio analysis is useful.

By comparing profitability and liquidity of a business over time and with other similar businesses, external accounts users can make more effective decisions.

Extend your analysis by explaining how this will benefit potential investors.

Profitability ratios will indicate the chances of profit in the future and shareholders will want rising dividends paid from profit over time. Increasing profitability is also likely to lead to higher share price. The liquidity ratios indicate how able the business is to meet its short-term debts. Investors are unlikely to buy shares in a company with very low liquidity ratio results.

Case study: Using accounts and ratios to help make decisions

Gloria Hotels is a public limited company that owns 3 hotels in the capital city. The tourist industry in the country is expanding but there are many competing hotel companies in the capital city. The company accountant has calculated the following ratio results from the latest published accounts:

Gloria Hotels	2024	2025
Return on capital employed	17%	13%
Gross profit margin	30%	35%
Profit margin	16%	12%
Current ratio	1.4 or 1.4:1	1.2 or 1.2:1
Acid test ratio	1.0 or 1:1	0.6 or 0.6:1

REVISION SUMMARY

Ratio analysis

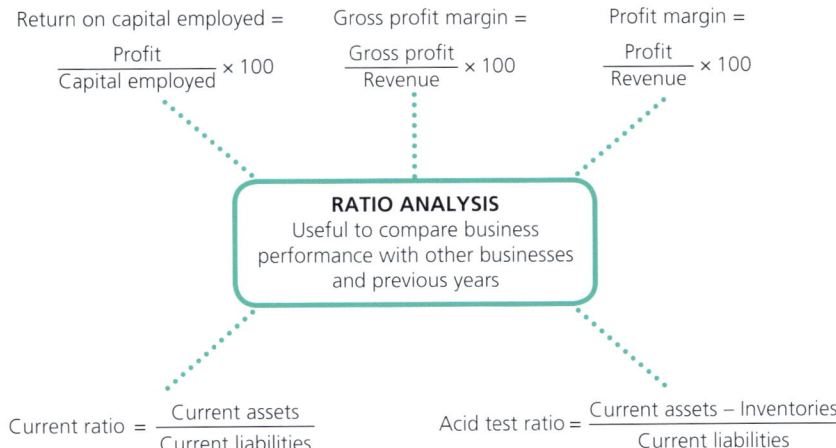

Return on capital employed = $\dfrac{\text{Profit}}{\text{Capital employed}} \times 100$

Gross profit margin = $\dfrac{\text{Gross profit}}{\text{Revenue}} \times 100$

Profit margin = $\dfrac{\text{Profit}}{\text{Revenue}} \times 100$

RATIO ANALYSIS – Useful to compare business performance with other businesses and previous years

Current ratio = $\dfrac{\text{Current assets}}{\text{Current liabilities}}$

Acid test ratio = $\dfrac{\text{Current assets} - \text{Inventories}}{\text{Current liabilities}}$

Limitations of using accounts and ratio analysis

All external and internal users of accounts and ratio analysis need to remember that there are limitations to this information. These limitations will reduce the usefulness of accounts and ratio analysis for both analysing business performance and for decision making.

These limitations are:

- Managers will have access to all accounts data but external users will only be able to use the published accounts, which contain only data required by law. Some important information will not be provided. For example, a business does not have to provide accounts information for each of its factories, shops or operations in other countries (if it has them). This information could be very useful to help analyse why the overall business is performing as it is.
- Ratios are based on past accounting data. Changes in business decisions or government policy may have a big impact on future ratio results. The existing information may not give a good indication of how the business will perform in the future.
- Accounting data over time will be affected by inflation, for example, rising prices of the main supplies of a business. Comparisons between years may therefore be misleading.
- Different businesses may use slightly different accounting methods, for example, in valuing their fixed assets. These different methods could lead to different ratio results, therefore making comparisons difficult.

International business in focus

Shell

Shell is one of the world's largest oil companies. But is it also one of the most profitable? Ratio analysis of the company's accounts leads to some interesting results which can be compared with other businesses in the same market sector.

In 2023 Shell's return on capital employed was 8.4%. This was lower than in 2022 when it was substantially higher than the average expected for the sector at 16.7%. The profit margin was 6% in 2023 which was a lower result than in 2022 when it was 11%.

Is Shell's profitability at the cost of low liquidity? It does not appear to be the case. In 2023 the company recorded an acid test ratio of around 1.1, the same as the previous year. It had a current ratio of 1.40 in 2023, about the same as the previous year of 1.37.

Will Shell be able to improve profitability and liquidity at times of world economic uncertainty and volatile oil prices?

Discussion points

- Which groups of Shell's stakeholders would be interested in these ratio results and why?
- Explain why it is important to compare ratio results with those of other years and other similar companies.

Chapter review questions: Short answer and data response

1. The table below is an extract from the accounts of Triton, a food canning and processing business. The company sells its products to the 3 main supermarket groups in the country.

	2024 ($m)	2025 ($m)
Gross profit	285	350
Profit	140	120
Revenue	2500	3000
Capital employed	900	1000

   a Define 'capital employed'. [2]
   b Outline **two** possible reasons why gross profit has increased from 2024 to 2025. [4]
   c Explain why **two** external users of the accounts would find Triton's financial information useful. [6]
   d Do you think the management of Triton should be satisfied with the profitability of the company? Justify your answer using suitable calculations. [8]

2. The table below is an extract from the statement of financial position of Hi Fashion. This is a private limited company that sells quality fashion clothes. It purchases from leading clothing manufacturers. It recently started offering its customers 2 months' credit. However, revenue has been falling due to increased competition. The bank manager is worried about the liquidity of Hi Fashion.

	2024 ($000)	2025 ($000)
Current assets	80	88
Inventories	35	48
Current liabilities	40	60

   a Define 'liquidity'. [2]
   b Outline **two** possible reasons why the current liabilities of the business are increasing. [4]
   c Explain **two** limitations to external stakeholders of using Hi Fashion's financial information. [6]
   d Do you think the bank is right to be worried about Hi Fashion's liquidity? Justify your answer using suitable ratios. [8]

Revision checklist

In this chapter you have learned:

- ✔ the concept of profitability
- ✔ how to calculate and interpret profitability ratios
- ✔ the concept of liquidity
- ✔ how to calculate and interpret liquidity ratios
- ✔ the internal and external users of accounts and ratio analysis
- ✔ how users of accounts might use financial information to help make decisions
- ✔ the limitations of using accounts and ratio analysis.

NOW – test your understanding with the revision questions in the Student etextbook and the Workbook.

Financial information and decisions: end-of-section case study

Case study: Fruity Smoothies

Fruity Smoothies is a public limited company which produces a range of fruit smoothies drinks. The business operates in many different countries around the world. Fruity Smoothies is a successful company but the Directors want to increase its market share of the fruit smoothies global market.

The following 2 ways of increasing market share have been identified:

- Option 1: Increase sales of its most popular brand of smoothies by selling it in 5 new countries. The investment required to get the smoothies launched into new markets is estimated to be $80 million. This includes market research, marketing campaigns and building a factory to produce the fruit smoothies to sell in the other countries.
- Option 2: Take over a competitor that sells a different range of brands of smoothies. The cost of the takeover to buy all the shares in the company is estimated to be $160 million.

Appendix 1

Extract of financial information for Fruity Smoothies 2025

Existing business	$m
Capital employed	800
Revenue	1600
Gross profit	1200
Profit	200
Option 1	**$m per year**
Predicted revenue from 5 more countries	400
Additional fixed costs	160
Total variable costs for additional sales	220
Option 2	**$m per year**
Predicted revenue from competitor's sales	400
Fixed costs of competitor	120
Total variable costs of competitor	220

Appendix 2

Information on Country X and Country Y

	Country X	Country Y
Average income per head	$6000	$40 000
Population	20 million	20 million
Competitors' sales	$20 million per year	$200 000 per year
Climate	Seasons (hot in summer and cold in winter)	Hot all year round
Average wage rate	$2 per hour	$20 per hour
Unemployment rate	24%	4%
Rents	Low	High

Financial information and decisions: end-of-section case study

Practice questions: Case study

1. **a** Explain, using examples, the difference between fixed costs and cost of sales for Fruity Smoothies. [8]
   b Using the information in Appendix 1, consider the **two** options for increasing the market share of Fruity Smoothies. Which option should the Directors choose? Justify your answer using suitable calculations. [12]

2. **a** Both Option 1 and Option 2 require capital for the expansion. Explain **four** suitable sources of finance the Directors of Fruity Smoothies could use. [8]
   b Consider how the competitor's statement of financial position and statement of profit or loss would help the Directors of Fruity Smoothies decide whether to take over the competitor. Should Fruity Smoothies take over its competitor? Justify your answer. [12]

Optional question

The questions below ask you to think about topics covered in earlier sections of this textbook. You can choose not to answer them if you prefer to focus on just the topics covered in this section at this time.

3. **a** Explain **two** objectives the Directors might have for Fruity Smoothies. [8]
   b Consider **three** disadvantages for Fruity Smoothies of entering a new market in another country. Which disadvantage will have the greatest effect on Fruity Smoothies? Justify your answer. [12]

4. **a** Explain **two** ways that Fruity Smoothies could create a brand image for a new fruit drink aimed at teenagers. [8]
   b Using Appendix 2, consider the advantages and disadvantages of each of the **two** countries where Fruity Smoothies could build a new factory. Which country should Fruity Smoothies choose to build the new factory in? Justify your answer. [12]

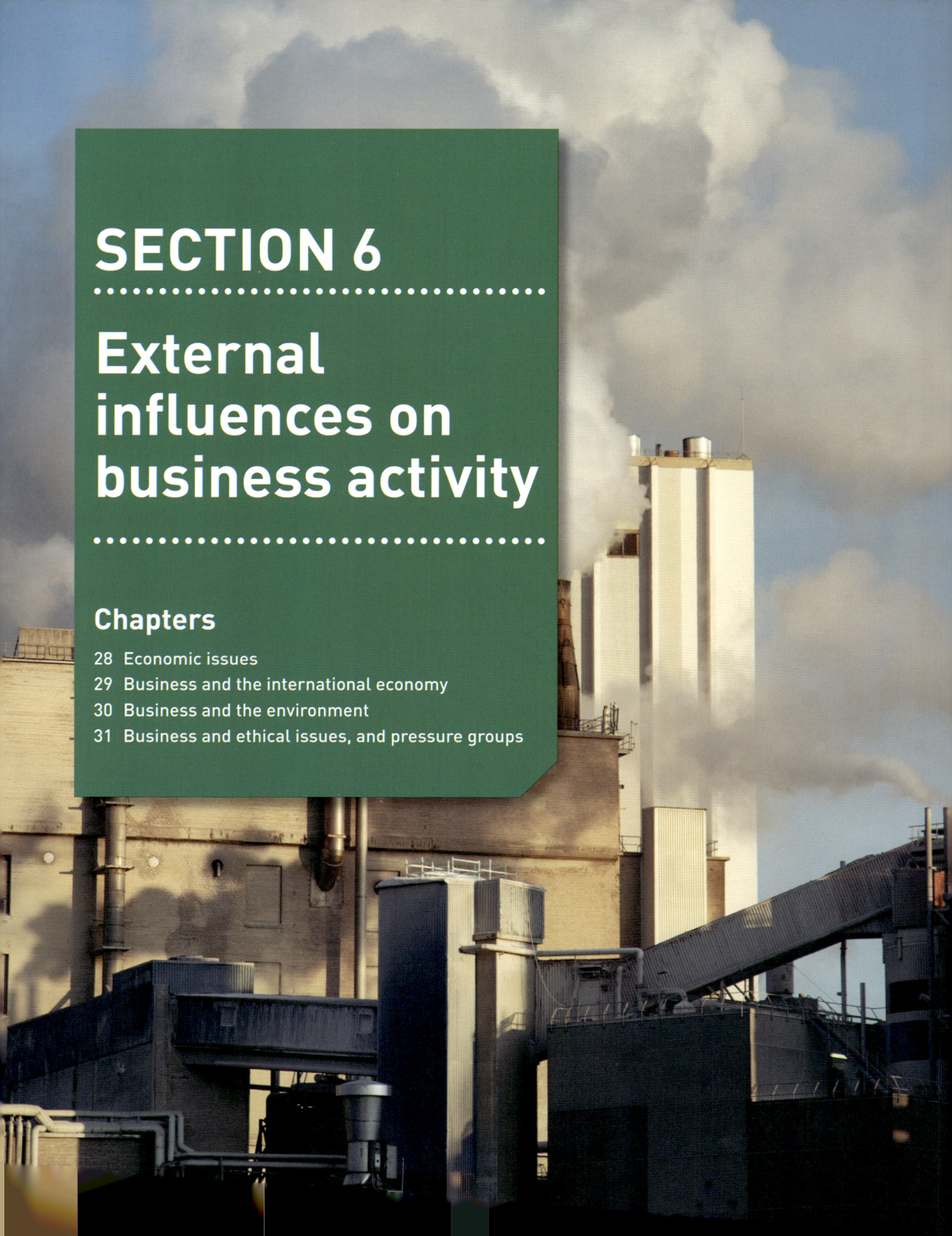

SECTION 6

External influences on business activity

Chapters

28 Economic issues
29 Business and the international economy
30 Business and the environment
31 Business and ethical issues, and pressure groups

28 Economic issues

This chapter will explain:

The business cycle:

★ the main stages of the business cycle
★ how each stage of the business cycle might affect a business
★ the effects of changes in the levels of employment, inflation and economic growth on a business.

The effects of government policy:

★ the effects of changes in taxes on business profit
★ the effects of changes in taxes on people's income
★ the effects of changes in government spending
★ the effects of changes in interest rates
★ how businesses may respond to changes in taxes and interest rates.

> **Definitions to learn**
>
> The **business cycle** is the fluctuations over time between periods of economic growth and economic contraction.
> **Gross domestic product (GDP)** is the total value of output of goods and services in a country in one year.

The business cycle

The state of a country's economy will affect businesses either directly or through the impact on their customers. One of the most important economic changes which occurs over time is the **business cycle**. Economic growth occurs when **gross domestic product (GDP)** becomes bigger, after allowing for inflation. Growth in an economy does not usually occur steadily. There will be periods of rapid growth and some periods of contraction. This series of fluctuations in the economy is illustrated in the figure below.

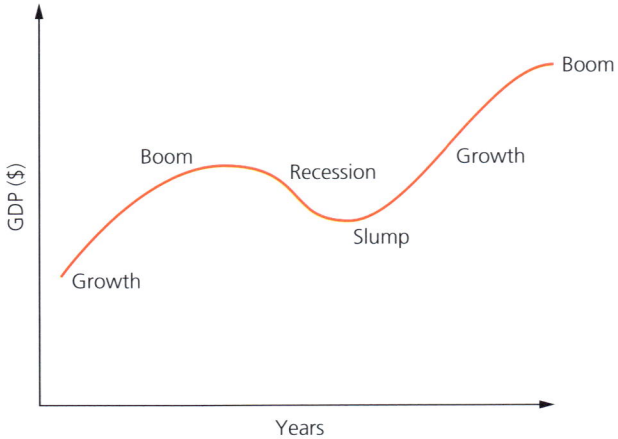

▲ A business cycle diagram

Main stages of the business cycle and the effects on a business

> **Definitions to learn**
>
> **Economic growth** occurs when real GDP increases, which is the value of GDP after taking inflation into account.
> **Unemployment** occurs when people who are willing and able to work cannot find employment.
> A **boom** is where the economy is growing very fast and costs and prices start to rise quickly.
> A **recession** is when there is a period of falling GDP.
> **Inflation** occurs when the average price level of goods and services rises over a period of time.
> A **slump** is a very serious recession with rapid falls in output and increases in unemployment.

» **Growth**. This is when real GDP is rising, **unemployment** is generally falling and the country is enjoying higher living standards.
  Effect on business: Most businesses will experience higher sales and profit. Many managers will be optimistic about the future and will plan to expand their businesses.
» **Boom**. This is caused by too much spending. Unemployment will fall to very low levels and prices start to rise quickly. There are shortages of skilled workers.
  Effect on business: Although demand for most products will still be increasing, many businesses will be affected by much higher costs. There will also be shortages of workers and vacancies will be difficult to fill. Demands for higher wages will add further to business costs.
» **Recession**. This is often caused by too little spending. This is a period when real GDP actually falls. Unemployment starts to increase.
  Effect on business: Demand for most goods and services will fall and business profits will decline. Some employees will be made redundant, increasing unemployment. Price rises will slow as the rate of **inflation** falls, so business costs will not be rising rapidly. Some businesses may fail.
» **Slump**. This is when GDP falls greatly and unemployment reaches very high levels. Average prices may fall.
  Effect on business: Rapid rises in unemployment will reduce demand for most products. Many businesses will have lower profits or even losses. Business failures will reach high levels.

Clearly, governments will try to avoid the economy moving towards a recession or a slump, but they will also want to reduce the chances of a boom. A boom with rapid inflation and higher business costs can often lead to the conditions that result in a recession.

Effects of changes in the levels of employment, inflation and economic growth on a business

Changes in the level of employment

This will impact on businesses in a number of ways:

» When employment levels rise and unemployment falls, more people will have incomes to spend. This will increase demand for most products, especially luxury goods and services, benefiting businesses with higher sales and profit. However, if unemployment falls rapidly and reaches a low level, then this will make it more difficult to fill job vacancies. Employees may ask for higher wages to stop them leaving for a higher paid job. Business costs will increase and this will make some businesses uncompetitive.
» When employment levels fall and unemployment rises, the opposite effects will occur. Some consumers who lose jobs will have less income to spend. Demand for many goods and services, especially luxuries, will fall. Business sales and profits will decline. However, higher levels of unemployment make it easier to retain employees and fill job vacancies. There will be less pressure to increase wages. Business costs may fall.

> **Key info**
>
> Unemployment in South Africa was 27.99% in 2023, while in India it was 4.17% and in New Zealand it was 3.74%.

Changes in the rate of inflation

This will impact on businesses in a number of ways:

> **Definitions to learn**
>
> **Real income** is the spending power of income. It falls when prices rise faster than money income and rises when incomes increase faster than inflation.

> **Key info**
>
> Inflation in Venezuela was said to be around 337% in 2023. However, it reached a peak of 63 000% in 2018.

- A higher rate of inflation means that average prices are rising faster than previously. A period of rapidly rising prices can make it easier for a business to increases its own prices. Consumers will almost be expecting prices to increase. If prices rise faster than wages, consumers' **real incomes** will fall, leaving them with less to spend on non-essential products.
- Higher inflation means that businesses will experience higher costs too. Higher prices for materials, components and energy will reduce business profit unless prices to consumers are increased too. Employees will demand higher wage increases to make up for higher prices and this will raise business costs.
- Not all businesses will be able to increase their prices easily. A business producing non-essential goods or services with many competitors may experience a big reduction in demand if they increase prices during periods of inflation. However, those producing essential products or services that consumers must purchase, such as energy for cooking and basic food ingredients, will not experience a big demand reduction when prices are raised.
- A lower rate of inflation is likely to have the opposite effect. If prices rise less than wages, consumers will have more to spend on non-essential products or services so demand for these could increase. There will be less pressure from trade unions to increase wages. Business costs will not be rising so quickly and this makes planning for expansion in the future easier.

▲ Rapid inflation means consumers have to spend a higher proportion of their incomes on essential products

Changes in economic growth

This will affect businesses in two ways:

- When economic growth occurs, the country's real GDP is increasing and more products are being produced. This is likely to increase living standards. Rising living standards means that consumers will have higher incomes and these are likely to be spent on non-essential products and services. So, demand for cars, kitchen appliances and holidays, for example, is likely to rise. Businesses will increase output and try to recruit more employees.
- When the economy is in recession, economic growth is negative. Demand for many products and services falls, unemployment rises and inflation will fall to low levels. If a recession lasts for some time, many businesses will fail as losses make it difficult to remain in operation.

28 ECONOMIC ISSUES

Key info
In 2024 the highest rate of economic growth in the world was in Guyana at 33.9%. In contrast, economic growth was 4% in Venezuela, 0.9 per cent in South Africa and −2.8% in Argentina.

▲ Youth unemployment reduces the country's economic growth

Study tips
It is a good idea to find out about growth, inflation and unemployment rates in your country.

Extend your skills of analysis

A question which asks for the effect of increased economic growth on a manufacturer of luxury cars could be answered as follows:

Economic growth means the total output of a country is expanding and people's living standards are rising.

Extend your analysis by explaining how this will affect the car manufacturer.

As people will have more income to spend, there will be increased demand for non-essential products such as luxury cars.

Extend your analysis by explaining how this will benefit the car manufacturer.

Increased demand for the luxury cars will increase revenue and the car manufacturer will consider expanding its operations.

Effects of government policy

All governments use economic policies to try to achieve the objectives of economic growth, low inflation and low unemployment. The main economic policies used by governments are:

» changes in taxes on business profit
» changes in taxes on people's income
» changes in the level of government spending
» changes in interest rates.

These policies all have effects on business activity and profit levels.

All governments need tax revenue to pay for spending on health, welfare, education, defence and other public services. There are many different types of taxes. Two which have the most direct effect on businesses are profit tax and income tax.

Effects of changes in taxes on business profit

Tax on business profit is sometimes referred to as corporation tax in some countries. It is a tax charged on the annual profit of a business. Tax on business profits is paid after interest expenses have been paid on loans, but before dividends are paid to shareholders. An increase in profit tax will leave less profit to be given to shareholders or retained in the business as a source of finance.

The two major effects of an increase in profit tax are therefore:

» Dividends to shareholders will be reduced. This could make them less likely to buy company shares. This would reduce the flow of finance into the company from the issue of new shares and lead to a fall in investment plans for the future.
» Retained profit will be reduced. This means that less profit is kept in the business for the purchase of assets. Again, this could force businesses to reduce plans for expansion and investment in the future.

Effects of changes in taxes on people's incomes

This will impact on consumers' spending power. Income tax can also have an effect on people's willingness to work. So, the two effects on business of an increase in income tax are:

» Consumers' disposable income after tax will fall. This leaves them with less to spend. Consumer demand for many products may fall, especially demand for non-essential goods and services. Businesses that produce non-essential consumer products and services such as hotels, restaurants, smartphones, high-priced branded clothing and cosmetics may experience substantial falls in revenue and profit.
» Employees will receive less 'take-home' pay. Work will be less well rewarded after tax. This could reduce workforce motivation and make it difficult for businesses to fill low-paid job vacancies.

The combined effect of increases in these two taxes is likely to lead to higher unemployment.

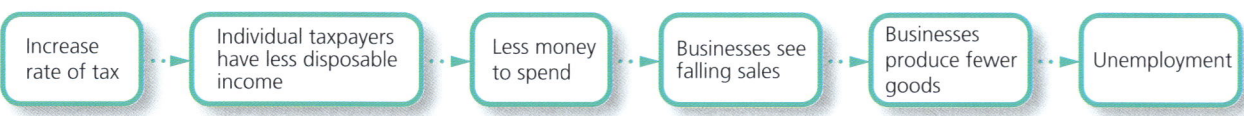

▲ Income tax flowchart

Key info

In 2024 the top rate of income tax in Belgium was 50%, while company tax was 25%. In Mongolia income tax was 20% and company tax was 25%. However, in Kuwait income tax was 0% and company tax was 15%.

Activity 28.1

a The GDP of Country A was $900 million in 2024. The population was 1 million. The average income per person was therefore $900. By 2025, as a result of economic growth, GDP was $1800 million. The population had also risen to 2 million. What was the average income per person in 2025?

b Joe earned $30 000 in 2024. He had a pay rise of 10% in 2025. Inflation was 15% in 2025.
  i How much did Joe earn in 2025?
  ii Did his real income rise or fall in 2025? Explain your answer.

> ### Activity 28.2
> Here are eight products:
>
> - rice
> - gas (petrol)
> - TVs
> - holidays in other countries
> - cooking oil
> - jewellery
> - salt
> - smartphones.
>
> The sales of four of these products are likely to fall following an increase in tax rates on people's income. Sales of the other four will not be much affected. Identify the **four** products likely to be most affected.

Effects of changes in government spending

Governments are the single largest spender in nearly all economies. The range of goods and services that governments buy is huge. In providing services such as health, education, defence, police and road networks, governments spend billions of dollars on products provided by businesses. Changes in the level and pattern of government spending can have big effects on different business sectors. Here are four examples:

» An increase in spending on health services, such as new hospitals, will increase demand for the construction industry and for products such as X-ray machines and ambulances. This will encourage businesses in these sectors to expand their operations and it will improve the health of the workforce.

» An increase in welfare spending, such as benefits for the unemployed, will increase the incomes of people with low living standards. This increase in welfare benefits will allow them to spend more, mainly on basic requirements such as 'value' low-priced food products, energy for cooking and warm clothes. Businesses in these or similar industries will experience an increase in sales.

» An increase in government spending on the road network could benefit many businesses, not just road building companies. Travel times for employees and transport costs for product distribution might be reduced as the infrastructure improves. Businesses (domestic or from other countries) might be more willing to invest in expanding their operations in the country because of these benefits.

» An increase in government spending on education should mean textbook suppliers and businesses making school furniture will experience increased demand. On a long-term basis, improving the education and level of qualifications achieved by young people will raise the quality of the workforce. Businesses should be able to recruit well-qualified workers more easily and economic growth will increase.

The level of total government spending has wide economic effects. Increased government spending should help to increase the rate of economic growth in many sectors of the economy. Obviously, if the government is short of finance and it reduces spending levels, all of the effects outlined above will be reversed.

Effects of government policy

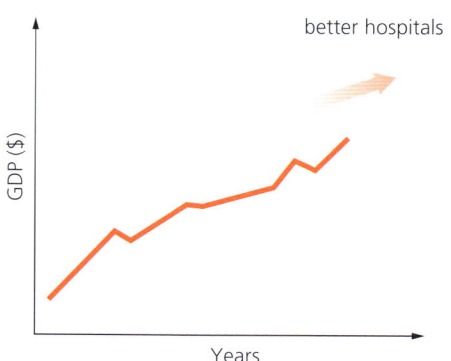
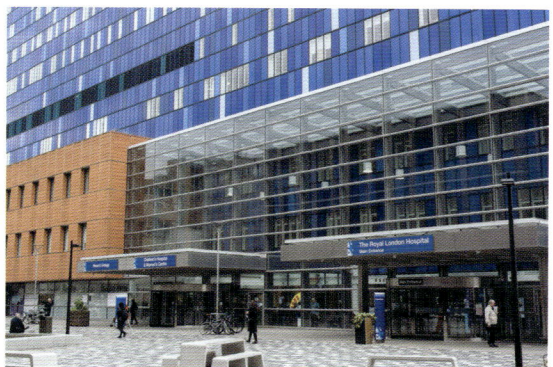

▲ Government spending on health benefits the population and also the businesses that build hospitals

REVISION SUMMARY

Government taxes and spending

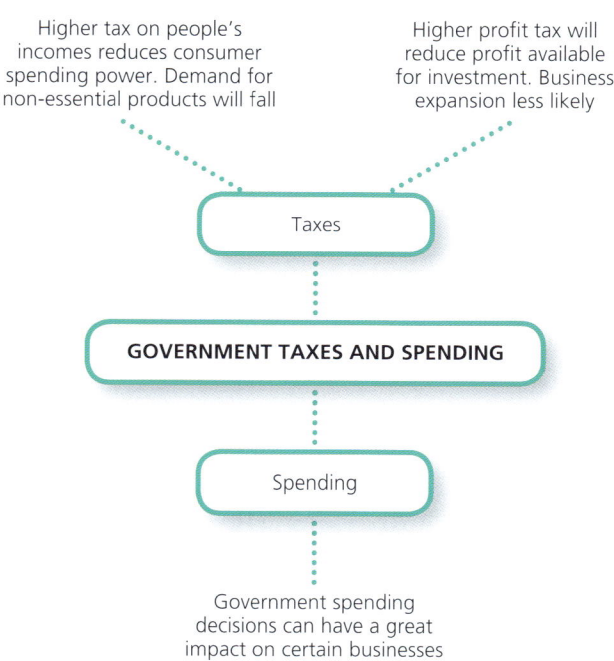

Effects of changes in interest rates

An interest rate is the cost of borrowing money. The following are the main effects of higher interest rates:

Study tips

When a question asks about the impact of tax or interest rate changes on a business, always refer to the type of good or service the business produces.

» Businesses with existing variable interest loans may have to pay more in interest to the banks. This will reduce their profits. Lower profits mean less is available to distribute to the owners and less is retained for business expansion.
» Managers planning to borrow money to expand the business may delay their decision. New investment in business activity will be reduced as the cost of borrowing has increased. Fewer new factories and offices will be built. Entrepreneurs hoping to start a new business may not now be able to afford to borrow the capital needed.

28 ECONOMIC ISSUES

Key info
Interest rates on loans in Sweden were among the lowest in 2024 at 3.5%. In the same year interest rates were: Uganda 10%, Zimbabwe 20% and Argentina 40%. The highest rate was in Venezuela at 59.25%.

» If consumers have taken out loans, such as mortgages to buy their homes, then the higher interest payments will reduce their available income. Demand for all goods and services could fall as consumers have less money to spend.
» Businesses that produce expensive consumer items, like cars or houses, will experience reduced demand for another reason. Consumers will be unwilling to borrow money to buy these expensive items if interest rates are higher. These businesses may have to reduce output and make employees redundant.
» Consumers may choose to save more and spend less as they will get a better return on their savings.

In summary, the impact of interest rate changes on a business will depend largely on its level of borrowing, its plans to expand and whether its consumers are affected by variations in interest rates.

REVISION SUMMARY Interest rates

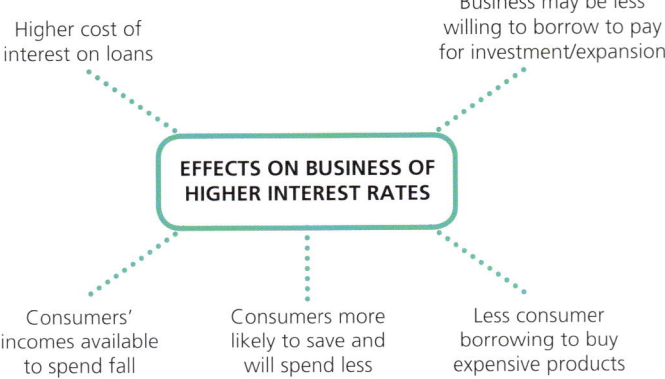

Activity 28.3

You are the Managing Director of the largest IT manufacturing company in your country. Your business sells products at home and in markets in other countries. Materials are imported from other countries. You employ hundreds of skilled workers to develop, assemble and test the IT equipment. Your business is planning a major expansion programme.

The government of your country has recently announced the following changes. Explain the likely impact of each of these changes on your business:

a A lower tax rate on people's income for high-income earners
b Lower tax on business profits
c Higher interest rates
d New training colleges to increase the supply of qualified workers

Case study: High levels of unemployment in Spain

The unemployment rate in Spain was 12% in 2023. This is the lowest rate unemployment has been since the worst year of 2013, when it was 27%. Spain still has the highest unemployment rate of all the European Union (EU) countries. However, GDP increased by 2.5% in 2023 and living standards are improving for those in employment in Spain.

Effects of government policy

> ### Activity 28.4
> Read the case study on the previous page.
>
> a Explain what is meant by 'GDP increased by 2.5%'.
> b Explain how improving living standards could affect:
>   i a farm producing milk
>   ii a manufacturer of leather goods.
> c Explain **two** reasons why the Spanish government might aim to reduce the level of unemployment.

How businesses may respond to changes in taxes and interest rates

Table 28.1 explains how businesses might respond to some major changes in taxes and interest rates. The business responses are likely to be reversed if the government decided to *reduce* taxes or *reduce* interest rates.

Table 28.1 How businesses might respond to changes in taxes and interest rates

Government policy	Business responses and their possible disadvantages
Increase in tax on people's income	• Reduce prices on existing products to increase demand now that consumers' disposable incomes are lower. *Disadvantage:* Less profit on each unit sold • Increase sales promotions such as vouchers, special offers and reward schemes to make products more affordable. *Disadvantage:* Increases costs of sales promotion • Produce 'value' products to be sold at low prices. *Disadvantage:* Consumers may think that quality is lower too, worsening the reputation of the business • Reduce plans for investment and delay or cancel expansion plans as falling demand does not justify expansion. *Disadvantage:* Slower business growth • Reduce employment levels by making some employees redundant as demand for products will be reduced. *Disadvantage:* Negative impact on the remaining employees' motivation • Plan to start marketing products in other countries where people's incomes are taxed less or where there are higher levels of consumer spending. *Disadvantage:* High cost of setting up marketing operations in other countries
Increase in tax on business profit	• Reduce dividends paid to shareholders so that retained profits are not much affected. *Disadvantage:* Share price might fall if shareholders decide to sell shares • Cut back on expansion plans as new investments will now be less profitable. *Disadvantage:* Slower growth and lower future profits • Plan to open operations in other countries where tax on business profit is lower. *Disadvantage:* Risks associated with being a multinational
Increase in interest rates	• Cut back on expansion plans if they were going to be financed by loans which now become more costly to pay interest on. *Disadvantage:* Slower business growth • Develop low-priced products that consumers will be better able to afford even when using loans. *Disadvantage:* Consumers may doubt the quality and business reputation could be damaged • Introduce special offers to consumers in the form of low-cost credit deals for high-priced consumer goods. *Disadvantage:* Business must finance these low-cost credit deals • Sell assets (or issue more shares if a public limited company) for cash to pay back existing loans. *Disadvantage:* Assets might be needed in future; issue of shares could reduce share price

The response of businesses to these tax and interest rate changes will depend upon:

- how big the changes to the taxes and interest rates are
- what actions competitors take in response to these changes
- the type of product the business produces.

> **Extend your skills of analysis**
>
> A question which asks how a housebuilding company might respond to higher interest rates could be answered as follows:
>
> Higher interest rates increase the cost of borrowing money.
>
> *Extend your analysis by explaining how this will affect the housebuilder.*
>
> Most people borrow money to buy a house. Higher interest rates mean that people are likely to borrow less so will be less able to buy large, high-priced houses.
>
> *Extend your analysis by explaining how the housebuilder could respond.*
>
> The housebuilding company could build fewer large houses and switch to building apartments instead. As apartments are sold at lower prices, consumers might still be able to afford to borrow enough to buy these instead of larger houses so revenue of the building company may not fall.

International business in focus

Indian motorbike industry powers ahead

India has overtaken China as the dominant Asian motorbike producer with total annual production of about 20 million units in 2023. Demand from most Asian countries is growing as economies continue to benefit from growth and rising incomes. South America is also seen as a growing market for the export of motorbikes from India.

The volume of motorbike sales in South America is expected to rise from US$13.84 billion in 2024 to US$18.54 billion in 2029.

Discussion points

- Why is the demand for motorbikes growing in Asia as local economies continue to grow?
- Explain how the business cycle in South American economies might affect the growth of motorbike sales.

Chapter review questions: Short answer and data response

1 The economy of Country A is growing rapidly. Unemployment is falling and the incomes of most consumers are rising. Businesses that produce low-priced food products have seen demand fall while businesses that produce high-priced products, such as cars, have seen sales increase. However, inflation increased to 8% last year. Many business owners are worried that the government could increase interest rates and taxes on incomes and profits.
   a Define 'inflation'. [2]
   b Outline **two** ways businesses in Country A might be affected by a higher tax on profits. [4]
   c Explain **two** ways in which an increase in interest rates could affect businesses in Country A. [6]
   d Do you think all businesses in Country A will benefit from economic growth? Justify your answer. [8]

2 The government in Country B is planning to reduce taxes on people's income and on business profits. It will also spend on building new roads and universities. The government aims to achieve a higher rate of economic growth and attract more tourists to the country. There was a recession in the economy last year and the government wants to avoid a slump. ADC produces exclusive high-priced branded fashion goods such as clothing and handbags. ADC managers are planning to respond to the government changes of lower taxes on people's income and on business profits.
   a Define 'slump'. [2]
   b Outline **two** effects on ADC of a recession. [4]
   c Explain **two** ways in which ADC could respond to lower taxes on people's income. [6]
   d Do you think that increased government spending on roads and universities will benefit all businesses? Justify your answer. [8]

Revision checklist

In this chapter you have learned:

- ✔ the main stages of the business cycle
- ✔ how each stage of the business cycle might affect a business
- ✔ the effects of changes in the levels of employment, inflation and economic growth on a business
- ✔ the effects of changes in taxes on business profit and on people's income
- ✔ the effects of changes in government spending
- ✔ the effects of changes in interest rates
- ✔ how businesses may respond to changes in taxes and interest rates.

NOW – test your understanding with the revision questions in the Student etextbook and the Workbook.

29 Business and the international economy

This chapter will explain:

The importance of globalisation:

★ reasons for globalisation
★ the opportunities and threats of globalisation for businesses
★ import tariffs and import quotas
★ the effects of import tariffs and import quotas on businesses.

Multinational companies (MNCs):

★ advantages to a business of becoming an MNC
★ advantages for the country where an MNC is located
★ disadvantages for the country where an MNC is located.

External costs and benefits:

★ external costs and external benefits of business decisions.

Exchange rates:

★ the appreciation and depreciation of an exchange rate
★ how changes in exchange rates can affect businesses which import and export products and services.

The importance of globalisation

Definitions to learn

Globalisation refers to increases in worldwide trade and the movement of people and capital between countries.

Reasons for globalisation

In many ways the world is becoming one large market rather than a series of separate national markets. The same goods and services can be bought in many countries around the world. Workers are finding it easier to move between countries and capital (finance) is also moving more freely from country to country.

There are several reasons for increasing **globalisation**:

» **Improved and cheaper transport links** have made it cheaper to transport goods and people around the world. Improved transport systems have made it cheaper to distribute products across the world. Larger container ships are just one example of the lower cost ways to deliver goods from one country to another. Cheaper air transport has also made it easier to send high value freight from one country to another.
» **Technological change**, including faster and more widespread communications between all parts of the world, have made it easier to buy and sell products globally. In addition, the internet allows easy price comparisons between goods from many countries. Online selling or ecommerce allows orders to be placed from anywhere in the world.
» Many **newly industrialised countries** are industrialising very rapidly. China and countries in South East Asia used to import many of the goods they needed. Now their own manufacturing industries are so strong they can export in large quantities – at very competitive prices.

▲ Huge container ships reduce transport costs and contribute to increased globalisation

The importance of globalisation

> **Definitions to learn**
>
> **Free trade agreements** exist when countries agree to trade imports/exports with no barriers such as tariffs and quotas.

» Increasing numbers of **free trade agreements** and economic unions between countries have reduced protection for industries. Consumers can purchase goods and services from other countries with few or no import controls such as tariffs or quotas.

Opportunities and threats of globalisation for businesses

Increasing free trade and the rising mobility of labour and capital, for example, the growth of multinational companies (MNCs), have many effects on businesses all over the world. Some of these effects are positive – opportunities – and some are potentially negative – threats.

Potential opportunities for businesses

These are explained in Table 29.1.

Table 29.1 Opportunities of globalisation

Opportunity	Impact on businesses
Start selling exports to other countries – opening up markets in other countries	This increases potential sales, perhaps in countries with fast-growing markets. Online selling allows orders for goods to be sent from other countries
	But it can be expensive to sell in other countries and there is no guarantee consumers in other countries will buy products, even if they are popular in the home market
Open factories/operations in other countries (become a multinational)	It could be cheaper to manufacture some goods in other countries than in the home country
	But will the quality be as good? Might there be an ethical issue (for example, over poor working conditions)? It can be expensive and/or difficult to set up operations in other countries
Import products from other countries to sell to customers in the home country	With no trade restrictions it could be profitable now to import goods and services from other countries and sell them domestically
	But the products will need maintenance and, perhaps, repairs – will the parts and support be available from the producer in the other country?
Import materials and components from other countries but still produce final goods in the home country	It could be cheaper to purchase these supplies from other countries now that there is free trade – this will help to reduce costs. These supplies could be purchased online
	But will the suppliers be reliable? Will the greater distance add too much to transport costs?

Potential threats to businesses

These are explained in Table 29.2.

Table 29.2 Threats of globalisation

Threat	Impact on businesses
Increasing imports into home market from competitors in other countries	If these competitors offer cheaper products (or higher quality products) sales of local businesses might fall
	But the increased competition could force the local businesses to become more efficient
Increasing investment from multinationals to set up operations in home country	This will create further competition – and the multinational may have economies of scale and be able to recruit the best employees
	But some local businesses could become suppliers to these multinationals and their sales could increase
Employees may leave businesses that cannot pay the same or more than international competitors	In some professions, employees will now have more choice about where they work and for which business – businesses will have to make efforts to keep their best employees
	But this might encourage local businesses to use a range of motivational methods to keep their employees
Can be disruption to the global supply chains e.g. problems with shipping routes	There may be delays or hold-ups to production. Businesses may not be able to produce any output or costs of transport may increase
	But this threat could be reduced by having more than one international supplier

29 BUSINESS AND THE INTERNATIONAL ECONOMY

Import tariffs and import quotas

Import tariffs are a type of tax that governments can use to raise revenue. **Import quotas** are government limits on the quantity of a product that can be imported. They are both forms of protectionism. They are used to protect domestic industries from competition from other countries that could otherwise force them to close down. Competitors from other countries might be able to produce products at a much lower cost. If they were allowed to import without any restriction then local businesses might be forced out of business. This would reduce employment and incomes.

> **Definitions to learn**
>
> An **import tariff** is a tax put on imported goods when they arrive into the country.
> An **import quota** is a limit on the quantity of a product that can be imported.

Effects of import tariffs and import quotas on businesses

» The effect of an import tariff is to raise the price of the imported product. If consumers have a locally produced, lower-priced alternative to the import, they might now be encouraged to purchase it. This should increase demand for the locally produced goods. If sales rise, then profits could increase and businesses are likely to create more jobs.

» The effect of an import quota is to lower the supply of the imported product. This usually leads to the price of the product increasing. If the quota is on a raw material or components, then the costs to local businesses will rise. In this case, the protectionism could damage local businesses. If the quota is on a consumer product, then consumers may switch to locally produced products instead. The lower supply may mean that the price of imported products increases. This will have the same beneficial effects on demand for locally produced goods as tariffs, explained above.

In the longer term, protectionism can have disadvantages for all businesses. Other countries might retaliate with their own import tariffs and quotas which would reduce demand for exports to them. Higher prices caused by tariffs and quotas might lead to inflation. The government might be forced to act to try to reduce inflation, which could lead to higher taxes or interest rates.

Many economists argue that all trade should be free from any protectionism. They suggest that consumers will benefit from lower prices and more choice. Businesses will have to become more competitive to survive, benefiting the economy.

> **Activity 29.1**
>
> Read the case study on the right.
>
> a Explain **three** opportunities to IBM of globalisation.
> b Explain **one** potential threat to IBM from continued globalisation.

> **Case study:** IBM takes advantage of globalisation
>
> IBM is one of the largest companies in the world, manufacturing and selling computer hardware, software and cloud computing services. It has taken full advantage of the opportunities offered by globalisation. Not only are its products sold in nearly every country but it has invested in factories and other operations in many low-cost countries with skilled IT employees – such as Romania and India. Most of the computers that it assembles in the USA use low-cost imported components. The company is well positioned to take advantage of growth in emerging market countries such as Brazil and Vietnam. However, IBM faces huge competition from newly developing computer businesses in China and India. IBM cannot ask the US government to protect its US market with tariffs because of free trade agreements.

Multinational companies

Definitions to learn

Multinational companies (MNCs) are those with factories, production or service operations in more than one country.

It is important to remember that a **multinational company (MNC)** is not a business which just *sells* goods in more than one country. To be called a multinational, a business must *produce* goods or services in more than one country. MNCs are some of the largest organisations in the world. They include:

- oil companies: for example, Shell, BP, Exxon Mobil
- IT companies: for example, Huawei, Samsung
- car manufacturers: for example, Toyota, General Motors, Stellantis.

> ### Activity 29.2
> Make a list of at least **four** businesses operating in your country which are a multinational. You can check this list with your teacher or by contacting the businesses themselves. Research which other countries they operate in.

Advantages to a business of becoming an MNC

Some advantages to a business of becoming an MNC are that it is able to:

- produce goods in countries with low costs, such as low wages. For example, most sports clothing is produced in South East Asia because wages are lower than in Europe
- extract raw materials which the company may need for production or refining. For example, crude oil from Guyana is needed to supply oil refineries in the USA
- produce goods nearer the market to reduce transport costs. For example, tiles and bricks are expensive to transport, so an MNC tile producer sets up a factory near the market in another country
- avoid barriers to trade put up by countries to reduce the imports of goods. For example, cars made in Japan have to pay an import tariff when sold in the European Union. Japanese manufacturers make cars in Europe to avoid these tariffs
- increase market share and expand into different market areas to spread risks. For example, if sales are falling in one country the business may move some operations to another country where sales are rising
- remain competitive with rival businesses which may be expanding in other countries to gain cost advantages
- gain government grants given to the business to set up operations in particular countries.

Key info

KFC has been successful in China. It has adapted its menu to Chinese customer tastes by adding local cuisine options such as egg tarts, soy milk drinks and rice porridge. In 2024 it had 10 000 restaurants in China, which is more than twice the number in the USA.

▲ Samsung operates in over 70 countries and is one of the world's leading technology multinationals

Extend your skills of analysis

A question which asks for an advantage to a car manufacturer and exporter of opening its first operations in another country could be answered as follows:

Operating in more than one country will mean that the business becomes a multinational company (MNC).

Extend your analysis by explaining why this might be an advantage.

As the car manufacturer exports its cars to other countries, setting up a factory in one of them should help to reduce costs.

Extend your analysis by explaining how this will benefit this business.

There are many car manufacturers so if this business can cut the high transport costs of exporting vehicles by operating within a country which is one of its main markets, then this will help to make it more competitive as it will be able to keep prices lower.

29 BUSINESS AND THE INTERNATIONAL ECONOMY

There are MNCs operating in nearly every country. There is much discussion about the effects on the countries where MNCs are located. There are both advantages and disadvantages to these countries.

Advantages for the country where an MNC is located

- **Job creation.** This reduces the level of unemployment. Toyota's operations in Mexico have created over 11 000 direct and indirect jobs in the country.
- **Increased investment.** New investment in buildings and machinery increases output of goods and services in the country. New technology can benefit the country by bringing in new ideas and methods. In just three months in 2023, South Africa received over $2 billion of investment from MNCs which helped to increase output and development in that country.
- **Increased exports.** Some of the extra output may be sold in other countries, which will increase the exports of the country. Also, imports may be reduced as more goods are now made in the country. Ford exports more than US$6 billion worth of cars and vans from its operations in Turkey each year.
- **Increased tax revenue.** The MNC will pay taxes to the government of the country where it is located.
- **More consumer choice.** MNC production of goods and services will increase consumer choice available.

> ### Key info
> South East Asian countries with low manufacturing costs include India, China, Vietnam, Thailand, Indonesia, Bangladesh, Philippines, Cambodia, Malaysia and Sri Lanka. These countries have had multinational companies locate their manufacturing operations there.

Activity 29.3
Try to identify **five** products available for sale in your own country which are produced by MNCs there.

Disadvantages for the country where an MNC is located

- **Unskilled jobs.** The jobs created are often unskilled jobs with assembly-line tasks. Skilled jobs, such as those in research and design, are not usually created in the countries where the MNC has its operations but in the MNC's home country.
- **Increased competition for local businesses.** Local companies may be forced out of business if consumers prefer products made by MNCs. Multinationals are often more efficient and have lower costs than local businesses.
- **Environmental damage.** The MNC's methods of production may be harmful to the environment with much waste and pollution created. Some analysts suggest that MNCs often ignore local environmental controls. It is suggested that they are so important to the economy that governments will not use legal controls against them.
- **Exploitation of natural resources.** Multinationals often use up scarce and non-renewable primary resources in the host country. When these are used up the MNC could leave the country. This means that the country loses the MNC and has much reduced natural resources.
- **Repatriation of profits.** Profits are often sent back to a multinational's home country and not kept in the country where they are earned. This reduces the benefit to the local economy.

> ### Key info
> In 2024 the government in Panama faced the prospect of a reduction in the country's GDP growth forecast from 5% to 1–2% after it ordered the closure of a very profitable copper mine operated by the Canadian MNC First Quantum. The decision arose after a dispute over the extension of the company's contract to operate the mine, which contributed around 5% of the country's GDP.

Multinational companies

Extend your skills of analysis

A question which asks for a disadvantage to a country of allowing an international chemical business to operate there could be answered as follows:

This is an MNC which produces chemicals in more than one country.

Extend your analysis by explaining why the location of a chemical business has a potential disadvantage to a country.

Chemical production is usually polluting with dangerous waste materials and polluting air emissions.

Extend your analysis by explaining why this is a disadvantage to the country where the chemical business locates.

The chemical business might not clear its own waste or reduce air pollution, leaving these costs for the government of the country and damaging the health of the population.

Activity 29.4

Should we allow the XYZ Company to set up a factory in our country?

- The XYZ Company is applying for planning permission to build a factory in your country. The factory is expected to be very profitable. 1000 new jobs should be created for assembly-line work. Many of the goods made could be sold in other countries. Some of the supplies for the factory will come from your country.
- Unemployment is high in your country, especially among skilled workers. The government cannot afford any new building projects. There are several local competitors producing goods similar to the XYZ Company. Imports are very high. Land for new building is very limited. New developments would have to be built in beautiful countryside.

a Identify **three** stakeholder groups in your country who may benefit from allowing the XYZ Company to build the factory.
b Identify **three** stakeholder groups in your country who may lose out from the building of the factory.
c Would you advise your government to allow the new factory to be built? Explain your answer by using all of the evidence.

REVISION SUMMARY — Advantages and disadvantages of multinational businesses

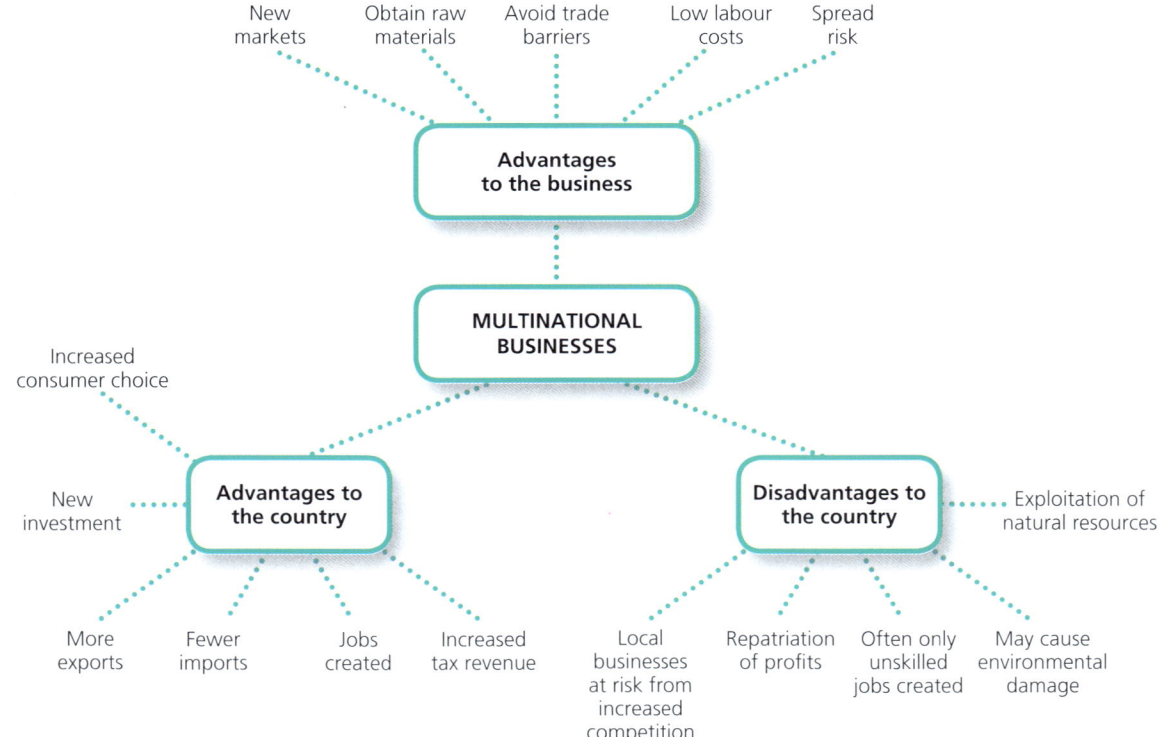

29 BUSINESS AND THE INTERNATIONAL ECONOMY

> **Definitions to learn**
>
> **External costs** are the costs imposed on a third party that are independent of the original economic transaction.
>
> **External benefits** are the benefits imposed on a third party that are independent of the original economic transaction.

External costs and benefits

External costs and external benefits of business decisions

Business activity sometimes has negative effects on the environment. At the same time, business activity can benefit the economy and the society it operates within in many ways. The importance of **external costs** and **external benefits** can be demonstrated by the following case study.

> ### ➡ Case study: Chemical business plans expansion
>
> A business producing chemicals plans to open a new factory. It has chosen a site which should help make the factory profitable. The revenue from selling chemicals made in the new factory will be greater than the costs of building and operating it. The site is in parkland a few kilometres from a major city. There is a high rate of unemployment in the city.
>
> However, the government is not willing to give planning permission until the external costs and benefits of the new factory are assessed. A government inspector has made a list of these as shown in the table.
>
> | External costs | External benefits |
> | --- | --- |
> | The construction and operation of the factory will cause noise and air pollution and much road traffic that will affect the local people | Jobs will be created, helping to reduce benefit payments paid by the government to the unemployed |
> | The cleaning up of waste from the factory, for example in rivers or in waste dumps, will be a cost to the local community or local government | Other problems often linked with unemployment, such as crime, might be reduced |
> | The health of the local population might be damaged and this will add to health service costs | Additional businesses might move into the area to supply services and materials to the new factory, creating more jobs |
> | The parkland cannot now be used by the local community for sport or recreation | Profit tax paid by the chemical business can be used by the government for social projects, such as improved health care |
>
> The government will try to give a value to these external costs and external benefits. This is not easy. For example, what is the cost of losing parkland which children used to play on? If the external costs are estimated to be much greater than the external benefits, then planning permission for the new chemical factory might never be given.

So you can see the external costs are the costs that are on a third party and are not part of the original economic transaction to produce or consume a good or service. The first and second parties are the business which pays the cost of producing the product or service and the consumer who pays to buy the product or service. For example, the producer of a car pays the costs of producing the car and the consumer pays the price to buy the car. However, it is *other* people who are affected by the pollution caused when the car is driven along roads and these people had nothing to do with the decision to produce or consume the car – they are third parties to this transaction.

You can also see the external benefits are the benefits that are for a third party and are not part of the original economic transaction to produce or consume a good or service. The first and second parties are the business which benefits from the revenue received after producing the product or service and the consumer who enjoys using the product or service. For example, the producer of a flu vaccine benefits from the revenue received from selling the vaccine and consumers benefit from not getting the flu after paying to have the flu vaccine. However, many *other* people will benefit from not catching flu as fewer people will have the flu virus. Therefore, these other people who were not part of the transaction to make or buy the flu vaccine will also benefit – they are third parties to this transaction.

> ### Activity 29.5
> Refer to the new chemical factory case study on page 352.
>
> a Define 'external costs'.
> b Explain why any **two** stakeholder groups will be worried about the external costs from a new chemical factory.
> c Explain why any **two** stakeholder groups will gain from the possible external benefits from the new chemical factory.
> d Assume you are the government minister responsible for planning decisions. Would you allow the new chemical factory to be built or not? Explain your answer.

Exchange rates

Appreciation and depreciation of an exchange rate

Definitions to learn

Exchange rate is the price of one currency in terms of another currency, for example 1 euro = $1.50.
Exchange rate appreciation occurs when the value of a currency rises – it buys more of another currency than before.
Exchange rate depreciation occurs when the value of a currency falls – it buys less of another currency than before.

If you have ever travelled to another country then you will know that it is usually necessary to change your money into foreign currency. To be able to buy things in another country you have to use the local currency. How much of another currency do you get in exchange for your own country's money? This will depend on the **exchange rate** between your currency and the currency of the other country you wish to buy.

Assume that the exchange rate between the US dollar ($) and the euro (€) is $1 = €0.90. This means that for each $1 being changed into euros, €0.90 would be received in exchange. This exchange rate is the price of one currency in terms of another.

Exchange rates between currencies change over time. This is because the demand for and supply of different currencies fluctuates. The value of a currency can rise or fall (go up or down) when compared with other currencies.

When the value of a currency rises, it is called an **appreciation**. An example would be if $1 = €0.90 increased to $1 = €0.95, then each dollar is now worth €0.95 instead of €0.90. This means that a given number of dollars buys more euros than it did previously. The value of the dollar has appreciated.

When the value of a currency falls, it is called a **depreciation**. An example would be if $1 = €0.90 decreased to $1 = €0.80, then each dollar is now worth €0.80 instead of €0.90. This means that a given number of dollars buys fewer euros than it did previously. The value of the dollar has depreciated.

29 BUSINESS AND THE INTERNATIONAL ECONOMY

Activity 29.6

	In 2023 one US$ buys	In 2024 one US$ buys	Appreciation or depreciation of the US$
Nigerian Naira	638 NGN	1340 NGN	
Kenyan Shilling	139 KES	140 KES	
Malaysian Ringgit	4.57 MYR	4.80 MYR	
Indian Rupee	83 INR	83 INR	
Mexican Peso	17.7 MXN	17.1 MXN	

a Complete the table by stating whether the dollar has appreciated or depreciated against the other currencies.
b Explain how a US importer of products could be affected by a depreciation of the dollar against other currencies.
c Explain how a US exporter of products could be affected by a depreciation of the dollar against other currencies.

How changes in exchange rates affect businesses which import and export goods and services

Price and costs

Most manufacturing businesses will import some of their materials and components. Many will also export some of their output. Supermarkets import many products, especially fresh food, to give customers a wide choice all year round. Changes in exchange rates will have an impact on the costs of imported goods and services and an impact on export prices in markets in other countries. These changes can impact on the competitiveness of a business.

Import costs

» Following an exchange rate *appreciation* the cost of imported goods and services in the domestic currency will *fall*. A given amount of the domestic currency will now buy more imported products than before the appreciation.
» Following an exchange rate *depreciation*, the cost of imported goods and services in the domestic currency will *rise*. A given amount of the domestic currency will now buy fewer imported products than before the depreciation.

Export prices

» Following an exchange rate *appreciation* the prices of exported goods and services in the foreign currency will *rise*. This is because if the old export price was kept unchanged, the business would be receiving less domestic currency for each item sold.
» Following an exchange rate *depreciation*, the price of exported goods and services in the foreign currency could be *reduced*. This is assuming the business wants to earn as much domestic currency of each unit sold as before.

Study tips

It is important to remember that an appreciation (or increase) in the exchange rate leads to exports also increasing in price (import prices do the opposite and fall). A depreciation (or fall) in the exchange rate leads to exports also decreasing in price (import prices do the opposite and rise).

Exchange rates

Competitiveness

Changes in costs and prices will impact on the ability of a business to compete – in both the domestic market and export markets. A business could try to protect its competitiveness.

A business which imports raw materials and components can increase competitiveness by:

» importing more raw materials and components if the exchange rate appreciates
» reducing imports of raw materials and components and switching to domestic suppliers if the exchange rate depreciates.

A business that exports goods and services can increase competitiveness by:

» reducing prices in exports markets when the exchange rate depreciates. If export prices fall this could increase export sales.

However, it is likely that the competitiveness of the export business will fall if it increases prices following an appreciation of the currency. The prices of foreign-based businesses will now be more competitive.

Study tips
You will not be asked to perform exchange rate calculations but you will have to remember what happens to import prices and export prices when currencies appreciate or depreciate in value.

Key info
The £ depreciated after the UK voted to leave the EU in 2016, making UK goods more competitive in overseas markets. By 2023 cars were the most valuable export from the UK, valued at approximately £36.6 billion. Mechanical power generators were the second-most valuable export with an export value of around £34.5 billion.

REVISION SUMMARY

Exchange rates

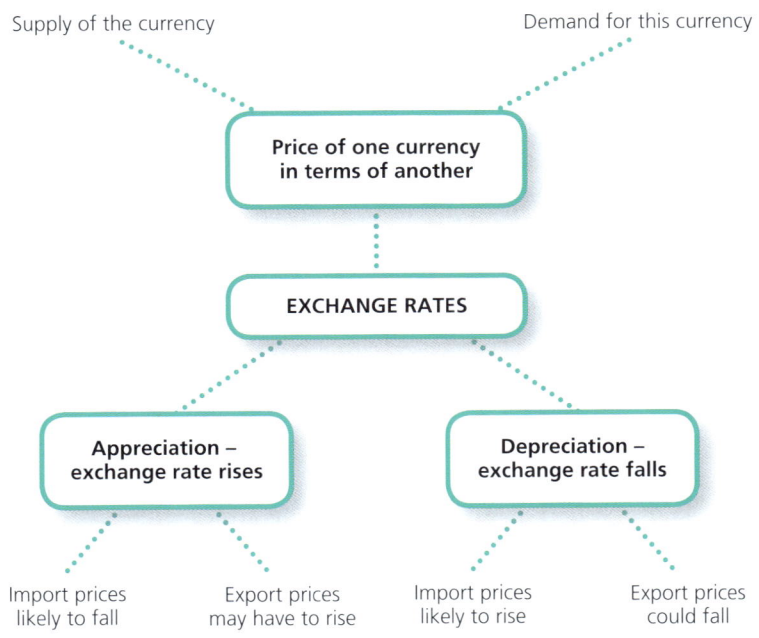

29 BUSINESS AND THE INTERNATIONAL ECONOMY

International business in focus

Starbucks and Argentina's cafe culture

The market for coffee in Argentina (both in-home and out-of-home) is expected to grow considerably in the coming years. Starbucks opened its first store in the country in 2008 and now has over 130 stores there, reflecting the shift of consumers towards global brands. The company's growth in the country is also expected to continue, but there are mixed feelings about the expansion of the huge multinational company in the country.

The cheerful and helpful approach to customer service and the speed of service at Starbucks have been welcomed. It has also been noted that the opening of a store can lead to local cafes improving their own service. However, some see multinational companies like Starbucks as a threat to the long-standing cafe culture in the country and have criticised its generic store design. As with other multinationals, decisions are taken outside of the country.

Discussion points

- Explain why Starbucks is referred to as a 'multinational'.
- Would you prefer to use a local cafe or one operated by Starbucks? Ask everyone in your class this question and see what the results are.
- On balance, do you think the expansion of Starbucks is good for countries such as Argentina?

Exchange rates

Chapter review questions: Short answer and data response

1. PaintCo manufactures specialist paints for aircraft. It has taken advantage of globalisation. The research department recruits scientists from several countries. Raw materials are imported and the paints are exported to aircraft manufacturers in the USA, Brazil and China. Until 10 years ago it only had 1 large factory in Europe. Now PaintCo has 4 factories in low-cost, low-income countries, including 1 in a nature reserve that gives access to a large sea port.
   a. Define 'globalisation'. [2]
   b. Outline **two** possible threats from globalisation to PaintCo. [4]
   c. Explain **one** external cost and **one** external benefit resulting from the factory being located in the nature reserve. [6]
   d. Do you think PaintCo should build its next factory in Europe or in a low-cost country? Justify your answer. [8]

2. Beema is a successful business that makes shoes in Country B. It imports some of the leather and the machines it uses, and exports 30% of its output. Recently the currency of Country B has fallen in value (depreciated). Beema's managers are planning to open a second factory. This will be located in Country C which already has several shoe manufacturers. Country C has just agreed to stop using protectionism by removing trade barriers such as import tariffs. Many of its industries are inefficient.
   a. Define 'exchange rate'. [2]
   b. Outline **two** likely reasons why Beema is planning to become a multinational business. [4]
   c. Explain **two** effects on Beema of a depreciation of Country B's currency. [6]
   d. Do you think the government of Country C should encourage businesses such as Beema to start operations in its country? Justify your answer. [8]

Revision checklist

In this chapter you have learned:

- ✔ the reasons for globalisation
- ✔ the opportunities and threats of globalisation for businesses
- ✔ about import tariffs and import quotas and their effects on businesses
- ✔ the advantages to a business of becoming an MNC
- ✔ the advantages and disadvantages for the country where an MNC is located
- ✔ the external costs and external benefits of business decisions
- ✔ the appreciation and depreciation of an exchange rate
- ✔ how changes in exchange rates can affect businesses which import and export products and services.

NOW – test your understanding with the revision questions in the Student etextbook and the Workbook.

30 Business and the environment

This chapter will explain:

Environmental issues:

★ how business activity can negatively affect the environment
★ why businesses may respond to environmental issues
★ how businesses may respond to environmental issues
★ the effects of legal controls over business activity affecting the environment.

Environmental issues

How business activity can negatively affect the environment

Business activity aims to satisfy customers' demand for goods and services – but it often has an impact on the **environment**. The 'environment' means our natural world.

Consider these two statements by different factory managers:

» Manager A: 'I know that my factory pollutes the air and the river with waste products but it is very expensive to use cleaner production methods. We make a profit from making low-cost products and these are what consumers want.'

» Manager B: 'We recently spent $10 million on new low-energy boilers that produce 90% less **pollution** than the old ones. We now recycle 75% of our waste – consumers prefer businesses that show **social responsibility** towards the environment.'

These two different opinions focus on the main issues with business activity and its impact on the environment. For reasons that will be discussed later, many businesses are moving towards the approach of Manager B. This does not mean, however, that business activity will have *no* impact on the environment, but its worst effects might be reduced.

> **Definitions to learn**
>
> **Environment** is our natural world including, for example, pure air, clean water and undeveloped countryside.
> **Pollution** is the introduction of harmful materials into the environment.
> **Social responsibility** is when a business aims to benefit stakeholders other than shareholders such as by protecting the environment by reducing pollution and using the most sustainable production methods.

▲ Air pollution damages the environment and harms peoples' health

▲ Rivers polluted by industrial waste are expensive to clean up

▲ Road transport creates noise and air pollution and adds to global warming

Here are some examples of how business activity can negatively affect the environment:

Pollution

Much business activity causes pollution in the form of waste products that have to be disposed of, dirty and dangerous air emissions and excessive noise from production methods. Here are some specific examples:

- Aircraft jet engine emissions damage the atmosphere.
- Pollution from steel foundries reduces air quality.
- Waste run-off from chemical works and farms pollutes rivers and seas.
- Transport of goods by ships and trucks requires the burning of fossil fuels, such as oil, that create carbon emissions which are linked to global warming and climate change.
- Use of plastic containers and bags that are not biodegradable can cause damage to marine life.

Depletion of resources

Business activity needs physical resources to allow for the production of goods and services. These resources are all obtained from nature. Examples include:

- steel, which requires coal and iron ore
- paper, which is produced from wood pulp
- plastics, which are made from refined oil products
- electricity, which is often produced from coal or natural gas or nuclear power (which requires uranium)
- meat production, which requires water, and agriculture is the world's largest user of fresh water.

The production of these materials used by business therefore leads to the consumption of natural resources. Nearly all natural resources have limits to their supply or production – they are said to be finite. Can the supply of any of these resources be replenished? Only in a few cases. For example:

- rain provides additional fresh water
- planting trees will allow wood to be obtained in future.

These two resources are renewable but the others mentioned above are non-renewable. This means that using them leads to the **depletion of resources**. They will eventually become very scarce.

Why businesses may respond to environmental issues

There are several reasons why a business might respond to environmental issues by becoming more environmentally friendly. They include:

- **Laws.** There are legal controls over business activities that damage the environment. See page 361. Businesses that do not comply with environmental laws may be fined.
- **Increased sales.** Consumer buying patterns in many countries are changing towards environmentally friendly products. If sales increase for this reason,

> **Study tips**
>
> You must make sure you understand what 'environmentally responsible' means. Be prepared to discuss whether a business should be more environmentally responsible or not.

> **Definitions to learn**
>
> **Depletion of resources** is when resources are being consumed at a faster rate than they can be replenished.

30 BUSINESS AND THE ENVIRONMENT

> **Definitions to learn**
>
> A **consumer boycott** is when consumers decide not to buy products from a business that does not act in an environmentally responsible way.
>
> **Environmental responsibility** is when a business considers the impact on the environment when taking decisions.

then it can be more profitable for a business to respond to environmental issues even if the short-term costs might be greater. Responding in these ways will reduce the risk of having damaging **consumer boycotts**.

- **Improved reputation.** 'Going green' or producing products that are better for the environment helps to create a positive brand image for a business. This can attract new consumers as well as increase the brand loyalty of existing ones.
- **Cost savings.** There may be lower long-term costs from environmentally friendly measures. Although the initial cost of fitting solar panels to a factory roof to generate electricity is high, the low cost of the power these generate can reduce long-term costs. This, and other similar measures, can increase long-term profit.
- **Recruitment.** Many employees prefer to work for a business that has a positive environmental image. It is often easier for these businesses to recruit and retain well-qualified employees.
- **Finance.** Some banks and other finance institutions are only lending to businesses that can show they are environmentally responsible. So failure to respond positively to environmental issues can make it more difficult to raise finance.

> **Key info**
>
> Nike is seen as a leader in **environmental responsibility** as well as in sales of sports clothing and equipment. Many of its products are made from environmentally friendly materials, such as recycled polyester, and the company aims to use 100% renewable energy by 2025. Central to Nike's environmentally responsible endeavours is its 'Move to Zero' initiative, which includes ending the use of single-use plastics at all of its sites.

How businesses may respond to environmental issues

As we saw at the start of this chapter, some business managers do not think protecting the environment is the responsibility of their business. This view is now very rare – for the reasons given in the previous section. How can businesses respond positively to environmental issues? These are the most common business responses:

- **Reduce waste.** By making the manufacturing production processes more efficient, fewer resources will be wasted. Food businesses can control their inventories more effectively so that perishable food products are not thrown away.
- **Reduce plastic use.** Plastic is a major environmental issue as it cannot easily be disposed of or reused. By businesses replacing plastic with more natural products, such as bamboo-sourced packaging materials, there will be environmental benefits.
- **Recycling.** Businesses are increasingly producing products that can be recycled (used again) and using production methods that use recycled resources. This includes using water in the production process more than once, after it has been filtered and cleaned.
- **Renewable energy sources.** Generating power by using solar or wind power is now widely done by many businesses. This greatly reduces the burning of fossil fuels which worsens climate change.
- **Buying from suppliers that use environmentally friendly production processes to make products.** Using these suppliers will reduce the overall damage to the environment caused by the business as it produces its products.

Environmental issues

> **Activity 30.1**
> Research the ways businesses in your country are trying to reduce their impact on the environment. Give examples of businesses that are using any of the five ways listed on the previous page.

Effects of legal controls over business activity affecting the environment

Governments can make it illegal for business activities which damage the environment or they can strictly control them. These legal controls are used to limit the following business activities:

» **How products are made.** For example, the government could legally control how electricity is generated by banning the burning of coal and oil in power stations. It could also make production methods that lead to pollution of rivers and the sea illegal – or at least impose high fines on businesses that do this. However, it is sometimes difficult to prove which business is responsible for these forms of pollution.

» **What is produced.** Many governments have made it illegal for gas (petrol) companies to add lead to fuels to improve the performance of cars because of the damage to peoples' health. Supermarkets can be forced to give consumers bags made from paper not plastic, because paper is biodegradable and plastic bags are not.

» **Where to produce and sell.** Governments can control the location decisions of businesses because of the need to protect the natural environment. So locating businesses in areas of great beauty or in national parks is very tightly controlled.

» **Influence on costs.** Business managers are often worried that these legal controls add greatly to the costs of operating their business. Developing products which use recyclable resources, cleaning up production processes and locating away from certain geographical areas – all of these factors can add to business costs. These higher costs will then lead to higher consumer prices. In some cases, however, long-term costs might actually be lower if the changes result in improved efficiency or lower energy costs from renewable resources. If the costs of a business do increase, this could make its products uncompetitive on world markets. This is because not all governments use strict legal controls over business activities that damage the environment. This keeps business costs in these countries relatively low and therefore the products more competitive. Why do some governments not use strict legal controls over environmental damage? Often, it is because the governments are more focused on economic growth and creating jobs than protecting the environment.

> **Key info**
> It is a criminal offence to break environmental laws in Australia. The maximum penalty varies depending on which law has been broken, but fines can be in the millions of dollars and/or up to four years in prison.

▲ It is often difficult for governments to find out which firms are responsible for dumping chemical waste

Do you think it is environmentally responsible for a business to locate in a country that does not have strict laws on protecting the environment?

30 BUSINESS AND THE ENVIRONMENT

> **Extend your skills of analysis**
>
> A question which asks why a soft-drinks manufacturer might respond to environmental issues can be answered as follows:
>
> A soft-drinks manufacturing business will affect the environment in a number of ways, such as using fresh water and transportation methods to distribute the products widely. It might respond because it is concerned about a poor public image and a possible consumer boycott.
>
> *Extend your analysis by explaining why the environment would benefit from the business responding to protect the environment.*
>
> Using electric vehicles to transport the soft drinks would be a lot less polluting than using vehicles powered by fossil fuels. Air pollution would be reduced and public health improved.
>
> *Extend your analysis by explaining how this would benefit the business.*
>
> The soft-drinks manufacturer could promote itself as being environmentally responsible and environmentally friendly. This would improve the reputation of the business, encourage new consumers to buy its products and increase consumer loyalty.

Case study: Should governments use laws to protect the environment?

In Country X, there are very few government controls on business activity. The government of Country X wants to encourage businesses to start up and grow. A government minister said: 'Legal controls over pollution and disposal of waste add to business costs. This will discourage production in our country.' Country X sells many products, such as cars, clothing and chemicals, in world markets at very low prices.

In Country Y, the government has very strict laws to control the ways in which businesses dispose of their waste, how much pollution they can produce and where new factories are located. A minister in the government said: 'We believe that businesses have a social responsibility to our community not to damage the environment. These laws have encouraged businesses to use much cleaner production methods. They have also developed products that pollute the environment much less than cheaper products. Many consumers in the world today will only buy environmentally friendly products.'

Activity 30.2

Read the case study above.

a Define 'environmental responsibility'.
b Explain **two** possible reasons why the government in Country X does not have strict controls on business activity that affects the environment.
c Explain **two** ways in which business activity can damage the environment. Use examples from your own country.
d Do you think that the government of Country Y is right to use strict laws against businesses that damage the environment? Justify your answer.

REVISION SUMMARY   Environmental issues

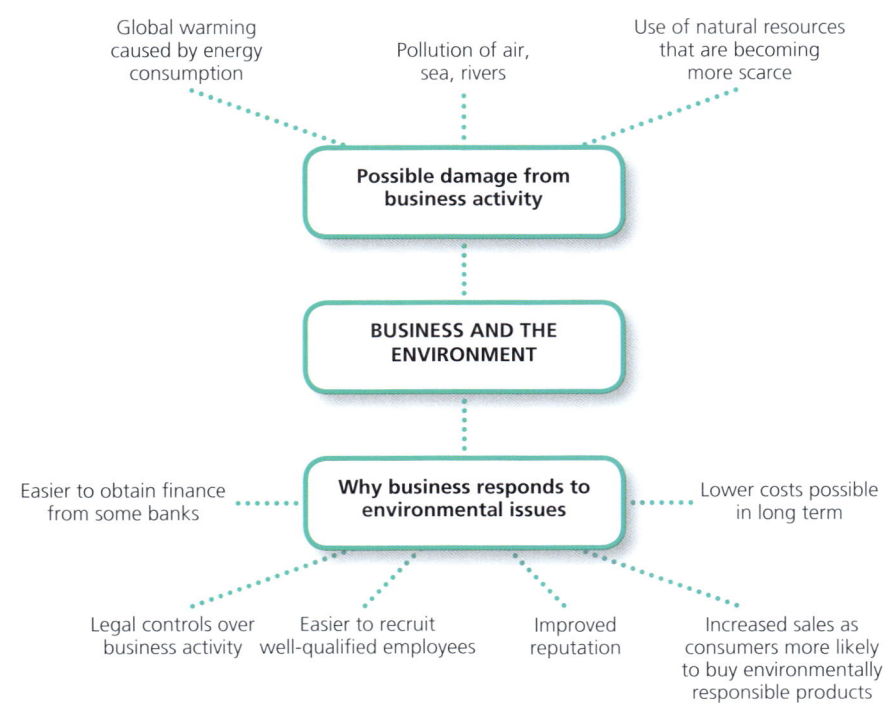

International business in focus

Airbus reduces environmental cost of air travel

Airbus Aircraft, the world's largest manufacturer of passenger aircraft, has produced a new range of planes. The Airbus A350 is more efficient than existing models in order to save fuel – it uses 25% less fuel and emits 25% less carbon dioxide. Its nitrogen dioxide emissions are 23% below industry standards and the aircraft has a quieter operation. The planes are expensive but by buying them airlines will save fuel and also improve their image of 'environmental responsibility'.

Plane makers and airlines are worried by Greenpeace pressure group activity. This organisation claims that only 1% of the world's population is responsible for more than half of global climate emissions from aviation and is calling for a ban on private jets. It is also asking governments to end the tax exemptions on kerosene fuel to make air travel more expensive.

▲ Fuel-saving planes are popular with airlines

Discussion points

- What are the environmental costs resulting from airline flights?
- Does all business activity lead to environmental damage?
- Why do businesses often want to seem to be 'environmentally responsible'?
- When do you think businesses should respond to pressure from groups such as Greenpeace?

30 BUSINESS AND THE ENVIRONMENT

❓ Chapter review questions: Short answer and data response

1 Jean-Luc is the Chief Executive of WFF, a furniture factory which employs 200 workers. He promotes his business as being environmentally friendly, as wood is better for the environment than plastic or metal. As new trees can be planted, wood does not have the same level of depletion of resources as other raw materials. WFF's furniture is sold in many countries. Wood is bought from the cheapest sources. Jean-Luc thinks it comes from renewable sources of timber but he does not ask the suppliers about this. Furniture is transported by trucks and ships. Waste wood is burnt as this is cheaper than sending it for processing into other products. Air quality in Jean-Luc's country is very poor but the government does not know who the major polluters are. It is considering more legal controls over business activity.
   a Define 'depletion of resources'. [2]
   b Outline **two** negative effects for people in the local area resulting from the operation of Jean-Luc's business. [4]
   c Explain **two** legal controls over WFF's activities that could benefit the environment. [6]
   d Do you think WFF would benefit from producing more environmentally friendly products? Justify your answer. [8]

2 AXX is a mining company. It operates the largest mine in Country X. It extracts metals such as iron and copper. AXX uses huge noisy petrol-powered machines to crush rock and move materials around the mine. The extracted materials are washed before sorting and grading. This process uses fresh water. The water becomes contaminated with deposits due to the washing process and it is then released into rivers. Pedro, the Operations Director, thinks AXX should respond to environmental issues. However, Jose, the Managing Director, wants to keep costs low. He thinks that legal controls over business activity that affects the environment will have no effect on AXX.
   a Identify **two** types of pollution created by AXX. [2]
   b Outline **two** reasons why Pedro is considering responding to environmental issues. [4]
   c Explain **two** ways AXX might respond to environmental issues. [6]
   d Do you agree with Jose that legal controls over business activity that affects the environment will have no impact on AXX? Justify your answer. [8]

Revision checklist
In this chapter you have learned:

- ✔ how business activity can negatively affect the environment
- ✔ why businesses may respond to environmental issues
- ✔ how businesses may respond to environmental issues
- ✔ the effects of legal controls over business activity affecting the environment.

NOW – test your understanding with the revision questions in the Student etextbook and the Workbook.

31 Business and ethical issues, and pressure groups

This chapter will explain:

Ethical issues:

★ ethical issues which may affect businesses
★ how businesses may respond to ethical issues
★ advantages and disadvantages of a business being ethical.

The role of pressure groups:

★ how pressure groups can influence business decisions.

Definitions to learn

Ethical decisions are based on a moral code and are sometimes referred to as 'doing the right thing'. An **ethical issue** is a situation where there is a possible conflict between moral standards.

Key info

Charities have had to become increasingly careful about how much they pay their senior executives after negative publicity and, as a result, lower contributions from some donors. Charities feel they still need to attract the best and most talented managers to run the charities efficiently and make the best use of the funds donated.

Study tips

Remember that there is no right or wrong answer when discussing ethical decision making. Be prepared to discuss the impact on a business of being less or more ethical in its decision making.

Ethical issues

Ethical issues which may affect businesses

Should businesses always 'do the right thing'? Should businesses always take decisions that are fair and moral? An increasing focus is being given to business decisions which involve an ethical dimension. Below are some examples.

Should businesses ever:

» employ child labour, even though it might not be illegal in some countries?
» pay unfair wages to their employees?
» use suppliers whose production methods damage the environment, for example, wood obtained from cutting down rainforests?
» force suppliers to accept low, unfair prices because the suppliers are in a weak trading position?
» pay directors large bonuses and owners of businesses high dividends at the same time as making some employees redundant?

If you answered NO to all of these questions then you would make a very ethical business manager! They are all examples of **ethical decisions** that many businesses have to make frequently. Business managers can have very different answers to the questions above. This is because people have different moral codes and therefore different ethical standards. The two most extreme views are:

» 'As long as a business does not deliberately break the law then any decision it makes is acceptable. The only measure of business success is whether it makes profits or not.'
» 'Even if certain activities are not against the law, it is unethical and therefore wrong to decide to do them despite any increase in profits that might result.'

How businesses may respond to ethical issues

As we noted above, it is still true that some businesses might ignore **ethical issues** when trying to make higher profit. However, in the long term, this approach could harm the image of the business so badly that negative publicity

31 BUSINESS AND ETHICAL ISSUES, AND PRESSURE GROUPS

drives many consumers away. So, if we assume that most businesses do want to 'do the right thing' when faced with ethical issues, how should they respond?

These are the stages a business might go through to make sure that its activities and decisions are ethically based:

1 Make it clear to all employees that there is a moral code of conduct for the business that they must follow. This could be printed and given to every employee. It might include:
   a Never employ children.
   b Always treat customers and suppliers fairly and be honest with them.
   c Make sure all employees are treated with respect at all times.
   d Treat all fellow employees fairly, showing no unfair treatment between them.
   e Tell your supervisor or a senior manager if anyone else in the business is breaking the moral code.
2 Train all employees in how the moral code should be applied in different situations. This could involve role play exercises where employees are put into situations where a decision has to be taken between an ethical and an unethical option. A discussion could then take place about how the business would benefit from the ethical option being chosen.
3 Ensure complete confidentiality if an employee tells a manager about another employee acting unethically. This will encourage more people to report if the moral code is being broken.
4 Ensure that all senior managers set an excellent example of ethical behaviour. If they are known to be avoiding tax or using expense accounts excessively, then these unethical examples will be assumed to be normal behaviour in the business.
5 Check regularly that all suppliers follow a similar moral code of conduct and switch to other suppliers if they do not.

▲ Western Union has been rated as one of the world's most ethical businesses

Advantages and disadvantages of a business being ethical

Assume a large multinational clothing business, Company X, buys clothes from a factory in a low-income country. The managers of Company X know that the factory employs child labourers to keep costs down, because it is not illegal to employ workers as young as 12 years old in the country it is based in.

Another business – Company Y – only buys clothes from suppliers who guarantee not to employ children. It also pays fair wages and offers good working conditions. Company Y managers check that its suppliers keep to these standards as well.

What is the potential impact on Company Y of this ethical decision? Table 31.1 explains the potential advantages and disadvantages of taking ethical business decisions.

Table 31.1 Advantages and disadvantages of Company Y being ethical

Advantages	Disadvantages
Consumers may be against buying clothing products made by children. The ethical image of Company Y might lead to increased purchases by consumers. They might buy less from Company X	There are likely to be higher costs for obtaining supplies from ethical suppliers. Adult employees will be paid more than child employees and good working conditions add to business costs too
Good publicity about Company Y's ethical decision will provide free promotion of its ethical image. Company X may suffer from bad publicity	Company Y's prices might have to be higher than those of Company X because of the higher cost of supplies. Some consumers are more interested in low prices than products bought from ethical businesses
Long-term profits of Company Y could increase as a result of higher sales, even though prices may be higher than those of unethical competitors	If most consumers are only looking for low-priced products, Company Y's sales and profit will fall
Many employees and shareholders want to be linked to an ethical business. Company Y may find it easier to recruit the best workers and raise capital from shareholders	If sales and profit fall, Company Y may have to make some workers redundant
There is less risk of legal action being taken against Company Y. Avoiding costly legal action because the business is operating ethically will help maintain profitability	It could be argued that, in some countries, if children are not employed the incomes of their families will fall to very low levels. Company X could use this to justify its unethical decision

Case study: Cocoa growers in Ghana

Ghana is the world's second-largest producer of cocoa beans, which are used to make chocolate. It grows around 15% of the world's cocoa beans but receives only about 1.5% of the estimated worth of the chocolate market. About two-thirds of the cocoa beans go to Europe. Even though cocoa farmers work extremely hard, up to 90% of them do not earn enough to feed their families, often surviving on $2 a day. The world's four largest chocolate corporations, Hershey, Lindt, Mondelēz and Nestlé, have continued to see their profits grow since 2020. Some of these companies are trying to help cocoa farmers to produce more cocoa but none of the programmes have increased production or incomes and many farmers have sold their land to illegal miners to supplement their incomes.

Source: Extracted from www.oxfam.org/en/press-releases/chocolate-giants-reap-huge-profits-promises-improve-farmers-incomes-ring-hollow

Activity 31.1

Read the case study above.

a What is meant by an 'ethical decision'?
b Explain **two** likely effects on cocoa production of cocoa farmers continuing to not be paid a living wage.
c Explain how the shareholders of the four large chocolate producers might have been affected by cocoa farmers being paid a low price for their cocoa beans.

Extend your skills of analysis

A question which asks how an aircraft manufacturer might be affected by its decision to force all small businesses that supply components to reduce prices could be answered as follows:

By forcing lower prices from small suppliers, a business is using trading power to achieve lower costs.

Extend your analysis by explaining why this might be unethical.

Small suppliers of components might depend on orders from the aircraft manufacturer. If these ended they could be forced out of business.

Extend your analysis by explaining why this might affect the aircraft manufacturer.

The manufacturer will receive bad publicity and a poor image for using its trading power. It might lose essential suppliers. Suppliers might try to cut costs with lower quality components. This could be a disaster for an aircraft manufacturer if an accident occurred as a result of this.

31 BUSINESS AND ETHICAL ISSUES, AND PRESSURE GROUPS

The role of pressure groups

How pressure groups can influence business decisions

Pressure groups are becoming increasingly active in their campaigns to encourage businesses to change their business activities. Pressure groups have, for example, been formed to protect workers' rights and reduce the impact of climate change from industrial production. These groups can take some very effective measures against businesses that are not acting ethically and are not being socially responsible. Pressure groups such as Greenpeace and Friends of the Earth organise consumer boycotts and Greenpeace has tried to block up businesses' waste pipes.

A recently established pressure group is Extinction Rebellion (XR). This is an international movement that demands governments declare a climate emergency, reach net zero emissions by 2025 and take action against the worst polluting businesses. XR members use non-violent direct action and civil disobedience to help stress the urgency of the climate crisis.

The most common forms of action taken by pressure groups to influence business decisions include:

- Organising consumer boycotts of businesses which damage the environment or act socially irresponsibly. *Business impact:* Loss of sales.
- Publicity stunts such as scaling tall buildings with banners or stopping the traffic in busy city centres. These stunts gain a great deal of publicity for the group. *Business impact:* Bad publicity.
- Media campaigns, especially using social media to engage young people in a group's campaign and to join the group. *Business impact:* Viral campaigns could change decisions made by businesses.
- Lobbying a government to make changes to the law, for example, to make felling of ancient trees illegal. *Business impact:* May have to stop activities that are now illegal.
- Opinion polls asking the public for their views on local business activities, such as an industrial location decision. If a majority of people are against it, the pressure group will use this result to influence business and the government. *Business impact:* Less likely that the business will be allowed to go ahead.

Pressure group activity is most likely to influence business decisions when:

- a business sells to consumers and it is very concerned about its public image being damaged by pressure group activity and negative publicity
- a consumer boycott leads to a substantial reduction in sales, especially of goods which cannot easily be stored for future sale
- the pressure group is well organised and has done much research to support its claims about business activity, for example, the damage it causes to the environment
- a business can make a change in its activities quickly and at low cost without affecting future profit greatly
- governments believe that taking action against a business activity criticised by a pressure group will win many votes at election time
- there is great public support for the pressure group's campaigns.

> **Definitions to learn**
> **Pressure groups** are groups of people who act together to try to force businesses or governments to adopt certain policies.

> **Key info**
> Greenpeace wants everyone to make the change to a safe, secure energy future for all, with 100% of energy being powered by solar, wind and other clean, renewable sources.

The role of pressure groups

▲ Demonstrations and protests help publicise the objectives of pressure groups

Case study: Achme Oil Company

For years, Achme Oil Company had been dumping waste products in the sea. The company argued that the dumping was far out at sea and so it harmed no one. It was a much cheaper method of getting rid of the waste than buying equipment to treat the waste. Low costs helped the company to keep down prices for consumers.

Environmental pressure groups had taken action against the business for not taking ethical decisions but it was ineffective. Then, thousands of dead fish and sea birds started to be washed up on the east coast. After examination it was found that they contained dangerous levels of oil-based poisons. Achme Oil denied all responsibility and blamed a recent oil spill from another business's tanker. Environmental pressure groups started to blockade Achme's gas (petrol) filling stations. They gained great support from the public. Achme's sales fell but it refused to change its policy. News reporters from other countries followed the story closely.

The Chief Executive was suddenly replaced and a press conference was announced for the following week. Perhaps the company was about to change its environmental policy after all.

Activity 31.2

Read the case study above.

a   Define 'pressure group'.
b   Why was Achme Oil Company unwilling to change its dumping policy after the fish and birds were washed ashore?
c   Explain **two** reasons why pressure groups might be successful in changing the business's decision in this case.
d   Do you think that Achme Oil Company should stop dumping waste and buy equipment to treat it? Give reasons for your answer.

Activity 31.3

Choose a pressure group that operates either in your country or internationally.

a   What is the pressure group trying to change or achieve?
b   What methods is it using to try to bring about change?

31 BUSINESS AND ETHICAL ISSUES, AND PRESSURE GROUPS

International business in focus

McDonald's switches to paper straws

McDonald's switched from giving out plastic straws to giving out paper ones, partly under pressure from environmental pressure groups and partly in preparation for the ban on the use of plastic straws in the UK. Environment America was one of the groups putting pressure on the company to stop giving out plastic straws. However, the paper straws it used were not recyclable, whereas the plastic straws were. To help reduce waste the paper straws will only be given out when requested by a customer. The restaurants have switched to biodegradable paper-based straws.

Discussion points

- Explain why you think McDonald's switched to paper straws in some countries.
- Do you think paper straws will be used in McDonald's restaurants in every country?

Chapter review questions: Short answer and data response

1. MST is a large steelmaking business. Sales and profits are falling. The Directors are under pressure from the owners to make the business more profitable. A Director has announced that MST will change many of its suppliers unless they immediately accept a 10% reduction in their prices. MST has recently closed 2 steelworks and opened a new steelworks in a low-income country. There are not many pollution controls in this country. Wages are low and some children are employed in the steel production process. 'Short-term profits must be increased as a priority,' said Marie, the Chief Executive of MST, 'ethical decisions can come later.' The international pressure group Ethical Business Action (EBA) is planning ways to try to influence MST's decisions.
   a. Identify **two** ways in which MST could be said to be operating 'unethically'. [2]
   b. Outline **two** possible disadvantages to the company of operating in these ways. [4]
   c. Explain **two** ways the EBA might influence MST's decisions. [6]
   d. Do you agree with Marie when she says: 'Short-term profits must be increased as a priority, ethical decisions can come later'? Justify your answer. [8]

2. CDK is a multinational clothes retailer. It purchases all of its supplies of clothes that it sells from low-cost manufacturers. CDK recently cancelled a contract with 1 of its largest clothing suppliers when it increased its prices. This led to the supplier making many employees redundant due to the cancellation of orders. CDK switched to another clothing manufacturer in another country that pays very low wages and offers no employment security for its employees. An international pressure group is using a social media campaign to try to organise a consumer boycott of CDK shops. CDK's Managing Director thinks this boycott will fail as most consumers do not care where clothes are made, only that they are fashionable and low priced.
   a. Define 'pressure group'. [2]
   b. Outline **two** ethical issues in this case. [4]
   c. Explain **two** ways in which CDK could respond to these ethical issues. [6]
   d. Do you think that the pressure group will succeed in changing CDK's approach to ethical issues? Justify your answer. [8]

Revision checklist

In this chapter you have learned:

- ✔ the ethical issues which may affect businesses
- ✔ how businesses may respond to ethical issues
- ✔ the advantages and disadvantages to a business of being ethical
- ✔ how pressure groups can influence business decisions.

NOW – test your understanding with the revision questions in the Student etextbook and the Workbook

External influences on business activity: end-of-section case study

Case study: FirstElectricity

FirstElectricity is a large company that generates electricity. The company has 10 power stations that use imported coal and 2 power stations that use water to produce electricity. The directors of FirstElectricity are considering building a new power station near Main City.

Main City is the capital of Country Z. It has been growing rapidly over the last 5 years as new businesses have set up and existing businesses have expanded. The population of the city has also grown as people from surrounding towns and villages have moved into Main City in search of jobs. Wages of skilled employees have been rising but unemployment for unskilled people is high. The supply of electricity has become a problem, with more and more power cuts occurring.

FirstElectricity is planning to build a dam across a wide river near the capital city if it gets permission from the government. A dam blocks a river and creates a reservoir of water. Electricity is made as the water passes through the dam. This new power station would provide all the electricity needed by Main City and would be very profitable.

The reservoir behind the dam, if built, will be used by FirstElectricity to provide leisure facilities for people from Main City. They are considering having either the hire of rowing boats or swimming facilities in the reservoir.

Appendix 1

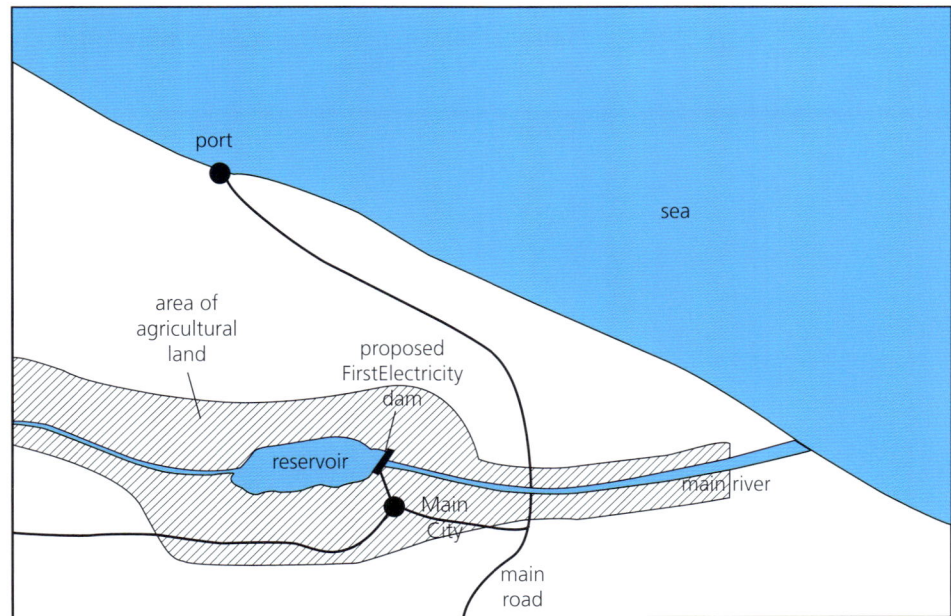

▲ Map of the proposed area for the dam

31 BUSINESS AND ETHICAL ISSUES, AND PRESSURE GROUPS

Appendix 2

Extract from *Main City Times*, 3 November 2024

Will we benefit from the new power station?

Environmental groups have been protesting as FirstElectricity plans to build a dam over the country's widest river. If the dam is not built then the government claims there will be more power cuts. Businesses may lose a lot of output and profit if they cannot manufacture products. Environmental groups claim the dam will destroy thousands of acres of excellent agricultural land and food supplies will be reduced. Food imports will increase and this might cause Country Z's exchange rate to depreciate.

Many people will be forced to leave their homes and move to another area. A government spokesperson said the future growth of the country could be reduced if the dam is not built. Multinational companies may be put off locating in Country Z if the power station is not built.

Practice questions: Case study

1. a. Explain **two** external costs and **two** external benefits of building the dam. [8]
   b. Consider the advantages and disadvantages for Country Z of having multinationals locate there. Should the government allow multinational companies to locate in Country Z? Justify your answer. [12]

2. a. Explain **two** effects on a food-processing business in Country Z if its exchange rate appreciates. [8]
   b. Using all of the information available to you from the case study, consider the advantages and disadvantages of building the dam. Should the government allow the dam to be built? Justify your answer. [12]

Optional questions
The following questions ask you to think about topics covered in earlier sections of this textbook. You can choose not to answer them if you prefer to focus on just the topics covered in this section at this time.

3. a. FirstElectricity will need to recruit construction employees to build the dam. Outline **four** stages of the recruitment and selection process FirstElectricity will need to follow to employ these people. [8]
   b. Consider **two** methods of training that could be used for these new employees. Which method should be used for the construction employees? Justify your answer. [12]

4. a. Explain how **four** different stakeholder groups will be affected by the building of the dam. [8]
   b. FirstElectricity plans to use the reservoir behind the dam to provide either the hire of rowing boats or swimming facilities for the people of Main City. Consider the advantages and disadvantages of using questionnaires and focus groups to find out which activity will be the most popular. Which of these market research methods should FirstElectricity use? Justify your answer. [12]

Glossary

3D printing Producing a physical three-dimensional object from a digital design.

Added value The difference between the selling price of a product and the cost of bought-in materials and resources needed to produce it.

Advertising A paid-for communication with potential customers about a product to encourage them to buy it.

Agent An independent person or business that is appointed to deal with the sales and distribution of a product or range of products.

Annual General Meeting (AGM) A legal requirement for all public limited companies. Shareholders may attend and vote on who they want to be on the Board of Directors for the coming year.

Assets Items of value owned by a business.

Autocratic leadership Where the manager takes all decisions in the business and expects to have their orders followed.

Automation The use of advanced technology to make a production method work automatically without employee control.

Average costs Calculated by dividing total costs by the number of units produced. Sometimes called cost per unit.

Bank loan A sum of money obtained from a bank which must be repaid and on which interest is payable.

Bank overdrafts A short-term source of flexible finance which allow more money to be drawn out of the bank account than there is money in the account.

Batch production Where a quantity of one product is made, then a quantity of another item will be produced.

Bonus An additional payment above basic pay as a reward for good work.

Boom Where the economy is growing very fast and costs and prices start to rise quickly.

Brand image An image or identity given to a product which distinguishes it from competitors' brands.

Brand loyalty When consumers keep buying the same brand instead of choosing a competitor's product.

Brand name The unique name of a product that distinguishes it from other brands.

Break-even charts Show how costs and revenue of a business change with sales and indicate break-even output.

Break-even output The quantity that must be produced or sold for total revenue to equal total costs.

Break-even point The level of output and sales at which total costs = total revenue.

Business An organisation that combines factors of production to make products (goods and services) which satisfy people's wants.

Business cycle The fluctuations over time between periods of economic growth and economic contraction.

Business objectives The aims or targets that a business works towards.

Business plan A written document that describes a business, its objectives, its strategies, the market it is in and its financial forecasts.

Capital The money invested into a business by the owners.

Capital employed The total amount of capital invested in a business for the purpose of generating profits.

Cash flow (of a business) The cash inflows and outflows over a period of time.

Cash flow forecast An estimate of future cash inflows and outflows of a business, usually on a month-by-month basis, showing the expected cash balance at the end of each month.

Cash inflows The sums of money received by a business during a period of time.

Cash outflows The sums of money paid out by a business during a period of time.

Chain of command is the way in which authority, control and instructions are passed down from senior management to lower levels.

Closing balance The cash held by the business at the end of each period of time.

Commission A payment linked to the number of sales made, often in addition to a basic wage.

Communication The transferring of a message from the sender to the receiver, who understands the message.

Communication barriers Factors that stop the effective communication of messages.

Competitive pricing When the product is priced in line with competitors' prices to try to maintain sales and market share.

Computer-aided design (CAD) The use of IT to help create, modify and improve designs.

Computer-aided manufacturing (CAM) The use of software and computer-controlled machinery to automate a manufacturing process.

Consumer Someone who buys goods or services for personal use – not to re-sell.

Consumer boycott When consumers decide not to buy products from a business that does not act in an environmentally responsible way.

Contract of employment A legal agreement between an employer and an employee, listing the rights and responsibilities of employees.

Contribution per unit (of a product) The selling price per unit minus variable costs per unit.

Cost of sales The cost of producing or buying in the goods actually sold by the business during a time period.

Cost-plus pricing The cost of manufacturing the product plus a profit mark-up.

Crowdfunding Funding a business venture by raising money from a large number of people who each contribute a relatively small amount, typically via the internet.

Current assets Assets that are owned by a business and converted into cash within one year.

Current liabilities Short-term debts that must be paid within one year.

Customer A person or business which buys goods or services from a business.

Glossary

Customer loyalty When existing customers continually buy products from the same business.

Customer relationships Communicating with customers to encourage them to become loyal to the business and its products.

Delegation Giving a subordinate the authority to perform particular tasks.

Democratic leadership Involves employees in the decision-making process but the final decision is left to the leader.

Depletion of resources When resources are being consumed at a faster rate than they can be replenished.

Directors Senior managers who lead a particular department or division of a business.

Diseconomies of scale The factors that lead to an increase in average costs as a business grows beyond a certain size.

Distribution channel The means by which a product is passed from the producer to the customer.

Dividends Payments made to shareholders from the profits (after tax) of a company. They are the return to shareholders for investing in the company.

Downsizing Permanently reducing the number of people a business employs.

Dynamic pricing When businesses change the price of a product, usually when selling online, depending on the level of demand.

Ecommerce (or electronic commerce) is the online buying and selling of goods and services using internet-linked devices such as laptops and smartphones.

Economic growth When real GDP increases, which is the value of GDP after taking inflation into account.

Economies of scale The factors that lead to a reduction in average costs as a business increases in size.

Email A digital communication tool used for sending messages, documents and other information to specific people or groups.

Employee selection The process of evaluating applicants for a specific job and selecting an individual for employment based on the needs of the organisation.

Entrepreneur A person who has an idea for a new business, starts it up and accepts the risks of the new business venture.

Environment Our natural world including, for example, pure air, clean water and undeveloped countryside.

Environmentally friendly products Products that do not cause damage to the environment when they are produced.

Environmental responsibility When a business considers the impact on the environment when taking decisions.

Ethical decisions Decisions based on a moral code and are sometimes referred to as 'doing the right thing'.

Ethical issue A situation where there is a possible conflict between moral standards.

Exchange rate The price of one currency in terms of another currency, for example 1 euro = $1.50.

Exchange rate appreciation When the value of a currency rises – it buys more of another currency than before.

Exchange rate depreciation When the value of a currency falls – it buys less of another currency than before.

Expenses The fixed costs of the business during a period of time.

Extension strategy A way of keeping a product at the maturity stage of the life cycle and extending the cycle over a longer period of time.

External communication Communication between the organisation and other organisations or individuals.

External costs The costs imposed on a third party that are independent of the original economic transaction.

External benefits The benefits imposed on a third party that are independent of the original economic transaction.

External finance Obtained from sources outside of and separate to the business.

External growth Growth that occurs when a business takes over or merges with another business. It is often called integration as one business is integrated into another one.

External recruitment When a vacancy is filled by someone who is not an existing employee and is new to the business.

External stakeholders Individuals or groups who are separate from the business but have a direct interest in the performance and activities of the business.

Factors of production Those resources needed to produce goods or services. There are four factors of production and they are in limited supply.

Feedback The reply from the receiver which shows whether the message has arrived, been understood and, if necessary, acted upon.

Finance Money or capital needed to pay for expenditure.

Fixed costs Costs which do not vary in the short run with the number of items sold or produced.

Flexible working Allows employees to choose when to start and stop work and where to work, as long as the contracted hours are completed.

Flow production Where large quantities of a product are produced in a continuous process.

Focus group A group of people who are representative of the target market, brought together to discuss opinions about products and promotions.

Franchise A business based upon the use of the brand name, promotional logo and product ideas of an existing successful business.

Franchisee A person who buys the licence to operate an outlet of an existing business from the franchisor.

Franchisor The original business that sells the right to a franchisee to use its name and idea. The franchisor sells the right to open stores and sell products or services using its brand name.

Free trade agreements When countries agree to trade imports/exports with no barriers such as tariffs and quotas.

Fringe benefits A form of financial motivation given in addition to an employee's regular form of payment.

Full-time employees Usually work 35 hours or more a week.

Glossary

Globalisation Increases in worldwide trade and the movement of people and capital between countries.

Goods Tangible products made by businesses to be sold to customers, such as cars and clothes.

Government grant A sum of money awarded to a business by the government which does not have to be paid back.

Gross domestic product (GDP) The total value of output of goods and services in a country in one year.

Gross profit Made when revenue is greater than the cost of sales.

Hierarchical structure A structure with different levels of authority and a chain of command.

Hire purchase Allows a business to buy a non-current asset over a long period of time with monthly payments which include an interest charge.

Home working Employees are given the option to work from home rather than at the normal place of employment.

Horizontal integration When one business merges with or takes over another one in the same industry at the same stage of production.

Import quota A limit on the quantity of a product that can be imported.

Import tariff A tax put on imported goods when they arrive into the country.

Incorporated businesses Companies that have separate legal identity from their owners.

Induction training An introduction given to a new employee, explaining the business's activities, customs and procedures and introducing them to fellow employees.

Industrial tribunal A type of court that makes judgments on disagreements between businesses and their employees, for example, complaints of unfair dismissal or discrimination at work.

Inflation When the average price level of goods and services rises over a period of time.

Internal communication Communication between members of the same organisation.

Internal finance Finance obtained from within the business itself or from owners, if it is an unincorporated business.

Internal growth Growth that occurs when a business expands its existing operations.

Internal recruitment When a vacancy is filled by someone who is an existing employee of the business.

Internal stakeholders Individuals or groups who work within or own the business. They have a direct interest in the performance and activities of the business.

Internet banking (also known as online banking) A system of electronic payment that enables customers of a bank to make a range of financial transactions through the bank's website.

Interviews Asking individuals a series of questions, often face-to-face or over the phone.

Inventory The raw materials, semi-processed goods and finished goods held by a business at any one time.

Job analysis Identifies and records the responsibilities and tasks related to a job.

Job description Outlines the responsibilities and duties to be carried out by someone employed to do a specific job.

Job enrichment Involves giving employees work tasks that require more skill and responsibility.

Job production Where a single product is made at a time, usually to a customer's specific requirement.

Job rotation Involves workers swapping jobs and doing each specific task for only a limited time and then changing jobs again.

Job satisfaction The enjoyment derived from feeling that you have done a good job.

Joint venture Where two or more businesses start a new project together, sharing capital, risks and profits.

Just-in-time (JIT) A production method that involves reducing or virtually eliminating the need to hold inventories of raw materials or unsold inventories of the finished product.

Kaizen A Japanese term meaning 'continuous improvement' through the elimination of waste.

Labour productivity The amount of work done or the number of units produced by a worker in a given time period e.g. one week.

Laissez-faire leadership Makes the broad objectives of the business known to employees but then they are left to make their own decisions and organise their own work.

Leadership styles The different approaches to dealing with people and making decisions when in a position of authority – autocratic, democratic or laissez-faire.

Lean production Aims to use fewer inputs, cut down on waste and therefore increase efficiency.

Leasing Allows a business to pay a regular leasing charge to use the asset without buying it.

Legal controls (on marketing) Laws passed by government to protect consumers from faulty goods, unsafe goods and misleading promotion.

Legal minimum wage The minimum wage rate per hour that employers must pay to employees.

Level of hierarchy Managers/supervisors/other employees who are given a similar level of responsibility in an organisation.

Liabilities Amounts owed by a business to be paid at a future date.

Limited liability The liability of shareholders in a company is limited to only the amount of money they invested.

Liquidity The ability of a business to pay back its short-term debts.

Long-term bank loan A loan that is repayable with interest over more than one year.

Long-term finance Provides capital which can be repaid over a period of time longer than one year.

Margin of safety The amount by which the current level of output or sales is greater than the break-even level of sales/output.

Glossary

Marketing Identifying customer wants and satisfying them profitably.

Marketing mix Used to describe all the activities which go into marketing a product or service. These activities are often summarised as the four Ps – product, price, place and promotion.

Market segment An identifiable sub-group of a whole market in which consumers have similar characteristics or preferences.

Market segmentation When a business knows that different segments of a market exist and it develops and markets different products to each segment.

Market share The percentage of total sales revenue for the whole market held by one brand or business.

Market research The process of gathering, analysing and interpreting information about a market.

Marketing strategy A plan with a marketing objective and details of the marketing mix that aims to achieve it.

Mass market Where a business sells to the largest part of the market, often where standardised products are being sold.

Mechanisation The introduction of machines into production methods.

Merger When the owners of two businesses agree to join their businesses together to make one business.

Message The information or instructions being passed by the sender to the receiver.

Motivation The reason why employees want to work hard and work effectively for the business.

Multinational companies (MNCs) Companies with factories, production or service operations in more than one country.

Net cash flow The difference between cash inflows and cash outflows during each period of time, usually one month.

Niche market A small, usually specialised, segment of a much larger market.

Non-current assets Property, machinery and other assets owned by a business which will not be turned into cash within one year.

Non-current liabilities Long-term debts owed by the business, repaid over more than one year.

Observation A method of market research that collects data about consumer behaviour by watching them and recording their actions when buying or choosing between products.

Off-the-job training Involves being trained away from the workplace, usually by specialist trainers.

On-the-job training Occurs when a trainee observes and practises with an experienced employee at the workplace.

Online shopping The action or activity of buying goods or services over the internet.

Online ticketing Booking a service such as a flight or cinema seat and receiving an online ticket which can either be printed out or stored in a device's memory.

Opening balance The cash held by the business at the start of each period of time.

Opportunity cost The value of the next best alternative given up when choosing one option over another.

Organisational chart A diagram that outlines the departmental and management structure.

Organisational structure The levels of management and division of responsibilities within an organisation.

Packaging The physical container or wrapping to protect a product and help in promoting it.

Partnership Formed when two or more people agree to jointly own a business.

Partnership agreement The written and legal agreement between business partners. It is not essential for partners to have such an agreement, but it is always recommended.

Part-time employee Someone who works fewer hours than a full-time employee. This is often less than 35 hours a week.

Penetration pricing When the price is set lower than competitors' prices in order to be able to enter a new market and gain market share.

Person specification A document which outlines the requirements, qualifications, expertise and personal characteristics a successful applicant should have.

Piece-rate An employee payment method that is paid for each unit of output produced.

Pollution The introduction of harmful materials into the environment.

Pressure groups Groups of people who act together to try to force businesses or governments to adopt certain policies.

Price skimming Where a high price is set for a new product on the market.

Primary market research (also called field research) The collection and collation of original data via direct contact with potential or existing consumers.

Primary sector The sector of industry that extracts and uses the natural resources from the Earth to produce raw materials used by other businesses.

Private limited companies Businesses owned by shareholders but they cannot sell shares to the public – only to family, friends or specialist business investors.

Private sector The part of the economy owned and operated by individuals and companies, usually for profit, and is not state/government controlled.

Product life cycle The stages a product will pass through, from its introduction, through its growth to maturity and then finally its decline.

Productivity The output measured against the inputs used to create a product or service and is a measure of efficiency.

Profit The surplus after total costs have been subtracted from total revenue.

Profitability Measures the profit of a business in comparison to its revenue or capital employed.

Profit sharing When a proportion of business profits is paid out to employees.

Promotion The advancement of an employee in an organisation, for example, to a higher job/managerial level.

Glossary

Promotion (marketing) The marketing activities of advertising and sales promotion which aim to raise customer awareness of a product or brand, generate sales and help create brand loyalty.

Public limited companies Businesses owned by shareholders but, unlike private limited companies, they can sell shares to the public. Their shares are traded on stock exchanges.

Public sector Organisations in the economy that are owned and controlled by the government.

Quality assurance Setting quality standards throughout the production process and checking these are reached at each stage of the process.

Quality control Checking for quality of a good or service at the end of the production process.

Quality products Of a standard which meets customer expectations.

Questionnaire A set of questions to be answered as a means of collecting data for primary market research.

Real income The spending power of income. It falls when prices rise faster than money income and rises when incomes increase faster than inflation.

Recession When there is a period of falling GDP.

Recruitment The process that starts with identifying that the business needs to employ someone up to the point at which applications have arrived at the business.

Recycling Takes previously used products and materials and reprocesses them so they can be used again.

Redundancy When an employee loses their job because the business closes down or the work done by the employee is no longer needed.

Redundancy payments Made to employees by the business when they are made redundant.

Renewable energy Power obtained from sources that are not used up in energy production, such as solar and wind power.

Retailer A business that sells products to customers in relatively small quantities.

Reusing Not throwing items away after one use but using them again or using them for another purpose.

Revenue The income of a business from the sale of goods or services during a period of time.

Salary Payment for work, usually paid monthly, and is not usually for a specific number of hours worked.

Sales promotions Incentives such as special offers or reward schemes aimed at consumers to achieve short-term increases in sales.

Sample A group of people who are selected to respond to a primary market research exercise, such as a questionnaire.

Secondary market research (also called desk research) Uses information that has already been collected and is available for use by others.

Secondary sector The sector of industry that manufactures goods using the raw materials provided by the primary sector.

Services Intangible products, such as banking or transport, that are provided by businesses to customers.

Shareholders The owners of a limited company. They buy shares which represent part-ownership of the company.

Short-term finance Provides the working capital needed by businesses for day-to-day operations and is repaid within one year.

Slump A very serious recession with rapid falls in output and increases in unemployment.

Social enterprise A business that has social objectives as well as an aim to make a profit to reinvest back into the business.

Social media Online platforms and networks that facilitate social interaction and content sharing with other users.

Social responsibility When a business aims to benefit stakeholders other than shareholders such as by protecting the environment by reducing pollution and using the most sustainable production methods.

Sole trader A business owned and controlled by one person.

Span of control is the number of subordinates working directly under a manager.

Stakeholder Any person or group with a direct interest in the performance and activities of a business.

Start-up capital The finance needed by a new business to pay for essential non-current assets and current assets before it can begin trading.

Statement of financial position Shows the value of a business's assets and liabilities at a particular time.

Statement of profit or loss A financial account that records the income of a business and all costs incurred to earn that income over a period of time, for example, one year.

Strike When a trade union tells its members not to work in order to put pressure on employers to meet trade union demands.

Sustainable production Needs businesses to minimise the use of natural resources and dangerous materials and to reduce waste and pollution.

Takeover When one business buys out the owners of another business, which then becomes part of the 'predator' business (the business which has taken it over/become the new owner).

Tertiary sector The sector of industry that provides services to consumers and the other economic sectors.

Time-based rate The amount paid to an employee for one hour of work.

Total assets Non-current assets plus current assets.

Total costs The addition of all fixed and variable costs of a business in a given time period.

Total fixed costs The addition of all of the fixed costs of a business.

Total liabilities Non-current liabilities plus current liabilities.

Total variable costs The addition of all variable costs at a certain level of output.

Trade credit When a business is allowed to pay a supplier some time after materials have been purchased.

Trade receivables Amounts owed to the business by customers who purchased products on credit.

Glossary

Trade union A group of employees who have joined together to ensure their interests are protected.

Training The process of improving an employee's skills.

Unemployment When people who are willing and able to work cannot find employment.

Unfair dismissal When an employer ends an employee's contract of employment for a reason that is not covered by that contract.

Unincorporated business One that does not have a separate legal identity to the owners of the business.

Unique Selling Point (USP) The special feature of a product that differentiates it from the products of competitors.

Unlimited liability The owners of a business can be held responsible for the debts of the business they own. Their liability is not limited to the investment they made in the business.

Variable costs Costs which vary with the number of items sold or produced.

Variable cost per unit The addition of all variable costs of producing one unit of output.

Venture capital Provided by investors who are prepared to take risks by offering finance to start-up companies or small companies that have good growth potential.

Vertical integration When one business merges with or takes over another one in the same industry at a different stage of production. Vertical integration can be forward or backward.

Virtual meeting A method of communication that enables people in different physical locations to use their mobile phone or internet-connected device to meet in the same virtual room.

Wage Payment for work, usually paid weekly.

Wholesaler A business that buys in bulk from a manufacturer and then sells to retailers in smaller quantities.

Working capital The finance needed by a business to pay its day-to-day expenses.

Index

3D printing 231

A

accounting
   analysis 321–30
   cash flow 293–302
   financial position 313–19
   profit and loss 304–11
acid test ratio 325
added value 2–4, 218
advertising 188, 191–3, 195
age
   ageing populations 135
   market segmentation 140
Agelvipa Online 13
Airbnb 203
Airbus 363
Alibaba Group 45
Alphabet Inc. 48
   see also Google
Amazon Web Services 112
Ambani, Mukesh 13
Annual General Meeting (AGM) 38
annualised hours 85
Apple 23, 28, 38, 160, 170, 187
application forms 67
appreciation 353–4
aptitude tests 67
Articles of Association 35
artificial intelligence (AI) 232
assets 314
   current 314, 317
   non-current 278–9, 314, 317
   sale of 282
AstraZeneca 29
autocratic leadership 92–3
automation 95, 219, 230
average costs 244–5

B

bank loans 285
bank overdrafts 284
banking 198, 200, 236
bar charts 156
barriers, to communication 109–12
batch production 225
bias 154
billboards 192
BMW 44
bonuses 120
boom 336
boycotts 360, 368
branding 160–2, 195
break-even 250–6
breakfast cereals 163
Brilliance Automotive Ltd 44
business activity
   factors of production 1–2
   stages of production 5–6

business cycle 335–6
business plan 15–18
business size 20–2

C

capital 1–2, 12, 278–83
capital employed 20–2, 316, 323
CapitaLand 291
capital-intensive production 218
carbon emissions 57
cash flow 293–302
cash flow forecast 296–300
chain of command 82–4
charities 45, 365
Chief Executive Officers (CEOs) 69
China
   Gracell Biotechnologies takeover 29
   joint ventures 43–4
   millionaires 17
   relocations 274
Coca-Cola 53, 165, 177
commission 120–1
communication 14, 100
   barriers 109–12
   effective 102–3
   external 101
   internal 100–1
   methods of 103–9
companies see private limited
   companies; public limited
   companies
competitions 189
competitive pricing 174
competitiveness 355
competitors 8, 29, 150, 179, 186, 207, 268
Compute 167
computer-aided design (CAD) 230–1
computer-aided manufacturing (CAM) 230–1
confidence 14
consumer 134
   see also customer
consumer goods 160
consumer protection 211–13
contactless payments 231
continuous improvement 222
contract of employment 72, 85, 88
cost of sales 306–7
cost-plus pricing 172–3
costs 172–3, 243–56, 264, 268, 307, 352, 361
COVID-19 pandemic 86
credit 284–5
crowdfunding 286
cultural factors 209–10
current assets 314, 317
current liabilities 281, 314, 317
curriculum vitaes (CVs) 67

customer 132
   loyalty 133, 161, 189
   needs 133
   protection 211–13
   spending patterns 134–5

D

data, analysis 154–7
delayering 83
delegation 91–2
demand 28, 95, 176
democratic leadership 93
departments see functional
   departments
depreciation 353–4
direct distribution 182
direct mail 192
directors 82
disabilities 73
discrimination 73
diseconomies of scale 248–9
dismissal 61, 72, 97
distribution 133
distribution channels 181–7
dividends 38, 48, 339
Domino's Pizza 210
downsizing 95–6, 98
dynamic pricing 175–6
Dyson 28

E

ecommerce 135, 198–203, 346
economic change 29, 47, 134, 337–40
economic growth 336–8
economic sectors 5–10
economies of scale 247–9
efficiency 219–20
electric vehicles 57, 136
electronic point of sale (EPOS) 232
email 104–5, 110, 112
email marketing 191
emerging markets 57
employee benefits 121–2
employee of the month 125
employee selection 61–2, 67–70
employment
   business size 20–1
   contracts 71–4, 85, 88
   full-time 88–9
   health and safety 73–4
   levels 336
   minimum wage 74
   part-time 88
   recruitment 61–71, 115
   redundancy 61, 95–6
   small businesses 27
   and technology 234–5
   see also unemployment
employment agencies 65

Index

enterprise 2
enterprise zones 19
entrepreneurship 12–19
environmental issues 56, 271, 358–63
   see also sustainable production
environmental objectives 49
equality 73
ethical issues 365–7
exchange rates 353–5
expansion 266, 268
   see also growth
expenses 307
export prices 354
extension strategies 166–9
external communication 101
external costs 352
external finance 281
external growth 23–5
external recruitment 68–9
external stakeholders 51–2
Extinction Rebellion (XR) 368

F

Facebook 13, 45
factors of production 1–2
failure, in business 28–9, 47
feedback 102, 109, 110
finance
   business plan 16
   department 82
   lack of 28
   needs 278–9
   sources of 281–91
financial objectives 48–9
financial position, statement of 313–19
fixed costs 244
flat hierarchy 83
flexible working 84–5
flow production 225–6, 230, 264
focus groups 146–8
franchises 41–3
free trade agreements 347
fringe benefits 121–2
full-time employees 88–9
functional departments 81–2

G

GDX Retail Stores 87
gender, and market segmentation 140
globalisation 135, 346
goods 1, 6, 160
Google 28, 48, 112, 122
government grants 285–6
government policy 338–41, 361
government sources, market research 150
Gracell Biotechnologies 29
grants 19, 285–6
graphs 157

Greenpeace 368
gross domestic product (GDP) 335–6
gross profit 306–7
gross profit margin 322, 324
growth 23–4, 48, 208–9

H

Haihambo, Victoria 13
Hayleys 319
health and safety, employment 73–4
Herzberg, Frederick 117, 122–3
hierarchical structures 82–4
hierarchy of needs 115–16
hire purchase 284–5
home working 85–6
horizontal integration 23–5
human resource management (HRM) 16, 61, 82
   see also employment

I

IBM 348
import costs 354
import tarrifs 348
income
   impact of taxation 339
   and market segmentation 140
   real income 337
incorporated businesses 34–5
independence 14
induction 76–7
industrial relations 61
inflation 336–7
Initial Public Offering (IPO) 37, 45
innovation 14
INOX Leisure 26
interest rates 341–4
internal communication 100–1
internal finance 281
internal growth 23, 25
internal recruitment 68–9
internal stakeholders 51–2
international markets 208–10
internet banking 198, 200
interviews 67–8, 146–7
inventory 220, 224

J

jargon 110
Jawbone 205
job advertisements 64–5
job analysis 62
job description 62–3
job enrichment 123–4
job production 224–5, 264
job rotation 124
job satisfaction 122–3
joint ventures 43–4

journals 151
just-in-time (JIT) production 221–2, 228

K

Kaizen 222
Kellogg 163
KFC 349
Kodak 302
Kraft Heinz 242

L

labour 1, 266, 268
labour productivity 114, 119, 218–19, 234
labour-intensive production 218
laissez-faire leadership 93–4
land 1
leadership styles 92–4
leaflets 192
lean production 220–3
leasing 284
legislation
   consumer protection 211–13
   new markets 210
letters 106
level of hierarchy 82
liabilities 314
   current 281, 314, 317
   non-current 314, 317
life cycle, product 165–9, 194–5
lifestyle, and market segmentation 140
limited liability 33, 35
liquidity 324–6
loans 19, 285, 288, 341–2
location 264–74
   and market segmentation 140
long-term finance 280
Louis Vuitton 175
loyalty, customer 133, 161, 189

M

Malaysia Airlines Academy 79
management
   delegation 91–2
   functions of 89–90
   leadership styles 92–4
   skills 28
manufacturing 6
margin of safety 253–4
Mari Petroleum (MPCL) 326
market changes 134–6
market reports 151
market research 16, 132, 144, 194–5
   analysing 154–7
   methods 145–51, 146–8
   primary 145–9
   sampling 149, 153
   secondary 149–51
market segmentation 138–42
market share 49, 133, 136

Index

market size 27, 271
marketing 16, 82, 132–4
   legislation 211–13
   strategy 205–10
marketing mix 159, 206–8
   place 159, 181–7, 207
   price 159, 172–9, 207
   product 159–70, 207
   promotion 159, 188–96, 207
markets, new 23, 167, 208–10
Maslow, Abraham 115–16, 123
mass markets 136–7
materials, cost of 3
Mauritius 10
McDonald's 179, 190, 210, 263, 370
mechanisation 230
Medi-Glow Aesthetics 13
meetings 103–4
Memorandum of Association 35
mergers 23–6
Microsoft 112
millionaires 17
minimum wage 74, 271
monopolies 8
Montage Technology Company 13
motivation 73, 83, 110, 114
   benefits of 114–15
   methods of 118–27
   theories of 115–18
multinational companies (MNCs) 347, 349–51

N

natural resources 1, 6, 238, 350–1
new markets 23, 167, 208–10
newly industrialised countries 346
newspapers 192
niche markets 136–8
Nike 115, 207, 360
non-current assets 278–9, 314, 317
non-current liabilities 314, 317
noticeboards 107

O

objectives 16, 47–9
   changing 50
   importance of 50–1
   and pricing 179
   of stakeholders 51–6
observation 148
off-the-job training 77–8
Oilco 55
online shopping 199, 200–1
online ticketing 199, 200–1
on-the-job training 77
operations department 81
opportunity cost 5, 12
organisation types 31
organisational charts 82–3, 87
organisational structures 81–4, 87
output 21, 116
overdrafts 284
over-processing 220
overproduction 220
overtime 119
Oxygen Media 13

P

packaging 56, 162–3, 168, 239, 242, 360
partnerships 32–3, 40–1
part-time employees 88
penetration pricing 174–5
perishability 185, 224
person specification 62, 63–4
personality tests 67
phone calls 106
pie charts 156
piece-rate wages 119
Pillsbury 165
planning 89
plastic packaging 56, 360
pollution 358–9
posters 106–7
praise 125
premises 19
pressure groups 368
price skimming 175
pricing 3, 159, 172–9, 207, 211
primary market research 145–9
primary sector 6
print advertising 192
private limited companies 34–6, 40–1, 45
private sector 7–8, 27, 36, 304–5
producer goods 160
product information 162
product life cycle 165–9, 194–5
production
   just-in-time (JIT) 221–2, 228
   lean production 220–3
   methods 224–7, 264
   overproduction 220
   processes 217
   stages of 5–6
   sustainable 237–42
   use of technology 230–6
productivity
   labour productivity 114, 119, 218–19, 234
   and technology 231–3
profit 48, 295, 304–11
   gross 306–7, 322, 324
   impact of taxation 339
   margin 322–4
   repatriation 350
   retained 281–2, 309, 339
   sharing 121
profit or loss statements 305–10
profitability 321
promotion (employee) 83, 125
promotion (products/services) 132–3, 159, 188–96, 207
protectionism 348
public limited companies 36–9, 40–1, 45
public sector 8–9
PVR Cinemas 26

Q

QR codes 199
quality 211, 258–62
quality assurance 260–2
quality control 260–2
questionnaires 146–7, 153
quotas 348

R

random sampling 149
Rangsutra Foundation 49
ratio analysis 326–30
raw materials 265, 272
real income 337
recession 47–8, 95, 336
recruitment 61–71, 115
recycling 360
redundancy 61, 95–6, 234
references 67
Reliance Industries 13
renewable energy 237, 360
resources
   depletion 359
   natural 6
retailers 182
retained profit 281–2, 309, 339
return on capital employed (ROCE) 323
reusing 238
revenue 246, 304, 306–7
reward schemes 189
risk 12, 14, 209
Rolls-Royce 262

S

salaries 120
   see also wages
sale of assets 282
sales, and business size 21
sales agents 183–4
sales promotions 189–90, 194
sales team 132
sampling 149, 153
Saudi Aramco 45
secondary market research 149–51
secondary sector 6
security 269
services 1, 6, 160
share capital 283, 319

Index

share price 48
   see also public limited companies
shareholders 33–4, 38, 339
shareholders' equity 314
Sheeran, Ed 196
Shell 330
short-term finance 280
size of business 20–2
skills tests 67
slump 336
small businesses 27
smartphones 135, 160, 170, 198
soap, market segmentation 139
social enterprises 45, 49
social media 101, 105, 191
social objectives 49
social responsibility 358
solar panels 237
sole traders 31–2, 40–1
sources of information 150–1
span of control 82–4
special offers 190
spending patterns 134–5
Sportsmaster 231
Spotify 98
stakeholders 51–6
Starbucks 4, 356
start-up capital 278–9
start-ups, support for 19
statement of financial position 313–19
statement of profit or loss 305–10
stock exchange 37, 38
stress 84
strike action 97
success, in business 28
Sunlife 311
survival 47–8
sustainable production 237–42

T

tables (data) 155
takeovers 23–4
tall hierarchy 83–4
target market 149, 194–5, 207
tarrifs 271, 348
taxation 339
Taylor, Frederick 116
team working 85, 88
technology
   and consumer choice 135
   investing in 279
   and market changes 142
   in production 230–6
television advertising 192
tertiary sector 6
Tesla 20–1, 256, 271
Tesseract Imaging 157
text messaging 105
time-based wages 118–19
Tose Somolekae, Wedu 13
tourism 10
Toyota 20–1, 28, 57, 210, 228
trade agreements 347
trade credit 285
trade magazines 151
trade receivables 314
trade unions 96–7
training 19, 61, 75–9, 219, 240
   induction 76–7
   on-the-job 77
   and motivation 124
   off-the-job 77–8
transportation 220, 266, 346
trust 85
Tunweni Drinks 241
turnover of staff 115

U

Uber 45
unemployment 336, 342
unfair dismissal 72, 97
Unilever (Malaysia) Holdings 184
unincorporated businesses 33
unique selling point (USP) 164
unlimited liability 33

V

value added 2–4
variable costs 244
venture capital 283
vertical integration 24–5
virtual meetings 103, 112
vouchers 189

W

wages 118–19, 271
Walmart 38, 184
waste, in production 220–2, 238, 360
websites 150
weights and measures 211
wholesalers 182–3
Winfrey, Oprah 13
working capital 280–2, 317
working from home 85–6

Y

Yang, Howard 13
Yeo's 213

Z

Zoom 112
Zuckerberg, Mark 13

Acknowledgements

The Publishers would like to thank the following for permission to reproduce copyright material.

p.274 © Hongyan Zhao. "Chinese Companies Are On the Move – Inland and to Southeast Asia" AMRO, February 6, 2024, https://amro-asia.org/chinese-companies-are-on-the-move-inland-and-to-southeast-asia; **p.367** The material "Chocolate giants reap huge profits as promises to improve farmers' incomes 'ring hollow' – Annie Theriault – 11th May 2023" is adapted by the publisher with the permission of Oxfam, Oxfam House, John Smith Drive, Cowley, Oxford OX4 2JY UK www.oxfam.org.uk. Oxfam does not necessarily endorse any text or activities that accompany the materials, nor has it approved the adapted text.

Photos

t = top, *b* = bottom, *l* = left, *r* = right, *m* = middle

p.viii © Rudy Balasko/Shutterstock.com; **p.2** *l* © withGod – Fotolia.com, *m* © artush – Fotolia.com, *r* © snapfoto105 – Fotolia.com; **p.4** © JHVEPhoto/stock.adobe.com; **p.5** *tl* © solerf/123rf.com, *tm* © hamik/123rf.com, *tr* © naughtynut/123rf.com, *bl* © mtoome/123rf.com, *bm* © mbongo/123rf.com, *br* © EyeMark/123rf.com; **p.6** *t* © bieszczady_wildlife/Shutterstock.com, *m* © Stasique/stock.adobe.com, *b* © Bohdan/stock.adobe.com; **p.7** *l* © forcdan – Fotolia.com, *m* © Imago/Alamy Stock Photo, *r* © frans lemmens/Alamy; **p.10** © Sara Berdon – Fotolia.com; **p.13** © T Mdlungu/peopleimages.com/stock.adobe.com; **p.22** *l* © svedoliver – Fotolia.com, *r* © gemenacom – Fotolia.com; **p.26** © Viacheslav Muzyka/Alamy Stock Photo; **p.29** © Drazen/stock.adobe.com; **p.38** *l* © zhang jiahan/Alamy Stock Photo, *r* © saiko3p/stock.adobe.com; **p.44** © VCG/VCG via Getty Images; **p.45** © Gorodenkoff/Shutterstock.com; **p.49** © www.Rangsutra.com; **p.57** © Toyota Motor Corporation. All Rights Reserved; **p.59** © JackF – Fotolia.com; **p.60** © insta_photos/stock.adobe.com; **p.77** *t* © auremar – Fotolia.com, *b* © sofiko14/stock.adobe.com; **p.79** © zapper/stock.adobe.com; **p.98** © Maria Vitkovska/stock.adobe.com; **p.112** © Kateryna/stock.adobe.com; **p.128** © Palie Massa/Shutterstock.com; **p.131** © martin berry/Alamy Stock Photo; **p.134** © Richard Levine/Alamy Stock Photo; **p.139** *l to r* © Rafael Ben-Ari – Fotolia.com, © Ladanifer/stock.adobe.com, © Jaak Nilson/Alamy Stock Photo, © Maria Sokor/Alamy Stock Photo; **p.141** *tl* © TeTe Song/stock.adobe.com, *tr* © VanderWolf Images/stock.adobe.com, *bl* © Zoran Karapancev/Shutterstock.com, *br* © Zoran Karapancev/stock.adobe.com; **p.142** *l to r* © fergregory – Fotolia.com, © patrikslezak/stock.adobe.com, © Nikolai Sorokin – Fotolia.com, © Science Photo Library/Alamy Stock Photo, © gangster9686/stock.adobe.com; **p.146** © Prostock-studio/stock.adobe.com; **p.147** © wavebreakmedia/Shutterstock.com; **p.157** © Anton Gvozdikov/Alamy Stock Photo; **p.161** © urbanbuzz/Shutterstock.com; **p.163** © esthermm/stock.adobe.com; **p.170** © Farknot Architect/Shutterstock.com; **p.174** © SFL Travel/Alamy Stock Photo; **p.176** © JackF/stock.adobe.com; **p.177** © meunierd/Shutterstock.com; **p.179** © Ming/stock.adobe.com; **p.184** © Sundry Photography/stock.adobe.com; **p.187** © Patrick Batchelder/Alamy Stock Photo; **p.189** *t* © khanisorn chalermchan/Alamy Stock Vector, *m* © Andrey Popov/stock.adobe.com, *b* © Kellogg's; **p.190** © Craig Stephen/Alamy Stock Photo; **p.191** *t* © Sutthiphong/stock.adobe.com, *b* © Chan Vectors/stock.adobe.com; **p.192** *t to b* © Art Directors & TRIP/Alamy Stock Photo, © Ninami/stock.adobe.com, © Tomispin/stock.adobe, © Gina Sanders/stock.adobe.com; **p.196** © bernardbodo/stock.adobe.com; **p.199** © Comauthor/stock.adobe.com; **p.201** *t* © IanDagnall Computing/Alamy Stock Photo, *b* © Sean Hsu/stock.adobe.com; **p.203** © elroce/stock.adobe.com; **p.210** © Homeland photos/Alamy Stock Photo; **p.213** © Yau Ming Low/Alamy Stock Photo; **p.216** © Jenson/Shutterstock; **p.218** *l* © photocrew – Fotolia.com, *m* © M.studio – Fotolia.com, *r* © mr.markin – Fotolia.com; **p.225** *t* © bst2012 – Fotolia.com, *b* © alephcomo1 – Fotolia.com; **p.226** © industrieblick – Fotolia.com; **p.230** *t* © Jenson/Shutterstock.com, *b* © Laurence Dutton/E+/Getty Images; **p.231** *t* © phonlamaiphoto/stock.adobe.com, *b* © Rido/stock.adobe.com; **p.237** © chayakorn/stock.adobe.com; **p.239** © ole999/Alamy Stock Photo; **p.242** © Feifei Cui-Paoluzzo/Getty Images; **p.256** © Kittyfly/Shutterstock.com; **p.258** © nnattalli/Shutterstock.com; **p.259** *tl* © Agencja Fotograficzna Caro/Alamy Stock Photo, *tm* © saiko3p/stock.adobe.com, *tr* © jim forrest/Alamy Stock Photo, *bl* © NurPhoto/Getty Images, *bm* © ton koene/Alamy Stock Photo, *br* © MANAURE QUINTERO/AFP via Getty Images; **p.262** © Christopher Barnes/Alamy Stock Photo; **p.263** © IB Photography/stock.adobe.com; **p.264** © industrieblick – Fotolia.com; **p.265** © kustov – Fotolia.com; **p.268** © JackF/stock.adobe.com; **p.269** © Oleg Zhukov/stock.adobe.com; **p.271** © Joanna Kearney/Alamy Stock Photo; **p.274** © Gloria chf/Shutterstock.com; **p.276** © Rob Pitman – Fotolia.com; **p.277** © Jirapong Manustrong/Shutterstock.com; **p.286** © Maurice Savage/Alamy Stock Photo; **p.288** © stocksolutions/stock.adobe.com; **p.302** *l* © Finnbarr Webster/Alamy Stock Photo, *r* © Paul Maguire/stock.adobe.com; **p.322** *l* © Iain Masterton/Alamy Stock Photo, *r* © Kees Metselaar/Alamy Stock Photo; **p.330** © markhall70 – Fotolia.com; **p.332** © tashka2000 – Fotolia.com; **p.334** © Alexander/stock.adobe.com; **p.337** © CRISTIAN HERNANDEZ/AFP via Getty Images; **p.338** © Allsorts Stock Photo/Alamy Stock Photo; **p.341** © Michael Kemp/Alamy Stock Photo; **p.344** © Elizabeth Bennett/Alamy Stock Photo; **p.346** © anitalvdb/stock.adobe.com; **p.349** © Oxana/stock.adobe.com; **p.356** © Jeffrey Isaac Greenberg 18+/Alamy Stock Photo; **p.358** *l* © corepics – Fotolia.com, *m* © Martin Diebel/Getty Images, *r* © mihi – Fotolia.com; **p.361** © kobah/123RF; **p.363** © dpa picture alliance/Alamy Stock Photo; **p.366** © Jeppe Gustafsson/Shutterstock.com; **p.369** © Tony Worpole/Alamy Stock Photo; **p.370** © ddukang/stock.adobe.com; **p.371** © Zechal – Fotolia.com